On May 8, 1945, the people of St. Helier gathered in the Royal Square to hear Churchill's historic declaration of victory over the Nazis.

For most of them, the highlight of the speech came with the words . . . 'Our dear Channel Islands will be freed today', and when the Union Jack was raised over the Courthouse the crowd was moved to a mixture of exuberant cheering and unashamed tears.

The five years of enemy occupation had brought hardship and sorrow to the people of the Islands; many had been imprisoned, many had died. All had suffered from lack of food, fuel, clothing—and freedom.

THE GERMAN OCCUPATION OF JERSEY is a contemporary account of those unhappy years, and of the courage and fortitude with which the Islanders bore them . . .

Compiled by L. P. SINEL

The German Occupation of Jersey

A diary of events from
June 1940 to June 1945

CORGI BOOKS
A DIVISION OF TRANSWORLD PUBLISHERS

THE GERMAN OCCUPATION OF JERSEY

A CORGI BOOK 552 08098 5

Originally published by *The Evening Post*, Jersey

PRINTING HISTORY

Jersey Evening Post Edition—First impression December 1945
Jersey Evening Post Edition—Second impression January 1946
Jersey Evening Post Edition—Revised Edition September 1946
Corgi Edition published 1969

This book is set in Plantin 9/10 pt.

Corgi Books are published by Transworld Publishers, Ltd.,
Bashley Road, London, N.W.10

Made and printed in Great Britain by
Richard Clay (The Chaucer Press), Ltd., Bungay, Suffolk

ILLUSTRATIONS

(between pages 160 and 161)

German troops marching into St. Helier *

St. Helier Town Hall: Offices of Kommandantur *

German posters declaring death sentences *

German funeral of an Allied airman †

Improvisation! †

A German relay race from West Park to F.B. Fields †

The German Band playing in the Royal Parade, St. Helier †

1945: The long lines of German prisoners embarking ready to be shipped to England †

 * Photographs reproduced by courtesy of Société Jersiaise.

 † Photographs reproduced by courtesy of the *Jersey Evening Post*. It is pointed out that the originals of these photographs are untraceable and it is not known who took them.

FOREWORD

Time has slipped away since this Diary was first published by the *Jersey Evening Post* in 1945, but interest in those fateful years of the German Occupation has been maintained and subsequent publications have found the Diary a basic necessity.

It would be foolish to claim that every incident which occurred is included, but it has proved to be a most useful reference book, care having been taken to present a sober statement of fact.

That Transworld Publishers have undertaken to reprint the Diary gives me great satisfaction, for there is still a demand. To keep it at an economic price has necessitated a certain amount of re-editing, but the basic facts remain and it is hoped that this book will find a place on many shelves waiting to receive it.

Jersey, 1969

OCCUPATION DIARY

THE month of June, 1940, must surely stand out as the most disastrous in Jersey history, both as regards the evacuation and the air raids which preceded the German Occupation. At the beginning of the month none of the men registered for national service had been called up; the Volunteer Defence Force was in operation and the Air Raid Precautions Organisation was in working order. After Italy's declaration of war the Italians resident in the Island were interned at Grouville, with the few Germans who were already there. During the month there were scenes in the Royal Square resulting from the potato deadlock owing to the lack of adequate shipping; this continued for several days, and on many occasions loads were taken back to the farms. There was an outbreak of foot-and-mouth disease at St. Lawrence which was quickly followed by another.

About the middle of the month—prompted by the news that Paris had been occupied by the Germans—English residents were leaving the Island, and there were queues outside the railways' offices. The approach of the German forces towards the French coast was viewed with anxiety; defence of the Island would mean a major effort for which it was unprepared. At this time French and British civilians were being evacuated from St. Malo, and in response to an appeal many local yachtsmen took their craft across to assist with their embarkation.

On June 15 troops and stores began to arrive from England for the Island's defence; this went on for three days, and some of the equipment was brought by train-ferry. Meanwhile, air raid precautions were put into effect; a curfew from 9 p.m. to 5 a.m. went into operation; women and children were being evacuated from St. Helier, and schools were closed until further notice.

Wednesday, June 19, was a day of wild rumours. The States met in special session in the afternoon, after Jurat Dorey had returned from the mainland, and it was announced that the British Government had come to the decision that the Channel Islands were to be declared a demilitarised zone. In accordance with this decision all troops and military equipment had to be withdrawn, and a voluntary evacuation was announced. The decision flung the Island into a panic, and people stood for hours in long queues waiting to register at the Town Hall for

9

accommodation on the boats; nearly half the population registered, but of these a great number decided to stay on the Island.

June 20. Evacuation proceeds. The piers are crowded with people, and many boats, including colliers, leave filled to capacity. There are heartrending scenes. The States meet and issue a reassuring proclamation, previous to which the Bailiff and Judge Pinel addressed crowds in the Royal Square, appealing to them to remain calm and stay on the Island. The States greatly deprecate the behaviour of farmers who abandoned their cattle, and the Volunteer Defence Force is officially disbanded. Hundreds of houses and farms have been abandoned, also cars, cycles and domestic animals. The total number of evacuees is considered to be between twelve and fourteen thousand.

June 21. Another 15 ships left today, and the Lieutenant-Governor—Major-General J. M. R. Harrison, C.B., D.S.O.—left. The last civilian plane also left the Airport. The Bailiff was sworn in as Civil Governor. Over 5,000 dogs and cats have been destroyed. The banks continue to be besieged with people wishing to make withdrawals, these being limited to £25 each.

June 22. The Island is recovering from its shock and life is more normal; many abandoned shops are being re-opened. Potatoes are being shipped again. *The Morning News* ceases publication. At a meeting of the States an 'Island Cabinet' is formed composed of the presidents of newly-formed departments which replace various committees. The air raid precautions and curfew continue.

June 24. The King sends a message of assurance to the Channel Islands, which is published in the Royal Square and posted in parish church notice boxes.

June 26. Potatoes are being shipped again, but we view the future with anxiety.

June 27. Today German planes flew low over the harbours during potato shipments, and this proved to be the last in a series of reconnaissance flights. At a meeting of the States there was a transfer of powers from the old committees to the new departments, and committees' credits cancelled. The curfew was abolished, and it was agreed that less printing be done, and that abandoned farms and goods be taken over.

June 28. At about 6.45 p.m., German planes swept across the south of the Island with machine-guns blazing and dropping bombs. Houses were wrecked at South Hill, stores set on fire in Commercial Buildings and hundreds of panes of glass were shattered in the Weighbridge vicinity, some stained-glass windows of the Town Church being also damaged. Bombs fell on the Fort, the District Office and in the harbour itself, which was primarily the German objective, several small boats and yachts being destroyed. Ten people were killed and several were injured. Those killed being Mr. J. Adams, Mr. T. Pilkington and Mrs. Farrell at La Rocque; Mr. J. Mauger at Mount Bingham; Mr. R. Fallis, Mr. L. Bryan and Mr. W. C. Moodie on the piers; Mr. E. H. Ferrand and Mr. A. Coleman in Mulcaster Street; while Mr. H. F. Hobbs was killed in the Guernsey lifeboat when on its way to Jersey. Guernsey was also bombed at the same time, the raid there being more severe, resulting in twenty-two people being killed and thirty-six injured.

June 29. Two air raid alarms were sounded today. German planes flew over the Island, but there was no attack. The States met and adopted three more defences regulations; measures of economy were adopted; the curfew re-imposed, and the use of motor vehicles restricted. During all this turmoil, *The Evening Post* reached its golden jubilee.

JULY 1940

July 1. Early in the morning German planes flew low over the Island and dropped messages to the local authorities. These called upon the Island to surrender peacefully. White flags had to be flown from all buildings as a sign of surrender, and a white cross had to be painted in the middle of the Royal Square; if this were done, the 'life, property and liberty of all peaceful citizens' was guaranteed. A German airman arrived at the Airport in the afternoon, having seen the signs of surrender, and was told the Island was ready to comply with the terms. He flew off, and later in the afternoon about a hundred German troops and officials arrived; these were under Hauptmann (Captain) Gussek, and were met at the Airport by the Bailiff, the Government Secretary and the Attorney-General. After that, soldiers were billeted at various hotels, anti-aircraft and machine-gun posts established, and many public buildings visited. The German Occupation of Jersey had commenced. During the day the German ultimatum was printed and published throughout the Island.

July 2, 1940. Previously, the German Commandant and other officials had called on the local Authorities. The white flags of surrender can now be pulled down, but the swastika flies over

11

Fort Regent! The Germans appear anxious to maintain the social life of the Island, and have issued late passes to persons working at dance halls, etc. One man was stopped by a zealous German patrol and promptly arrested when the name on his pass was read as 'Churchill'!

July 3. States discuss several important items. Closing hour of licensed houses reverts to the old time (10 o'clock). About ninety members of the British Forces attending at the Town Hall today to give their names to the Germans.

July 4. Island life is almost normal again, with the occupying troops trying to be friendly. There is still a run on the purchase of goods, and German soldiers buy heavily in exchange for 'Occupation' reichsmarks, which must be accepted at the rate of seven to the pound sterling.

July 5. Petrol is to be allowed only for essential services, by permit from the German Commandant; groceries, etc., are to be delivered to various depots and fetched from these by customers. All cycle shops are sold out. Irishman sentenced at the Police Court for assaulting a German soldier. The occupying troops commence to organise public dances. The States adopt more Acts and establish a Pensions Department to deal with sums formerly paid by the British Government. The labour problem and the growing of foodstuffs are also dealt with.

July 6. Important changes in rationing: Butter, sugar and cooking fats, 4 oz. per person per week; meat, $\frac{3}{4}$ lb. per person per week. The Germans bring barges from France and take them back laden with potatoes; tomatoes are also being taken, these in transport planes. Many yachts and high-powered cars are commandeered, several of the latter being taken to France.

July 8. Labour schemes put into operation. Service men on leave in the Island at the time of the Occupation are interned in a camp at Grouville, from which the German and Italian internees have been released. Communal meals served daily at the Technical School, Phillips Street, at the price of 6d. German films shown at all cinemas.

July 9. A third 'proclamation' issued, as a result of which further petrol restrictions are enforced. With all private cars off the roads and a minimum of essential service vehicles running, horse-drawn vehicles make an appearance and cycles fetch enormous prices at auction sales. The German Commandant takes up residence at Government House.

July 10. German proclamations read at the foot of the statue in the Royal Square. All orders and official notices must now be approved by the Commandant and signed by him (or a deputy) and the Bailiff, and several cars have been requisitioned.

July 11. New milk delivery system put into operation, but this does not work ideally. The Germans are buying up all they can.

July 12. Jersey and Guernsey linked up again; communications restored and mail services are to function. Stores are being collected from abandoned shops. There is much movement of German planes to and from Guernsey and France, which becomes an everyday affair. A.R.P. services are instructed to carry on.

July 13. A ship arrived today from Granville.

July 15. Paraffin rationed and restrictions imposed on the purchase of goods. Removal of ban on listening to English broadcasts. The Germans bring some anti-aircraft guns and equipment from France, this being the first of many consignments. Another outbreak of foot-and-mouth disease.

July 22. On the orders of the German Authorities, *The Evening Post* publishes a daily edition for distribution among the troops in occupation of the Channel Islands; this bears the title *Deutsche Inselzeitung*, the text of the front page being in German. The editor (Dr. Kindt) said that this was the first German newspaper issued in the British Empire 'for the moment'; when reminded that, though the Island was well stocked, the winter was coming, he said that there was no need to worry as the war would be over in three weeks, the subjugation of England being 'just a manoeuvre'!

July 26. Cooking-fat ration reduced from 4 oz. to 2 oz. Public meeting held to discuss organised sport and recreation.

July 27. Service men in Jersey who were interned by the Germans are transferred to France. Trenches being dug at the Airport and other air raid precautions put into full operation. Several private residences have now been taken over by the troops (mostly Air Force personnel), including Villa Millbrook. First sitting of the States for three weeks: Act passed for the payment of £44,000 due to farmers and £29,000 due to merchants—this to put money into circulation. All remaining potatoes in the Island to be purchased at £2 per ton and stored. An Act is passed dealing with the taking of a census and a law respecting the adjustment of rents is lodged au Greffe.

July 28. Civilian stabbed by a German soldier at the Alexandra Hotel, St. Peter's, during a disturbance; this affair, like many others involving the German military forces, is dealt with and hushed up by them. Rowdyism at a local cinema during the showing of a German film provokes a warning by the occupying authorities.

July 29. German Commandant declares that the public must learn to use the roads properly, and drops a hint to cyclists and pedestrians.

July 30. Reports that many Five Mile Road bungalows have been burgled; by whom it is not definitely established.

July 31. After a month of German occupation the life of the Island is more or less normal, but stocks of certain commodities are diminishing and purchases of some goods are restricted. The tugs and barges used by the Germans have taken away potatoes, spirituous liquors, motor cars and other goods on a small scale, while the troops have made substantial purchases, mostly of clothing, jewellery and tobacco, especially cigars; new arrivals are to be seen standing in front of shop windows with their mouths open! Rabbit-keeping is now an Island-wide proposition.

AUGUST 1940

August 1. Guernsey internees arrive on their way to France; several Belgian priests from Maison St. Louis leave for their native land.

August 2. There is a shortage of eggs, which increases seriously as time goes on, this partly due to the inferiority of feeding stuffs and partly to commandeering by the occupying troops.

August 3. Germans announce the inauguration of passenger services to Granville, Carteret and Guernsey by the SS. *Holland*, the SS. *Hust Jersey* and the tug *Duke of Normandy*. Two meatless days are ordered—no meat to be cooked or eaten on Thursdays and Fridays; this order, like many others, was observed for a time and then gradually forgotten.

August 8. The Germans take over many more hotels and private dwellings. Motor cars are again being commandeered and taken to France in barges.

August 9. Colonel Schumacher assumes duties as Field Commandant of the British Channel Islands. Parade of occupying troops through the streets of St. Helier, led by a German Air Force band; the strength of the occupying troops is estimated to be in the neighbourhood of two thousand.

August 10. Census taken; the figures subsequently published show that the civil population is 41,101 (males 18,773, females

14

22,328)—a decrease of 10,361 compared with the census of 1931.

August 11. Much activity among the occupying troops following the bombing of Guernsey; guns and equipment brought from France and the Island is being strongly fortified. Horse-drawn buses commence a Sunday service, there being no motor buses on that day, but this does not continue.

August 12. More potatoes and cars being shipped, and the barges bring over army waggons and gun-carriages. Road signs in German make their appearance in various parts of the town, especially those directing to the 'Rathaus'—Town Hall—which soon became known as 'the rat-house'.

August 13. Another outbreak of foot-and-mouth disease. *The Evening Post* inaugurates an Exchange and Mart column, which proves very useful as commodities get scarce.

August 15. Fishermen with gear on the Minquiers proceed there under escort to bring it back to the Island, by order of the Germans.

August 17. 'Feldkommandantur 515' commences duties at Victoria College House, to deal with matters of civil administration. Boat fishing again permitted, but the only distance allowed is 1½ miles from the shore! German Authorities command A.R.P. services to be put in full working order; if volunteers are not forthcoming there will be compulsory service. Prizes presented at West Cinema for a cycle-trailer competition. Channel Islands' delegation leaves for France to purchase essential commodities.

August 18. Some prize cattle are being taken away, in addition to potatoes, cars and other goods. Cinemas of Jersey and Guernsey arrange a film exchange of stock, the only German films now obtainable being shorts and news-reels. German Authorities commence full censorship of *E.P.*

August 20. Two-day visit by a German band. Retail prices of potatoes and tomatoes fixed at 7 lb. for 3d. and 1d. per lb. respectively. All official notices regarding civil matters now signed by the Field Commandant and the Bailiff. Fishermen must obtain permits with photographs.

August 21. Old Victorians' Association suspends activities for the duration. The Jersey Mechanics' Institute decides to carry on.

August 22. Germans play Jersey XI at football. Swimming Club gala held at the Pool.

August 23. Proclamation issued regarding punishment for circulating 'enemy' propaganda. Several Italians visit the

15

Island, these being officers and a few journalists.

August 24. By command, German soldiers are allowed to purchase fruit and vegetables only; other goods must be obtained by special permit, which, by the way, appears to be very easy to obtain. Many people are being evacuated from the immediate vicinity of the Airport. At the only States session of the month the financial position was reviewed and Income Tax was fixed at 4s in the £, instead of 9d., to be retrospective from January 1, 1940.

August 25. Early in the morning a British plane flew over the Airport and dropped a bomb on a gun emplacement, causing several casualties.

August 26. Germans give warning that lights showing at night will be fired at. The Island was shaken in the early morning by a terrific explosion; it was, subsequently learned that this occurred during depth-charging by the Royal Navy in an attempt to break the cable between Jersey and France.

August 27. Consignment of grass seeds, etc., arrives from France for local farmers. Guernsey's census reveals that about 20,000 people left the Island during the evacuation—about half the normal population.

August 29. Orders issued regarding bread; only 2-lb. and 4-lb. loaves to be sold—no breadcakes, breadrolls or fancy bread; 20 per cent. of the dough must be of mashed boiled potatoes. Gas consumption cut by one-third. Jersey Chess Club decides to carry on.

August 30. Liqueurs now added to the list of what may be sold on licensed premises. Germans prohibit all dances, it being thought that too much information is gleaned from the troops.

August 31. Although details are lacking, several German planes have been damaged or destroyed in the vicinity of the Island. A boat is reported as having left Rozel for the mainland, manned by a party making a getaway. Every day there are sounds of heavy gunfire or bombing along the French coast. August weather has been perfect.

SEPTEMBER 1940

September 1. Large exodus of German Air Force personnel and machines. General Milch visits the Island.

September 2. Rate of exchange for Reichsmarks fixed at 9.50 to the £, instead of 8 as previously. Guernsey orders 10,000 tons

16

of potatoes.

September 3. Second year of war commences. Rabbit craze continues, and the *E.P.* offers prizes for the heaviest buck or doe.

September 4. Wests Pictures suspended for a week for showing a film contrary to German orders. General von Richthofen visits the Island.

September 5. Germans cancel football matches that had been arranged with them, and an absolute blackout is ordered for two nights.

September 7. Fishing now permitted up to a distance of three miles from the Island. Cycles again allowed to be ridden through the town on Saturday afternoons, after being prohibited for some time.

September 9. The Germans commence taking clothing, bedding, etc., from unoccupied houses 'for the German poor'.

September 11. Milk must be boiled immediately on purchase there being danger of infection as all milk is now pooled.

September 12. Fires of refuse prohibited. The Field Commandant takes up residence at Belmont, Mont-au-Prêtre, moving later to Beauvoir, St. Saviour. Peat fuel is being dug by the Labour Department in St. Ouen's Bay and is to be stored and dried.

September 13. Department of Labour undertakes tree-felling service. Germans bring concert party from Germany to entertain the troops.

September 14. Food supplies arrive from France, purchased by the Essential Commodities Committee.

September 15. Troops and equipment leaving the Island, but others arriving; changes being made in the German administrative personnel.

September 16. Registration of all motor vehicles which were in the Island on July 1, 1940.

September 17. Communal meals for children commence at the Chelsea Hotel, and are subsequently spread to other centres throughout the Island, reaching the figure of some 3,000 daily.

September 19. Dr. Dannenberg appointed new Island Commandant in place of Captain Gussek, who is leaving the Island. St. Peter's Parish Assembly approves the plan for a new road to the Airport. Through the Red Cross, a few people receive news of relatives and friends in England.

September 20. Books not approved of by the Germans are removed from the Public Library and other libraries, some of them being burned. There are several Gestapo men—or Secret

Police—here now, although the Germans would not admit that they are Gestapo.

September 21. Stock being taken of all cereals in the Island. Local lady sentenced to a month's imprisonment by the German authorities for the alleged insulting of a German officer. Béghin's commence making boot polish.

September 22. On this day (Sunday) and other Sundays throughout the month the usual harvest festival services are held.

September 23. Fishing permitted from registered boats only, and all boats must operate from St. Helier's Harbour. Stocks of textiles being taken by shopkeepers for submission to the local authorities. Meat ration temporarily reduced to half a pound. All advertisements concerning meetings, etc., must be approved by the Germans.

September 24. Leaflets dropped by the R.A.F. In spite of the ban on and risk of spreading propaganda, the leaflets are read by almost everybody.

September 25. Large consignments of foodstuffs arrive from France. Visites du Branchage carried out in horse-drawn waggonettes.

September 26. Many more troops arrive in the Island, together with large quantities of military stores and equipment; several large hotels and garages requisitioned. Green Room Club puts on a show at The Playhouse. The Jersey Electricity Company commences to make salt.

September 27. New changes again in military personnel: Graf von Schmettow appointed Commandant for the Channel Islands, and the Prince zu Waldeck and Pyrmont becomes Island Commandant for Jersey. High prices being paid at sales for livestock—pullets sell for 17s. each, cockerels 20s. and a doe in kindle 32s. 6d. Two Germans killed in a car crash at Mont-à-l'Abbé.

September 28. Military order issued regarding motor cars: all vehicles are to be mustered for inspection and requisition by a German purchasing commission, to provide credits for purchase of food in France by the States.

September 30. Owners of 1939–1940 models cars ordered to parade their vehicles for inspection. Fruit and vegetables are plentiful, but the shops are emptying rapidly; much cider is being made and consumed, and many people are making hay-boxes for cooking. The Germans have purchased men's clothing from evacuated houses to the value of £700.

This was the month which was subsequently to be remembered for the Battle of Britain. Every day we used to watch large numbers of planes flying en route for England; it was always a pleasure to count many less on what we took to be the return journey.

OCTOBER 1940

October 1. Weather turns very cold and wintry. Restriction placed on the sale of drugs, invalid foods and surgical appliances. Large cargo of flour arrives. Fishing again permitted from the Island bays, but in rowing-boats only.

October 2. Important German Order issued by the Royal Court: 'For the purpose of taking an inventory', boot shops, draper, outfitter and soap shops are to close for ten days; there must be no reduction in staffs or wages. Opening hours of shops are fixed from 10 a.m. to 12.30 p.m. and from 2 to 4 p.m. These announcements are followed by another wave of buying.

October 3. The town is a place of desolation, and deputations of certain shopkeepers (such as barbers) wait upon the Germans and local authorities for extensions of hours, some of which are granted.

October 4. Census figures published (see August 10). Meat ration restored to three-quarters of a pound.

October 5. Owing to a delay in shipping the purchase of cars is suspended until further notice. At the last moment the announcement that Winter Time would commence was cancelled. Woolworth's closes down, but the remainder of the stock is being sold on other small premises.

October 6. Church services held in the afternoon instead of the evening.

October 7. Prices fixed for the sale of fowls, rabbits and eggs, and certain days appointed upon which potato haulms may be burned.

October 8. Another batch of R.A.F. leaflets picked up, some of them being printed in French. Cars again being purchased for shipment to France.

October 9. Notice given that inquiries for relatives in England will be forwarded through the Red Cross. The Germans advertise for crews for 'steamship and motor boat'.

October 11. Full Court registers three Orders from the German High Command, these being more or less a repetition of

Orders already issued. In the evening about a hundred persons were taken off the streets in St. Luke's district and placed in various hotels for an hour or so, this consequent on the light at Mont Ubé having been accidentally switched on and the Germans thinking it was a signal!

October 12. Orders issued by the Department of Essential Commodities regarding rationing of leather and textile goods.

October 14. On this and subsequent days large queues form outside Burton's premises to obtain ration cards for textiles—the ration cards were much easier to obtain than the goods they were intended to purchase! Cars of 1938 model now being requisitioned.

October 15. The Full Court registers the following Order from the German Commandant: 'By reason of acts committed in Guernsey against the safety of the German Army,' as a warning all male British subjects of the Channel Islands between the ages of 18 and 35, inclusive, are ordered to report for official registration. Another Order deals with wireless transmitters and accessories.

October 17. French, Belgian and Dutch subjects ordered to register at the Aliens Office. The Germans are buying up all the expensive brands of cigars.

October 18. Registration of males begins at the Church House. Italians who wish to return to Italy are invited to apply at the Commandant's office—there was no rush!

October 19. *Les Chroniques de Jersey* published and issued as usual, after having been suspended for a fortnight while a copy was sent to Paris for the Jersey–French to be deciphered! Horse-drawn bus commences for town suburban area, but runs only for a few days; motor bus services cut to a minimum. Cars of 1937 model now required.

October 21. More Orders registered by the Royal Court: all Jews or descendants of Jews must register, and all Jewish business premises must bear special notices; the other Order deals with the prohibition of photography. Department of Essential Commodities places restrictions on the sale of motor tyres.

October 22. Opening of communal restaurant at St. Helier House Hotel, under the auspices of the States; three-course meals (including meat) served for a shilling. Everybody interested in a B.B.C. broadcast to the Channel Islands.

October 23. Official German Order issued concerning the possible hiding of members of the British armed forces, and the public warned not to use motor vehicles without a permit.

Piggeries opened at a site near the Sports Stadium, Victoria Road.

October 24. Official German Order issued regarding demonstrations at cinemas. Announcement of last days upon which farmers may burn haulms. Free potatoes are being distributed.

October 26. Essential Commodities Department issues new rationing Orders: No more cooking fats obtainable, but the butter ration increased to 6 oz.; tea ration reduced to 2 oz.; wheat flour rationed, the allowance per person to be 4 oz. Amendments made to the Orders concerning poultry and rabbits, potatoes and tomatoes. Case of scarlet fever at St. Ouen's; school closed for short period.

October 28. Schools commence at 10 a.m. and bus services commence at a later hour. Island Commandant orders the creation of a Military Zone in certain coastal areas; inhabitants in the zone must be indoors between the hours of 8 p.m. and 7.30 a.m.

October 29. Wood from trees felled by relief workers made available for the deserving poor at 6d. per sack. Permits being issued for entry into the Military Zone.

October 30. German authorities give notice that wreaths may be placed on the Cenotaph and soldiers' graves on All Saints' Day and All Souls' Day. Another notice deals with German vehicles having right of way in the vicinity of the Airport. French Consul-General announces that he can pay out pensions.

October 31. Notice given of tobacco rationing: retailers of tobacco must be licensed. Most luxury articles are scarce or non-existent, barter is becoming the order of the day, and there is a considerable amount of 'bootlegging'. Three women have been in prison for alleged espionage activities on behalf of the British Government. The German Propaganda Office is established at Les Carrières, Claremont Road, and a propaganda van has been parading the Island.

NOVEMBER 1940

November 1. German plane crashes at La Pulente while on a practice flight over St. Ouen's Bay. The demarcation line for the Military Zone has now been painted and in some districts is regarded as having created a farcical situation.

November 2. A new Order is issued regarding fishing, which is again permitted by boat from certain harbours at specified times. German soldiers are visiting pigeon-fanciers and destroying the birds. German troops pay a visit to the Museum, but several valuable objects have been removed to a place of safety.

November 4. Order issued forbidding the activities and meetings of societies, unions and associations, the wearing of distinguishing marks and the display of flags; certain exceptions may be granted.

November 5. German Court sits at the Royal Court Buildings. Natives of Eire must give notice of their nationality to the Attorney-General.

November 7. One of the big German troop-carriers crashes at the Airport; there were well over twenty casualties, the majority being pilots who had finished a course of training.

November 8. More rationing changes: children under 6 to have an extra 4 oz. of sugar (some has arrived from France); 4 oz. of wheat flour, 4 oz. of oat or barley flour and 2 oz. of salt per person per week.

November 9. Alcoholic spirits (whisky, gin, etc.) released for consumption on licensed premises by German troops; this does not apply to civilians. The Germans are establishing a detector station near St. Martin's Arsenal, and in consequence of this several residents have been temporarily cut off from the electricity and telephone services.

November 11. Armistice Day: German authorities allow wreaths to be placed on the Cenotaph, but no processions or gatherings.

November 12. The Royal Court registers an Order from the Germans dealing with the confiscation of wireless sets, which are to be registered and handed in by the 20th inst.

November 13. Order issued enlarging the Military Zone in the Five Mile Road district. The construction of a pavement is commenced along the length of the Five Mile Road by the Labour Department. In the evening the fringe of a cyclone strikes the Island—the fiercest gale within living memory; at its peak gusts of more than 100 miles an hour were recorded.

November 14. German troops assist in clearing roads barred by fallen trees. British planes pass over the Island but are not fired upon. Persons made prisoner by the Germans in Guernsey transferred to France via this Island, being accommodated at the prison; others follow at subsequent intervals.

November 15. Germans commence wiring the beaches and areas of the Military Zone, and a barge has arrived with hundreds of land-mines.

November 16. Alterations made in the price of milk and potatoes. Large queues form for the registration of wireless sets. Royal Court registers two more Orders dealing with sabotage and Jews. Attention of the public is drawn to the alleged wastage of bread.

November 18. Although as yet not officially published, it is learned that the confiscation of wireless sets is not to be put into effect; Colonel Schumacher has intervened and appealed to the German authorities in Paris on Jersey's behalf. Currency difficulties arise in shops owing to the hoarding of silver.

November 20. Cyclists riding two abreast are stopped by members of the German Military Police. Germans try to purchase ingredients for making Christmas puddings. Incendiary bombs dropped by a plane at St. Ouen's; one farmhouse fire resulted.

November 21. The Bailiff appeals for boots, etc., for working men and children. All cars manufactured since August 1936 are to be called in for purchase.

November 22. States issue an official announcement regarding proper rentals for agricultural land. Motor cycles are to be presented for purchase.

November 23. States issue a request to the public not to hoard silver coinage and to hand it over to the banks. The 4-oz. butter ration must suffice for all fat, and butchers are to send any surplus fat they have to the Abattoirs. Germans issue new Order about open fires, which are not permitted between one hour after sunset and one hour before sunrise. Another horse-drawn bus commences from Samarès Post Office, but does not run for long; return fare to town was 1s. 6d.!

November 25. French gruel available for invalids and for infants under nine months. Advocate H. W. Giffard arrested and then sentenced to two months' imprisonment alleged defamatory remarks about the Germans.

November 26. German Order in regard to cycling officially registered by the Royal Court and strong warning also given to pedestrians. Two German soldiers arrested for rape at St. Martin's; they were taken to France. The French Consul-General leaves the Island.

November 28. Public officially warned that retention of wireless sets is dependent upon good behaviour and a loyal attitude. Slight amendment made to the Tobacco Rationing Order.

November 29. Grocery shops ordered to send in returns of tinned goods and cereals (if any).

November 30. More Orders issued: One concerns the killing

of game, which is the sole right of occupying troops; another deals with the rationing of feeding stuffs, and a third makes it compulsory for dogs to be on the leash and muzzled when not on the owner's enclosed premises; this because of rabies prevalent in France and which it was feared would be carried here by dogs of German soldiers. The States meet for the first time since September 7, and a report is presented by the Department of Finance and Economics showing that the estimated deficit for the year commencing February 1, 1941, will be £423,177. Various recommendations to meet this were made.

DECEMBER 1940

December 1. The line 'By Permission of the Bailiff' must be deleted from all advertisements.

December 2. The Impôt takes stock of all kinds of spirits following the new duty order; persons with over a dozen bottles must declare them. Electricity now being rationed.

December 3. Following the departure of the French Consul-General arrangements are made for the payment of pensions to French nationals.

December 4. Many of the German and Austrian servant girls are being sent back to the Reich; some Italians must also return to Italy. The identity cards issued for permission to enter the Military Zone must be taken back to the various parish halls to be stamped once again, in accordance with a German Order.

December 6. Superior Council of the States issues a statement concerning the prices to be paid for 1941 crops.

December 8. Incendiary bombs dropped by aircraft in the Five Mile Road district; no damage reported. Death of Lt.-Col. H. H. Hulton, D.S.O., Government Secretary.

December 12. Amendments made to the Feeding Stuffs (Control of Retail Sales) Order, whereby all merchants dealing in the same have to obtain a licence. Prices of jam are fixed, but the quantities that may be purchased are negligible.

December 13. Free soup being distributed to men employed by the Department of Labour or under States-controlled schemes. Locally-made toys are on sale.

December 14. Germans issue warning that land-mines have been laid at different places along the foreshore of the Island.

December 15. Young man sentenced to a month by the Germans for reading a pamphlet dropped by the R.A.F. Soap is now being made locally, and German periodicals are at the Public Library.

December 16. Last States session of the year, at which it is announced that by a German Order new identity cards are to be issued for everyone over the age of 14, bearing a photograph. Radical changes are made in the system of parochial taxation; the Foncier Rate is abolished and rateable value of property and land is based on rental value, the occupier of same being deemed to be the landlord for the purposes of taxation. This measure aims at giving relief to persons substantially affected by the increase in Income Tax, the surtax amendment to which is adopted. A new schedule is introduced, fixing the number of quarters per £ rental, 30 quarters entitling the ratepayer to a vote at parish meetings. Upkeep of main roads is to be borne by the States; also the cost of unemployment, thereby enabling the parishes to keep their expenses down. The maximum interest on loans is fixed at 4 per cent., a financial amendment to the duty on wines and spirits is adopted, and among other items is a measure providing for the protection of growers against legal proceedings for debts incurred prior to 1941.

December 17. Appeal made from the Town Hall for women and children. More arrests made for infractions of the Curfew Order.

December 18. Official warning given to the public regarding the hoarding of silver. It is learned that the SS. *Antwerp*, plying between Jersey and France, has sunk after a collision in the fog.

December 20. Notice issued by the Department of Essential Commodities dealing with coal, etc., all distributors having to obtain a licence. A welcome increase in the meat ration is announced for Christmas week, from 12 oz. to 16 oz. A few highly-priced turkeys have arrived from France.

December 21. Extension of shopping hours announced: 9.30 to 12.30 and 2 to 5.50 p.m. Curfew for Christmas Eve and New Year's Eve not to begin until 3 o'clock next morning, the closing down of public houses to be 2.30.

December 22. Captain of the steamer which collided with the SS. *Antwerp* arrested for alleged sabotage; he was put on parole, then tried and exonerated.

December 24. Registration with milk retailers ordered. Labour at fixed rates of pay is made available to growers.

December 25. Christmas Day. In spite of all our fears, with a bit of saving, scheming, or wangling, mostly the latter, the general provision of festive cheer was nothing short of wonderful. Although poultry was very scarce, the Germans consuming a good deal of it and supplies from France almost unworthy of mention, for some time now there had been a lot of secret pig-killing, which meant that pork which was not sold by the legitimate butcher found its way to consumers.

December 26. Boxing Day. Dances were held at the Pavilion and The Plaza, the German troops attending in large numbers; at the last moment the curfew was extended until midnight.

December 28. Vouchers made available for the deserving poor to obtain textile goods at a reduction of from $33\frac{1}{3}$ to 50 per cent.; these are the goods being made at 'Summerland' by more than 300 girls for supply to the shops. *E.P.* Christmas Fund creates a record.

December 29. Visit of Hans Freidrich Blunck, one of the best-known German poets.

December 30. Particulars published regarding the registration of all persons over 14 years of age.

December 31. Maximum prices fixed for eggs, the first-grade price being 4s. 3d. per dozen retail. New Year's Eve dances held at the Pavilion and The Plaza; troops attend in large numbers and there are several disturbances by them late at night in various parts of the town. During the month several mass treats have been given to children, including visits to cinemas. Although not plentiful, quantities of oranges and nuts have reached the Island, and certain goods held back have been released. On New Year's Eve local people held parties at home, the curfew being extended to 3 a.m.; midnight, however, was not observed by Central European Time—we all waited for Big Ben!

1941

JANUARY

January 1. New Year's Day. Germans entertained a hundred children at the Continental Hotel.

January 2. Instructions issued regarding the new Island registration.

January 4. Price of sugar increased to 5½d. per lb.; price of oat and barley flour increased to 10d. per lb. Cooking fats (2 oz. per person) placed on the list of rationed foods again, but not available until further notice.

January 5. Beauvoir, St. Saviour's, burned to the ground by a fire that could be seen for miles; this was the residence of the Field Commandant and he then took up residence at Linden Court, Bagatelle.

January 6. More German Orders registered at the Royal Court: Curfew hours are altered—10 p.m. to 6 a.m. in the Parish of St. Helier; 9 p.m. to 6 a.m. in all other parishes. Another Order again related to the prohibition of pigeon-keeping, and the Court registered twelve Acts recently passed by the States. New ration books commence.

January 7. Shopping hours, which were extended for the Christmas period, now back to previous times—Hours of cinema performances altered to accord with the new curfew hours.

January 8. Ice-bound roads make conditions difficult for horse and motor traffic. Quantity of letters received through the International Red Cross are being realt with by the 'Bailiff's Enquiry and News Office', over Burton's in Halkett Place.

January 9. Second-crop potatoes being bought by the States for seed. Captain Sowden, of the SS. *Normand*, arrested by the Germans in Granville for refusing to carry munitions, and is placed on parole.

January 11. Economy in bread urged and the eating of more potatoes advocated. Appeal made for old or unserviceable clothing. Germans announce restoration of postal communication between the Channel Islands and Occupied France, through their Field Post Office; also with Germany, Belgium and Italy. Notice received by ex-Service men's clubs that they must close down.

January 13. Important notice issued affecting societies and

27

clubs; those with permission to function temporarily must furnish all particulars of activities and lists of members, but annual meetings of limited liability companies are allowed to take place. A deputation from various clubs waited upon the German authorities. Only one cinema is allowed to have a matinée every afternoon of the week.

January 14. No rationed goods are allowed to be offered in the *E.P.* 'Exchange and Mart' column. Orders issued cutting to a minimum lights on motors and cycles.

January 15. By order of the German Harbour Commandant, owners of damaged boats in St. Helier's Harbour must remove them immediately, and owners of boats in the Old Harbour must remove them at once to allotted berths.

January 21. Germans prohibit fishing of all description until further notice. Potatoes are being shipped to France.

January 22. Several ships arrive in the inner roadstead, they having come from Cherbourg to shelter in Channel Islands waters. Fishing permitted again but not boat fishing.

January 23. New ration orders: butter reduced to 2 oz. per person per week (instead of 4 oz.) and sugar ration for juveniles from six to eighteen years is increased to 8 oz. (instead of 4 oz.).

January 24. Boat fishing again permitted. *E.P.* Almanac published in abbreviated form.

January 25. Curfew altered again—11 p.m. to 6 a.m.; cinema performances altered accordingly. Salt ration comes to an end.

January 28. States offer subsidy to farmers to encourage pig-breeding. Germans ransack the Masonic Temple and send their loot to Germany.

January 29. Farmers are asked to provide 20,000 boxes of seed potatoes for Guernsey; these were forthcoming within twenty-four hours.

FEBRUARY 1941

February 1. Germans ban the Salvation Army. They also issue a notice asking the public to give immediate notice of any landings or leavings around the Island, rewards being offered. Mr. H. P. Turpin, a St. Ouen's man, shot in the back and killed by a German patrol while in the Military Zone after curfew.

February 3. Registration of bakers announced as a preliminary to bread rationing. Germans hold a two-day trial in the Old

Committee Room of the Royal Court, the case concerning 16 young Frenchmen who escaped from France in a boat and who were captured off Guernsey; sentences of death and penal servitude are passed.

February 4. Vegetable prices are to be controlled. The bread ration is announced: Persons born on or before June 30, 1931—male manual worker, 6 lb. 2½ oz.; any other male, 4 lb. 10 oz.; female manual worker, 5 lb. 6¼ oz.; any other female, 4 lb. 10 oz. Persons born on or after July 1, 1931—male or female, 3 lb. 1¼ oz. The weights are based on the metric system.

February 7. Amendment made to the Rationing Order whereby holders of a Reich-German's ration book are entitled to larger rations.

February 8. New Orders: Electricity must not be used between 11 p.m. and 7 a.m., and the sale of electrical apparatus is prohibited. Children are to be allowed a jam ration of 1 lb. per fortnight. Important changes made in the meat ration—new ration cards are to be issued, each weekly coupon being divided into eight sub-coupons; all available meat is to be sold cut up and issued in the form of stewing meat or obtained in the form of bottled stew, this being prepared at the Sun Works, First Tower, and obtainable at specified depôts on presentation of one sub-coupon per half-pint. Beef is to be the normal issue from the butcher, but other meat may be obtainable occasionally. A sub-coupon must be exchanged for a meat meal at a restaurant. The tobacco ration is reduced to 20 cigarettes and only 1 oz. of tobacco, instead of 2 oz.

February 10. In order to save electricity, cinema performances are curtailed, each cinema taking it in turn to remain closed.

February 12. Amendment made to the Bread Rationing Order, whereby a Reich-German gets a quarter ration more than anyone else.

February 13. Petrol ration reduced, to three-quarters of a gallon per coupon.

February 14. Instructions again issued regarding a re-issue of coupons for the new meat-rationing scheme. Telephone conversations must not exceed three minutes' duration, in order to save electricity. German authorities give permission for ex-Service men's clubs to re-open.

February 15. Announcement that there is to be one issue of cooking fat—2 oz. per person.

February 17. Bread rationing commences, some families receiving much less than their normal supply. Play presented at the

Opera House by Messrs. Britton and Whinnerah, under the auspices of the Green Room Club.

February 19. Much activity among the troops. Practically the whole of the Air Force leaves and many of the residences and hotels containing personnel are emptied; stores and equipment are also being taken away in small ships.

February 21. More Orders: the butter ration is to be increased to 4 oz. from 2 oz. and that 'Channel Islanders are forbidden to leave the Islands for the Continent'!

February 22. Tobacco running out; many tobacconists supply their customers with cigarettes only. Several horses arrive from France for States work. Germans take over more accommodation at the General Hospital; maternity cases are transferred to the Dispensary.

February 23. Captain 'Ben' Bennett, of the SS. *Spinnell*, a vessel plying between the Islands and France, falls between his ship and the harbour at Guernsey and is drowned.

February 24. New meat rationing in force, the stew being issued at the price of 3d. per half-pint (one half-pint per sub-coupon). Buses further restricted and no return tickets are issued for journeys of less that 1¾ miles.

February 25. German Purchasing Commission now requires lorries (1936–1940 Models). Ration of 100 saccharins available to adults over 16 years of age. Department of Transport and Communications makes arrangements for a parcel delivery service by Messrs. Le Riche, Orviss and Tregear to their country depôts. Child patients at the General Hospital must not be visited owing to the prevalence of influenza.

February 26. Miss M. A. L. Carter appointed Matron at the General Hospital.

February 28. Public telephones are suspended. The Order concerning dogs being muzzled comes to an end. One bright spot in the month has been the large number of letters received through the International Red Cross.

MARCH 1941

March 1. Another ration of cooking fat and salt is to be issued, but the butter ration is again cut down to 2 oz. Germans hold a dance at West Park Pavilion. The installation of a radio beam station at Les Platons has now been completed.

March 3. Textile and boot shops are to shut two days a week

—Mondays as well as Thursdays. There is a rush on summer shoes, which have been released.

March 4. Germans order all persons possessing old rubber tyres or inner tubes not on serviceable vehicles to deliver them to a collecting depôt, payment to be made as follows : Motor tyres, 1d. for 3 lb.; tubes, 1d. per lb.; cycle covers, 1d. for 5 lb.; tubes, ¾d. per lb.

March 5. Germans visit marine-store dealers to make inquiries regarding scrap metal.

March 6. Disastrous fire at St. Ouen's Manor (occupied by the Germans): drawing-room and oldest wing completely gutted; historic treasure and valuable furniture destroyed.

March 7. German Purchasing Commission now requires all private cars, irrespective of year of manufacture, particulars to be sent to the Transport Office. Charles Cuzner knocked off his cycle and killed by a German driving a car down Bath Street.

March 8. New Orders issued concerning the control of pigs. Amendment made to the Building Materials (Control of Supply) Order.

March 11. Petrol supplies must be obtained from only one pump, which is situated in David Place. Curfew hours for the Military Zone are shortened in view of the longer period of daylight. Inspector appointed under the meat rationing scheme. Meeting of interested persons held and scheme submitted to stimulate interest in the Island's fish supply.

March 12. Limited number of letters may now be sent through the Red Cross to relatives from whom no messages have been received.

March 13. Number of German personnel leaving the Island, together with stores and equipment. The petrol shortage causes more cuts to be made in the number of buses—season-tickets discontinued and travel within a three-mile radius is not guaranteed on Wednesday and Friday afternoons and all day on Saturdays, preference being given to the aged and infirm. A horse-drawn ambulance is being constructed and private cars are cut to a minimum. Another extra ration of butter is announced.

March 14. Cinemagoers now notified that comedians or heroes may be applauded. Potatoes and tomatoes brought under the scope of the Vegetables Order.

March 15. German Order presented regarding 'postal traffic and telecommunications in the occupied territories in the West'. Serious accident at Seven Oaks, St. Brelade's, ends fatally for Mr. C. W. Machon, a cyclist who collided with a

31

German-driven car. Tobacco ration now consists of 20 cigarettes and a packet of French tobacco at 1s. 6d. for less than two ounces.

March 16. Mother and two children injured when a landmine explodes at Fliquet Bay.

March 17. François Scornet, one of the Frenchmen sentenced by the Germans on February 3rd, is taken to St. Ouen's Manor to be shot.

March 18. The Superior Council of the States issues an Order that all attics and roof-spaces must be cleared of inflammable material; this Order to come under A.R.P. supervision.

March 20. Several notices chalked on walls in the town—'The workers want more food; search the houses of rich hoarders' and 'Down with Hitler and his riff-raff'.

March 21. Allotment scheme started at Grouville. Cycle park and parcel delivery service started. Large steamer arrives from France with material for road-making, including sand! A considerable amount of flour and wheat has also arrived, as well as two tons of chocolate for culinary purposes.

March 22. Petrol is 2s. 2d. per gallon and the paraffin ration is temporarily stopped. The public may now obtain soup at the Chelsea Hotel, Gloucester Street, at 1d. per pint. A new cigarette is to be sold—a mixture of Virginian and French tobacco—at 10d. for 20; French matches are also on sale. The butter ration is 4 oz. for the second week in succession.

March 23. Many people visit the grave of the young Frenchman at Almorah Cemetery and place flowers there in profusion. Some churches make reference to the National Day of Prayer.

March 26. The use of coal for heating purposes is forbidden; the use of gas or electricity for heating and a variety of other purposes is also forbidden. Licences may be obtained, however, in cases of extreme necessity. The juvenile sugar ration is to be reduced from 8 oz. to 4 oz.

March 27. Victoria College gymnasium display held as usual. Chamber of Commerce annual meeting.

March 28. B.B.C. announces that a German supply ship, the SS. *Diament*, a small vessel plying between the Islands and France with military stores, was badly damaged, but was not sunk. Nationals of Czechoslovakia are to attend at the Feldkommandantur with their papers.

March 29. To encourage pig-breeding, the Department of Agriculture announces that the farmer or owner of a pig may keep 10 per cent. of the animal if it is taken to be slaughtered at the Abattoirs, the remainder to be sold to the Department of

Essential Commodities. The butter ration is again back to 2 oz., and the tobacco ration consists of 20 cigarettes only. Gift arrives through the International Red Cross at Geneva of foodstuffs for sick children and babies.

APRIL 1941

April 1. Unique event—Jersey issues her first postage stamp (1d. value); these were printed at the *E.P.* office and there was a rush by philatelists to secure first-day covers. The stamps—in carmine—embodied the Jersey 'coat of arms', being designed by Major N. V. L. Rybot, D.S.O., F.S.A.* The issue of soup made at the Sun Works is a great success. A hundred tons of crude oil arrives for the Electricity Company.

April 2. Amendment made to the Agricultural Wages Bonus; married workers employed by more than two farmers may now obtain it.

April 3. About forty Italians leave for Italy, taking their families with them; Czech and Swiss nationals also leave. The Germans in the Island have been threatened with 15 years' imprisonment for listening to British propaganda. States Technical Instruction Department appeals for boys to learn the bakery trade.

April 4. The system of cut-up meat comes to an end and new schedules are issued controlling the retail prices of pork and beef. Alterations in the sugar ration: Adults are to have 3 oz., instead of 4 oz.; juveniles, 6 oz., instead of 8 oz.; children, 6 oz., instead of 8 oz.; Reich-Germans, 5 oz., instead of 6 oz. Hairdressers' hours fixed: 9 to 12.30 and 2 to 6.

April 5. Salt ration of 2 oz. to be available until further notice, a large quantity having arrived from France. Additional depôts opened for the distribution of soup. The distribution of

---

* On being asked by the Bailiff to design the first local penny stamp, Major Rybot was told that his drawing was to be based on that of the first Guernsey stamp, for the German authorities would sanction no other design. His design, however, differed from the original in that he gave the King of England's shield of arms a more correct heraldic treatment. He also inserted in the corner four very small 'A's, which stood for 'Ad Avernum, Adolphé Atrox', that is to say, 'To hell with you, atrocious Adolf!' On the halfpenny stamps, issued later, Major Rybot altered this lettering to 'A', 'A', and 'B', 'B', meaning 'Atrocious Adolf' and 'Bloody Benito'. Major Rybot's services as a draughtsman were given gratis, and the chief beneficiaries of the issues were German and local speculators.

jam to the juvenile population is discontinued temporarily.

April 9. This being Holy Week, nearly all the textile and boot shops have closed this afternoon (Wednesday) until next Tuesday morning.

April 10. Announcement of second rationing period for textiles and leather goods, if stocks are available, but these are very low. For one week only there is to be a ration of potato flour.

April 11. Good Friday. No buses running today; the usual parties of low-water fishermen were in evidence, and Passion music was rendered in the various churches.

April 12. The tea ration is to be reduced from 2 oz. to 1 oz., and, except under the authority of the Department of Transport and Communications, the Department of Agriculture or the Department of Essential Commodities, no person shall sell or offer to sell, or buy or offer to buy, by auction, any price-controlled article; this to stop the fabulous prices being paid at auctions.

April 13. Easter Sunday. Curfew altered to 1 a.m.

April 14. Easter Monday. Curfew again altered to 1 a.m.

April 15. First prosecution under the Jams and Savoury Pastes Order: Royal Court imposes fine of £10 and £2 costs on a butcher for making 'vegetable brawn'. Department of Agriculture issues a Plant and Plant Seeds (Maximum Prices) Order, prices to be issued periodically; this in view of the profiteering of late. Jam again distributed to juveniles, but now only one pound per month.

April 16. German Order warns holders of fishing permits and registration papers for their boats to return them to the Harbour Office by the 23rd inst., after which they will be invalid.

April 17. Very large quantities of military equipment arrives; this included field kitchens and searchlight units, also a lot more cement.

April 18. One ration of block chocolate (2 oz.) for making cocoa to be issued to adults, and new tobacco ration cards commence.

April 19. Two-ounce ration of cooking butter to be issued for one week in addition to the usual 2 oz. of butter on ration. German Harbour authorities demand security deposit of 100 reichsmarks from fishermen for motor and sailing boats and 50 reichsmarks for rowing boats, the notice declaring that 'by proved spying, sabotage or flight', fishing will be stopped and all deposits confiscated.

April 20. German film *Victory in the West* is shown to the troops at The Forum on the occasion of Hitler's birthday, the building being decorated both outside and inside.

April 21. Lorries, cars, motor cycles, commercial tractors (with rubber tyres) of models from 1936 to 1940 are to be produced to the German Purchasing Commission. Amateur Dramatic Club presents straight play at the Opera House.

April 22. Medical Board makes known its decision for the disposal of Red Cross supplies, much of which is to be kept in hand for the winter. Price of petrol increased to 3s. 2d. per gallon.

April 23. German Befehlshaber moved from Monaco, St. Saviour's Road, to the Metropole Hotel, Roseville Street.

April 24. An Impôt notice warns would-be growers of tobacco that a licence must be obtained. Germans issue notice that all boats on shore, in garages, private houses, etc., have to be taken to the harbours of St. Helier, St. Aubin or Gorey.

April 28. Meat rations are to be cut down for one week to 8 oz. for adults and juveniles; 4 oz. for children, and 10 oz. for Reich-Germans. Fishermen and boat-owners are invited by the Harbourmaster to co-operate in an attempt to provide fish for the general public. Messages through the Red Cross may again be sent from Jersey.

April 30. Price of old potatoes (Royals) fixed at 1s. 6d. per cwt. wholesale. On the 'black market', which is in full swing, tea is being offered at 10s. per pound, sugar at 3s. and fowls for the table in the neighbourhood of 25s.; pork and other meat is about 4s., and there is a rush to get rhubarb when it is exposed for sale. Inspection of attics has begun by A.R.P. personnel.

MAY 1941

May 1. States of Jersey Textile Department announces that a workshop has been established at 'Summerland' to undertake clogging—the fitting of wooden soles and heels to boots and shoes. The Germans have not published a paper today (May Day). A 21-year-old bicycle fetches £25 at an auction sale, and £3 10s. is paid for rabbit-hutches.

May 2. Dud coins are being circulated; there is a shortage of silver and many business houses are obliged to use German paper money. Butchers' shops are to open three days a week only—Wednesdays, Fridays and Saturdays. There is to be a ration for one week of one tablet of soap.

May 3. First issue of a tobacco ration for a month; the ration is of one ounce, priced at 1s. The States give notice that they will take possession of all gardens and small plots which, after May 31, are found to be in a neglected state. A German Order prohibits the removal of works of art, and a notice warns all foreigners that they must report any change of residence within two days.

May 4. Two extra ounces of cooking butter to be issued again this week, the meat ration is now 4 oz. for adults and juveniles, 2 oz. for children, an extra ounce for manual workers, and 5 oz. for Reich-Germans.

May 5. Potato crop seriously burnt by frost. Official prices of coal issued.

May 9. Curfew hours altered slightly—10 p.m. to 6 a.m. in the Military Zone. There is to be one 4-oz. ration of barley semolina.

May 10. Order issued concerning the defacing of German posters, and a meeting of Constables fixed special posting places for official notices, ninety-nine in number.

May 11. Drapery and boot shops are to open only three days a week—Tuesdays, Fridays and Saturdays. Major Haas has now taken over duties as Island Commandant.

May 12. Kenneth Britton and Richard Whinnerah present Noel Coward comedies at the Opera House. Mr. A. C. Sarre appointed Guernsey representative in Jersey.

May 13. States Committee of Markets gives notice that all vegetables and produce brought to the public markets must be properly dressed and ready for sale before being admitted; a stall-holder has been prevented from selling poultry and rabbits in the market.

May 14. German Order prohibits boat fishing from Gorey Harbour, but permits the use of La Rocque Harbour instead; fish is very scarce, and whenever there is any for sale there is almost a fight to get it.

May 15. Several new Orders. The outside painting of woodwork with paint, varnish, etc., can only be done by permit; all motor vehicles which have been abandoned are to be offered for sale to the German Purchasing Commission, and the infants' food which has been used as breakfast meal is now available for infants only, other meal being provided for adults. There is to be another 2-oz. ration of potato flour issued and also a ration of tinned beans.

May 18. Fishing from Elizabeth Castle Breakwater is prohibited by the Germans.

May 21. The Bailiff warns the inhabitants about interfering

with military signposts, some of which have been found turned the wrong way.

May 22. Extra rations of barley semolina (3 oz.) and coffee substitute (4 oz.) to be issued for one week. Shop hours extended to 4.30 p.m. on Fridays and Saturdays. Lifting of potatoes prohibited for four days. Messages from Jersey are now arriving in England.

May 23. The butter and meat rations are to remain at 4 oz. each until further notice. Footwear from France is now on sale, but is very dear. At an auction sale £30 was paid for a gent's cycle.

May 26. Postal traffic, including small parcels, is now established between Jersey and Holland, Denmark and Norway.

May 28. Colonel W. A. Stocker killed by a German car in Hill Street.

May 29. Another Order issued regarding the declaration of motor tyres for delivery to the authorities, and all cars, lorries, motor cycles, etc., 1935 to 1940 models, are to be presented to the German Purchasing Commission for purchase, whether previously rejected or not. A tin of tunny fish is to be issued on ration.

May 30. Royal Court approves and sanctions two States Acts —extension of school-leaving age and issue of 2s. notes. Germans give notice that any flotsam or jetsam found around the shores of the Island is the property of the Army of Occupation. Curfew hours for the whole Island, inclusive of Military Zone, fixed from 11 p.m. to 5 a.m. Georgetown Methodist School-room becomes a soup depôt.

JUNE 1941

June 1. Whit Sunday.

June 2. Whit Monday. As bad a day as one could wish for— cold and raining: nothing to do, nowhere to go, no papers to read.

June 4. Special bonus to be paid to farm workers during the summer months—14s. per week to workers earning not less than 36s. per week.

June 6. Market greengrocers petition the Essential Commodities Department that growers should not supply town grocers with vegetables. Another German Order demands that motor vehicles from numbers J10,000 to J12,000, 1935 to 1940 models, be produced for purchase; failure to comply means imprisonment.

June 7. The attention of the public is drawn to a clause of the Rationing Order whereby it is an offence to obtain rationed goods by barter; windows of exchange shops have been full of these goods lately.

June 9. Farmers urged to take precautions regarding blight, and the Department of Labour issues rates of pay for potato and harvesting seasons. The Imports and Exports Advisory Committee gives notice that it will consider applications from trade organisations for the importation of strictly essential supplies. Warning issued by the Bailiff concerning the loitering of persons near Fort Regent.

June 10. Scale of charges issued for the carriage of goods. Salt ration increased to 3 oz., instead of 2 oz. Horse-drawn ambulance now acquired by the Public Health Department.

June 11. Motor cars from J9,000 to J10,000 are wanted by the Germans.

June 12. Jam ration of 1 lb. per head to be issued alphabetically.

June 13. Farmers are invited to apply for liquid fuel for the mowing of hay. Weekly bonus of 7s. to be paid to young men under 19 working on the land. Motor cars from J8,000 to J9,000 now required.

June 16. Farmers are warned not to mix morning and evening milk on account of the hot weather turning it sour. The Island learns with regret that the destroyer H.M.S. *Jersey* has been sunk, and, following that, the former G.W.R. mailboat *St. Patrick*.

June 17. Buying of motor cars by the German Purchasing Commission is temporarily suspended.

June 18. This being Derby Day, several sweeps were organised and also a number of 'books'.

June 19. Public warned not to take dogs in the Military Zone unless on a lead, on account of them running over land-mines; dogs not on a lead are liable to be shot.

June 20. Tobacconist's shop broken into and 500 rations stolen. German troops arrive in very large numbers—the figure mentioned being 3,000; many more houses and hotels have been requisitioned, including West Park Pavilion, Highlands College and Springfield; some soldiers are being billeted with private families.

June 23. Messrs. Kenneth Britton and Richard Whinnerah present 'Sally' at the Opera House.

38

June 24. Important notice issued concerning the use of gas, which is to be cut off except during the following hours: 7.30 to 8.30 a.m., 11.30 to 1.30 p.m. and 5.30 to 7 p.m. Another important Order: All traffic must be driven on the right-hand side of the road!

June 25. The Superior Council issues the Forestry (Jersey) Order, 1941, empowering the Department of Labour to purchase trees either felled or standing, and to pay for same at the rate of 10s. per ton, and 5s. per ton if the roots are removed. The price of tobacco is increased to 1s. 2d. per ounce. Butcher shops are to open only two days a week—Fridays and Saturdays.

June 28. Germans take over Merton Hotel as hospital for venereal cases.

June 30. Long German Order issued concerning the regulation of traffic, whereby certain speeds are fixed for certain areas, and, of course, German forces have road priority. The daily ration of tobacco for the troops is cut down to 3 cigarettes or 2 cigars, or 2 cigarillos or $\frac{1}{2}$ oz. of tobacco.

July 1941

July 1. The Germans are very annoyed. 'V' signs have been painted on certain houses and walls in the Rouge Bouillon district and a slogan on the roadway at the top of Midvale Road. This is considered to be sabotage, and if the responsible persons do not give themselves up the following penalties are to be imposed in the affected district: (1) All radio sets will be confiscated; (2) A fine will be imposed on the inhabitants, and (3) A civilian guard will be required nightly to prevent a recurrence. It has been pointed out to the Germans that the slogan on the roadway—'Victory is British'—was very well done but quite ungrammatical, making it suspiciously like the work of a foreigner. Many people today wore a rose for England or a black tie in mourning for liberty.

July 2. Rabbit disease is prevalent in the Island; due to interbreeding. German Order concerning fishing: 20 per cent. of each catch must be sold to the occupying troops, the remainder to be sold in the Fish Market.

July 3. To save fuel, laundries give notice that blankets and heavy articles cannot be accepted. Large quantities of fish arrive from France in French boats. School of Physical Culture gives display in Howard Davis Park.

July 4. New Order restricts the buying and selling of certain fertilisers. The price of pork mince is fixed at 1s. 6d. per pound, but this commodity does not last for any length of time. The Germans try out the air raid siren in order to find a suitable 'invasion' signal.

July 5. More German Orders registered: Administrators and legal representatives of persons who evacuated from the Island must forward a list of furniture and household effects which were left behind by the said persons and where they are to be found. An amendment to the Rationing Order reduces the flour ration to 2 oz., the issue of wheat flour being discontinued, the whole ration consisting of 6 oz. of either breakfast food or infants' food. A civil guard has been instituted in the district where the 'V' signs were found, but the other two penalties are held in abeyance for the time being. The Germans are now exporting large quantities of potatoes. Mayfair Hotel has become a soldiers' recreational hostel.

July 7. The Airport is to be greatly enlarged, large numbers of men being drafted there. Valuers are busy taking inventories of furniture left by evacuees. The public is warned that they must burn only one-third of the last ration of gas allotted to them. New ration books commence.

July 8. Another warning issued regarding the consumption of gas, this time in connection with the cooking of food for animals; wood fuel is advocated for heating water. Imports and Exports Advisory Committee gives instructions to trade associations desirous of purchasing essential supplies from the Continent.

July 9. Through the initiative of a Jerseyman, several English-speaking films have arrived, the German authorities having made contact with American cinema agents in Paris.

July 10. Germans issue notice dealing with 'V' propaganda; the requisitioning of wireless sets as set out in paragraph 1 of the penalties for persons in the Rouge Bouillon district is put into operation, they being given one day in which to hand-in their sets to depôts in St. Helier and St. Saviour.

July 11. German Field Marshal von Witzleben arrives on a visit. More fish arrives for the Germans from France; they make much capital out of releasing three-quarters of a ton to 700 families, but omit to mention that the fish would not have kept!

July 12. Twenty-six days of drought comes to an end—a period beaten only once since 1894.

July 14. German Order issued requisitioning all single mattresses belonging to evacuated persons, these for the large number of troops arriving.

July 16. Germans take over the Town Terminus buildings. There is to be a one-week issue of coffee substitute (4 oz.). St. Mary's Parish fixes the Rate at 7s.

July 17. The bread ration of children up to two years of age is cut down to 1 lb. 8 oz. Quantity of coal arrives.

July 21. The Germans putting up the 'V' sign themselves, occupied buildings and motor vehicles receiving most attention.

July 23. Large number of Red Cross letters arrive.

July 25. Amendment to the Rationing Order by which the meat and butter rations of Reich-Germans are increased. The Germans are now trapping the pigeons in the Royal Square.

July 26. The public is informed that there will be no sugar available for jam-making, but jam in proportion is to be made with the available supply of sugar and released to the public on ration.

July 28. Confiscated radio sets of persons in the Rouge Bouillon district are to be returned. At the same time a German notice announces that two female residents have been sentenced to nine months' imprisonment each for 'V' propaganda—they picked up pamphlets and stuck them on a wall; the sentences are to be served in France.

July 29. Germans show the film *Victory in the West* again, this time with English captions.

July 30. Bread ration reduced all round, as follows: Male manual worker, 6 lb.; any other male, 4½ lb.; female manual worker 5¼ lb.; any other female, 4½ lb. males or females born between January 1, 1932, and December 31, 1938, are allowed 3 lb., and males or females born on or after January 1, 1939, are allowed 1½ lb.

July 31. *Morning News* office becomes Red Cross centre for messages.

August 1941

August 1. The German Feldgendarmerie—is trying to catch civilians for infringements of petty road regulations, fining them a mark (2s. 1d.) on the spot. Curfew in the Military Zone is now from 10 p.m. to 6 a.m.

August 4. August Bank Holiday. One packet of soap powder is to be issued on ration.

August 5. All U.S.S.R. nationals over 15 years of age are warned to report at the Feld Kommandantur. Rewards are offered to persons reporting crashed aeroplanes.

August 6. Germans give warning of the death penalty for persons harbouring crews of 'enemy' aircraft. Huelin's depôt at Five Oaks becomes an ammunition dump. Grouville fixes the Rate at 6s. 6d.

August 9. First prosecution by the Royal Court for painting without a permit. Germans advertise for 200 men for constructional and digging work at the Airport. The tobacco ration for this week is ten cigarettes only.

August 11. Issue of a small piece of soap per person and 4 oz. of macaroni. Germans bring over a large number of horses for transport work.

August 13. The lifting of main crop potatoes prohibited. Owing to there being no more paraffin, the public is warned that road lamps on repair work, scaffolding, etc., can no longer be lit at night.

August 14. Large quantities of French plums on sale in the markets at 1s. 3d. per pound.

August 15. Sexcentenary of St. Helier's Parish Church.

August 18. Full particulars of all motor cars, lorries, etc. (1935 to 1940 models) not exempted by the German Purchasing Commission must now be submitted. Ration of 4 oz. of semolina issued.

August 19. Public warned about gas consumption; some gas appliances in private houses have been disconnected. Department of Agriculture issues Order whereby it can purchase potatoes at prices exceeding the prescribed maximum prices.

August 20. Steps taken for the control of the Island's fuel supply, registration forms being issued upon which householders must state the quantities of fuel they possess, after which ration cards are to be issued; there is now a Fuel Registration Office in Halkett Place.

August 21. Department of Agriculture fixes prices at which it will purchase cereal grain; the Germans order farmers to work on Sundays if this is necessary to gather the harvest. First prosecution before the Royal Court for an infraction of the Electricity Order—that is, having a light after 11 p.m. The tobacco ration back to 10 cigarettes and 1 oz. of tobacco.

August 24. Large number of melons arrives from France.

August 25. Butter ration reduced to 2 oz. again. Issue of 4 oz. of macaroni, and 4 oz. of barley flour for juveniles and children.

August 26. Six horses sold in the Cattle Market for the total sum of £1,005; one horse was sold for £210. Urgent appeal for labour to turn and ventilate stocks of harvested crops, to prevent germination.

August 30. Department of Agriculture fixes price of home-grown straw at £4 per ton.

August 31. During the month friendly societies have ceased payments, but money for pensions is being loaned by the States. Work is proceeding on enlarging the Airport and part of St. Peter's Barracks has been demolished; volunteer labour has been asked for by the Germans, but there has not been a great response, they having to adopt various ruses to give the impression that private individuals require the work. Beer is being manufactured and a small quantity is allotted to public houses and clubs, but this is not for long. The black market is still flourishing, among the soaring prices is £50 for a hundred-weight of sugar. Graf von Schmettow, the Military Commandant, has returned to the Island, and the Germans are now 'rounding up' blankets.

SEPTEMBER 1941

September 1. Ration issued of 4 oz. of semolina and 100 saccharins, thousands of which are being hawked around the Island at exorbitant prices. Householders may obtain ¾ lb. of wheat flour per week in lieu of a 1-lb. loaf. Milk ration is ½ pint for adults and 1 pint for children and juveniles per day.

September 2. New arrangements for the cinemas—the one which has to close in turn will now show a German film for the troops, they having to pay when seeing the film elsewhere when it is screened for civilians.

September 4. The beginning of the month has brought beautifully hot weather, which, after the appalling conditions last month, is proving excellent for much-delayed harvesting.

September 5. Petrol shortage; supplies curtailed until further notice, except for the following: medical services, flour deliveries, milk deliveries, wholesale grocery and wholesale bread deliveries, the amount being allowed being very small. The sale of potato flour is prohibited.

September 6. Bus services are cut further, no midday buses being run. Quantity of coal arrives. Royal Court fines a person £10 for obtaining a duplicate ration book. Football matches commence at the F.B. Fields.

September 7. Harvest festivals begin, there being more fruit in the churches than in the shops.

September 8. Ration issued of 8 oz. of barley flour. Large consignments of tomatoes arrive from Guernsey for canning.

September 9. A charcoal-bus makes a trial run; a small quantity of petrol has arrived, and the midday buses run again.

September 10. Two parishes fix the Rate—St. Martin's at 7s. and St. Ouen's at 6s.

September 11. Holders of Weighbridge tickets for cereals or potatoes of 1941 crop are notified to present them for payment. Extra rations are to be issued for heavy and very-heavy workers; the former are to receive 1 lb. of meat and 10½ oz. of fat per month and the latter 2 lb. of meat and 21 oz. of fat.

September 12. Persons with surplus fruit are urged to let the authorities have it for jam-making.

September 13. The tobacco ration again back to 10 cigarettes only. Order issued that, after the end of the month, specified articles (mostly unobtainable foodstuffs) cannot be exchanged or offered for sale without a special licence. Germans bring over a fife-and-drum band.

September 14. The Germans open a cabaret at The Plaza named 'Bel Ami'; this consists of Continental artistes, and champagne is served galore at ten marks per bottle (21s. 8d.); this cabaret was for the troops, but was eventually opened to the public.

September 15. Issue of 4 oz. of macaroni. A charcoal bus is now running a regular schedule service to St. Aubin's. Three notices issued concerning licences for the distribution and rationing of coal.

September 16. Two soup distribution depôts opened in the La Rocque district. Robberies of cycles are increasing.

September 18. High prices being paid at auction sales: candles are fetching more than a shilling each. Department of Agriculture advises farmers to dig main crop potatoes; of every 22 barrels delivered to a specified depôt the farmer will be allowed to retain five, and one on every additional 22 barrels up to a total maximum of 15 barrels.

September 19. Comprehensive notice issued regarding coal rationing; ration coupons issued bear different 'class letter', and monthly directions are to be issued as to the amount of fuel obtainable by each class. Jews and descendants of Jews must hand in their wireless sets.

44

September 22. Owners of trees again reminded that it is punishable to fell or lop trees without the necessary permission. The Germans establish themselves on the J.M.T. premises. Issue of 4 oz. of semolina and a piece of soap.

September 23. Trinity fixes the Rate at 5s.

September 25. New gas rationing scheme comes into operation for the winter period, based upon the number in a household; 200 cubic feet is allowed for one person per week, 300 for two, then advances of 50 feet up to six and 75 for each additional person; this is for cooking only, but extra is available for persons whose only means of lighting is gas.

September 26. Elderly local resident sentenced by the Germans to 12 months' imprisonment for defending his wife when an officer snatched at an R.A.F. brooch she was wearing. Numbers of Frenchmen arrive here for work on various German schemes.

September 27. All infants up to two years of age are to be allowed an extra half-pint of milk per day, making 1½ pints in all; and children up to two years are to receive a ration of French gruel. Persons applying for permission to fell or cut trees are warned that they must present their ration books. Male German civilians are ordered to attend at once at the Paris headquarters.

September 28. Many churches revert to afternoon services instead of evening. Several more robberies of cycles. St. Paul's Church holds jubilee services.

September 29. Superior Council issues an Order forbidding a person to sell or buy by retail, on any one occasion, more than one hundredweight of potatoes. The deposit paid to the German authorities by fishermen as a guarantee is to be refunded to them. Ration issued of barley flour (8 oz.) and coffee substitute (4 oz.).

September 30. Sudden death of a man at St. Luke's: inquest verdict of death from malnutrition and heart failure. Request received from Jersey prisoners of war for a football. Night exercises have been held, and a canteen at St. Martin's has been opened which may or may not be patronised by residents of the parish. Wedding rings cannot be purchased at any price, and couples getting married are allowed to have six pounds of wedding cake. Threshing is going on throughout the Island, the machines being augmented by French ones. Elderberries are on sale in the markets at 1s. per pound, and some apples have arrived from France, where over 300 francs are being paid for a £1 note, this being roughly 30s. It has been a good month for

Red Cross letters. The main topic has been the getting away from the Island in a boat of a Jerseyman—Denis Vibert—right under the noses of the Germans.

OCTOBER 1941

October 1. Curfew altered—11 p.m. to 6 a.m.; 9 p.m. to 6 a.m. in the Military Zone. Small quantity of paraffin has arrived and is to be allotted to persons with no other means of lighting. St. Saviour's fixes the Rate at 2s.

October 2. Visite du Branchage held throughout the Island. Thursday football commences. Fuel rationing begins: only wood is obtainable, and three in a family receive one hundred-weight, the ration increasing in proportion, but persons with stocks are not granted any until these are used up.

October 3. Rationing of textiles is to be placed on a coupon basis. All retailers of clothing, footwear, accessories and materials—new or second-hand—must obtain a licence.

October 4. Colonel Knackfuss arrives to take up the duties of Field Commandant from Colonel Schumacher, who has resigned owing to illhealth. Poultry-keepers advised to kill off birds over two years of age as there is insufficient grain available; a lot of wheat, however, is being given to poultry after the threshing. Robbery at the Bailiff's residence.

October 6. Ration issued of semolina (4 oz.) and another issue of jam (alphabetically).

October 10. Carbide for cycle lamps arrives from France. Two pints of paraffin are allowed to households without gas or electricity. A second-hand cycle fetches £36 at an auction sale.

October 11. Issue of new tobacco ration cards.

October 12. Houses in the Samarès district are requisitioned and tenants turned out at short notice.

October 13. In view of the new rationing period, a list of textiles and footwear, which can only be obtained with coupons, is published. Several more private houses taken over by the Germans at short notice, especially in the vicinity of the Airport. Macaroni (4 oz.) issued, and rice (4 oz.) for juveniles and children only.

October 14. St. John's fixes Rate at 3s.

October 15. The Germans take over Victoria College to billet cadets—Hitler Youth—for a period of (they say) eight weeks; the scholars are transferred to Halkett Place Girls' and Infants'

School, which split up, some of the children being accommodated in Grove Place schoolroom.

October 16. Poultry-keepers are notified that they must send in a return of the number of head of poultry in their possession under two years of age. Farmers are asked to send in quantities of seed Royal potatoes for Guernsey at 9s. per hundredweight.

October 17. The Germans take over Woolworths, the C.W.S. bakery, the Sports Stadium, and many more houses. Another German notice dealing with the registration of used or unused tyres.

October 18. German Order warns the public to be more careful with black-out observance. Local resident opens a nautical and marine engineering college.

October 19. Large numbers of Hitler Youth are arriving in the Island.

October 20. The exchange of many specified articles is prohibited either in shops or through advertisements in the Press. St. Helier Community Restaurant opens from 5 to 6 p.m. for the sale of vegetable stew, not to be consumed on the premises. Two ounces of cooking fat issued for one week—the first for months—and four ounces of barley flour. Messrs. Kenneth Britton and Richard Whinnerah present a revue at The Forum.

October 21. Many houses requisitioned in the Mont Félard district; also some in the vicinity of David Place. St. Brelade's fixes the Rate at 3s.

October 22. Notice issued to inhabitants of St. Ouen's that mines have been laid in the l'Etacq district. More 'V' signs have made their appearance. At an auction sale £320 was paid for a horse.

October 24. British plane drops bombs in the early hours of the morning and is fired upon by the Germans; part of a bomb rack was later found, and nobody was injured; the general opinion is that the plane did not drop the bombs intentionally.

October 25. Germans impose penalties for the re-appearance of 'V' signs; three districts affected include a large part of the town; patrols are to be supplied nightly by inhabitants of the districts concerned and wireless sets are to be handed-in. The tobacco ration is now 10 cigarettes and 1 oz. of tobacco; fabulous prices are being paid for cigarettes.

October 26. Curfew altered again—10 p.m. to 6.30 a.m.; 9 p.m. to 7 a.m. in the Military Zone. Germans give special film show at Wests for the Irish community; this was purely anti-British propaganda and identity cards were carefully scrutinised at the doors to make sure that only Irish patrons were admitted.

October 27. The *E.P.* circulation is cut by 15 per cent. owing to the shortage of paper. Leaflets picked up, mostly in the St. Lawrence and St. John's area; these were in French and probably those intended for Nantes, the B.B.C. announcing that the R.A.F. had dropped some there the previous night. Evening meals are to be served at the Chelsea Hotel, Gloucester Street, from 5.30 to 7 o'clock. Another ration issued of 4 oz. of semolina. Notice given to householders in the penalised districts as to where they must deliver up their wireless sets. Amateur Dramatic Club presents a play at the Opera House.

October 28. Another depôt for soup opened in the Samarès district at Baverstock's Stores. Germans issue notice that wreaths may be placed upon the Cenotaph and upon soldiers' graves on All Saints' Day, All Souls' Day, and Remembrance Day; there must be no processions, marches past or public speeches. Planes flew over the Island during the evening and there was anti-aircraft firing by the Germans.

October 29. The public is warned by the A.R.P. authorities to keep indoors when there is any firing of anti-aircraft guns and not to show any lights from careless opening of doors or windows. Labour Department grants a 10 per cent. increase in the wages of its employees.

October 31. The Germans have stated that Jersey is to be made as strong as Gibraltar. Furniture is again being requisitioned in large quantities. They have brought over stores of food, and, although using a lot of local potatoes, stocks from Roscoff (Brittany) have been clamped on the People's Park. Tunnels are being made in St. Peter's Valley and other places for the storage of ammunition, and whatever properties the Germans have taken over are subjected to ruthless alterations to suit their needs. Some more cattle have been brought from France for consumption by the occupying troops, and these have been put to graze until required; it is a pity they do not bring milk as well, for they are consuming well over 4,000 pots a week—local people have to queue up for skim! Civilians are still being put in jail by the Germans for minor offences; this month's batch includes a man who made sneering remarks when the Germans were clearing Woolworths, and another who took photographs without a permit. The Germans are starting to take down the 'V' signs with which some of their billets have been adorned.

November 1. New textile rationing books come into operation; these are based on the coupon system. The Germans issue notice relating to resolutions of company meetings, and another notice deals with the surrender of sporting guns, etc. The November fuel ration includes a small amount of coal or coke, in addition to wood.

November 3. Criminal Assize Court deals with a case of aiding and abetting a robbery; as the Court was not heated, blankets were issued to officials to wrap round their legs. No more dry-cleaning can be undertaken as the necessary materials are no longer available.

November 4. Germans hold a hunt and races at St. Peter's. The wireless sets handed in by residents of certain districts have been taken to College House, the German Field Command Headquarters.

November 5. St. Helier's Parish Assembly summarises the financial position and the Rate was fixed at 3s. 9d., with promise of help from the States Finance Department. Verdict of suicide while of unsound mind concerning a Mrs. Herteaux, of Valley-des-Vaux; it was revealed that the Germans had gradually taken over the whole of the farm worked by this woman and her husband and that she was greatly worried, these facts being suppressed by the Censor.

November 6. Owing to heavy mining of the Island, persons are not permitted on the beaches or shores at parts of the coast named in a special notice, this in addition to areas already prohibited. The Gas Light Company, by German Order, is to disconnect all gas fires and radiators.

November 7. Germans are absolutely pouring in, including civilians; stores are arriving galore and there were over forty different steamers and barges in the harbours today, all unloading.

November 8. Gas consumption restricted—7.30 a.m. to 2.30 p.m. and 5 to 9 p.m.—the pressure being cut right down outside these times. Germans announce that the only legal tender is the British £ Sterling and the German Reichsmark; this does away with the use of French francs. Another German Order calls upon all persons who were residing here only temporarily previous to July, 1941, to report to the Chief Registration Officer. Tobacco ration again down to 10 cigarettes only per week.

November 9. B.B.C. announces that the Channel Islands were

included in an R.A.F. sweep; British planes are known to have been in the vicinity lately, and an E-boat recently sunk off the Island by a Spitfire had several high German officials on board, not one being saved.

November 10. In consequence of the new regulations concerning gas, the *E.P.* is published each day at 2 p.m. Semolina (4 oz.) issued again.

November 11. Armistice Day; wreaths were placed on the Centotaph and other soldiers' graves.

November 12. The Germans take over the Jersey Girls' College, the scholars being eventually accommodated at Coie Hall, Janvrin Road; Mont Cantel was taken over at the same time, as was Teighmore, Gorey.

November 13. To conserve paper, the *E.P.*, by German orders is not to be published on Thursdays, making a total cut in circulation of over 30 per cent. Mr. A. E. Perrée, an elderly man, knocked down and killed by a German lorry at St. Aubin's; the inquest was adjourned sine die.

November 15. German Billeting Order registered by the Royal Court: Every occupier of a dwelling house in the Island must fill up a form containing particulars of inhabitants, number of bedrooms (furnished and unfurnished), other rooms, light, heating and sanitary arrangements; other forms issued deal with houses evacuated by persons prior to the Occupation, requiring information as to whether furniture, fittings, etc., are stored on the premises. Tea ration ceases to be available and retailers have to give notification of existing cards. Tea is fetching as much as £3 a pound in the black market, and carrot tea is becoming popular.

November 17. Farmers of St. Helier are asked to send in returns of potatoes for disposal, with a view to meeting the great shortage of potatoes for the retail trade. The Germans cut their milk supply to ¼-pint per day. Ration of barley coffee issued (4 oz.).

November 18. Another spate of robberies, the latest being the theft of a baker's cycle with 18 lb. of bread; the cycle was later recovered.

November 19. Alterations made to supplementary rations of heavy workers, whereby they may obtain an extra 2½ oz. of butter and 3½ oz. of meat per week.

November 20. Smoking in cinemas by civilians is forbidden; this Order has already been in force for a few days for the troops, whose tobacco ration is now very meagre. Parish of St. Clement fixes the Rate at 3s.

November 21. Heavy troop movements go on during the night, a large number leaving for France.

November 22. Warning given to the public concerning the buying and selling of potatoes at prices higher than the maximum.

November 24. Department of Agriculture announces proposed financial assistance to farmers for the cultivation of their land, at the rate of £6 for each vergée, the applicant being directed to cultivate cereal and potato crops. Ration issued of half a pint of cooking oil; also another jam ration (alphabetically).

November 25. The Germans propose taking over Ommaroo Hotel, and the residents there are given eight days to make arrangements.

November 28. Owing to the potato shortage and in order to find what supplies are available for the public, all persons must send in a return of potatoes held by them at midnight on the 29th.

November 29. Royal Court imposes fines on farmers who did not dig their potatoes, and a farmer and trader were fined for selling potatoes above the maximum price. In the afternoon the third States meeting of the year was held. The Estimates were presented by Jurat Dorey. The total estimated revenue for the financial year beginning February 1, 1942, was fixed at £267,350, and the expenditure at £748,534; this, with the statutory reserve under Article 23 of the Finance Law (£10,000), showed an estimated deficit of £491,183. After various recommendations had been approved, among them that Income Tax remain at 4s. in the pound, the Estimates were adopted.

November 30. There are not nearly as many troops here as at the beginning of the month. There is very little air traffic, and about the only planes seen are those carrying high officials and escorted by fighters. One thing that amuses is the variety of uses to which the Germans put Red Cross waggons, some for the carting of coal! The skipper of the SS. *Normand*—a Jerseyman —has been put in jail in France for carrying letters from Jersey and posting them in that country en route for England, and a local policeman has been fined for not saluting a German officer. Several private dances are now being held by various clubs, but these have to finish at 9.30. Cider is fetching enormous prices, and a small quantity of cognac and Dubonnet has arrived from France. A lot of black market meat is being sold, beef at about 4s. a pound and pork anything up to 6s. 6d.

December 1. Bus services cut down in order to save petrol for ploughing. The Medical Officer of Health advises expectant mothers to have their confinement either at the Dispensary or at a nursing home, so that heating and lighting difficulties may be overcome and also to save doctors using petrol. This week's extra ration is a small piece of soap.

December 2. A big black market case receives the attention of the Royal Court; three accused are heavily fined—£125, £60 and £25 respectively. The fuel ration is the same as for November; many trees are being felled and those in the Parade have been greatly thinned.

December 3. The meat ration is to be doubled—8 oz. for adults and juveniles and 4 oz. for children; the Germans have brought over many head of cattle of late.

December 4. Ommaroo Hotel is now providing accommodation for numbers of labourers who have been brought here from the Continent.

December 5. The butter ration is to be doubled to 4 oz. for everybody, and it is announced that bread ration books are to be issued so as to get bread rationing on a coupon system similar to that prevailing for other rationed foodstuffs. German Order registered which means in effect that anyone working for the Germans is not allowed to leave his employment of his own free will.

December 6. The M.O.H. informs the public that local flour analyses are very satisfactory, such flour containing the entire vitamin content of the original wheat, especially Vitamin B, which protects against diseases of the nervous system. The price of butter and sugar increased—7d. per ration of 4 oz. and 1½d. per ration of 3 oz. respectively. The Royal Court fines farmers again, and the price of home-grown hay is fixed at £20 per ton.

December 8. Inspectors appointed to visit premises to obtain information in connection with the Potatoes (Sales and Returns) Order.

December 12. Salt ration increased to 4 oz. instead of 3 oz. Meat may now be purchased in more than one portion at a time.

December 13. Maximum prices fixed for home-grown potatoes: 9s. 6d. on a sale to the Department of Agriculture;

10s. 6d. on a sale by the Department of Agriculture; 11s. 6d. on a sale of wholesale; 1½d. per lb. on a sale by retail.

December 15. A hundred saccharins issued this week, and the extra rations for Christmas Week are announced as follows: Sugar ration doubled for adults to 6 oz.; 2 oz. of tea for everybody over the age of six; chocolate for children and juveniles; cocoa for children; the tobacco ration is 50 cigarettes and 2 oz. of pipe tobacco (instead of 10 cigarettes only). A quantity of dried fish is also available.

December 16. German Order forbids farmers and producers to sell foodstuffs directly to German soldiers or to civilians employed by them. The coupon system for textiles and footwear is revised, which in the main reduces the number of coupons required for various articles. Order issued whereby newly-born calves must be slaughtered within 14 days of birth, in order to relieve the milk shortage. Merton Hotel, which has been a German military hospital for some time, is cleared by the Army and taken over by the Air Force. Last States meeting of the year, a continuation of the sitting of November 29. By order of the Germans, Freemasons' and Odd Fellows' property is transferred to the States. The proposed amendment to the Parish Rate Law was again considered, and it was decided to re-introduce the Foncier Rate, the abolition of which has caused so much adverse comment; a person qualifying for a vote at a parish assembly must pay 'not less than 50 quarters', and the amended law will operate from January 1, 1942.

December 17. The Department of Agriculture gives notice that it may purchase 60 calves a month during the next three months, and the Department of Essential Commodities is empowered to make further directions to deal with rationing, including that of potatoes. U.S.A. nationals are ordered by the Germans to report at the Feldkommandantur. Butcher shops and textile and footwear dealers announce Christmas shopping hours.

December 18. Germans visit Boots' and other libraries and demand that all books with unfavourable references to Germany shall be cleared by December 30.

December 19. Farmer sentenced by the Germans for overcharging for eggs—100 Reichsmarks or ten days' imprisonment. Notice issued appealing to administrators to hand to the Controller of Textiles and Footwear any used clothing or footwear that may be in their possession. Livestock sales are forbidden. A small quantity of walnuts is on sale.

December 20. Two German notices issued—one dealing with

the keeping of pigeons, the penalty for which is death or imprisonment, the other giving the change of curfew for the Christmas period : Christmas Eve, Christmas Day, New Year's Eve and New Year's Day curfew does not begin until 1 o'clock next morning (Military Zone excepted). German military hospital established at La Haule Manor. In the early morning leaflets in French were picked up in the St. Martin's district.

December 22. The gas hours are to be extended until midnight instead of 9 o'clock on December 24, 25, 26 and 31, as also the electricity hours; there has been a number of gas poisoning accidents of late through persons not turning off taps when the gas has been cut off.

December 23. A case concerning the robbery of tobacco from German Depôts has been investigated by the military and heavy sentences imposed on civilians implicated, varying from 21 months to 12 months.

December 24. Christmas Eve. The shops are attempting to make a brave display, but articles are very scarce; there is a quantity of second-hand articles for sale, however, but in most cases very big prices are demanded. Hundreds of labourers of all nationalities are arriving in the Island, some of them being rather pathetic looking and certainly most of them badly clad.

December 25. Christmas Day. Everybody tries to make the best of it, but the proper Christmas spirit is lacking. The food situation is, in the majority of cases, better than was expected. The children have had everything done for them and sweets have been made and distributed; wooden toys and other playthings have been on sale and have proved that there is much ingenuity in the Island. We all heard the broadcast by Channel Islanders, but were greatly disappointed that no actual message was sent. The usual services were held in the churches, the Germans holding their own. and today, as throughout the whole of the Christmas period, the weather has been fine and very mild, roses even being in bloom.

December 26. Boxing Day. Apart from a couple of football matches and the cinemas, one of which staged a variety show, there was very little doing today, the curfew again being back to 10 p.m.

December 27. After the increase for Christmas, the tobacco ration is once more ten cigarettes only. More foreigners are arriving for labour operations.

December 28. Serious assault on the licensee of the Oxford Inn, Union Street, by a party of Germans who tried to enter after hours; the licensee sustained injuries and shock, but his wife rendered one of the soldiers unconscious for two hours by a well-timed blow with a stick; there was also a similar disturbance at Gorey, but a phone call brought speedy assistance. The two cases were kept out of the Press by the Censor.

December 29. German plane crashes at St. Ouen's close to the Airport. Messrs. Kenneth Britton and Richard Whinnerah presents a comedy at the Opera House; on this occasion, as indeed on almost every date fixed for a local production, the Germans decided to stage some show of their own, with resultant inconvenience to producers and public alike.

December 30. *The Evening Post* Christmas Fund reaches a new record total—£320. Two Irishmen sentenced by the Royal Court to four months' hard labour for infractions of the Rationing Order.

December 31. The public may obtain potatoes only with the dealer with whom they are registered, and no member of a household may register if there is an amount of potatoes in that household exceeding 28 lb. per member. Stocks of paraffin being almost exhausted, it is not possible to issue any to householders, but a small quantity will be released for stable lighting or in cases of sickness; in certain instances of farmers relying solely on paraffin, the Jersey Electricity Company has recently been installing its service. Late at night German soldiers were very noisy in various parts of the town; most local people, as last year, waited for Big Ben to chime 12 to usher in the New Year—one hour later than Central European Time.

The end of the year finds us quite cheerful and quietly optimistic for the next twelve months, although local conditions have greatly deteriorated. The Germans appear to be very depressed and they are all wishing for a quick finish to the war; the number of Air Force personnel has increased lately, and seems to be greater than that of the Army. Thousands of foreign workers—directed by the Todt Organisation—are being poured into the Island; these are of all nationalities and include Spaniards who, during the Civil War, were interned in France. The troops are still buying everything they can lay their hands on, floor furnishings, scent and woollen articles—the latter presumably to be sent to comrades in Russia. One of the greatest problems at the moment is the acute shortage of small change, it is very rare that an English silver coin is seen, and even copper is hard to obtain. The general health as a whole is quite good, but there have been many cases of diarrhoea, or colitis, which is thought to be due to the bread. There were 458 births and 671 deaths in 1941, big increases considering that the population was 41,101, according to the 1940 census, as compared with 50,455 in 1931.

1942

JANUARY

January 1. New Year's Day. The weather is fine and there is a note of hope in the air.

January 2. German plane crashed at Bouley Bay—the second within a week; it was subsequently learned that the first one was shot down by the R.A.F. Fuel ration for January is less, the coal ration being cut by half which means that a small family receives two hundredweight of wood and half a hundredweight of coal or coke. One pound of oranges may be obtained by children up to six years of age. The Germans take over The Playhouse, New Street, to be used as a store.

January 3. The tobacco ration becomes 10 cigarettes and 1 oz. of tobacco, alternating each Saturday throughout the month with 20 cigarettes. French gruel may be obtained by children up to three years of age, and housewives may obtain 6 oz. of flour per week instead of 8 oz. of bread; previously, exchange could be made only at 12 oz. of flour instead of 1 lb. of bread. Petrol retail price is fixed at 4s. 2d. per gallon, and the Department of Labour offers inducements to owners of motor lorries journeying to town to take return loads. The Department of Agriculture is directed by the German Field Command to lower from £3 to £2 the salary offered to part-time milk inspectors, who had been advertised for by the Department. Big military parade through the town, and afterwards an Air Force band plays in the Royal Square.

January 5. United States nationals—less than a dozen from Jersey and Guernsey—are taken to France for the internment; a number of men who have been kept in custody by the Germans for purchasing black market tobacco are also taken to France for imprisonment. A boy employed at a chemist's shop is charged at the Police Court for stealing 'sweets' which were in reality opium tablets; these were given to children who were made ill. This week's extra rations consist of 4 oz. of cocoa substitute and a piece of soap.

January 6. German guns blaze away at a British plane, presumably returning from a night raid; later in the morning leaflets printed in French were picked up in various parts of the Island. There are not so many soldiers about, many of them

57

having left the Island during the past week; more motor vehicles, however, are being imported from France, these including a number of delivery vans. Mr. A. H. Coutanche appointed Parish Secretary and Registrar of St. Saviour's in succession to Mr. A. Briard.

January 7. Owing to an outbreak of chicken-pox, the General Hospital is closed to visitors until further notice. More milk inspectors advertised for. Germans put up a terrific barrage when British planes pass over during the evening on their way to and from France; it was the heaviest yet known.

January 8. Germans bring over mechanical shovels for use by their labourers; these are on caterpillar wheels.

January 10. Royal Court passes sentence of two months' imprisonment upon a woman for a serious rationing fraud, she having obtained rations of every description for a man who evacuated 18 months ago.

January 12. Department of Agriculture issues several Orders concerning milk control; the price of milk to be increased—11¼d. per pot wholesale, 1s. 2d. per pot retail at dairy, 1s. 4d. per pot retail delivered (3½d. per pint); returns must be made of the quantities of milk given by cattle, all of which must be registered. The Germans forbid the felling or removal of trees and shrubs, applications for exemption having to be made to the Field Command; another Order calls upon all owners of motor lorries or motor cycles, models from 1930 to 1940, to furnish particulars, as these are needed by the military. Another issue of jam is to be made (alphabetically), a large quantity having been purchased from German stores by the States, and this week's extra rations consist of a packet of 'Lessive' washing powder and a piece of toilet soap (6d.), the latter being sold in the black market recently at the price of 4s. and 5s. per tablet! A small quantity of chestnuts is on sale at some of the grocers' shops, but there is not enough to give everybody a fair-sized ration.

January 13. After several days of cold weather, snow falls fairly heavily and makes things very unpleasant, especially for poor families with little food and the sparse fuel ration; a lot of the wood that is being issued is very wet and cannot be easily kindled.

January 15. More 'V' signs have made their appearance, this time at Millbrook and at St. Ouen's, in the consequence of which local civilians from the districts concerned have to supply guards at night for two weeks; it is extremely doubtful that these 'V' signs are put about by local persons, but by the German soldiers themselves, for it is alleged that the latter have been seen doing so. In the last instance of 'V' signs wireless sets were requisitioned and have not yet been returned, although in a few cases where owners have written for them, their requests have been granted.

January 16. Licences have been withdrawn from certain shopkeepers for charging exorbitant prices for rationed or un-rationed goods.

January 17. Clifton Park Estate, Georgetown, which was to have been a building site at one time, is allotted to the public in five-perch plots for the growing of foodstuffs. The second *E.P.* Occupation Almanac is issued. Windows broken by bottles thrown by soldiers leaving the German cabaret 'Bel Ami' at night; lately, there have been many instances of this sort of thing.

January 19. The Germans commence clearing out metals, rags, bones, etc., from the marine-store dealers, and a German play is being presented in various parish halls. Potatoes to be issued by shopkeepers to registered customers is 7 lb. per person per week; large quantities of potatoes are needed for Guernsey. This week's extra rations include 2 oz. of cooking fat, 4 oz. of chocolate and 4 oz. of coffee substitute. Mr. 'Sonny' Godbolt presents a review at the Opera House.

January 21. The Milk Control Department announces that, owing to the recent severe weather, the quantity of milk sup-plied to the public may have to be reduced: this is put into effect in some days, dairymen being cut 15 per cent. on supplies.

January 23. German court-martial, held locally, publishes findings in a Guernsey black market case: sentences varying from 12 to 15 months and fines from 3,000 to 1,200 marks were imposed for the illicit slaughter of cattle. The local black market in meat is expected to decline now that the registration of cattle has come into operation, and there have been several narrow escapes lately from German police. One half-pint ration of liquid saccharin is to be issued.

January 24. Persons registered for potatoes are cut down to 5 lb. per head per week. The General Hospital is re-opened to visitors. German military band gives performances to the general public at The Forum.

January 26. The M.O.H. announces that, owing to the small suppy of insulin, none can be supplied to out-patients, and that diabetics obtain it at the Hospital. The *E.P.* announces it is necessary to make a cut from four pages to two pages each Tuesday and Wednesday.

January 28. The German Censor complains to the *E.P.* about

the bad English that is allowed to pass in the German news. Death of Mr. C. E. Malet de Carteret, a former Bailiff of Jersey.

January 29. Issue of Jersey's own half-penny stamp, printed at *The Evening Post* offices; this was similar to that issued on April 1, 1941, but green in colour, and there was again a great rush of dealers and private collectors anxious to secure first-day covers.

January 31. The Germans put up a terrific barrage at night when British planes pass over; it is noticed that there is plenty of activity when St. Nazaire is bombed. Great fortification works are going on in all parts of the Islands, and funny little railways have been constructed for these operations, particular at Gorey and at La Pulente, while an anti-tank wall is being built on the beach at Le Hocq. A de-lousing hut has been constructed in the grounds of the Hospital for some of the foreign labourers. There has been a large number of deaths during the month.

FEBRUARY 1942

February 1. The fuel ration contains a little more coal than last, and in addition there is peat and faggots for those persons who fetch same. It is estimated that each month's wood ration amounts to about 1,500 tons. The tobacco ration is the same—20 cigarettes alternating with 10 cigarettes and 1 oz. of pipe tobacco.

February 2. This week's extra rations consist of a tin of tunny fish for everybody, 1 lb. of oranges for juveniles and 6 oz. of walnuts for adults. By German order, the *E.P.* publishes an obviously inspired report from the Guernsey *Star* dealing with the recent R.A.F. raid. It is learned that four members of a British bomber which was shot down by the Germans on the night of January 31 have been found in a dinghy off the Island; the pilot died and the others were eventually taken to a prison camp in France, being lodged in the Air Force Hospital at Merton Hotel for two days, during which strong guards were posted in the vicinity.

February 4. Four German Orders registered by the Royal Court: one deals with deep-sea fishing and the policing of ports, another prohibits the manufacture of official stamps and seals of the German Armed Forces, a third contains executive regulations under a pervious Order dealing with postal communications, and the fourth relates to the declaration of American property. The B.B.C. announces that light naval forces have sunk two fully-laden German supply ships off the Channel Islands.

February 6. The Superior Council issues an Order notifying members of the public that they will be photographed, so that a copy may be affixed to their identity cards.

February 7. Numbers of bodies of German sailors and soldiers are being washed up around the coasts of the Island, these being from the supply ships which were sunk three days ago. German Air Force orchestra gives symphony concert at The Forum. Arrival of over 6,000 Red Cross letters.

February 9. Issue of 4 oz. of coffee substitute, and 1 lb. of oranges to children; substitutes for tea and coffee are now being largely used.

February 10. As certain supplies ordered from France have not arrived, the *E.P.* printing arrangements have to undergo revision, it now taking ten hours to print a two-page paper which would normally be done in less than half an hour. The Germans test the air-raid siren.

February 13. Two daylight robberies of bread from a baker's shop are reported, as also robberies of food.

February 14. Tobacco prices increase: 1s. 4d. for 20 cigarettes and 1s. 4d. for 1 oz. of pipe tobacco.

February 15. Death of the Rev. J. A. Balleine, Rector of St. Brelade's since 1892, and Vice-Dean of Jersey.

February 16. This week's extra rations consist of ship's biscuits and a piece of soap. Essential supplies having been received, the *E.P.* goes back to normal printing. The meat ration is reduced by half from 8 oz. to 4 oz. Green Room Club presents a comedy at the Opera House. British plane sweeps over the Airport and the Five Mile Road.

February 20. In the middle of the morning British planes come in from the sea and fly over the harbour and towards Noirmont.

February 23. The work of taking photographs for identity cards commences, St. Helier being the first parish. This week's extra ration is 4 oz. of cocoa substitute per person. Germans give a 'Variety spadoni' at the Forum. We learn with interest that the Bishop of Winchester has been appointed Archbishop of York.

February 24. Farmers whose lands have been taken over for German military purposes and who have not received a requisitioning order are asked to inform their Constables of the facts; of late there has been a lot of manoeuvring by troops, whether the ground is cultivated or not; in one instance an elderly farmer who lost his temper with some soldiers has been sentenced to two years' imprisonment, this being his second term, although he was greatly provoked. A German notice calls attention to the fact that wood shall neither be supplied to the civil population without a permit from the Island authorities, nor to the forces without a permit to purchase issued by the Field Command; this is to try and stop purchases of wood other than the official ration, which everybody is trying to augment.

February 25. Owing to the inclemency of the weather, schools are closed; many of the children are insufficiently clad and large numbers of wooden-soled shoes with only canvas tops are being worn; added to this, there is a lack of fuel for school fires. The public is asked to give up any horse hair that may be available, for the making of brushes; some small brushes—toothbrushes, etc.—are being imported from France.

February 27. The severe weather conditions affect the milk supply, and the public is notified that there will be a 25 per cent. decrease in their already meagre ration. Several foreign labourers die from poisoning after having eaten hemlock under the impression that it was edible; these poor men are half-starved and eat anything resembling food, irrespective of where it is found. German band plays in the grounds of the General Hospital and outside the military hospital at Merton Hotel.

February 28. Amendment made to the Footwear Rationing Order whereby rubber used for repairs is put on the same coupon basis as leather. Persons now desiring new footwear must sign a form and declare before a panel that they are entirely without serviceable footwear. There has again been a large number of deaths, especially among elderly people, and almost everybody has suffered severely from chilblains. The bread has improved of late, and at the moment 60 tons of Jersey wholemeal, to which is added 25 per cent. of French flour, is used each week by the bakers. The allotment scheme at Georgetown has had to be revised because the Germans have taken over a large section of the site as a store dump, huge wooden buildings being constructed; only 30 out of the 105 plots originally marked out are now available. The Germans have opened a brothel for the troops at the Maison Victor Hugo, and there have been so many windows broken at night that several shops in the town are permanently boarded up. Shopkeepers have on sale a certain quantity of goods recently imported from France, Mostly in the cosmetic and toilet line, and a certain amount of brandy has also arrived. During the month two boys from a private school stole two revolvers from German officers who were exercising at the F.B. Fields; the latter visited the school concerned, but took it in good part and did not press for punishment. The Dean is having a difficult time in trying to keep some of the churches open owing to the small number of clergy now available, and more lay preachers have been forthcoming. Many private socials are being held, usually with a charitable object, and there is a very large clientèle at the various 'dancing classes'. The A.R.P. personnel now turns out after a severe anti-aircraft barrrage when British planes pass over at night.

MARCH 1942

March 1. British planes are observed flying off the harbours, where activities cease for a time; later in the day leaflets in French are picked up. Fuel rations for March are similar to those for last month, with the addition of a little coal. Butter ration reduced from 4 oz. to 2 oz. per week.

March 2. This week's extra rations consist of 2 oz. of cooking fat or margarine, a tin of tomatoes per head (1s. 7d.) and a jam ration starts again; many poor people find it difficult to purchase all their extra rations in one week, so most shops are allowing them to draw them at their convenience. A quantity of honey is being issued at 4s. 9d. per lb.; shopkeepers have been notified to increase the potato ration by 1 lb., making it 6 lb. per head, and breakfast meal is increased by 1 oz. A long German Order deals with the notification to them of property belonging to nationals of the British Empire who are not residing in the Island.

March 3. Arrival of a large number of Red Cross messages, including many replies to those sent from here at the end of last summer.

March 4. German notice calls the attention of the public to the fact that the metric system is operative in all dealings with the Army of Occupation. Normal milk ration resumed owing to better weather.

March 6. The cost of electricity increased by 50 per cent., in view of the high cost of oil purchased by the company; the price per unit for lighting purposes is now 9d., as compared with 6d.

March 7. Order issued revoking all licences granted under the

Milk Control (Jersey) Order, 1941, this mainly affecting farmer retailers.

March 8. Milk ration cut down again for a few days owing to a resumption of cold weather, the cattle being unable to go out.

March 9. This week's extra rations consist of a tin of sardines and 4 oz. of coffee substitute. The Germans commence their own newspapers again after an interval of a month owing to their direct printer breaking down and having to be sent to Paris for repair.

March 10. Issue of what is expected to be the last paraffin ration until October, at the price of 7d. per pint.

March 12. The Germans commence a series of night manoeuvres. German officials arrive in a plane with Red Cross markings and escorted by Messerschmitt fighters.

March 13. Germans give variety show at The Forum, and an Air Force band plays outside the German Military Hospital. Prices of French baking powder fixed at 1½d. per packet; there has been a ramp in this commodity for a long time, as much as 7d. a packet being charged.

March 14. Issue of cycle tyres to persons who are greatly in need of them; these are 7s. 6d. each, plus fitting charge. Two German Orders registered by the Royal Court, one relating to the medical treatment of the personnel of the German Armed Forces, the other dealing with sales of medical prescriptions. Tobacco ration for this week is 20 cigarettes only.

March 15. British planes in the vicinity of the harbours; all work temporarily suspended.

March 16. This week's extra rations consist of 4 oz. of cocoa powder, a packet of 'Lessive' washing powder, a piece of toilet soap, and 7 oz. of dates. Messrs. Britton and Whinnerah present a thriller at the Opera House. Germans hold one of the heaviest gun practices we have yet heard.

March 17. Hours of gas supply altered—7 a.m. to 2 p.m. instead of 7.30 to 2.30 (evening hours remain the same: 5 to 9); nearly everybody has exceeded the gas ration for this month the more vegetables we eat the more have to be cooked. The Irish community run a dance in celebration of St. Patrick's Day at The Plaza, from 9.45 p.m. to 6 a.m.

March 18. German Order registered reducing the speed limit of all motor vehicles in the centre of St. Helier to 15 miles per hour.

March 19. Arrival of another batch of Red Cross letters.

March 20. Appeal made for cardboard for use in the manufacture of slippers made by 'Summerland'; some of the goods manufactured there are of very serviceable quality, especially socks and stockings.

March 21. Tobacco ration again 20 cigarettes. Hours of electricity altered, none to be consumed between 11 p.m. and 6 a.m. Two farmers fined by the Royal Court—one for failing to declare the death of a heifer and the other for refusing to give information under the Milk Order. German band plays in the Royal Square.

March 23. Germans issue notice reminding the public that they are not allowed outside their houses following the sounding of an alarm; this Order applies to alarms by sirens and/or A.A. fire. Retail price of new potatoes, of which there is only a small quantity available as yet, fixed at 1s. per lb. for ware and 10d. for mids. Issue of 2 oz. of cheese for adults and juveniles and half a pint of cooking oil for everybody.

March 25. The Germans bring over about a dozen heavy tanks, these being preceded for some days by personnel. They are stationed near Tabor Chapel. British planes pass near the Island on their way to St. Nazaire, about midnight, and heavy gunfire from the French coast is heard.

March 26. The Germans commence a series of night manoeuvres; there is no doubt that the Island is a proper training depôt.

March 27. Further curtailment of the bus services; return travel not guaranteed, only single tickets within a 3½-mile radius of town. Notices issued by the Department of Agriculture—(1) Farmers allowed artificial fertilisers to the extent of 18 lb. per vergée of the area allocated to hay and grazing on their Cultivation Order; (2) Growers with a surplus of seed potatoes must notify the Department; (3) Potatoes grown under glass can be lifted only under licence; (4) Any farmer growing cereal crops who considers his crop to be a failure must report immediately, and (5) The price of milk is fixed at 1s. 4d. per pot—4d. per pint retail, delivered or fetched.

March 28. Just after midnight, for nearly three hours, severe anti-aircraft fire was directed against British planes, it was learned from the B.B.C. that a raid by the three Services had been made on the submarine base at St. Nazaire. Soldiers give a concert at the Forum, and a military band plays in the Royal Square, which is usual at week-ends. Tobacco ration alternates again for the next four weeks—20 cigarettes with 10 cigarettes and an ounce of pipe tobacco. Textile Department urgently appeals for box nails to be used in the manufacture of children's sandals, etc.

March 30. This week's extra rations consist of half a pound of dried beans, half a pint of liquid saccharin, and, for juveniles only 4 oz. of dates or 5 oz. of walnuts. The 'Fifty-Fifty Club' presents a comedy at the Opera House. Potato ration reduced to 5 lb. per person.

March 31. The retailing of milk by farmers comes to an end, except in a few isolated instances; this affects about 7,000 customers, who have now to get their milk from other depôts. Many of the labourers brought from the Continent are so hungry that in certain parts of the Island there is a shortage of cats! These men—a large number of whom are Spaniards—are paid in Occupation money, which is plentiful, but they cannot buy anything, and some have been known to offer 10 marks (£1 0s. 10d.) for a cup of coffee! The Bel Ami Cabaret for the Germans has been closed down owing, it is stated, to inability to obtain liquor. There have been suicides of some German officers during the month, and one was killed by the explosion of a land-mine. Part of the Five Mile Road is now mined. Foreign labourers who die are given a Protestant or Roman Catholic funeral and are buried in the Strangers' Cemetery, the burial ceremony being made the occasion for several political speeches. Work at the Airport has been accelerated and the airfield has been greatly enlarged; the streets of the town, which were getting in a shocking state, have now been patched up with cement. The Germans have forbidden the publication of the local rainfall figures as they might be useful to the 'enemy'! Figures of births and deaths for the three months ending March 31 were 113 and 320 respectively.

APRIL 1942

April 1. Fuel ration for this month consists of wood only, with a few exceptions. The Germans issued a notice prohibiting the use of motor vehicles on Sundays, except for some essential services (this is really funny!).

April 2. The Department of Education advertises for examiners in an effort to organise a local School Certificate Examination.

April 3. Good Friday. Passiontide music was performed in the churches.

April 4. In connection with A.R.P., all 'authority cards' have to be returned immediately to the A.R.P. Office for submission to the Field Command, College House. Another German Order requires the Island to furnish 50 gents' cycles, of which 20 is the quota of St. Helier. Personnel of the German Army have had their petrol cut down again. The markets are full of Easter flowers, of which the Germans buy large quantities. The Germans bring over an anti-aircraft float from France and berth it in the harbour. Public Library issues 625 books from the lending department—a record.

April 5. Easter Sunday. Islanders cheered by B.B.C. message to the occupied peoples. The churches were well filled and the Germans held their own services.

April 6. Easter Monday. Apart from a football match, there was very little doing; no buses were running today. Extra rations for this week consist of a slab of chocolate (approximately 4½ oz.) for everybody.

April 7. Following an appeal by a Jerseyman prisoner of war, Anglican prayer and hymn books are being sent.

April 8. German Order published warning all Reich nationals who are not as yet in the armed forces to report to German headquarters in Paris within one week: this Order does not apply to many persons, but it includes a number of interpreters. A hundred plots are now available in a part of the F.B. Fields and are being handed over to allotment holders by the Jersey Allotments Council at a charge of 10s. per plot for the season.

April 11. German Order registered by the Royal Court concerning motor vehicles; every inhabitant having one in his custody must furnish full particulars to the Department of Transport and Communications; meanwhile, all batteries are to be removed, and if it is impossible to raise the car off the ground, the tyres are to be removed and sent to a storage depôt. Woman sentenced by the Royal Court for the worst ration fraud to date.

April 13. Issue of 4 oz. of coffee substitute and a piece of household soap. Green Room Club presents opera at the Opera House.

April 15. An article in the *E.P.* urges the growing of more foodstuffs, especially by persons who still have large lawns and flower gardens.

April 16. Early in the morning British planes fly over the north-east of the Island and machine-gun a party of Germans. German notice warns the public that they must take cover immediately on the sounding of the air-raid siren, and must remain there until the 'all-clear'.

April 18. The Germans arrest two local growers for alleged sabotage of crops by neglect of greenhouses which were planted with potatoes and tomatoes; they were eventually released after being fined 1,000 R.M. and severely reprimanded.

April 20. Issue of local currency notes in denominations of £1, 10s., 2s., 1s. and 6d.; these are quite attractive, having been designed by Edmund Blampied. Extra rations this week of 8 oz. of macaroni per head, five boxes of matches per household, and the jam ration commences again in alphabetical order. Today being Hitler's birthday the Germans have had special celebrations, it was learned that at a German billet in the evening, when a sergeant-major was addressing his men on the qualities of 'the Fuehrer', one of them shot him and then committed suicide.

April 22. German notice issued concerning the renewal of fishing permits, which are to be granted to fishermen only on condition that 90 per cent. of the catch is placed at the disposal of the States. Tobacco ration for the next four weeks remains the same. The Islanders learn with appreciation that Lord Portsea has asked Parliament if it were possible to send a food ship to the Channel Islands.

April 23. Orders issued by the Department of Agriculture revoking certain Orders relating to animal bedding and the stabling of cattle. German company gives a variety show at The Forum.

April 24. Farmers informed that a top dressing of artificial fertliser for cereal crops is available at the rate of 16 lb. per vergée; a small amount of French seed potatoes (late variety) is also available for planting. Great interest aroused by a postscript to the B.B.C. News dealing with Channel Islanders who evacuated from the Islands nearly two years ago.

April 25. Three Orders registered by the Royal Court: (1) Declaration of Members of Households, whereby all such must have their names on a list which is to be hung behind the main door for inspection at any time by officials; (2) Prohibition of Training of Radio-Telegraphists and Wireless Technicians and (3) Withdrawal from Circulation of German Copper Coins (these are pieces of 1 and 2 pfennig). German band gives performance in the Royal Square.

April 27. Another serious ration fraud before the Royal Court, a husband and wife sentenced to nine months and three months respectively. This week's extra ration is a can of dwarf beans per head. During last month 5,000 trees were planted to replace trees felled for use as fuel; more are to be planted as time goes on. Island School of Dancing and Elocution gives display at the Opera House.

April 28. The J.M.T. announces that, it is only possible to run buses on Tuesdays and Saturdays. The Department of Agriculture gives notice that all gardens and small plots in a neglected state will be taken in hand without compensation.

April 29. German notice issued that all persons are forthwith forbidden to wear A.R.P. coat badges and arm badges; furthermore, all A.R.P. signs are to be removed from buildings; members of A.R.P. are only allowed to wear arm badges when specially called upon during action.

April 30. British planes fly over the Island, and in consequence all work on the quays is stopped for a period. Foreign workers, some of whom now have their wives with them, are working on railroads (one from Ronez to St. Peter's), blockhouses, gun emplacements, etc. A lot of work is going on at some of the slipways adjacent to the town, where blockhouses are being constructed; one cannot walk anywhere without seeing a gun position, sentries, barbed wire and sandbags. Apart from the official ration, nearly all the tractors in use in the Island are being run on stolen petrol.

May 1942

May 1. German Order issued whereby all persons owning livestock of any description (excluding rabbits) must send in a list thereof. Ration of wood issued for May, with a few exceptions. Heavy gun practice has been going on this week, part of the East Coast Road being closed to traffic and pedestrians for a short period.

May 2. First States session of the year held, the main business being the Budget. (The cost of the Army of Occupation under various heads was £138,413 3s. 10d.). Other items included the adoption of a proposal to maintain the school-leaving age at 15 years; removal of restrictions on the sale of milk, whereby shops may now open at any hour all the week, and a tribute to the late Mr. J. E. Le Huquet (Deputy Greffier). A German Order was also registered forbidding camping out in tents, etc., at night. The Germans are celebrating May Day today, and all work on the various fortifications schemes is stopped.

May 3. An attempt to leave the Island ends in tragedy when the boat containing three youths overturns off the south-east coast, and one of them (named Audrain) is drowned; the other two (named Hassell and Gould) were taken prisoner by the Germans. It was subsequently learned that the attempt was made from Green Island, and that when the boat was taken there a party of Germans helped the boys to launch it!

March 4. Criminal Assizes acquit a States official charged with perjury in connection with the removal of a small quantity of grain from one of the boats. Issue of 4 oz. of coffee substitute.

May 5. German concert given at The Forum, to which civilians are invited. In the early hours several Guernseymen and the crew of a German store ship climb ashore after the vessel had struck a rock off Grosnez, the result of fog: part of the cargo was eventually salvaged. Among the cargo was a quantity of yeast for the Ann Street Brewery, where the Germans are to make beer.

May 6. Inquest opened and adjourned on the lad named Audrain, drowned in the attempt to escape on the 3rd. The Germans take a serious view of the affair as photographs and a special chart which had been prepared for them were found. A lot of the photos were of gun positions.

May 7. Largest German naval force yet seen visits local waters; this consisted of five destroyers (three of which entered harbour), two E-boats, two anti-aircraft vessels, and two supply ships of approximate 12,000 and 5,000 tons. During the day the town was full of sailors and the quays were as busy as during a normal potato season. The ships left early in the evening, and all day everybody prayed that they would be spotted by the R.A.F. Large batch of Red Cross messages arrive. The S.C.S. bus service is to be cut in the same way as the J.M.T. owing to the lack of fuel.

May 8. German Order issued prohibiting persons over 16 who were engaged on May 1, 1942 in agriculture or horticulture to leave their employment without permission of the Department of Agriculture; penalties up to six weeks' imprisonment or a fine up to 30,000 reichsmarks (over £3,000) are threatened. Air-raid warning given on the quays—the R.A.F. is about!

May 9. The Germans issue a warning to the inhabitants against further attempts to leave the Island and threaten severe penalties: parents and guardians are to be held responsible in future, and in the event of a similar event occurring, measures will be taken affecting all men of military age in the Island, e.g., internment on the Continent. A further notice requires that all boats not in the four specified harbours of the Island shall be declared in writing to the Harbour Kommandant, and the Constables of the various parishes are held responsible for the declaring of all boats whose owners have left the Island. The penalties are, six week's imprisonment or a fine of 30,000 reichsmarks.

May 10. Mr. Churchill's speech cheers us up; the German version of it gave proof of what credence can be attached to any of their propaganda.

May 11. Alterations made in the hours during which gas is cut off—from 2 p.m. to 5 p.m. and from 8 p.m. to 6 a.m. The price of new potatoes is fixed at 4½d. per pound, and those who can afford to purchase these for the whole of their ration are asked to do so. This week's extra ration consists of a tin of tomatoes per head. Messrs. Britton and Whinnerah present a play at the Opera House.

May 12. At the last session of the Royal Court it was decided that in cases of persons dying outside the Island, the death of whom was reported by the Red Cross, there should be an administrator appointed who would apply for the registration of the Will of such deceased person.

May 15. In view of the danger of smallpox, the Department of Public Health urges the public to be vaccinated; this service is free, and may be performed by one's own practitioner. Another large batch of Red Cross letters arrives.

May 16. Department of Essential Commodities advises all builders, contractors and traders that accounts for payment by the German authorities must be made out in German, and may be translated for them at the Department's office in Mulcaster Street. The Germans have forbidden the sale of spirits in public houses and are also checking supplies held by the various merchants. This affects persons holding doctor's certificates for supplies of liquor for medicinal purposes. Cider has arrived from France recently; the Ann Street Brewery is making beer for the German troops only and half has to be sent to Guernsey.

May 18. Until the end of the month the price of home-grown potatoes is fixed at 23s. 6d. per cwt. on a sale by a grower, 24s. 6d. on a sale by wholesale, and 3d. per lb. retail; the ration remains at 5 lb. per person per week. The Honorary Police are visiting houses to make sure that the recent Order regarding the placing of names of household members near the main door has been carried out. The bread now contains 50 per cent. of French flour and 50 per cent, of local flour. This week's extra rations consist of ¼ lb. margarine and a piece of household soap, and two French eggs for children under six years of age. Fish shops

71

may keep open until 6 p.m.

May 19. Owing to the full quota not having been met, three parishes warn cyclists to take their machines (within specified numbers) to their respective parish halls, so that some of these may be picked out. Notice is also given by the German Harbour Kommandant that all boats, including canoes, must be taken by their owners to one of the four specified harbours, with severe penalties for non-compliance, the Constables being made responsible for boats belonging to persons who are at the moment non-resident here. Yet another notice prohibits the public from using certain streets in the neighbourhood of the Weighbridge after 9.15 this evening: the Germans are to have an invasion practice. Victoria College Playing Field is to be let out as allotments under the auspices of the Jersey Allotments Council.

May 20. British planes over again, the Germans putting up a fairly heavy barrage; it is presumed that a plane had its bomb rack hit, as in a field at Trinity 11 small high-explosive bombs were dropped, but without doing any damage.

May 22. Growers are advised to spray their potatoes, in view of the very wet weather which has prevailed of late. Owing to the temporary exhaustion of the supply of lymph, there is to be a short lull in the vaccination campaign, practically the whole of the population taking advantage of the service.

May 23. British planes pass over again in the early morning on their way to and from St. Nazaire. Department of Agriculture announces a scheme by which farmers requiring the services of additional agricultural labourers (male), with a guarantee of four months' work, will pay a weekly wage of 40s. for a 56-hour week as their share of the wages paid. The tobacco ration remains the same for the next four weeks.

May 24. Whit Sunday; miserable day, with high wind and rain squalls.

May 25. Whit Monday; weather worse than previous day. This week's extra rations consist of 8 oz. of macaroni, 4 oz. of coffee substitute, and 10 boxes of matches per household. Amateur Dramatic Club presents *The Wind and the Rain* at the Opera House, an apt title.

May 26. Owing to the Germans alleging that their telephone cable has been cut at Five Oaks, an area of two kilometres radius from the point involved has to supply guards for a period of 14 days, six men (between the ages of 18 and 55) patrolling at a time in two-hour shifts. The Germans open a store at Burton's, at which the troops may purchase presents, etc., and it is understood that the prices demanded are very high, but Occupation money cannot be expended in Germany and must be got rid of.

May 28. German court passes sentence on the manager of a local grocery store who has been in custody since the middle of April for black-market activities; this was 12 months' imprisonment and a fine of £150, his firm being fined £650; two other men implicated were fined £80 or 50 days' imprisonment. A case dealing with the sale of black-market brandy was also disposed of, two men being sentenced to 3 years and 2 months, and another to 1 year and 10 months. It is also learned that during the month six men were condemned to short sentences for alleged sabotage in connection with some compressors on a job for the Germans in St. Peter's Valley. Another man has been sentenced to 5 years for possessing a revolver and ammunition. Sentences of more than two or three months' duration have to be served in France.

May 29. Notice from the Essential Commodities Committee gives the public reason to think that a fish ration may be available in the near future. Department of Agriculture increases the number of calves per month that may be exempted from slaughter; this is now 80, with no more than three bull calves. Burial by the Germans of a Belgian worker, aged 19, who was killed when bird-nesting on the north coast.

May 30. Two German Orders registered by the Royal Court; one deals with the use of scrap film, old film and cut film intended to be destroyed, and the other relates to the regulation of working hours. The Court also imposed fines on some well-known residents who were concerned with incorrect declarations regarding the ownership of cows. Tobacco prices increased to 1s. 7d. for 20 cigarettes and 1s. 7d. for 1 oz. of tobacco. Four boxes of matches were issued with this week's ration of 20 cigarettes. A large number of farmers who have established reputations for vegetable growing have been notified that they are to supply the German forces only, clearing depôts being established in town.

May 31. We learn with satisfaction of the R.A.F.'s first big raid with 1,000 bombers over Cologne; as a consequence of this the German troops billeted at Highlands have been forbidden to use their wireless sets. Many people have suffered severely owing to the effects of vaccination. Although a few cricket matches are being played it has been decreed that Victoria College boys will not take part in any of the normal sports, as conditions prevent them being physically fit. The troops are now forbidden to attend churches where services are being held in English. Red Cross messages are now coming regularly.

JUNE 1942

June 1. Price of potatoes altered: 14s. on a sale by a grower; 15s. 2d. on a sale by wholesale and 2d. per lb. retail; the ration per week is 7 lb. per head (officially). This month's fuel ration consists of wood again, with bundles of faggots if desired. This week's extras consist of 8 oz. of dried split beans per head, and two date sticks and a bar of chocolate for everyone up to the age of 18 years.

June 2. The Germans institute a new one-way traffic system in the town area. The Royal Court takes a serious view of the farmer withholding all his milk supply, and imposes a fine of £100. Supplies of paper failing to arrive from France, the *E.P.* has again to resort to printing a single sheet every day on an old hand-fed press; on account of this the Germans cannot publish their own newspaper.

June 5. Notification is given of six cases of diphtheria, and in consequence a school is closed in St. Ouen's Parish.

June 6. The Traffic Order is causing much confusion, and the German Feldgendarmerie (known as the 'Chain Gang' because of a chain worn around the neck) are fining people on the spot for pretty offences against the regulations.

June 8. All wireless sets belonging to the civilian population are to be handed in and retained by the Feldkommandantur; infractions of this Order are punishable by imprisonment up to six weeks and a fine of 30,000 reichsmarks (over £3,000). It is said that this Order is 'decreed by a higher command', and it is believed that efforts have been made by the local German authorities to have the Order rescinded. This week's extras consist of a new jam ration (commencing alphabetically), 3 oz. of cheese, and a packet of washing powder. Messrs. Britton and Whinnerah present a musical comedy at the Opera House.

June 9. Further details are given concerning the delivery of wireless sets, which is to be completed by June 13. A delegation waited upon the German authorities to plead for the retention of the sets, and although they were sympathetically received there was no hope given that the Order would be recalled. German court martial sentences two girls to two months' imprisonment, for stealing beef and butter from a building in which they worked and where German troops are billeted. Late in the evening the Germans carry out a practice, for the repelling of a British invading party.

June 10. The Germans issue a notice to the effect that the confiscation of wireless sets is not to be regarded as a punishment but as a measure taken for military reasons; they also add that the sets will be kept in safe custody and that in order to ensure orderly collection the date of delivery has been extended to June 20.

June 12. Further details issued regarding the collection of wireless sets: depôts are named, and persons with surnames commencing A to K must hand their sets in up to the 17th, L to Z up to the 20th; the public is also informed that it will be useless to make application for exceptions. Registration for fish is announced, but regular supplies cannot be guaranteed; this measure has as its object the prevention of persons going from one place to another and obtaining supplies from each.

June 13. The *E.P.* gives notice that publication is to be suspended owing to supplies of paper not having arrived, but a consignment is delivered during the day and saves the situation. German band plays in the Royal Square during the afternoon. Today being Derby Day, several sweepstakes are run.

June 14. A lot of week-end shipping has been noted; numbers of the Todt Organisation are leaving the Island. Several persons who had been sentenced either in Jersey or Guernsey were taken to a German prison in France.

June 15. Notice given by the Department of Public Health regarding arrangements made for free vaccination at A.R.P. first-aid points and posts. The Department of Agriculture announces that boys over the age of 14 may be released from school for the summer holidays after June 15 if they wish to assist with agricultural work. Fish may now be obtained from dealers with whom one is registered. German notice concerning motor cycles; particulars are to be forwarded of make, horse-power, condition, etc., with the usual penalties for non-compliance. This week's extras consist of 8 oz. of coffee substitute per head and a piece of toilet soap. The potato ration is now fixed at 10 lb. per head per week.

June 16. Among the articles stolen in recent robberies are several wireless sets; this handing-in of our sets has certainly cast a gloom over the Island.

June 17. A typewritten pamphlet is being circulated headed Bulletin No. 1 of the British Patriots; this urges us not to give up our wireless sets and refutes the German assertion that the confiscation is covered by the Hague Convention.

June 19. The public is urged to be careful in the use of water, in order to save fuel oil used for pumping; the price of gas fixed at 6s. per 1,000 cubic feet, an increase of 7d. A policeman who supplied petrol to the boys who recently tried to get away has been sentenced by the Germans to two months' imprisonment. All telephones within a mile of the north of the Island have been cut off; the Germans are very jittery.

June 20. After a morning of wild rumours, the Germans issued a notice that, following a further act of sabotage of telephonic communications and a distribution of leaflets, they had ordered the arrest of ten persons; in the event of the perpetrators not being discovered, these ten people would be taken to a Continental internment camp, and if a repetition of such incidents occurred, twenty persons would be dealt with this way. Tobacco ration remains the same for the next four weeks.

June 21. The German troops held several sporting events, including a relay race through the streets of the town; prizes were presented in the Parade and a band played there: one of the prizes was a photograph of Hitler. Growers are prohibited from digging owing to there being a glut of potatoes. The Germans are tapping telephone wires and interrogating people who give cause for suspicion. Over 10,000 wireless sets have been handed in; representations are being made in Paris for their return.

June 22. The Germans have given until the 30th for the perpetrators of the act of sabotage and the distribution of leaflets to come forward: in the meantime, the ten hostages are still in jail—Messrs. Frank Tregear, 'Tony' Huelin, Geo. Le Cocq, Phil. Le Cornu, H. Vallois, W. H. Kennett, H. Ferguson, Advocate H. W. Giffard, Dr. C. Mattas and Col. Wellbourne. Schools closed for a week in consequence of the children having been vaccinated. Extras for this week: 8 oz. of cocoa substitute per head, half a pint of vinegar, and ten boxes of matches per household. Old Victorians' Sports Club present a comedy-thriller at the Opera House.

June 23. The German Feldgendarmerie carry out a search of the *E.P.* premises in an effort to discover where the leaflets were printed; other printing offices have also been searched and some private houses have been visited.

June 24. Several persons detained and interrogated in connection with the leaflets affair.

June 24. Large numbers of troops and workers leave the

Island including an Air Force contingent, which was played down to the quay by a band.

June 26. The author of the leaflet has now been discovered and the German police are pursuing inquiries in order to trace those persons who were responsible for circulation; several already arrested in connection with the affair, have been let go.

June 27. German Order issued whereby all fishing boats must, before July 5, be painted with the colours blue, white and red, in that order, from the bows, across the boats' sides and fore-decks, extending from the waterline on one side to the waterline on the other, each strip of colour to be a foot wide. The salt ration ends until further supplies are available from France, and this week's tobacco ration is supplemented by five boxes of matches. The Germans stop the publishing of messages to relatives and friends through the Red Cross which have for some time been a regular feature in the *E.P.* German band plays in the Royal Square in the afternoon. The ten hostages were released from prison, where they had been made as comfortable as possible, their meals being supplied every day from Gaudin's Restaurant. It is now a week since the wireless sets were handed in.

June 28. Early in the morning British planes pass over on their way to and from St. Nazaire; the Germans fired upon them and claim to have brought one down off the north of the Island.

June 29. Planes over again in the early morning and also in the afternoon. The Germans announce that five other persons are under arrest because of the distribution of another leaflet, and that these will be set free likewise if the distributors are found by July 10. Most of these five are masters from Victoria College, and this has necessitated the temporary closing of the school. Many persons are also being apprehended and interrogated. A German Order states that, photographic materials of all kinds, including cameras, film cameras and enlargers, are to be taken into custody by the the military authorities by July 11. Price of potatoes lowered: 12s. on a sale by a grower; 1½d. per lb. retail. This week's extras consist of 8 oz. of macaroni per head and a stick of shaving soap for the male adult population; there was also a large quantity of French apricots on sale at the greengrocer shops at 1s. 6d. per lb.

June 30. Alterations made to the Rationing Order, whereby certain goods hitherto on the controlled articles list are placed on the list of rationed articles. German court martial sentences two girls, aged 14 and 15 years of age to three days' imprisonment; it was alleged that they spat out some cherry stones at Germans who were passing at the time.

It may be interesting to quote from the leader published in the *E.P.* at the end of two years of Occupation, which, although printed in accordance with German demands, gives an accurate picture of what an awkward time we have passed through . . . 'looking back to that fateful 1st of July, 1940, we now realise how few of us, if any, visualised a separation from our kith and kin extending over two years, and how little prepared the Island was for such a new and dramatic experience. From Britain we were accustomed to draw the great bulk of our supplies; to Britain we sold our surplus products—that country was our only customer. With the complete cutting off of communications, therefore, the whole economic structure of the Island was changed, and now ways and means had to be devised for the maintenance of the life of the community. The local authorities were now set a difficult problem, and while there are critics who will aver that the methods evolved could have been improved upon, the great majority of the inhabitants will agree, we feel sure, that those responsible for administration of the Island— who received the full co-operation of the German Forces of Occupation—have done extremely well in circumstances without precedent in local history. We can now look back on those two years and say that although at times the food situation has been difficult, it has never reached that acute stage it might very well have done had the organisation of our supplies been less intelligently carried out. Of the forces of Occupation, we can only repeat the words used in our editorial of twelve months ago, "the behaviour of the military rank and file has been exemplary". So we pass on to the third year and all that it may hold for us. Our hope, which we know full well is that of all our readers, is that during the coming twelve months the peace for which we all long will be proclaimed throughout the world.'

JULY 1942

July 1. At the beginning of the third year of Occupation some people wore a rose for England and a black tie in mourning for freedom. The Germans celebrated it by having a double-number of their newspaper, with special articles calling attention to the day. The fuel ration for July and August consists of half the wood available in the previous months.

July 3. Alterations made under the Textile and Footwear Order, whereby imported sandals and slippers are to be rationed; a quantity of wool is also available at 4s. 2d. per oz. Building contractors are warned by the German authorities that it is prohibited to undertake, or complete, building operations of a total cost exceeding £500, except where a permit has been obtained from the Department of Public Health.

July 4. The Germans advertise for a master, engineer and one deckhand for the s.t. *Duke of Normandy*. Arrival of a large quantity of greenhouse carrots from Guernsey; the prices of local vegetables are still very high. German Order issued requiring that the following articles not in the possession of the German Forces shall be declared to the German authorities by July 18: New and used accumulators for motor vehicles; accessories for motor vehicles; electrical material for motor vehicles; spare parts and constituent parts of motor vehicles; oil paints and cellulose varnishes for motor vehicles—with the usual penalties for non-declaration.

July 6. Extra rations for this week are half a pint of cooking oil per head and one pint of liquid saccharin. Messrs. H. B. Coley and Max Le Feuvre present a comedy at the Opera House. Victoria College (still at Halkett Place) re-opens; the places of the masters who are still in jail are taken by prefects who have been teaching at elementary schools.

July 7. A German court martial has passed sentence on two brothers in connection with the first leaflet, five years' imprisonment and two years' imprisonment respectively.

July 8. Two French members of the Todt Organisation found accidentally gassed at their billet; they were father and son, and at the subsequent funeral large numbers of the French colony were present.

July 10. Without any explanation, the Germans release the hostages who were incarcerated some days ago in connection with the second leaflet.

July 11. The Germans bring over from France a full-size steam railway engine, and this is used on the lines running all round the harbours and along the track running to Bel Royal: the children are in their element! In the afternoon an Air Force band played in the Royal Square.

July 12. The Germans invite the public to a variety concert at the Forum; invitation is one thing—acceptance another.

July 13. Father and son sentenced to six months and twelve months respectively at the Assizes for the theft of a cow for black market purposes. This week, 20 boxes of matches and 4 oz. of cheese are the extra rations, while a much-appreciated gift for children and juveniles under 18 is a pound of biscuits from the French Secours Nationale.

July 14. The Germans undertake blasting at 1,500 metres south-east of Havre-des-Pas, and all householders in the vicinity are warned to open their windows. The meat ration is to be increased by 2 oz., i.e. to 6 oz., for adults and juveniles, with 3 oz. for children. Bigwood's publish a ready reckoner for British–German money.

July 15. What must rank as one of the greatest jokes of the Occupation took place today. With all solemnity, the Germans officially opened the new railway, which at present connects the piers with Millbrook; a special platform was erected and speeches were made by various German officials, the Military Commandant of the Channel Islands blowing a whistle for the train to start and the latter—after a couple of attempts to get away—cutting a decorated tape as it commenced its journey. A band enlivened the proceedings, and afterwards the officials adjourned to the Pomme d'Or Hotel for a special commemorative dinner! The Germans declare that it is only the beginning of a railway which is in due course to be run practically right round the Island. For the moment it will be used solely for the transport of material and troops, later on it will be available for the use of civilians. And to think that we scrapped our trains because they were out of date.

July 17. At night the Germans carry out an evacuation practice.

July 18. Man charged at the Royal Court and fined £10 with costs for selling a reel of cotton—at 2s. 6d.! without holding a licence under the Textile and Footwear Order. Tobacco ration (fixed the same for next four weeks) supplemented by 10 boxes of matches. German Air Force band plays in the Royal Square.

July 20. The Germans give publicity to the findings of a recent court martial: The Court dealt with excessive prices of tobacco, certain dealers having been heavily fined; imprisonment had been imposed in several cases for careless driving which resulted in accidents, and sentences of five years' imprisonment had been passed on the distributor of the leaflet dealing with wireless sets. With reference to this the Germans quote Article 53 of the Hague Convention, as follows: 'All appliances adapted for the transmission of news, or for the transport of persons or goods, may be seized, even if they belong to private individuals.' The Germans also give warning that any accidental cutting of cables or wires during the harvesting of crops must be declared immediately, in order to avoid severe punishment. This week's extra rations consist of approximate 6½ oz. of cocoa and a piece of household soap; the salt ration (2 oz.) commences again, and a cheap wood ration at 1s. 6d. per cwt. is to be made available for the deserving poor of the Parish of St. Helier. Mr. E. Vivian Marett presents a comedy at the Opera House.

July 22. Huge quantities of material still arriving from France, the latest including about 800 tons of barbed wire. Some more railway engines also arrive; they are to be overhauled before being put into service.

July 24. More cycles are needed by the Germans and official notice to that effect is given, owners of machines within certain numbers being required to present them at several parish halls in order to have some picked out. Hundreds of frying-pans are on sale in the shops today, having arrived from France, and there is a rush to buy them; articles of this sort are fetching enormous prices at sales and in the second-hand shops; those sold today were at the reasonable price of 2s. 1d. (a mark).

July 25. The usual band performance took place in the Royal Square in the afternoon. The train running around the piers jumped the rails today, and it is suspected that some children are continually putting stones on the line.

July 27. German Order issued dealing with the harvesting of grain crops and protecting them from aerial attack; the public are warned to keep a look-out for incendiary leaves and to report same. Bus services are slightly augmented. This week's rations are supplemented by 3 oz. cheese and 8 oz. coffee substitute per head.

July 28. The *E.P.* suspends publication owing to the exhaustion of the paper supply. Knowing that this may be the last paper for some time, the Germans take the opportunity of inserting several notices. We are reminded that the death penalty will be inflicted in cases of espionage, sabotage or treason, and owners of dogs are again told not to let them stray into minefields. The military patrol having had orders to shoot such animals.

July 29. The Germans bring over a 100-ton floating crane, and this is followed later by some steam cranes, which are placed on the New North Quay.

July 30. German Feldgendarmerie has again started going around at night to see if any lights are lit after 11 o'clock; several people have been fined, the Germans going up into the bedrooms to feel the electric bulbs. Large catches of mackerel are being made, sometimes in the region of two thousand.

July 31. Well, the end of the month finds us without wireless and no *E.P.*; Any special notices are posted in the *E.P.* windows, and those dealing with vegetable prices or rations may be seen outside the Food Control Office. The Germans have taken for their own use 250 of the wireless sets which they assured us would be kept in safe custody, and for still having one, a man has been fined £50 and another sentenced to 12 months' imprisonment, to be served when notified. The Germans have also set up their own shop where troops may take photographs to be developed. The farmers have been allowed a small quantity of petrol for reaping and have started on oats, but the wheat crop is not yet quite ready. An enormous amount of coal has been brought to the Island; consignments of building material are arriving, and the work of messing up the Island goes on. Among the many blasting operations which are taking place is a huge tunnel being made at the bottom of the Victoria Pier under Mount Bingham.

AUGUST 1942

August 1. Large consignment of French plums on sale in the market.

August 2. The Germans hold a big sports meeting at the F.B. Fields which lasts all the afternoon and part of the evening.

August 3. August Bank Holiday: beautiful weather, but no holiday spirit. This week's extras consist of 8 oz. of macaroni and a packet of washing powder. Mr. 'Sonny' Godbolt presents a revue at the Opera House.

August 5. The public warned to be careful with the water supply and to note certain restrictions on use. A list is to be made by the various Constables of persons who are willing to volunteer their services for the gathering of the harvest. German Order compels farmers to parade their horses in order to have them inspected and some earmarked for subsequent requisitioning: the first three parishes to do so included St. Helier, where the horses were lined up all along the Parade. Parish of St. Mary fixes the Rate at 1s. 6d. per quarter, compared with 7s. last year; this is due to the reversion to the old system of Occupiers' Rate and Foncier.

August 8. German Orders published in *Les Chroniques* deal with potatoes and the sending in of returns of motor oils. A notice published by the Department of Transport and Communications advertises for the services of temporary assistant valuers of motor vehicles.

August 10. A supply of paper having arrived, the *E.P.* resumes publication. This week's extras consist of a bottle of red wine for everybody over 18 years of age and 100 saccharin tablets for all.

August 11. More gents' cycles are to be requisitioned from the Parish of St. Helier, and the Germans also advise nationals of the Irish Free State that they must report at the Feldkommandantur by the 20th inst., taking with them their passports and the passports of the members of their family.

August 13. Big fire at a house occupied by the Germans, Les Silleries, Grouville, which was practically destroyed. As usual the Germans refuse publication of the newspaper report. Hundreds of Russians arrive; they made a pathetic sight, and many of them were mere boys, the majority with no footwear and some with bleeding feet; they were under escort of the Todt Organisation and were very badly treated.

August 14. Price of cider apples fixed at 3d. per lb. and honey at 5s. 6d. Among recent robberies, someone has cut and taken away a portion of the rubber floor covering in the entrance to Messrs. Le Gallais' Bath Street premises, presumably for boot repairs.

August 15. More Russians arrive, including some women; these are also in a sorry state, and are reputed to be some of the guerilla band. Of German Orders registered by the Royal Court, one relates to telegraphic and postal communications with Sweden, one concerning further measures against the Jews, and six others with financial affairs. The issuing of photographs for identity cards officially ends, having been in process since February 23.

August 15. The milk ration now half a pint per day. Large consignment of tomatoes arrives from Guernsey; large quantity of flour arrives from France, and coal (from Belgium) is still being unshipped in large consignments.

August 17. Department of Agriculture fixes the prices of the cereal crops as follows: Wheat, 28s. per cwt.; oats, 22s. 6d.; barley, 32s. 6d.; rye, 39s. The wheat crop this year is exceptionally good, but gleaners have caused a lot of trouble by cutting off the ears of wheat, and some farmers have even charged a price for permission to glean. The Germans demand more cycles from the parishes of St. Helier and St. Saviour. This week's extra is a 4-oz. packet of chocolate. Messrs. Britton and Whinnerah present a murder play at the Opera House.

August 18. The Germans issue instructions that all diseased potatoes must be removed immediately after digging; notice is given as to which slips may be used for access to beaches for the gathering of vraic. High German naval official pays a brief visit.

August 19. We learn with interest of the Dieppe raid. During the day the Germans have been running around as if they expected a landing; sentries were doubled, all posts manned, and for a time telephones were cut off.

August 20. The Germans have taken a lot of precautions consequent upon the Dieppe raid, among them being the lengthening of curfew, which is temporarily fixed from 10 p.m. to 6.30 a.m. St. Martin's fixes the Rate at 2s. 6d. per quarter.

August 21. Publication of two Department of Agriculture Orders concerning the cultivation of lands; revised delivery charges for fuel are also issued. Inquest concluded and a verdict of 'found drowned' passed in the case of the lad named Audrain, who made an attempt to leave the Island on May 3 last; the other two lads were subsequently sent to France.

August 22. Preliminary notice given of potato rationing, which is to be 5 lb. per week. Usual Saturday band performance in the Royal Square.

August 24. More cycles are to be requisitioned from the Parish of St. Helier. Large consignment of paper arrives for the *E.P.* This week's extra rations consist of half a pint of cooking oil and ten boxes of matches.

August 26. More allotment holders affected by the further taking over of ground at the Clifton Park Estate, Victoria Road, by the Todt Organisation. Grouville Parish Rate fixed at 2s. 1d. per quarter.

August 28. The Germans call attention of parents to the fact that children have been observed placing stones and pieces of wood on the railway lines of what we now call the Todt Express. The Guernsey papers have carried a German-inspired article dealing with the disrespect of people in Jersey, who ignored the playing of the German National Anthem at the opening ceremony of this railway.

August 29. Five boxes of matches were issued with today's tobacco ration, for 6d. Heaviest thunderstorm for some time floods roads and causes subsidences; in places more than 1½ inches of rain were registered in about half an hour. German soldiers rescue children from drowning at West Park.

August 30. Harvest festival services being held. The Germans hold sports meeting at the F.B. Fields and open a café in

Colomberie where soldiers may take their 'friends'. St. Saviour's Honorary Police do guard at Beauvoir, where the Germans have found that fruit in the garden, reserved for them, is being stolen. German soldiers are carrying their gas masks.

August 31. Extra rations for this week are 8 oz. of coffee substitute and a piece of toilet soap; two spools of lisle thread are available for females. The Fifty-Fifty Club presents a comedy-thriller at the Opera House. The threshing of cereals is now in full swing; the wheat crop is a good one. Night manoeuvres have been carried out on a large scale and the Dieppe raid certainly frightened 'our friends'; it is understood that if the raid had lasted a few hours longer many units would have been evacuated from the Island. The Censor has made things awkward at the *E.P.* and the Italians living in the Island have had to hand in their wireless sets. A shopkeeper has been sentenced by the Germans to one month's imprisonment and fined £100 for overcharging for second-hand goods. Motor cars which have not yet been requisitioned are being valued. The Russians are now working in various parts of the Island; those who have died have been buried in lime, and it is believed that there have been cases of typhus. The A.R.P. activities are almost nil; this month all helmets have had to be handed in. Some of the current prices in the black market are: butter, 16s.; beef, 10s.; pork 15s.; tea, £8 (all per lb.).

SEPTEMBER 1942

September 1. Fuel rationing commences again, this month's quota for most families being a hundredweight of wood.

September 2. By German order, several farmers, mainly in the Coin Varin Vingtaine of St. Peter's, are notified that they must make preparations to evacuate their farms within 48 hours if called upon to do so; the effect of such an order can hardly be imagined. The Germans have also taken over St. Matthew's R.C. Church, the Presbytery and hall.

September 3. Everybody is rallying around the unfortunate farmers with offers of help; it is not known for what reason their farms are to be requisitioned.*

---

* These farmers never actually received notice to quit, but were always in a state of apprehension. Soon afterwards the Germans commenced to construct concrete blockhouses in this district, which were to serve as military headquarters in the event of invasion.

September 4. Amendments made to the Livestock (Jersey) Order, 1942; any person wishing to transfer the ownership or custody of cattle can now only do so under licence. Small amount of French crockeryware on sale at fixed and quite reasonable prices.

September 5. Department of Agriculture issues notice in compliance with an Order of the Field Commandant: all cereal crops in the necessary dry condition, unless bad weather makes it impossible, must be gathered into stacks or brought under cover within the next two days; volunteers are asked for, and the Feldgendarmerie will act as a control to see that the necessary work is done. Another German notice notifies farmers that they will be allowed to cultivate fields which are enclosed in barbed wire entanglements, having obtained permission. Order is registered by the Royal Court regarding the jurisdiction of German police over persons not themselves subject to German Military Law. Department of Agriculture issues further directions under the Livestock (Jersey) Order, 1942. The Department of Public Health advertises for crutches.

September 6. All the farmers are busy attempting the impossible, and there is no lack of volunteers. During the morning the agricultural inspectors were summoned to the Feldkommandantur and the order of the previous day was extended so that the farmers would have another six days in which to do the work; if necessary, work must not cease until 8 p.m., and the threshing machines must also continue until that time.

September 7. Potato rationing commences with a ration of 5 lb. per head; nobody is supposed to register where there is an amount exceeding 56 lb. per member of a household, and an emergency stock may be purchased by persons who have less than 28 lb. per head. Prices of bottled and unbottled cider officially fixed—$7\frac{1}{2}$d. and 5d. respectively. Carbide arrives from France; a large number of hand torches and cycle dynamos on sale. This week's extra ration is 6 oz. of cocoa substitute per head. During the lunch hour some British planes passed over the Island and the Germans fired on them—this is the first instance for some time. New grade instituted in the Police Force with the appointment of two detective-constables. Tobacco ration remains the same for the next four weeks; the locally-grown tobacco is quite good and large quantities are being cured.

September 8. Trinity Parish fixes the Rate at 1s. 6d. per quarter. The Germans warn fishermen not to take their boats across St. Aubin's Bay between Elizabeth Castle and West Park slip at high tide, so as not to damage the telephone cable which runs on poles from the castle to the shore.

September 9. The Germans are on the warpath regarding wireless sets and several persons have been caught and sentences imposed, mostly of three weeks' imprisonment; informers are offered payment by the Feldgendarmerie. A man has also been sentenced to a long term of imprisonment for being mixed up in a petrol racket.

September 11. St. Lawrence fixes the Rate at 1s. 10d. per quarter.

September 12. Another notice issued regarding the gathering of the harvest on Sunday.

September 14. Ration issued of 3 oz. of cheese: this was hardly necessary, as of late the Island has been flooded with Camembert, purchasers being allowed to obtain an almost unlimited quantity. Island School of Dancing and Elocution presents a show at the Opera House.

September 15. The Germans give publication to the following:

NOTICE

By order of higher authorities, the following British subjects will be evacuated and transferred to Germany.

(a) Persons who have their permanent residence not on the Channel Islands, for instance, those who have been caught here by the outbreak of the war;

(b) All those men not born on the Channel Islands and 16 to 70 years of age who belong to the English people, together with their families.

Detailed instructions will be given by the Feldkommandantur 515.

Der Feldkommandant:
KNACKFUSS, Oberst.

The effect of such an Order cannot be described. It is learned that it is a direct order from Hitler and that speed must be applied in carrying it out. The Bailiff, Attorney-General and the Constables were summoned and the Germans gave their orders. The Bailiff and Attorney-General made vigorous protests and the Constables refused to be the ones who would tell people they must be sent away to Germany. No logical reason can be thought of for this distressing order. Early in the evening and continuing throughout the night cars were rushing around the Island with German and local officials armed with lists of the first people to be sent away. Those concerned were handed a document of which the following is a copy:

Feldkommand 515.   Jersey, 15. Sept., 1942.
          Mr. John William Bacon,
                St. Lawrence, 10 Rue Verte Villas, Mont Félard.
    In pursuance of a Higher Command, British subjects are to
be evacuated and brought to Germany.
    You have to appear, therefore on 16–9–42 not later than 4
o'clock at the Garage, Weighbridge, St. Helier, wife and minor
children.
    You have to take with you all papers proving your identity.
    It is necessary to outfit yourself with warm clothes, strong
boots, and provisions for two days, meal dishes, drinking
bowl, and, if possible, with a blanket.
    Your luggage must not be heavier than you can carry and
must bear a label with your full address.
    It is further left to you to place ready, for each person, a
trunk packed with clothes to be sent afterwards, labelled with
full address.
    It is also left to you to take with you an amount of money
not exceeding R.M. 10 in German notes for each person in
Reichcredit notes.
    All valuables (jewels) must be deposited as far as possible
with the banks. Keys of the houses are to be handed over to
the Constables.
    Should you fail to obey the order sentence by court martial
shall be effected.
                              Der Feldkommandant:
                                  gez. KNACKFUSS, Oberst.

    There are to be several exemptions in cases of persons em-
ployed by the essential services, etc., but there is no definite
statement as regards the length of these exemptions. Words fail
to describe the wretched state of the Island at the moment, for
those not affected have scores of friends who are.
    September 16. Heart-breaking scenes were witnessed all over
the Island today as friends said good-bye to one another. Many
of the Germans themselves expressed their sympathy for those
affected by the latest order; it is felt also that the German
authorities at College House are not at all happy in carrying out
their instructions, for they know as well as we do that there is
not the slightest excuse. The deportees themselves were magnificent, and England can be proud of them; they sang and joked
on their way to the quay, and for all the world seemed to be
going on a great picnic. For about two hours previous to the
time of assembly at the Weighbridge (4 o'clock) a large crowd of

sympathetic onlookers gathered near the New Cut and the Le Sueur Obelisk to wave good-bye and pass on words of good cheer to friends passing by, many on foot and others from the country parishes in buses. German troops controlled the crowd, being armed with rifles and machine-guns at certain places, but they appeared to be very shamefaced; entry to the Weighbridge from Conway Street and Mulcaster Street was barred to persons other than deportees. At the Weighbridge Garage a panel of doctors (three local and three German) examined all doubtful cases, and a number of last-minute exemptions were granted because of ill-health or where families included very young children. Refreshments in the form of hot milk and bread and jam were provided during the long hours of waiting, and each person received from the States of Jersey a 1-lb. loaf of bread, a tin or jar of paste, a slab of chocolate, a tin of milk and a packet of cigarettes. Buses conveyed our departing friends down to the boats, these being two quite decent little craft in which everyone was made as comfortable as possible. The total number of passengers was 280. St. John Ambulance members were there to attend those in need, and the German sailors were most considerate and sympathetic, especially with children and old people. As the vessels drew away from the quay the deportees raised cries of 'Are we downhearted? No!' and sang patriotic songs such as 'There'll always be an England'. At 9 o'clock people on Mount Bingham could hear the singing as the vessel left the harbour and went towards the breakwater. Many marriages are taking place between young English women and men who are Jersey-born, and a gassing tragedy is reported from Beaumont involving a man and wife; the latter does not recover, and at the subsequent inquest a verdict was recorded of 'suicide during temporary insanity'. The College re-opened today for the autumn term, and fees have been reduced. The Royal Court has been very busy swearing-in attorneys to persons who are being deported. St. Ouen's Parish fixes the Rate at 2s. 1d.

September 17. Many businesses are in a state of confusion owing to depletion of staffs, and the banks are busy with clients depositing their jewellery and other valuables; silver and pound notes have been pouring in. The first shock of the Deportation Order has passed, but there is apprehension regarding the next batch to be sent. There is not long to wait, for in the afternoon further notices were served, similar to the first ones, with the exception of the first two paragraphs, which read:

For the purpose of evacuation you have to appear with

your next members of family (parents, husbands, and children of any age) on the 18th of September, 1942, at the Garage, Weighbridge, at 4 p.m. o'clock.

The competent Constable will provide for punctual transport to this collecting place, as far as country parishes are concerned;

and four additional paragraphs:

In case of your being fully occupied for a longer period at a German office, you have to report immediately to the Fieldkommandant (room 11 K. V. Ass. Hertig) with a certificate of the authority concerned.

Growers of agricultural produce, that is farmers who are themselves in full charge of their farms, planters, gardeners and hands on such farms, the employers of mills and dairies, and the manufacturers of foodstuffs, have to report to the Fieldcommand (room 20 K.V.R. Pelz).

All employers and workmen of the electricity works, waterworks and gasworks have also to report to the Fieldcommand (room 16) enclosing a certificate of their work.

All employees and workmen of the electric works, waterworks and Fieldkommandantur. People may call here up to the 18th September, 11 a.m.

September 18. Another exodus takes place. Crowds line the approaches to the harbour and cheer those leaving, the latter showing a fine spirit which the Germans cannot understand. In the evening large crowds assemble around Mount Bingham and the biggest patriotic demonstrations since the Occupation takes place; this prompts the German patrols to clear the roadway, but the crowd only moves to the top of Pier Road, overlooking the harbour. The old cries of 'One, two, three, four; who the hell are we for?' were vociferously answered by 'Churchill!', 'England!', 'Jersey!', etc., and patriotic songs ended with 'God Save the King'. As one of the boats left with 436, those on board were in high spirits and tried to outshine their friends on land in the matter of patriotic fervour. A second boat was to have left, but at the last moment those who were to travel by her were sent home, as the Commandant had inspected the vessel and declared that it was not in a fit state for travel. About 300 people were sent home for a week, with instructions to be there at the same time on the 25th; this also meant that the curfew could not be enforced, as cars and conveyances had to be requisitioned for people returning home. Many found themselves in queer straits, as they had given away their provisions, and some of their furniture had been split up for custody among friends; in some cases neighbours gave them a right royal welcome, and many parties were held. All sorts of rumours are abroad as to the cause for postponing the sailing of the second boat, and people were sceptical as to the reason given, for later in the night the ship left for France with German soldiers. It is learned that the first batch of deportees was well received at St. Malo by members of the International Red Cross and were given a meal before being entrained for Paris, en route for Germany. They were accompanied to St. Malo by personnel of the St. John Ambulance Brigade. Those who were to have left today declare that the way they were looked after when they were waiting to embark was splendid. The Germans have temporarily prohibited fishing around the Island, and today have issued a long Order concerning traffic regulations, both in Jersey and Guernsey, one result of this being that more and more road signs are being added to the already vast number now in existence. The Germans also announce the farewell performance at The Forum of the Air Force Band.

September 19. The Royal Court is still busy swearing-in attorneys and many businesses are suffering acutely owing to the recent deportation of English members of staffs. The Germans publish a notice reminding those deportees who were sent back to their homes that they must assemble again at the Weighbridge on the 25th inst. Large quantity of apples arrives from France; at the moment there is a glut of apples.

September 20. The Parish of St. Clement has to furnish civilian guards to watch a telephone cable in a meadow along Blinerie Lane, which the Germans allege has been cut, but which everybody else recognises as having been broken by stray cows; the guards work in four-hour shifts and are unlucky enough to have been picked for the worst wet spell of the year. The Germans hold another big sports meeting at the F.B. Fields.

September 22. Arrival of 3,000 Red Cross messages; this is the first batch to arrive for six weeks. St. Brelade's fixes the Rate at 2s. per quarter.

September 23. Although numbers of residents are still being notified that they are to be deported to Germany, the Germans publish a notice requiring that persons who were already registered for the last ship but whose embarkation was cancelled, as well as those persons ordered to appear on September 25, 'shall hold themselves in readiness for the new date, which will be duly published in the newspapers', the reason for postponement being given as bad weather. The Textile Department factory at 'Summerland' is working full out in order to provide deportees with much-needed winter garments. About 3 o'clock in the morning the air-raid siren was tried out, being sounded continuously for the best part of an hour.

September 25. The Germans alter the rate of exchange for the mark, which is now fixed at 9.36 to the English £, to date from the 21st of August, 1942 and 'for retrospective calculation the date of transaction shall be valid and not the date of application of settlement'. This change, which in effect increases the value of the mark from 2s. 1d. to 2s. 1½d., causes widespread confusion and inconvenience, further increasing the problem of small change, which has been a bogey to shopkeepers for some time. The Germans issue instructions that acorns must be gathered for feeding pigs; this is to be done by persons upon whose land there are oak trees.

September 26. The English residents who were registered to leave on the 25th are warned to appear at the Weighbridge again on the 29th, together with others who have been warned since. When the Deportation Order was first issued it applied in the main to men with or without families, but now even single women and widows are included. Persons in need of winter wear (underclothing, footwear, etc.) are being sent to 'Summerland', where noble efforts to meet the demand are being made. Many more attorneys are being appointed at the Royal Court.

September 27. Members of the Todt Organisation appear to have had a gala day today; in the morning hundreds were attending a performance at The Forum, and in the afternoon and evening many of them were seen drunk in the streets and causing unpleasantness.

September 28. More people receive warning for deportation tomorrow, included in the number being about twenty Jersey people; these are some who have at various times been sentenced to imprisonment by the Germans or found guilty of petty offences. One hundred saccharin tablets is the extra ration for everyone this week. The Amateur Dramatic Club presents a comedy-thriller at the Opera House.

September 29. The third batch of persons to be deported to Germany leaves the Island—560; arrangements similar to the other two occasions are put into operation and crowds line the streets to wish their friends good luck. The Germans have taken further precautions in the vicinity of the harbours and more streets have been barred to the public, especially in the Mount Bingham area. Assembly was at 2 p.m., but a few persons had been warned to arrive a little later; the majority of these, as well as many others, were lucky, for it was found that there was not sufficient accommodation for all of them on the two ships which were to be used and they were sent back home again. When the complements of the boats were complete a German official announced that the remainder could 'return to your normal occupations' and that that was the end of the evacuation 'for the time being'. Those returning were welcomed with open arms by their friends who a few hours previously had bade them farewell. When the boats were due to leave (about 8.45) a large crowd of young people assembled at the top of Pier Road and commenced to sing patriotic songs, but the Germans chased them away. Parties of youngsters commenced singing and shouting in various parts of the town, and when the German patrols interfered the situation became ugly, especially near Bond Street and in Kensington Place; the Germans chased some young boys, and one of them unloosed a beautiful right hook and laid out a German officer; others played football with a German's helmet, and many spectators added volume to the epithets being hurled at the German soldiers who attempted to interfere, the latter eventually chasing the boys with their bayonets and revolvers. Fourteen boys, the majority of whom were from private schools were arrested and taken by the Germans to their section of the prison in Gloucester Street, pending the decision of the German authorities in the matter of punishment. St. Helier Parish Assembly fixes the Rate at 3s. 2d. per quarter.

September 30. Some of the Italian colony have to leave the Island and proceed to Italy for military training; this causes no regret among us, for many of these Italians, who were formerly waiters glad to get a twopenny tip, have become quite prosperous as proprietors of cafés where the Germans congregate to drink their ersatz coffee. The Germans advertise a film of the Dieppe raid which purports to show the actual landing of the troops and the development of the attack. Department of Essential Commodities warns the public that loose coupons will not be accepted in the shops, but must be accompanied by the ration books: due to the number of people who have left the Island, there has been a fair amount of wangling extra rations from shopkeepers.

German is being taught compulsorily in the higher forms of the colleges, where there has been a certain amount of 'stalling'

93

for some time. The Germans are proceeding with the railways running from Gronez to the Airport and to the Five Mile Road, and have brought over some more railway engines, these being the biggest ever seen locally and on the style of the smaller G.W.R. type. The G.W.R. sheds on the New North Quay have been demolished to make room for the railway which is being laid down, and the end of the upper promenade of the Victoria Pier has also been demolished to make room for what appears to be a blockhouse or gun emplacement, of which the harbours already have their full quota. Many of the Russians have died during the month and are still abominably treated by the Todt officials; there have been reports of some of these officials being attacked, and in at least one case there must have been some such instance, for one of these officials who was buried with full Nazi honours was afterwards exhumed and a full-scale inquest held at which were several doctors and shorthand typists.

OCTOBER 1942

October 1. The fuel ration for this month is the wood allowance, supplemented by a small amount of coal, an average family receiving 2 cwt. and 1 cwt. respectively.

October 2. Following German notification, the Department of Agriculture announced the discontinuance of the agricultural workers' bonus; growers must pay men with families a minimum weekly wage of £2 10s. 0d., and single men £2 0s. 6d.; financial assistance will be granted only in respect of wages of men with dependents, and growers who are unable to pay the wages may apply for such assistance, the applications to be submitted to the Feldkommandant for final approval.

October 3. The Germans announce that the question of communications with the persons recently deported from the Island is under consideration and that it is hoped to make a definite statement shortly. This is the first instance where reference to the 'evacuation' has been allowed; up to now censorship has been rigidly imposed. It is learned that the last batch of deportees travelled under appalling conditions, the weather being very rough and the accommodation insufficient; many were seasick and there were only two lavatories.

October 4. The first of a series of monthly Sunday evening charity concerts given at the Opera House, which was absolutely filled.

October 5. Issue of 8 oz. of coffee substitute per head; a wine ration, which was commenced alphabetically, has been suspended owing to the supply becoming exhausted. A quantity of beer made at Ann Street, is available to public houses. Very heavy fog prompts the Germans to take a lot of precautions; guards are doubled at night and the crews of barges are taken up to Fort Regent for the night, together with the local harbour police who are on duty.

October 6. The Germans are out all night again, and during the day more bombing is heard.

October 7. We are very interested in the B.B.C. announcement that a small raid has been made on Sark in order to ascertain whether English persons had been deported to Germany; apparently the raid was a success and the desired information obtained, for the broadcast gave the correct details, including the Order signed by Knackfuss.

October 8. Further news gleaned from the B.B.C. regarding our English friends. We are pleased to learn that the International Red Cross will see to their welfare and supply the names of everyone so that their relatives or friends can get in touch with them. St. John's Parish fixes the Rate at 1s. 3d.

October 9. The Germans given publicity to the Sark raid. German must now be taught in all forms at the colleges.

October 10. Several persons, in particular those accused of spreading news, are released from jail with a caution that they must keep their mouths shut. At their period there are over seventy prisoners in the German jails. The tobacco ration remains the same for the next four weeks; large quantities of local-grown tobacco are on sale, and some is excellent if properly treated, the price being on an average 3s. 6d. per oz.

October 11. The curfew altered now being from 9 p.m. to 6.30 a.m. instead of commencing at 10 p.m., this as a reprisal for the raid on Sark on the 4th inst. Nearly all the churches commence holding their usual evening service in the afternoon, and all entertainments are advertised to start at 6 p.m.

October 12. The boys who were taken to prison for causing a disturbance on September 29 after the departure of deportees were tried today by court martial; the majority were released, but those over 18 were given varying sentences; a man who was alleged to have incited them was sentenced to three years. A man and wife have recently been sentenced to six months each for 'consorting with prisoners of war'. German notice draws attention to dealings with the Army of Occupation, which must be transacted in Reichsmarks. The metric system has to be

95

applied to measures of length, square measures, cubic measures and weights. This week's extras consist of a piece of toilet soap and 20 boxes of matches per household, while persons depending on paraffin for lighting purposes are to have two pints. Messrs. Britton and Whinnerah present a concert-party entertainment at the Opera House. The farmers are being circularised with a notice appealing to them to give the maximum quantity of milk to the Department of Agriculture; this in order that the Island shall be self-supporting as far as milk and butter are concerned, the Superior Council prefering that no butter should be imported from France rather than that all milk should be skimmed, with the exception of that intended for children under 14 years of age. The Germans have been trying to force the skimming of milk for some time, but the local authorities have so far succeeded in evading the issue. It is believed that Jersey is the only place in occupied territory in which milk is not skimmed.

October 14. In the early hours of the morning terrific gunfire is heard somewhere off the Island, culminating in a gigantic explosion; it was subsequently learned from the B.B.C. that a German convoy between Guernsey and Cap La Hague had been intercepted by British E-boats and that an ammunition ship had been blown up.

October 15. The Island suffers a great loss in the death of Mr. Arnold S. Ferguson, M.R.C.S., L.R.C.P., the well-known eye, ear, nose and throat specialist.

October 16. Young girl fractures her skull in falling downstairs in a house run by females for the entertainment of German soldiers.

October 17. Department of Agriculture warns consumers and producers against accepting or retaining milk in respect of persons who have been evacuated from the Island. Ten boxes of matches issued this week. Newly-arrived German band resumes the usual Saturday afternoon concerts in the Royal Square.

October 19. This week's extra ration is half a pint of cooking oil.

October 20. Arrival of a large number of troops (about 2,000); these were met by a band and marched through the town; several companies have recently left the Island.

October 22. Visite du Branchage held throughout the Island. Arrival of more Gestapo men; inquiries are in progress concerning the robbery of large quantities of petrol which had been sold to farmers mostly for tractor use, the allotted ration being inadequate. The Germans take over many houses in the Mont

Félard district, tenants being turned out at short notice.

October 23. German notice calls attention to carelessness in regard to the blackout, with the usual threat of punishment; in some cases military police fine householders on the spot. St. Peter's Parish fixes the Rate at 2s. per quarter.

October 24. More robberies reported, mostly in the country parishes; it is alleged that many of these are perpetrated by foreign workers, who have insufficient to eat, or by German troops. German Orders gives permission for wreaths to be placed on soldiers' graves on All Saints' Day, All Souls' Day and Remembrance Day.

October 25. German variety concert given at The Forum, civilians being invited; travelling companies visit the Island from time to time on the style of the British E.N.S.A.

October 26. Dr. E. A. C. Drecourt, recently Ophthalmic Surgeon to l'Hôpital de Bon Secours de Paris, who has been a resident here for some time, re-opens the eye clinic at the General Hospital, where the death of Mr. Ferguson has been acutely felt. Another big robbery reported from a farm at Mont Cochon, goods valued at £140 being stolen. This week's extras consist of a packet of chocolate and a piece of household soap; the salt ration is increased to 4 oz., but it is still of the variety that has to be boiled before being used. Green Room club presents a comedy at the Opera House.

October 27. Thirty-two cases of medicaments have arrived for distribution between Jersey and Guernsey, the gift of the International Red Cross; the insulin, for use in cases of diabetes, of which there are many at the moment without proper treatment, was most unfortunately stolen from the consignment somewhere between Paris and Granville. Nine more cases of robbery reported, five from St. Martin's and four from Trinity.

October 28. Department of Public Health makes arrangements for the taking over of the property known as Les Vaux, Grand Vaux, as an annexe to Overdale Isolation Hospital, where accommodation is now severely taxed. Department of Agriculture invites applications from persons who are willing to carry out tractor-ploughing during the coming season; no applications will be entertained in respect of tractors over 14 h.p.

October 31. More robberies reported from the Parish of St. Martin. The month has seen the virtual wind-up of A.R.P. as such, by German order, but behind the scenes the service is still to be kept in some sort of order in case of emergency, such as the sudden departure of 'our friends', with a certain amount of trouble likely through the destruction of vital plants, etc. The Germans evidently expect an invasion here, and all precautions are proceeding with a view to meeting it, almost every slipway has had a wall built across it. More goods are arriving from France, notably tools and small farm implements, but all of inferior quality; electric torches find a ready sale, but the difficulty is to get re-fills. Black-market goods from France are getting very scarce; butter has been changing hands at 25s. per pound, saccharins are almost right out of the market. More houses are being requisitioned, and the troops have to attend their own dentists instead of civil ones, additional clinics being opened in various districts; the Germans have a mania for gold teeth—in fact for anything gold—and anyone possessing a sovereign is being offered as much as £8 for it—in paper money, of course! A brothel has been opened for the Todt officials at the Abergeldie Hotel. A big petrol racket has been investigated by the Gestapo, and large sums of money have been collected from numerous farmers who are alleged to have been receivers. A young man suffering from T.B. who was among the recent deportees to Germany has been sent back owing to his state of health! it is learned that the evacuees are in Bavaria and are being treated reasonably well, and apparently not forced to do any labour.

NOVEMBER 1942

November 1. Thank goodness! the gas hours are extended by two hours, the supply now being turned on from 7 a.m. to 2 p.m. and 5 p.m. to 10 p.m.; people who had only gas for lighting were in the dark after 8 o'clock. The fuel ration remains the same and new textile ration books come into operation, with many changes in coupon values. Germans invite civilians to a variety show at The Forum, and the second Sunday evening charity concert takes place at the Opera House.

November 2. Central European Summer Time comes to an end and our clocks now conform with British time; this is a boon for people who have to be about in the early morning. Elementary schools re-open for the autumn term after a few days' holiday; the children are to be medically examined and German must now be taught. Details are issued by the Textile and Footwear Control concerning the 'Jersey' shoes which has been manufactured at 'Summerland'; this consists of a neat and well-constructed article with an oil-dressed leather upper, wooden sole protected by metal toe-plates, metal heel-plates, and rubber strips; the first of these will be made available to schoolchildren and women agricultural workers, the latter to obtain an employer's certificate. The wine ration is re-commenced alphabetically at letter E, where it was discontinued owing to lack of supplies; this week children and juveniles receive 15 tablets of 'Consomox' soup as an extra ration.

November 3. Department of Agriculture fixes the price of sucking-pigs at £3 sterling each. Department of Essential Commodities makes a new Order dealing with the manufacture and sale of cider. Today being the first shopping day after the issue of the new Textile Ration Books, large queues form, especially outside the Textile Office, where permits for footwear are to be obtained; another much-sought-after article is ladies' stockings, the next pair not being obtainable for six months. Annual meeting of Brig-y-Don Children's Convalescent and Holiday Home, which is still carrying on and doing excellent work.

November 4. As several cases of lead poisoning have been reported, the Official Analyst reminds the public that samples of well water which passes through lead pipes will be tested free to ascertain if it is injurious.

November 6. Several official notices published by the Department of Essential Commodities dealing with licences to sell cider. The Germans repeat their variety concert at The Forum —civilians invited.

November 7. Textile and Footwear Control announces that no more applications for footwear can be received until further notice. The Royal Court registers a German Order concerning 'the loading and unloading of railway waggons'; the Court also fines a farmer for keeping unregistered cattle—an infraction of the Livestock Order—£40 fine with £10 costs. The tobacco ration for the next four weeks is to be the same.

November 8. This evening (Sunday) the cinemas flashed notices on the screen calling on all soldiers to report at once; a general alarm was given, as there were unidentified boats in the vicinity.

November 9. Issue of ½ lb. macaroni, and jam ration again (alphabetically). Green Room Club presents miscellaneous concert and operetta at the Opera House. Messages are commencing to arrive from people who were evacuated to Germany, these being on the style of the field postcard.

November 10. The Department of Agriculture advises farmers to take every precaution to safeguard the Island's milk supply, especially stressing the need for cleanliness. Two pints of paraffin are to be allowed to householders with no other means of lighting; the lighting problem for those who have neither gas nor electricity is really acute.

November 11. Remembrance Day: wreaths are laid on the Cenotaph by the Bailiff, the Constable of St. Helier and representatives of bodies of ex-Service men. The Germans warn the civil population against giving food to foreign workers, especially Russians; these workers have been begging and people give them food on compassionate grounds.

November 12. All German guards are doubled everywhere; all soldiers on duty carry arms, and The Forum, which is used exclusively by them, is closed every evening. The excellent news from Egypt and North Africa has bucked us all up, and many wireless sets which were buried have been brought into service again, although care has to be taken as the German plain-clothes police are on the prowl.

November 13. The *E.P.* publishes an interview with the returned deportee who was sent back from Germany on account of ill-health. While this article was allowed to be published from a propaganda angle, there is every reason to believe that the deportees are fairly well housed and fed; they are camped in wooden huts, but it is anticipated that as the weather gets colder they will be accommodated in brick buildings. Recreation of various kinds is arranged for them, and the Jersey people do the cooking. A letter was also published which was sent to the *E.P.* by Captain J. A. Hilton, who has been nominated 'Camp Senior'.

November 16. Issue of 1 lb. of coffee substitute for everybody; adults only receive 6 oz. of onions and 100 saccharin tablets. Huge German convoy, which includes the largest tanker yet seen, appears off the Island, probably seeking shelter from bombing.

November 17. German variety concert given at The Forum in the afternoon, to which civilians were invited.

November 18. Two more items put on the list of controlled articles—black butter and toilet paper: there is very little that is not on this list. British plane (an old-type Spitfire) receives damage in a flight over Guernsey, and makes a forced landing here in the grounds of Diélament Manor, Trinity. The pilot, a young Frenchman, whose home is at Brest was eventually taken prisoner, but several people procured souvenirs from the plane before the Germans arrived.

November 20. British plane attacks a German patrol boat off

Corbière, killing eight of the crew and riddling the ship with bullet holes; the sailors were subsequently buried at St. Brelade's. Arrival of a Red Cross plane with a commission to inquire into the conditions affecting Russian prisoners. The Germans issue a long Fishery Order which deals with the passage of fishing vessels in and out of harbours in connection with 'herring fishing', which is calculated to begin in the month of October!

November 21. At the corner of La Motte Street and St. James Street a huge German trailer failed to take the turning successfully and one of the two anti-aircraft guns with which it was laden fell off; great excitement prevailed, especially when high officials arrived on the scene and voiced their opinion of the driver; eventually a crane was set up and the gun removed. At night German Feldgendarmerie raided the cafés to find people without their identity cards. The 100-ton crane which arrived some weeks ago has been taken away.

November 22. By German order, the Fire Brigade is busy washing down certain streets of the town which have been made very dirty with coal dust. Many troops are leaving the Island; the Grand Hotel is almost empty and at several other places billets are being cleared.

November 23. This week's extra ration consists of a small tin of tunny fish. The price of petrol is increased to 4s. 9½d. per gallon. Messrs. H. M. de Ste. Croix and J. H. Le Sueur present a thriller at the Opera House.

November 27. Re-opening of the Ear, Throat and Nose Department at the General Hospital.

November 28. The Germans give notice that arrangements are being made to forward trunks containing winter clothing to people who were deported to Germany in September last; these trunks are to be taken to the Corner House, King Street, and will be despatched in due course.

November 29. Third Sunday evening charity benefit concert held at the Opera House, a repeat performance being given.

November 30. Meeting of the States—the first since May 2. Consideration of the Estimates was deferred and the Order of the Day was the consideration of two amendments to the Parish Law. The Parish of St. Helier was given authority to borrow money up to an amount not exceeding £45,000 and among other items on the agenda were the extension of the term of office for Deputies for another year, water service charges, various pensions, the issue of currency notes and the appointment of Income Tax special commissioners. The only extra issued this week is a packet of washing powder. This month we have been greatly cheered by the news from North Africa, and the Germans have had the jitters badly, being continually in a state of alarm; the cafés they frequent and their own cinema (The Forum) have been closed almost every evening. Many foreign workers have left, and some of the work which was in progress has been stopped. The Co-operative Wholesale Society's bakehouse in Don Road, which was used exclusively by the Germans, has ceased to function, and many houses where they were billeted are empty. The clothing problem is felt keenly this winter, for although 'Summerland' is doing excellent work, the demand by far exceeds the supply and the goods are very expensive; many women have solved the difficulty of obtaining a new winter coat, however, for 'blanket coats' have become an Occupation vogue! People are continually being arrested for spreading B.B.C. news or having a set. The jail is full, the condemned portion being also requisitioned, and conditions are said to be appalling. We seldom see a German plane nowadays, but the harbours are still very busy with shipping, concrete being the most popular import. The Germans say that several Russians are missing and are at large in the Island.

DECEMBER 1942

December 1. Shocking tragedy at St. Peter's. In the early hours Mr. Ernest Le Gresley, who, with his sister, kept a shop at the cross-roads near St. Peter's Windmill, heard someone downstairs; taking a heavy stick with him, he found two men near the fowlhouse; one of the men struck Mr. Le Gresley on the head, the sister also being badly injured. The men made off, and when help arrived Mr. Le Gresley was found to be dead. A search was commenced by the local police and the German Feldgendarmerie, the Germans saying the marauders are foreign workers. Price of electricity increased, now being 10½d. per unit for light and 7½d. for cooking or heating. This month's fuel supply is more than usual, an average family receiving 2 cwt. of coal and 2 cwt. of wood; bundles of faggots are also available.

December 2. Inquest opened concerning the St. Peter's tragedy and postponed for a post-mortem examination; the country is being combed for the assailants and the Germans have interrogated many Russian workers. Arrival of 7,000 Red Cross letters. The Dispensary is being fumigated and cases have been transferred to other nursing homes, as there has been an outbreak of septic throats and hands.

December 3. Resumed inquest on the St. Peter's victim; post-mortem examination reveals that Mr. Le Gresley was stabbed several times and died of heart failure caused by loss of blood; the inquiry was further adjourned 'sine die', in order that the evidence of Miss Le Gresley, who is recovering from her injuries at the General Hospital, might be heard. It is learned that C.I. deportees in Germany have received parcels from British prisoners of war; many letters are arriving from these people, but it is difficult to get a true picture of conditions, as the views expressed are widely divergent.

December 4. The German state of alarm appears to be over, as the cafés and The Forum are open again in the evenings. Arrival of a further 5,000 Red Cross letters. The Department of Agriculture gives notice that the Field Command blames farmers for the recent thefts in the country parishes by foreign workers; they declare that the practice of selling or giving agricultural produce to these men has encouraged them to break out of camp, and that conditions will not improve until these sales or gifts are stopped.

December 5. The Bailiff makes an appeal for gifts for fellow-Islanders in Germany, in the form of books, toys, music and games, which will be despatched with the luggage which is to be sent; it is made clear that no letters or money can be enclosed. Supplies having become exhausted, the tobacco ration comes to an end until further notice. It is learned that Mr. Morrison (the Home Secretary), in a reference to the Channel Islands, has said: 'Be patient; have courage; the day is coming.'

December 6. After a long period, British planes pass over the Island at night; German anti-aircraft batteries open fire for a few moments.

December 7. About 2 p.m. today British planes attacked a German convoy off Noirmont and inflicted heavy damage; two ships were sunk (one of them of 700 tons was comparatively new and had recently been brought from Holland); two barges were also sunk and another ship was brought into harbour very badly damaged, the whole of the gun-crew having been wiped out. It is presumed that there were many drowned from the other ships, one of which was observed to break in half and sink in a matter of seconds. The response to the Bailiff's appeal for gifts for Channel Islanders in Germany has been more than adequately met. This week's extra rations consist of half a pint of cooking oil and a tablet of toilet soap. The Green Room Club presents a play at the Opera House.

December 8. Amusement is caused by a notice issued by the German Harbour Commandant, the first paragraph of which reads as follows: 'As results of fishing have become less and less in recent months, and, according to past experience, will start to increase only in April, I decree that fishing between 15.12.1942 and 31.3.1943 is prohibited for the entire Island of Jersey.' A lot of timber is being washed up from the boats sunk yesterday and the Germans are collecting it. All the local honorary police were forced to collaborate with the German Feldgendarmerie today to search for a large number of foreign workers (mostly Russian) who have been roaming the countryside for some time; only about two dozen were caught.

December 9. More and more Red Cross messages are arriving. The Department of Essential Commodities fixes the official price for flints for mechanical lighters at 6d. per tube; there has been a ramp in this article for some time and all sorts of fancy prices were being charged. It is learned that two more ships have been sunk in the vicinity of the Island.

December 10. St. Clement's Parish fixes the Rate at 2s. per quarter. German troops going on leave, including the Censor, were turned back from the harbour today owing to R.A.F. activity over France.

December 11. An advertisement published by a local firm of wireless dealers, with the approval of the German authorities, states that it is willing to purchase sets which are now deposited at the parish halls, etc., at the best possible prices. This is said to be 'in view of the fact that the sale of receivers directly to members of the military forces is forbidden, and they are not allowed entrance in halls where radios are stored'. This bears out the fact that of late the troops have not been permitted to listen to the wireless within certain hours, under pain of very severe punishment. The banks have stopped taking French francs as legal tender, and there has been a racket going on in the buying and selling of English £ notes and silver: the Germans are offering about £12 in paper money for a sovereign and about 26s. for a £1 note. Tomato puree can now be purchased at 2s. per pint.

December 12. The public is asked by the German authorities to co-operate in apprehending escaped Russian prisoners and to report their whereabouts. For the information of those people who are reluctant to give these men away for fear that they will be given over-rigorous punishment, it is stated that such punishment is not in any way severe, but 'consists merely of closer confinement and the deprivation of certain privileges which the well-behaved enjoy'! The Royal Court deals with a farmer who kept a bull calf and fed it on eggs and milk, in contravention of the Calves (Slaughtering) Order; a fine of £10 and £2 costs was imposed, the destruction of the animal being ordered.

December 13. The Germans stage a variety show at The Forum, to which the civilian population is invited.

December 14. Meeting of the States; a few minor items were dealt with, and the purchase of various pieces of land in the parishes of St. Mary and St. John, to be incorporated in the making of the new 'North Road' from Sorel to La Saline, was approved. More daring robberies reported, these including 175 boxes of seed potatoes and several cases of tunny fish from the Essential Commodities store. Extra rations for Christmas may be purchased between now and Christmas Eve, these being: 8 oz. of coffee substitute and 7 oz. of breakfast meal (or infant food) for everybody; those under 18 are to have 4 oz. of sweets and 4½ oz. of cocoa powder; those over 18, 4 oz. of sugar and 4½ oz. of chocolate.

December 15. Tobacco rations are announced for the Christmas period: 10 cigarettes, available from December 19, 30 cigarettes and 2 oz. of pipe tobacco, available from December 23. The price of paraffin is now 8½d. per pint retail, a quart to be issued to householders and farmers dependent on this commodity for lighting purposes.

December 16. German order published concerning the surrender of wireless sets.

December 18. Reports of more robberies, including another outrage at St. Mary, when thieves assaulted an householder who was disturbed. Many German soldiers going on leave, and among the vessels plying to and from France are two paddle-steamers.

December 19. The Royal Court disposes of two cases of illegal threshing, the farmers concerned being fined £60 and £30 respectively, each with £10 costs in addition. The Germans issue notices regarding the curfew over the holiday period, which is fixed to begin at midnight on December 24, 25 and 26, and January 1, and at 1 p.m. on December 31; these notices are only to be displayed in the parish boxes and must on no account be mentioned in the local Press. The gas and electricity hours are also extended until 1 a.m. on each of the above occasions.

December 20. 'Music Hall' presented at Wests on Sunday evening; these concerts, as well as the charity concerts held at the Opera House, are proving very popular on Sunday evenings.

December 21. An additional ration this week is 3 oz. of cheese. The Amateur Dramatic Club presents a comedy at the Opera House.

December 22. The Germans carry out heavy artillery practice in a south-easterly direction, persons living in the danger zone, unless prevented by age or illness, being advised to move out while the firing is in progress.

December 23. The General Hospital is closed to visitors owing to an outbreak of diphtheria.

December 24. Christmas Eve. The streets are crowded, but there is very little to buy except second-hand goods, although even with these some shops are making a brave display. There is one thing that is plentiful; namely, wooden toys which have been made for the children, but the prices are almost prohibitive for poor folk. Raffles have been run by the hundred; some of the prizes are really astounding after two and a half years of Occupation. Black-market foodstuffs are very expensive: Butter, 24s. per lb.; pork, 15s. per lb.; eggs, 24s. per dozen; sugar, 15s. per lb.; salt, 12s. 6d. per lb. Fowls have fetched about £3 each and geese and turkeys about £8 and £20 respectively. Cigarettes, too, are at a premium, some having changed hands at more than a shilling each! Several so-called 'political' prisoners were released today from the German portion of the prison, including some who were waiting sentence for being in possession of a wireless set.

December 25. Christmas Day. The weather is cold and dry, but dull. Our spirits are not dull, however, for everyone is agreed that there is a good chance that this will be the last Christmas under Occupation. The poorer folk have been helped by various funds and the *E.P.* Christmas Fund has broken all previous records, with a total sum of £493. The King's Speech was listened to by those who still possess a wireless set, and the note of optimism was commented upon.

December 26. Boxing Day. A football match was held at the F.B. Fields and in the evening several public and private dances took place. These dances are on the increase and there is much more entertainment than there was during the first two years. The Germans stage a variety show at The Forum again, to which civilians are invited.

December 27. Many of the churches held their annual carol services; the fourth Sunday evening charity concert is held at the Opera House.

December 28. No extra rations are issued this week. The public is warned to be very careful with the use of matches, as this commodity is getting more difficult to obtain.

December 31. Diphtheria is on the increase and the dampness is not very helpful. During the month the Germans have lost a tanker in St. Ouen's Bay, but, as usual, details are lacking. Work on making gun-emplacements, etc., is still going on apace, and the latest site is at the bottom of Green Street. The railways are also being further extended. The manufacture of sugar-beet syrup is more widely undertaken than last year, some people making a commercial proposition of it, the price averaging 5s. per lb. Among the goods imported from France is a large number of mackintoshes, which are being sold at £8 5s. each; clothing generally is fetching enormous prices, these being especially offered by the foreign workers, who are well paid but have nothing to buy. The *E.P.* suspends publication today owing to lack of certain supplies from France. Those who had kept their wireless sets heard Big Ben strike at midnight.

JANUARY

January 1. New Year's Day: raining and windy, but not cold; our spirits are bright, and we are full of hope. Many parties and dances are held, and the Green Room presents a pantomime at the Opera House. This month's fuel ration consists of 2 cwt. of wood and 1 cwt. of coal for an average family; the wood is very wet, and getting the fire going is a full-time job. The new penalties on persons who have still retained their wireless sets came into force today, but it is not learned whether anyone took advantage of the German promise to take no proceedings against persons who handed in sets of their own free will.

January 2. Very rough weather interferes with shipping, but a small amount of material arrives for the *E.P.* and publication is resumed. The Germans issue a list of articles which must not be included in parcels to be sent to deportees in Germany. The vegetable prices list has now to be published in German as well as English. The tobacco ration is fixed again at 20 cigarettes, this alternating with 10 cigarettes and 1 oz. of pipe tobacco. The Lending Department of the Public Library sets up a new record with 657 issues in one day.

January 4. New Food Ration Books come into operation. This week there is an issue of 8 oz. of dried beans and the jam ration commences again (alphabetically). From directions issued under the Rationing Order it is interesting to learn that fish is no longer rationed; as fish has been almost unobtainable since the beginning of the Occupation, this amendment seems to be only of academic interest.

January 5. In the small hours distress signals are sent out by a German ship (the *Schottland*, 1,500 tons) which had struck the rocks known as Grande Grune, about a mile to the south-west of Noirmont Point. The ship had left here with the *Holland* the previous evening and had been waiting for an escort before proceeding to France, via the western passage; she had a Dutch skipper, and there were 370 passengers, the majority being soldiers going on leave. Boats going to the wreck were not very successful at rescue work, for only 40 were saved, 330 being lost. Many were in the water for several hours, including the

Guernsey Censor (who was rescued), and all day today bodies have been washed up at various points along the south coast. A number of wooden spars has also been washed up, many of them being seized by inhabitants before they were seen by the German authorities.*

January 6. More bodies are being washed up, and wreaths and coffins have been ordered by the Germans; many of the dead have been taken to the General Hospital, and most of the burials are to take place at St. Brelade's Cemetery, where already there are scores of soldiers. The Germans take over Icho Tower, the tenants of which have had to remove all their belongings. Diphtheria is on the increase and the various clinics in connection with the General Hospital have also been closed; the weather is not very helpful for this complaint.

January 7. The Germans demolish the Martello Tower at Bel Royal to make room for one of their fortification schemes; inhabitants in the vicinity were warned to be out of their houses during the time of the demolition, and this latest piece of vandalism was attended by much ceremony.

January 8. Many letters have been received from the deportees to Germany; the trunks that were supposed to have been sent have not yet been recieved. More bodies are being washed up and burials carried out, several in the Strangers' Cemetery.

January 11. Many Regular Army officers on the retired list, from a captain upwards, have had to present themselves today at College House, and those who were medically fit (only five in all) were to hold themselves in readiness to be deported to Germany, with the option of taking their wives and families. More bodies from the wreck are being washed up and it is learned that a raft with four German soldiers on it has been found at the Minquiers, with the occupants all fairly well after a severe buffeting. This week's extra rations consist of a piece of household soap for everybody and five boxes of matches per household.

January 12. The Germans have sent notices to a large number of persons to attend at College House for interview; of these are some who had been sentenced by the Royal Court for various offences during the last 15 years; others were persons who have been sentenced by the Germans for offences since the Occupa-

---

* About a year after Liberation, a Spaniard called to inform me that his comrade—also a Spaniard, who was working on the quays under the Todts—had made a bomb, and placed it in the hold of the *Schottland*. He said the fuse was set to go off at 1.30 a.m., and he helped to steal dynamite for this purpose.—L.P.S.

tion or upon whom they may have 'had their eye' for one reason or another. Until more is known of this latest move there is much apprehension, and, of course, the usual crop of rumours is current. During the morning a large four-engined British or American bomber flew very low over the harbour vicinity and the south coast, escorting planes being well above; the Germans opened up with everything they had, but the plane went along quietly on its course; this is the first time such a barrage has been put up in the daytime, apart from practice. Planes were also heard at night. Owing to lack of supplies, the *E.P.* again ceases publication.

January 13. About 5.30 a.m. the Germans open up as British planes pass over the Island; the firing went on for some time. Several of the persons warned yesterday attended at College House today; some were told that they were to stay in the Island and others that they must hold themselves in readiness to be sent to Germany. All sorts of people have been warned, including officials of some of the friendly societies (which are thought by the Germans to be secret organisations). The inquest is resumed and concluded on the body of Mr. E. Le Gresley, the victim of the affray at St. Peter's, who was stabbed by one of the foreign workers; the verdict was that death was due to loss of blood caused by several pocket-knife wounds inflicted by some persons unknown.

January 14. Among the latest robberies is one at the Co-operative Wholesale Society's store at Charing Cross, the articles stolen including over 100 lb. of butter, 92 lb. of jam, 40 lb. of sugar and 75 tablets of soap; from St. Martin's also comes the news of the robbery of another cow. German minesweepers are busy outside the harbours.

January 15. The Germans examine a lot more people today at College House, but the number picked out to be sent to Germany is very small; these are mainly young single men; married men have been given the option of taking their families with them. They have been told to await official notice, either individually or through the medium of the Press. In the evening German batteries open up in several of the coastal areas and intermittent firing goes on for about an hour; it was learned that the R.A.F. had made a heavy attack on Cherbourg.

January 16. The harbours are re-opened to shipping again and supplies arrive from France which enable the *E.P.* to resume publication after four days without an issue. The impression is gained that the local German authorities are by no means enamoured of the order, and in many cases the deportee concerned has been allowed 'to get away with it' on some trifling pretext—in fact, some of the German doctors have suggested minor ailments which did not exist, with a view to the 'sufferer' being classed as medically unfit. After being closed for some time, due to the prevalence of diphtheria, the General Hospital is again to be opened to visitors. The German Food Office inserts a notice in the *E.P.* for cats and dogs, good mousers and ratters.

January 17. A statement issued by the Committee appointed by the States on January 9 to go into the question of sending food, clothing, etc., to deportees, was read in the churches today; it stated that permission to function had been granted to the Committee by the German authorities; receiving centres and a packing depôt are to be established, but the public is asked to be patient and await developments.

January 18. The Department of Public Health gives notice that children of 14 years and under may be inoculated against diphtheria at the General Hospital; the service is free, and private inoculation may be done at the practitioner's usual fee. Issue of 100 saccharin tablets and ½ lb. of coffee substitute per head. The Fifty-Fifty Club presents a thriller at the Opera House.

January 19. By order the Field Command, all dances are cancelled owing to the prevalence of contagious diseases (mainly diphtheria). Tobacco prices increased; cigarettes 9d. for 10; pipe tobacco 1s. 6½d. per oz. The salt ration is again issued as a finished article.

January 20. About 50 natives of Eire who left here some months ago to work in Germany have returned to the Island; it is stated that they were not very satisfied with conditions there and asked to be sent back.

January 21. Victoria College Spring Term commences at the College again, having been at Halkett Place Schools since October 1941, when the Germans requisitioned the College for 'eight weeks'! The Girls' College also commences at Mount Pleasant, the former Victoria College Preparatory building. Two pints of paraffin issued to householders relying solely on that means for lighting purposes.

January 22. So as to prevent the spread of diphtheria, children under 14 years of age will not be permitted to attend public performances, parties, meetings, etc., until further notice. A dozen horses, the property of the Department of Transport and Communications, put up for sale in the Cattle Market; prices ranged from £200 to £300. Large number of Red Cross letters arrives; those from deportees are much more cheerful, by reason of the fact that the British Red Cross has sent them much-needed foodstuffs.

January 23. The Jersey Internees Aid Committee issued a public statement, by sanction of the German authorities; parcels up to 15 kilos (about 32 lb.) may be sent at fixed postal rates, declaration forms to be obtained at the British Post Office; special collecting centres are established in the various parishes. The parcels must contain 'only winter clothing, underwear and small articles of daily use'; they must be handed in at the German Field Post Office. Further details will be issued regarding the sending of money.

January 24. Fifth Sunday charity concert held at the Opera House.

January 25. Issue of piece of toilet soap and 8 oz. of macaroni per head.

January 26. The meat ration reduced from 6 oz. per head to 4 oz.

January 28. Many persons who were recently exempted by the Germans after examination have attended again today for further medical examination; almost everyone got off again. The Germans invite civilians to a military concert at The Forum.

January 29. Between 8 and 9 o'clock in the evening some very heavy explosions are heard which are thought to be either mines or an ammunition ship. Among goods from France on sale in the shop's are men's black leatherette mackintoshes at £5 each.

January 30. Instructions are issued by the military authorities that all private felling and lopping of trees must cease. Notice published by the Department of Essential Services reminds the public that the consumption of electricity is prohibited between 11 p.m. and 6 a.m. The Germans have informed the Department of Agriculture that Pontac slipway will be opened to farmers for the collection of vraic on February 1. Farmers are also notified that clover and rye grass seed is obtainable. An appeal by the M.O.H. for probationer nurses for Overdale.

January 31. We learn with interest of a special service for Channel Islanders held at St. Martin-in-the-Fields, London, with an address by the Archbishop of York, former Bishop of Winchester. Second Sunday charity concert held at Wests; the Germans give a light orchestral concert at The Forum, to which civilians are invited. The month goes out with a gale, but it has been the mildest January for several years, though very wet. The number of troops in the Island has greatly decreased; among recent arrivals are some from the Russian front. There has been a serious fracas between Russian workers and Todt men on the Five Mile Road; the former are alleged to have attacked the latter, who turned machine-guns on them. The Germans are laying a cable across the Island from west to east; construction of gun emplacements still goes on, and plans have been prepared for the laying of a railway to Gorey from St. Helier, commencing at the Victoria Pier and keeping as far as possible to the track of the old Eastern Railway. The work of fencing in the whole of the harbours is now complete, and there is a submarine net across the harbour mouth, with a special winch to draw it up.

FEBRUARY 1943

February 1. Fuel ration for this month the same as last. This week's extra ration is a tin of dwarf beans; the price of sugar is increased from 2d. to 3d. per 3 oz. (a ration). Beryl and Norman Hockmuth present a variety show at the Opera House.

February 2. Owing to the non-arrival of essential supplies, the E.P. again suspends publication.

February 3. Very heavy gales have affected shipping and the harbours are almost empty. In the evening the Germans clear The Forum of soldiers, following an order for three days' mourning for the defenders of Stalingrad. Publication of the E.P. Almanac. After a long interval, Camembert cheese is on sale again in the shops in large quantities.

February 4. Ships commence arriving again. Over fifty German women arrive to take the place of men in some of the German offices, canteens etc.

February 5. The E.P. published again. In the early hours of the morning the Germans put up a terrific barrage as planes pass over the Island for a rendezvous (it was subsequently learned) at Lorient.

February 6. Sixty-three persons are warned to hold themselves ready to be deported to Germany on Tuesday next (the 9th); the majority of these are 'undesirables' from the German point of view. The Royal Court fines a farmer £20 for selling milk from which the cream had been removed. The Germans publish an article dealing with the value of learning languages.

February 7. About 400 lb. of flour stolen from a bakery at St. Ouen's. A resident of Grouville who had been warned for deportation to Germany is found in a bath with his throat cut.

February 8. The Germans again warn farmers that it is forbidden to sell rationed or controlled goods to members of the forces. Persons who are to be deported are notified, the date of departure being postponed to the 10th inst. The Germans give notice that vraic may be gathered in Grouville Bay below Fort William; there is no slipway at this spot, but the bank is level with the beach. The Department of Agriculture informs farmers that artificial fertiliser may be obtained at the rate of 3 cwt. to the vergée, the price being 3s. per cwt, ex-store. Another official notice fixes the price of cycle tyres at 12s. for the cover and 6s. for the tube; this is exclusive of the fitting charge, and the goods are not guaranteed. This week's extra rations consist of $\frac{1}{4}$ lb. of margarine and 8 oz. of dried beans per head.

February 9. The deportees are notified of yet another day's delay.

February 10. Again the date of deportation is extended—until the 12th inst. Letters arriving from deportees already in Germany express the hope that they may be repatriated to England.

February 11. Gestapo agents inspect incoming mail from France at the General Post Office, in particular letters addressed to foreign workers, for there is suspicion that French Marquis are active here. Another six hundred-weight of flour stolen from a bakery at St. Ouen's.

February 12. Amendments made to rationing orders. One deals with potatoes, whereby in an household having an amount exceeding 28 lb. per member no person of that household may register for supplies. Quantity of wool arrives, female holders of Textile Ration Books being able to obtain eight ounces at 1s. 6d. per ounce. The deportees assembled at The Plaza at 2 p.m. and were taken to the harbour at 5 o'clock; after they had gone aboard engine trouble developed and they were sent home again until the next day; those who had been taken from jail were locked up for the night.

February 13. The deportees were warned to be at The Plaza at 5 o'clock; they were taken to the harbour and the boat left at about 7 o'clock, St. John Ambulance personnel having attended to persons desiring comfort. The Internees Aid Committee publishes information concerning private parcels for internees, which have to undergo inspection at a depôt before being taken to the German Field Post Office. Money may also be sent in reichsmarks to the value of £10; remittances will be made within the scope of existing International Clearing House agreements. The Royal Court fines another farmer £20 for milk adulteration.

114

February 14. A circular letter read in the various churches appeals for text-books for use among children who were deported to Germany; a depôt has also been established for the reception of clothing, etc. It is learned with satisfaction that goods already sent from here have been received.

February 15. Issue of 8 oz. of macaroni per head; the butter ration of 2 oz. has been increased to 4 oz. The Green Room Club presents a drama at the Opera House.

February 16. British planes pass over at night; Lorient is now one of the main targets and bombing can be heard from all parts of the Island.

February 17. The Germans are sending out notices to more probable deportees. The leather ration for this month has not arrived, and the trade is informed that there will be no allocation for shoe repairs. Six French horses sold in the Cattle Market by auction, the prices averaging £270.

February 18. Several people attend at the German military doctors' office at Westbourne Terrace, Wellington Road, for examination with a view to being deported to Germany; about 50 people have been warned this time. Numbers of men who have at some time or another worked for the Germans, at the Airport, as drivers, etc., and who have left their employment, are being rounded up and are given the option of working for them again or being sent away.

February 19. A German Order deals with the display of lights in Occupied France and the Channel Islands; the hours of blackout are now from sunset to sunrise.

February 20. The Textile and Footwear Control open a Footwear Exchange Depôt at No. 9 Beresford Street; persons wishing to exchange footwear may do so on payment of a registration fee of 1s. 0½d. (half a mark); there is no guarantee, however, that footwear will be returned in the event of an exchange not being possible. Apples, onions etc., are still to be found in various shops, but at a price and 'under the counter'; of course, it is not safe to display too much as the Germans buy up everything they see. About 250 Russian workers are taken back to France; these were in very bad health and some could hardly walk up the gangway of the boat.

February 21. The Germans bring over a large consignment of ready-made coffins. Sunday Charity Concert No. 6 at the Opera House.

February 22. States meeting deals with a few minor items, the chief of which is an increase in accident benefits for workers covered by the Social Assurance scheme. In connection with the forthcoming Assizes, an Act was adopted exempting jurors from the obligation of sleeping away from their homes. This week's extra ration is a tin of green peas, and the jam ration recommences (alphabetically). Notices are still being sent to persons to attend at College House for interrogation with a view to their deportation to Germany.

February 23. There is to be a further paraffin ration of one pint per household for those relying solely on that means of lighting (8½d. per pint), the last issue until October. A fowl has laid an egg weighing 4½ oz. and measuring 6¾ in. in circumference.

February 24. Big conference of German officials of the Channel Islands Command held at Military Headquarters (Hotel Metropole, Roseville Street), known as the Befehlshaber; visiting officers were housed at the Ommaroo Hotel, and during their stay guards were doubled in the vicinity at night and buses were ordered to be ready for requisitioning at a moment's notice.

February 25. About 25 more persons are deported to Germany; the great majority of these are 'undesirables'. The Plaza was the meeting place, and streets in the vicinity were barred off.

February 26. German court martial passes sentence on a Nonconformist minister (the Rev. C. N. Mylne), his wife and daughter, the parents to serve 12 months' imprisonment and the daughter 10 months', in addition to each being fined 300 reichsmarks (about £30); it was alleged they were in possession of a wireless set and the daughter has disseminated news; it is expected that an appeal will be made. Another local resident has been fined £50 recently for being in possession of a loud-speaker and wireless parts. The Germans re-publish the Order requiring that applications and communications sent to them should be in the German language! It is hoped this will prevent a large number of anonymous letters which some despicable persons are sending to College House. The G.P.O. staff opens suspected anonymous letters and warns the person concerned to get rid of anything which may be incriminating.

February 27. Another German Order published today requires that all electric fires, etc., shall be handed in 'for custody' at the various parish halls. Hospitals and nursing homes, are exempted, and the usual threat of six weeks' imprisonment or a fine up to 30,000 reichsmarks (about £3,000) is mentioned. In consequence of the heavy calls which have recently been made on stocks (the Germans have had another 150 tons), the Department of Agriculture appeals to persons holding potatoes in excess of their actual needs to hand them over to the nearest greengrocers or grocer. The Germans are apparently also getting short of petrol, as several essential services have been warned of an impending stoppage unless supplies arrive; in order to cut down petrol consumption, milk is to be collected once a day (mornings) instead of twice. A new roadway was opened at St. Lawrence from the foot of Charrière Nicolle to Hamptonne, in the upper portion of the Waterworks Valley.

February 28. Death of J. E. Pinel, Esq., Judge, in his 80th year. Two German submarines are seen off the north-east coast of the Island. Temperatures have been about the average for February. The fine weather has enabled farmers to plough and in many cases potatoes are already planted; at farms in the west, however, newly-planted potatoes are robbed at night by foreign workers. Local institutes are still closed on account of the danger of diphtheria, but the number of deaths generally is not as large as during last winter. A few more local men who served with the French Army and were taken prisoner have been released and returned to the Islands. Goods arriving from France nowadays include ladies' coats and frocks, which are sold at high prices. French business men visiting here and the crews on the barges offer better value if they are paid for goods in English £1 notes; some are making a trade of buying these notes; the price offered at the moment is about 15 marks—£1 12s. Many of the soldiers in the Island today are men who have served in Russia, and Jersey has become a rest-base, particularly for those suffering from frostbite. There seems to be a general tightening-up concerning the conduct of the general public; persons talking in groups are dispersed by the Feldgendarmerie and asked individually what their conversation was about. Cases are also reported of men using cigarette lighters being asked where they obtained the petrol, while to be out after curfew or riding two abreast may mean names taken and added to the list of 'undesirables' to be deported to Germany!

MARCH 1943

March 1. Extras for this week consist of ½ lb. of dried split green peas and a piece of household soap per head. Hot vegetable stew is obtainable each evening from 5.30 to 6.30 from the St. Helier House Community Restaurant (Sundays excluded) at 3d.

per pint. Batch of Red Cross letters delivered. The Chamber of Commerce is made the medium for circulating a questionnaire to various shops, etc., in connection with an 'economic chart' required by the Germans; names of business principals and numbers of staff have to be declared. Overdue supply of meat, petrol and other goods arrive from France. March Assize opens; two cases are down for trial, the first concerning extensive burglaries from the States store with a view to selling the goods in the black market. Sentences of two years' hard labour were passed on two of the accused, the third receiving one year's hard labour. The Island School of Dancing and Elocution presents a revue at the Opera House.

March 3. Opening of the second case before the March Assize—two men charged with larceny of goods from the stores of the Mental Hospital; a third who should have been on trial has been deported by the Germans as an 'undesirable'; sentences were passed of two years and 15 months respectively.

March 4. After being in prison for some time, Advocate Ogier and his son are taken to Paris to await trial on a charge of espionage; the latter is alleged to have been in possession of an Ordnance map on which he had marked various German gun positions, and the father is charged with 'harbouring a spy'. The hunt for wireless sets goes on and fresh arrests are reported; the Gestapo headquarters are now at Silvertide, Havre-des-Pas. Electric fires are today being taken to the various parish halls.

March 6. More information is published by the Jersey Internees Aid Committee following further German alterations concerning the dispatch of letters and parcels; only ten lb. may be sent at a time. The Superior Council appeals again for surplus stocks of potatoes to be handed in as there has not been a very good response. A Department of Agriculture notice reminds growers that, except under licence, they must not sell potatoes, wheat, oats, barley or rye to any person other than to the Department.

March 7. British planes were in the vicinity of the Island today; they were fired at from a few points along the north coast.

March 8. Names of roundsmen (bakers, milkmen, etc.) handed to the German authorities: this is for special permits should the emergency plans have to be put into operation and the civil population have to stay indoors for a lengthy period. An area extending in a ring around the Abattoirs is put out of bounds for cattle, this being a precaution against foot-and-mouth disease. The cinema which has to show a German film alternately now has to commence the screening on Mondays instead of Wednesdays. Issue of ½ lb. of coffee substitute and a piece of toilet soap per head. The Germans want the names of 21 men to be sent for work of a non-military character in Alderney.

March 9. Shrove Tuesday; in spite of everything, many people made pancakes! A special sitting of the Royal Court fines a farmer £20 for milk adulteration and the abstraction of fat; this was the second offence. The German Commandant (Colonel Knackfuss) pays a visit of inspection to 'Summerland'; much excellent work is being done there, and Guernsey is receiving some of the goods manufactured.

March 11. The German Commandant pays a visit to Victoria College; he stays for a time, being specially interested in the German language period.

March 12. Notices issued by the Department of Agriculture fix the price of potatoes grown under glass at 6d. per lb. when sold by the grower, and warn against the warble fly, foreign cattle having been found to be infested with maggots from it. Report published by the Forestry Section of the Department of Labour concerning re-afforestation; during 1942 the number of trees planted was 5,246. Entry forms are being issued for the forthcoming School Certificate Examination, to be held in July. A section of the Strangers' Cemetery in which Russian workers are buried has today been consecrated by a Russian Bishop, who, with his chaplain, came from Paris specially for the ceremony. The general public was excluded except for about half a dozen officials, but six Russians from each of the ten camps attended and were addressed by the Bishop; a Requiem was beautifully sung by a choir composed of workers. This seems sheer hypocrisy on the part of the Germans, for the 'Russians are treated very badly. Over sixty have already been buried in the Strangers' Cemetery, where five graves must always be kept open. Three German soldiers have also been buried there after being exhumed from the German section of St. Brelade's Cemetery for 'dishonouring the flag' by committing suicide.

March 13. The Germans are on the trail of persons who are spreading wireless news; several well-known residents of St. Saviour's Parish, from the church district, are in prison for this 'offence'; these include the Acting Rector (Canon Cohu, who is also Hospital Chaplain), the Deputy (who is also a Church-warden), the Parish Clerk, a Vingtenier and his son, and the gravedigger. An alteration is announced in the rationing of electricity, which comes into operation after the 31st inst.; basic ration per week per household—April to September (inclusive), 3½ units; October to March (inclusive), 5 units; adjustments have to be made, but no ration cards will be issued where the basic ration applies; additional rations are to be granted to consumers who are licensed to use cookers, refrigerators, pumps, etc. Fertiliser for grassland is obtainable at the rate of 56 lb. per vergée, the price being 21s. 4d. per hundredweight.

March 15. The Germans issue a notice announcing that fishing will be permitted again from the 22nd; all fishermen have to attend at the German Harbour Office (Pomme d'Or) to renew their permits. A hundred saccharins issued to everybody, and persons who did not receive their wine ration in the last issue may now do so (I to Z). Early in the evening heavy bombing is heard, the B.B.C. later announcing that the airport near St. Malo has been visited by the R.A.F.

March 16. More people are being arrested and put into prison for the alleged spreading of news; altogether, eighteen from the St. Saviour's Church area are locked up; the Germans think that the set was hidden in the church.

March 17. The Germans are bringing over many horses; extra stabling is being acquired or built.

March 18. It is learned through the B.B.C. that Lord Portsea has appealed to the British Government to send a food ship to the Channel Islands.

March 19. Permission has been granted by the Field Commandant for farmers to cut branches overshadowing their crops to a height not exceeding three metres from the ground (about 10 feet). The Germans have demanded 160 men for work in the Channel Islands, the majority to come from the Labour Department and the others from textile shops; employers of labour have to supply names. Amendments made to the Controlled Articles Order whereby more articles are added to the list which cannot be sold at auction sales; second-hand dealers are also informed that they cannot undertake sales on commission. The meat ration for this week is cancelled; a small quantity of Camembert cheese has been released, and rabbits are being 'bumped off' galore.

March 20. More people are being arrested in connection with the St. Saviour's wireless case, and the Rev. C. N. Mylne, his wife and daughter, who were sentenced last month, are now serving terms at Gloucester Street. Fertiliser for cereals is obtainable at 56 lb. per vergée, the price being 20s. per hundredweight.

March 21. A new Roman Catholic chapel was opened today at Samarès; this is an old Army hut which has been made serviceable by willing workers and it is to be known as the Church of St. Patrick. The Germans celebrate Heroes' Memorial Day, a wreath-laying ceremony taking place at St. Brelade's Cemetery. Sunday Charity Concert No. 7 held at the Opera House.

March 22. Following the German demand for men, over a hundred have been picked out by the Department of Labour and today about twenty of them were taken over by the Germans; these men are to be replaced by volunteers who are being appealed for in the following Department of Labour advertisement published today:—

The Occupying Authority, availing itself of its right under Article 52 of the Hague Convention, to requisition labour for work of a non-military nature, has demanded the immediate services of 160 men and women for such work in the Island. The pay offered is similar to that at present given to men employed on building constructional work. Persons willing to offer their services for the work in question should communicate with the Department of Labour, Conway Street, where full particulars as to rates of pay and conditions of work will be available.

A tin of green haricot beans is available to everybody, and five boxes of matches per household; these are getting very scarce, and as much as a shilling a box is being offered for them.

March 23. Over a hundred men have volunteered for work and the Germans have accepted only a few; they are to be used on store work or on the two-horse waggons, and sympathy is extended to those who have to ride on one of these vehicles with a German soldier as driver. Fish rationing is to commence again. Victoria College terminal service held at St. Helier's Parish Church—the first since the Occupation.

March 24. A farmer at St. Ouen's who found workers trying to get into the house between midnight and 1.30 a.m. attacked them with a heavy stick and knocked two of them unconscious; one man was later found to be dead; the case is being investigated. This is the second of its kind, another man who broke into a farm at St. Mary's last month being the victim of wounds inflicted by a pitchfork. Two more arrests made today by the Germans in connection with the St. Saviour's wireless case—the

Steward and the Secretary of the General Hospital.

March 25. Death of the second man connected with the farm robbery at St. Ouen's.

March 26. The Germans announce that a farmer has been sentenced to three days' imprisonment and fined 150 reichsmarks for an infraction of the Maximum Prices Order. Attention is called to the fact that setting foot on the Aerodrome is by special permit only. Department of Agriculture publishes a schedule for the return of crops for the 1943 season. No meat ration again this week, but a tin of tunny fish is being issued.

March 27. The Todt Organisation appeals for baby clothes for pregnant Russian women. A number of cattle arrives for slaughter and over a hundred tons of potatoes, mostly seed. Representatives of agriculture have attended two meetings at College House in connection with the requisition of cattle for slaughter, and the growing of vegetables, the Germans complaining that the troops do not get enough variety.

March 29. The clock advanced one hour to conform with Central European Summer Time, which for one week from now will be one hour ahead of British time. The curfew is also altered—from 10 p.m. to 6.30 a.m. This week's extras consist of 4 oz. of cheese and a packet of washing powder per head; a ration of red wine is to be issued again (alphabetically) over a period of three weeks; some churches are appealing to members for some of this wine for use in the Sacrament of Holy Communion. The Germans have asked that administrators be appointed to take care of farms belonging to farmers arrested in connection with the St. Saviour's wireless case. Messrs. Britton and Whinnerah present a play at the Opera House.

March 31. Sudden death of the German Harbourmaster. Robberies are still going on on a large scale; foreign workers who are found stealing are severely punished by the Germans, who put them in a pillory and then take them to Elizabeth Castle. At St. Ouen's a hut which had been occupied by workers has been burned because of fear of infection, and the Germans are turning the Girls' College into a hospital. Cables are being laid in several parts of the Island, and it is learned that the Germans contemplate making a power-house in St. Peter's Valley for their own use. A horses' hospital is being established at La Pommeraie, St. Saviour's. Among the goods from France there is a quantity of material for ladies' frocks and men's suits; the former has been released and the price of a kind of marocain is 37s. 6d. per yard! Our bread now consists of 100 per cent. of Jersey flour and is quite palatable.

April 1. The fuel ration for this month is 2 cwt. of coal and 1 cwt. of logs for an average family, the coal to be kept in reserve for next winter. Change made in the hours during which the gas is turned on, these now being: 6 a.m. to 1.30 p.m., 5 to 7 p.m., and 8.30 to 10 p.m. The Spanish workers give an entertainment at The Forum for Jersey folk only.

April 2. Meat ration to be issued this week.

April 3. New tobacco ration cards come into operation; the ration is now permanently fixed at 20 cigarettes one week and 10 cigarettes and 1 oz. of pipe tobacco the next. Local tobacco is almost unobtainable, even at the exorbitant prices being charged. The Royal Court sentences a man to 12 months' imprisonment for ration book frauds extending over a prolonged period, he having obtained food, illegally or fraudulently, for five persons, in addition to himself, over a period of two years. A grower was also fined £10 for selling new potatoes without a licence.

April 4. The first Sunday in April—beautiful weather, everything in the garden being a month in advance.

April 5. In the evening a tragedy occurs on Grève d'Azette beach, when a boy aged 14 is killed and two others injured as the result of playing with explosives. This week's extra ration is ½ lb. of dried split beans.

April 6. Inquiry held into the Grève d'Azette tragedy.

April 9. A meat ration is issued again this week; this was mostly of French meat, but a scheme has been launched whereby each parish has to supply six animals for slaughter each week. The Germans have held the trial today of 17 persons implicated in the St. Saviour's wireless case; sentences were passed ranging from three years to two weeks, and many of those concerned were charged with 'receiving news'! The trial was held in the Old Committee Room, and numbers of people were in the Royal Square awaiting the outcome.

April 10. Early in the morning a British plane damaged over France, came down in St. Ouen's Bay; the crew were brought ashore on a German tug—two were dead, two badly injured, and the other airman had slight injuries; he was put into Gloucester Street Prison. Interesting meeting of the States: A statement was made on behalf of the local committee acting in connection with the Jersey Internees (or deportees) in Germany; from this it was gleaned that they were being sent parcels by the British Red Cross and the Canadian Red Cross, and that the Channel Islands Fund contributed liberally. The Superior Council of the States, or any person authorised by the Council for the purpose, can direct any male between 16 and 50 or any female (umarried or a widow) between 18 and 35, to perform such duties as the Council might think proper. The principal item on the agenda was the Budget. The state of the Public Debt on January 31, 1943, was £2,847,540 10s. 8d., largely created by borrowings on Treasury Bonds and Notes since July, 1940, of £1,508,800 10s. 8d.; of this amount £678,886 had been borrowed during the year under review.

April 12. Department of Education invites entries for scholarships at Victoria College and Jersey College for Girls. Half a pound of macaroni issued per head and the jam ration commences again (alphabetically). The Amateur Dramatic Club presents a comedy at the Opera House.

April 13. The Germans publish the following notice under the heading of 'Heavy Punishments for Wireless Order Infractions':

Although in June, 1942, i.e., 10 months ago, the handing over of wireless sets was ordered, and, furthermore, in December, 1942, another Order was published by which persons who at that time were still in possession of apparatus were given the opportunity of delivering up the same without suffering punishment, wireless sets are still being found in possession of the local population.

Therefore, at the sitting of the court martial last week-end, it was necessary to inflict heavier punishment than given last year on those persons retaining wireless sets.

Furthermore, the news bulletins broadcast by the B.B.C. have been spread both verbally and by leaflets, although the persons concerned were well aware of their criminal actions. The three persons chiefly concerned were, therefore, sentenced to punishments ranging from one year to three years' imprisonment, while the rest received lighter sentences.

In the case of two elderly female persons, the Feldkommandant, as confirming officer of the court martial, deferred their sentences until the end of the war provided they do not commit any further culpable action.

April 14. Resumed inquest concerning the Grève d'Azette beach tragedy; the verdict was one of accidental death following multiple injuries.

124

April 15. The Germans advertise for skilled labourers to undertake work in Alderney.

April 17. A farmer is fined £10 for selling seed potatoes above price. Supplies of vegetables were requisitioned by the Germans. An exhibition of works of art, etc., by members of the German forces stationed here has been opened at the premises formerly occupied by the Fifty-Shilling Tailors, which is now a book depôt. Some of the persons who received lengthy sentences in the recent St. Saviour's wireless case are being sent to France; others who had served part of their sentence then had the remainder remitted are also to be sent.*

April 18. Sunday Charity Concert No. 8 held at the Opera House.

April 19. This week's extra rations consist of 4 oz. of margarine, 8 oz. of coffee substitute, and a piece of toilet soap per head. Children also receive five bars of cream chocolate.

April 20. A small quantity of assorted woollen fabrics available today for men's suitings, women's suitings, coatings and dress materials; although the prices ranged between 20s. and 30s. per head, the materials were sold in a very short time. Hitler's birthday is being celebrated by the Germans, who have a special edition of their own newspaper.

April 22. The Germans stage an international variety show by visiting artistes; this was held at The Forum exclusively for the civilian population.

April 23. Good Friday: very heavy but much-needed rain in the morning. The usual Passiontide music was rendered in the various churches, and a three-day musical festival was concluded with 'The Messiah'.

April 24. Easter Saturday. There is a profusion of flowers this year, and these are purchased in large quantities. The price of new potatoes has been fixed at 7½d. per lb. retail, and today tons of greenstuffs have arrived from Guernsey. The Lending Department of the Public Library has set up a new record today with the issue of 735 books.

April 25. Easter Sunday: rain practically all day, and a very cold wind. The churches were well attended. The German troops also held special services.

April 26. Easter Monday: Football attracted a large crowd, and the Green Room Club revived 'Les Cloches de Corneville'. The extras for this week were ½ lb. of dried split green peas and

---

* Four of these unfortunate people never returned to Jersey, they having died in German concentration camps—Canon C. J. Cohu and Messrs. J. Tierney, J. Nicolle and A. Dimmery.

a piece of household soap per head.

April 27. Inquest opened and adjourned on a 14-year-old boy who was knocked from his cycle and killed by a car on the 24th inst. at Vauxhall. Great excitement in the early evening when a convoy from France en route for Guernsey was attacked by British planes in the vicinity of Noirmont. A supply ship named the *Helder* and a patrol boat were sunk, while another patrol boat which was towed into harbour eventually sank; a fourth ship—the *Marz*—was laden with coal, and though badly damaged in the stern was towed to the New North Quay for discharge. Residents assert that about twenty planes were seen. Among the vessels machine-gunned was an oil barge on which were three Guernsey buyers returning from France.

April 28. Early in the morning British planes were fired on by the German batteries and later on the air-raid siren was sounded, the all-clear being given within a matter of seconds. An accident has occurred at Grands Vaux, where the Germans have been tunnelling for some time. Today the Germans began demolishing the Abergeldie Hotel, Havre-des-Pas, to make room for the railway that is being laid through the eastern parishes; the hotel had been used as a brothel for the Todts—known as the O.T. Café—and this was now moved to Norman House, First Tower. The price of the tobacco ration further increased to 10d. for 10 cigarettes and 1s. 9d. per oz. for pipe tobacco.

April 29. Variety programme by international stars again presented at The Forum for the civilian population.

April 30. The Germans publish this notice, which causes great indignation:

Wherever German forces have occupied territory they have safeguarded the supplies of foodstuffs and essential commodities for the civilian population. To this the British Channel Islands have been no exception.

The British Command, on the other hand, does its worst to hamper and interrupt the steady flow of supplies to the isles, regardless of the fact that the population of the Islands are their own fellow-countrymen. Since, as a result of these nuisance raids, the rations of the civil population have to be reduced, they may thank their countrymen across the Channel for such measures.

Mr. Churchill and the men behind will not achieve any military results with their nuisance raids. But it is typical of their well-known ruthlessness and lack of consideration that they do not refrain from exposing their own countrymen to hardships and sufferings which might well be avoided.

At least, however, the Island population ought to know the guilty party!

Der Oberbefehlshaber der Armee.

The Germans have been putting pressure on the local authorities to reduce the rations and the attack on their shipping on the 28th inst. has given them an opportunity to say that it is not their fault. Boats leaving for Guernsey again this evening were machine-gunned off Corbière and two were damaged and had to turn back; the skipper of one was wounded and the three Guernseymen were again on board one of the attacked vessels. Far from depressing us, these attacks are welcomed, for we always believed that when shipping in the vicinity of the Island was attacked it would herald greater events. The month has ended on a note of optimism, and we observe that the Germans in our midst are very gloomy. Guards from among the civilian population have been ordered to watch over the Russians working in various parts of the Island, especially in connection with the railway from Havre-des-Pas to Le Bourg. It is learned that a German soldier has committed suicide on learning that his wife and children had been killed in a recent air raid. A big 'sweep' has been organised by a committee of local doctors, the proceeds of which are to be allotted for the purchase of extra rations needed by children suffering from ill-health. The trading in £1 notes still goes on, and crews of boats plying between Jersey and France are offering about 17 marks for them (£1 16s. 3d.).

MAY 1943

May 1. The Royal Court registers an Order of the German authorities reducing the hours of curfew for the civil population, from 11 p.m. to 5 a.m. and 10 p.m. to 5 a.m. in the Military Zone. The Court also fined a farmer £40 for milk adulteration by the abstraction of fat up to 45 per cent. The fuel ration for May consists of a small quantity of wood and coal, it being pointed out that this should be reserved for use next winter. Today being a German holiday, all the work carried on by the Todt Organisation was suspended, but the celebrations which are usually held on this day were conspicuous by their absence. Two British fighters and a bomber swept over the Island at a low altitude and shot up a couple of German

127

machine-gun posts in the St. Lawrence area; the German batteries put up a terrific barrage.

May 3. A large number of young men between the ages of 18 and 25 have been called up today under the Compulsory Civil Duties (Jersey) Regulations 1943, recently passed by the States. The primary object of this is to find labour for farmers during the coming busy period. The public is again reminded that all small gardens must be properly cultivated otherwise they will be taken over without compensation. A quantity of galvanised goods from France is on sale in various shops, and this week's extras consist of a tin of vegetables (beans, peas, etc.) and a bottle of red wine. Wests put on a stage show with the title *The Old Town Hall*.

May 5. The Germans are investigating a case involving several local residents and some German soldiers in connection with the robbery of about a ton of sugar for disposal on the black market.

May 6. Salvage efforts are under way to raise the patrol boat which sank in the harbour following the recent R.A.F. raid. St. Paul's defeat Corinthians in the Open Cup Final at the F.B. Fields.

May 7. The following notice is published in today's *Evening Post*:

STATES OF JERSEY

During the past few days the Field Commandant and a delegation of the Council have held conferences with reference to the sinkings of ships by Allied Forces in the waters adjacent to the Channel Islands and to the possible effect of such sinkings on insular supplies.

The delegation received the assurance of the Field Commandant that the 20 per cent. reduction of the present bread rations of the entire civil population over 21 years of age is indicated by the existing war situation and is in no sense a punishment against the civil population.

Future events will show the time during which it may be necessary to continue this reduction.

On behalf of the Council,

A. M. COUTANCHE, Bailiff.

May 5, 1943.

BREAD RATIONING

As from Monday, May 10, 1943, the bread ration for the civil population is, until further notice, fixed as follows: —

Manual Worker, male, over 21 years of age .	4 lb. 12 oz.
Manual Worker, female, over 21 years of age	4 lb. 4 oz.
Other Adults, over 21 years of age . .	3 lb. 12 oz.

The bread rations of the rest of the civil population remain unchanged.

E. P. LE MASURIER,
President, Department of Essential Commodities.
Zur Veroeffentlichung genehmigt
Jersey, 5. mai 1943.
Fuer den Feldkommandanten:
DR. CASPER, O.K.V.R.

This is the outcome of a long series of meetings held between the Superior Council and the German authorities.

May 8. An official notice states that it is hoped to forward at an early date any luggage which was left behind by persons who were 'interned' on the Continent. The Germans remind that the felling of trees is prohibited except under special permission, and threaten with punishment any persons who feed or hide Russian prisoners escaping from camp. The weather has turned quite cold and a strong gale is blowing; this has meant the turning back from the harbour of several persons sentenced by the Germans who were to be taken to France.

May 10. This week's extra is a stick of shaving soap for the male population; this is the first issue for about twelve months. Messrs. John Le Sueur and H. M. de Ste. Croix present a thriller at the Opera House. The potato ration has now to be made up largely of new potatoes; this is a hardship for many families, however, as the price is 7½d. per lb. The reduced scale of bread rationing came into force today; it is hoped to save about ten tons of flour per week. This evening a disturbance occurred at the Ritz Hotel, where German troops are billeted; the news from Tunisia prompted many of them to shout anti-Hitler slogans and to throw his photograph out of one of the windows; a fight ensued and the military police only restored order after a considerable time.

May 11. The Department of Agriculture gives notices that the Field Command has arranged for the importation of about 450 tons of late variety seed potatoes suitable for winter storage. The Jersey Allotment Council at the same time reminds plotholders that as per agreement 25 per cent. of their plot must be planted with potatoes. Several groups of Allied planes have been seen today, especially in the north. The sailing of a ship with troops for France was cancelled. Searches have been made by the German military police today for deserters in the neighbourhood of Westmount and First Tower.

May 13. The SS. *Normand* is discharging a large cargo of aerial torpedo-bombs, which are being taken by lorry to the Airport. A very large cargo of coal is being discharged; this is being stacked in the field under the Fort in Pier Road, and residents in the vicinity have collected considerable quantities from lorries that have tipped going around corners. A number of local workmen leave for work in Alderney: The Dean dedicates a new cemetery at St. Brelade's; the old cemetery is now very full, the German section having taken up a large area.*

May 15. Early in the morning Allied planes fly around the south and west coasts of the Island and a German patrol boat was sunk off St. Brelade's, another being slightly damaged. The Royal Court registers a German Order relating to Civil Defence; this was published and dealt *in extenso* with measures to be adopted in connection with A.R.P., although for some time now A.R.P. has been a dead letter. The Constables are designated as being in charge of A.R.P. in their respective parishes, and the States have today issued instructions for dealing with incendiary bombs. To celebrate its 70th anniversary, the Société Jersiaise opens a branch for junior members at a special annual subscription of half a crown. A high German official is on a visit to the Island—the Commander of the Forces in Northern France.

May 16. German hospital ship arrives in harbour and leaves again during the day. Sunday Charity Benefit Concert No. 9 held at the Opera House. An orchestra composed of foreign workers entertains a crowd of spectators in front of West Park Pavilion during the evening.

May 17. Fire guards are being instituted for various buildings under the German Order recently registered by the Royal Court. Leaflets dropped by Allied planes have been found in the First Tower district; these were in French and contained the text of a speech made in Ottawa by Mr. Anthony Eden; fishermen returning to harbour were searched for leaflets by the Germans. This week's extra rations consist of $\frac{1}{2}$ lb. of macaroni and 100 saccharin tablets for adults. During the evening the Germans held a mock invasion with sham fights in some of the streets of the town. The ban on dancing has been lifted in so far as it applied to social clubs. Large quantities of greens from Guernsey are on sale. Tomatoes sold on the black market are 5s. per

---

* This was made necessary because the Germans had commandeered all the valuable space in the parish church cemetery for a soldiers' burial ground.

lb. and strawberries 20s. per lb.

May 18. About 2 a.m. large numbers of planes were heard passing over the Island; the Germans appear to be using the Airport again for raiding. German officials are visiting the schools to find out what progress is being made in the teaching of German; several teachers have been to College House recently, having been sent for by the Germans to be sounded regarding their views on teaching the language. The gas hours have again been changed; these are now from 6 a.m. to 3 p.m. and 5 to 8 p.m.; the object being to enable the Germans to issue a two-page newspaper daily in place of a one-page and to include the day's communiqué which is issued about 1.30 p.m. The enlarging of their newspaper appears to be designed to sustain the moral of the troops. A German notice issued today warns the public that sharpshooting on targets in the air will take place from 9.30 a.m. to 12 (noon) and from 2.30 to 5.30 p.m. daily until the 30th of this month; 'the population is requested to take shelter in a house or a splinter-proof place if there is shooting in their vicinity'.

May 19. Attempted burglary at the States Treasury.

May 21. The Germans held a very concentrated anti-aircraft practice and pieces of shrapnel flew in all directions, doing considerable damage to glasshouses. The workers on the harbours now come under the direction of the German Harbour Authority.

May 22. In the early hours a large cargo vessel of about 4,000 tons (the *Ostland*) strikes the Grunes aux Dardes rocks, which are between Elizabeth Castle and Noirmont; she eventually settles down and breaks in two. The vessel was on her way to Guernsey and had a cargo of hay, coal, timber and a large number of bombs for aircraft. There is an immense quantity of shipping still coming and going, and the harbours are very busy.

May 23. Bales of hay are being washed up from the wreck on the Grunes aux Dardes: a local pilot asserts that bad navigation was the cause of the trouble and the German crew panicked when she struck.

May 24. Advocate Ogier returns to the Island after trial with his son in France for alleged spying activities; the former was sentenced to six months' imprisonment, but had part of the sentence remitted, and the latter is staying in France in a sanatorium. Some of the bombs which were on the wreck have been taken off and landed at the New North Quay. A Rat Week commenced today, the damage caused by these vermin having become a serious problem. Issue of 4 oz. of margarine per head;

another red wine ration is also available to adults. The Fifty-Fifty Club presents a comedy at the Opera House.

May 26. Blasting has been going on at the end of the Victoria Pier near the Harvey Monument; this is in connection with the tunnel which has been bored under Mount Bingham for the railway to run through. In today's operations a large part of the wall coping on the top road was blown away and will have to be replaced.

May 27. Arrival of another large consignment of coal, and, after a long interval, quantities of Camembert cheese are again available. A variety show at The Forum run for the German troops gives a special performance for the civil population only.

May 28. The German Admiral in Command of the Northern France area pays a visit to the Island and stays at the British Hotel, where a double guard is placed and barbed wire barricades are erected on the pavement.

May 29. Departments of Agriculture and Essential Commodities issue the Livestock (Amendment) (Jersey) Order, 1943; this deals with pigs and calves, and is aimed at ensuring a sufficient quantity of meat to supply the present ration fixed for the civil population. Pigs born before January 10, 1943, must be offered to the Department of Essential Commodities not later than October 10, 1943, and pigs born on or after January 10, 1943, must be offered for sale to that Department within nine months of their birth. Calves born on or after June 1, 1943, must be offered for sale to the Department between the 18th and 21st days next following their birth. This replaces the provision requiring calves to be slaughtered within 14 days of their birth. Another Order is published increasing the price of pork by 3d. per lb.; this causes much amusement, as the ration of meat is only 4 oz. per week, and pork is almost unobtainable.

May 31. German notices issued to the effect that all public or private businesses, shops, farms glasshouses, artisans, etc., are ordered to increase their working hours to a minimum of 48 hours per week, and, in special cases, to 60 hours per week, if public or private customers' orders, or dates formerly agreed to, or the upmost utilisation of the soil, should make such an increase necessary; any person ... not making the fullest use of his own working capacity or that of his employees is liable to imprisonment not exceeding six weeks and to a fine not exceeding 30,000 reichsmarks (about £3,000). The price of new potatoes is 2d. per lb. retail; this is a drop of 5½d. per lb., but the ration remains at 5 lb. per head. This week's extras consist of ½ lb. of coffee substitute per head, 5 boxes of matches per household and the jam ration commences alphabetically. Local workers for the Todt Organisation are being enticed with the prospect of extra rations. The railway which is to run from Gorey to town is almost complete; it runs through fields, gardens and all around the walk at Havre-des-Pas from Green Street to the Harbour Works, part of the headland having been blasted to make room for the track; from there it proceeds through a tunnel under Mount Bingham to the Victoria Pier opposite the Lifeboat House, past La Folie, and over a bridge which is being erected across the little harbour at the foot of Commercial Buildings; there the track meets the one running from the West, but the two gauges are different!

JUNE 1943

June 1. The first two stamps ($\frac{1}{2}$d. and 1d.) of a new pictorial series issued today, there being a busy time at the G.P.O., caused by the rush of persons anxious to obtain first-day covers. These are designed by Mr. Edmund Blampied, and have been printed in Paris; the $\frac{1}{2}$d. stamp bears a picture of Vinchelez Lane and the 1d. stamp one of Portelet. Farmers and growers are ordered by the Department of Agriculture to spray potato and tomato crops as the Colorado beetle has been found in the Parish of St. Helier by Dr. Pelz, a German officer attached to the administrative staff; depôts from which arsenate of lead may be obtained have been established and spraying must be effective between the third and tenth days of this month. The fuel ration for June consists of a little wood. White cotton is available to the public from today on a ration of one reel. Messrs. G. Ahier and L. Landick are presenting a week's variety at Wests.

June 2. Parcels of clothing are being received by some residents from friends of relatives in Germany who were deported, the garments being from supplies sent by the British Red Cross. Letters from deportees state that the Red Cross is looking after them very well, but the supplies for one camp have been delayed for some time.

June 3. The body of an R.A.F. sergeant has been picked up at La Pulente and then to the Hospital mortuary. Identified as that of Sergeant D. C. Butlin, whose home was in Leeds; he was a married man and 27 years of age. More troops are leaving the Island, and many of the houses in which they were billeted are empty. Some of the anti-aircraft gun crews have Russians forming part of the crew. Today the bank managers had to attend at College House to be informed that the Germans are going to inspect safe deposits at the various banks.

June 4. Arrangements have been made for a military funeral for the R.A.F. sergeant; this is to take place tomorrow (Saturday) from the Hospital Chapel. All the big firms of the Island and scores of private individuals are sending flowers and making subscriptions towards a headstone. The Germans are reticent about it all and even the undertaker is not permitted to divulge the time of the funeral.

June 5. Large numbers of people made their way to the Hospital Chapel this morning, but it was learned there had been a postponement as the body of another airman had been picked up at Samarès, and in consequence there would be a double funeral. This airman was also a sergeant and his name was A. Holden. List published of parish representatives who have been nominated to make arrangements for the extra labour required by farmers for the harvest. A German infantry band gives a concert in the Royal Square. For the third time within a fortnight, various members of textile shop staffs have been visited by German officials and warned to present themselves at a German office to be given employment: this time a few men were given a job, but no females have yet been taken on. Some of the persons who have been sentenced by the Germans have now been fetched to undergo their punishment. A policeman was today reported by the German Commandant for 'showing disrespect by failing to salute him'; he was subsequently fined 30 reichsmarks (about £3).

June 6. The funeral of the two R.A.F. sergeants took place this morning; the service was held at the Hospital Chapel at 7 o'clock, and hundreds of people had gathered in the vicinity and all along the route leading up to Mont-à-l'Abbé Cemetery. The service was conducted by the Dean of Jersey, who was assisted by the Rev. W. J. Ward, Chairman of the Methodist Church in Jersey. The Bailiff, Jurat P. M. Baudians, and the Attorney-General represented the States of Jersey; Dr. H. J. Shone the Red Cross; and Mr. A. E. Mossop the British Legion and the Royal Air Force Association. The Constable of St. Helier was also present, and a German officer represented the German military authorities. The coffins were each covered with the Union Jack and bore wreaths from the States of Jersey and the German Air Force. Only three Germans followed the hearses as they left the chapel, but at the cemetery German Air Force personnel acted as bearers and there was also a firing party.

Among the wreaths were two laid by the Bailiff—one in the name of the King and the other in the name of the States of Jersey. Nobody was allowed into the cemetery, apart from the officials, during the burial. Later in the morning two lorry loads of wreaths were sent to the cemetery from the Hospital Chapel, where the public had been admitted the previous evening to view them, and in the afternoon hundreds filed past the grave.

June 7. Many wreaths were still being taken to Mont-à-l'Abbé Cemetery, and it is learned that eventually all the inscriptions are to be removed and a list sent to the widows of the airmen. One striking feature of the ceremony was the absolute lack of ostentation with which the Germans allowed the funeral to be carried out, for everyone expected a lot of military pomp. Today, German officials commenced visiting the banks and safe deposits had to be opened in their presence; a note was made of various valuables. Issue of 8 oz. of soup semolina for everybody, and 8 oz. of sweets for children and juveniles. Green Room Club presents a play at the Opera House.

June 8. This afternoon the Germans had an alert; double guards were posted at various places and fishing boats recalled. During the evening soldiers were turned out of the cinemas.

June 9. A boat laden with potatoes which were to be sent to France has been sent back; the potatoes are being unloaded and returned to various depôts, whence they are to be supplied to shopkeepers for the public to have an extra ration. The 100-ton floating crane which was here some time ago returned to the Island.

June 10. Tragedy occurs at Le Mourier, St. John's, when a farmer is knocked down and killed by a train which runs through his fields; he went to move his cows, and, being stone deaf, did not hear the train's approach. The inquest, at which none of the German forces or the Todt Organisation gave evidence, resulted in a verdict of accidental death. A young lady in the neighbourhood of the Victoria Pier today was wounded in the leg by a stray bullet; this is not surprising, for almost every day the Germans hold firing practices in any place they think fit. The Todt workers staged a variety show at The Forum today, to which the civilian population was invited.

June 11. Three persons sentenced by the Royal Court today for serious ration frauds extending over the whole period of the Occupation; a man and a woman each received six months and another woman three months. The Germans had another alarm during the evening, the cinemas being cleared of soldiers again. Large cargoes of cement are being unloaded and huge gun cupolas or turrets are being unloaded by the 100-ton crane.

June 12. At the Royal Court, 240 inspectors for the Colorado beetle were sworn-in. The Labour Office advertises for 11 lorry drivers for Alderney. Potatoes are being loaded to be sent to France. A quantity of men's working trousers has arrived and facilities are afforded for these to be obtained by persons who are in real need. A German infantry band played in the Royal Square during the afternoon. The Germans open a Soldiers' Home at Seafield, Millbrook. There are five in all, the others being at the Mayfair Hotel, Fort d'Auvergne, the British Hotel and St. Brelade's Bay Hotel. A circular letter has been issued to greengrocers warning them that all vegetables, etc., must be displayed and sold straight away—nothing must be kept under the counter.

June 13. Whit Sunday: weather dull all day. A German seaplane comes down off the north of the Island to pick up a British airman who had been in a rubber dinghy for several days. The airman was landed at Greve-de-Lecq and taken to the German military hospital at Merton Hotel.

June 14. Whit Monday: Among soldiers going away are many who have told people that they are being sent to the Turkish frontier; it is learned that German circles expect Turkey to come into the war at any moment. This week's extra rations consist of $\frac{1}{2}$ lb. of macaroni and a piece of toilet soap; the salt ration is reduced to 3 oz., the potato ration is doubled this week to 10 lb. Mr. John Dunmore presents a variety show at Wests.

June 16. The Constable of St. Helier calls attention to the recent notice regarding air-raid precautions, and the public is again warned that when aerial target practice is taking place all persons must seek shelter.

June 17. In pursuance of the policy of planting all available land with main-crop potatoes, part of the Davis Park was today ploughed up. The Commandant of the Forces in the Channel Islands, General Mueller, who is stationed in Guernsey, is on a visit to this Island.

June 18. Alteration again in the gas hours, cuts the hours of consumption by one hour, from 6 a.m. to 2.30 p.m., and 5.30 to 8 p.m. Warning that all cabbage, lettuce or soft fruit which may have been in contact with anti-Colorado beetle spray should be washed before it is eaten. The public is advised to make use of curds, a shop for the sale of which has recently been opened under the direction of the Milk Control.

June 19. Three years today since the States sat and issued the evacuation notice! German band plays in the Royal Square during the afternoon. Aerial target practice takes place also during the afternoon when the town is crowded—again without warning. Mackerel is being caught in fairly large quantities, but not much of it reaches the market.

June 20. A young Frenchman working for the Germans is killed on the quay when hit by a scale-board laden with bags of cement. Local young French residents are sent for by the Germans and informed that they must work for them.

June 21. The Germans are calling up all civilian German girls in the Island between the ages of 19 and 20; a few of these are acting as maids, clerks, etc., in German billets or offices. Quantity of tomatoes arrives from Guernsey. This week's extras consist of 4 oz. of margarine and a piece of household soap per head. The Amateur Dramatic Club presents a play at the Opera House.

June 22. The Bailiff issues a notice that all dance permits are cancelled until further notice; for medical reasons. Cinema managers have been warned against allowing remarks, cat-calls, etc., during the showing of the German news films, and the Feldgendarmerie is to attend performances.

June 23. The Germans give a sacred concert in Grove Place Chapel, to which the civilian population is invited. Work commenced today on running a branch line of the railway from the east from Grève d'Azette, up Plat Douet Road to the Todt depôt at the corner of Victoria Road. A court martial sentenced a resident of St. Mary's to a year's imprisonment for being in possession of a wireless set.

June 24. International variety concert held at The Forum, the afternoon performance being especially for the civilian population.

June 25. Distant bombing heard in the early hours. More trousers for working men have arrived; these, of very good quality, are the same as supplied to the French Navy.

June 27. Large convoy leaves in the evening; a band played some troops down to the quay. Local men who are to work in Alderney also left.

June 28. Large consignment of tomatoes arrives from Guernsey, but the Germans commandeer the lot. Issue of ½ lb. of dried haricots and a packet of washing powder. The ration of potatoes is still 5 lb.

June 29. Allied planes heard passing near the Island, Lorient being the objective. A high Nazi official is visiting the Island in connection with labour, the Germans asserting that not enough workers are being found. New pictorial stamp issue made available today; these were the 2½d. and 3d., bearing views of Mont Orgueil Castle and St. Ouen's Bay respectively.

June 30. Fifty head of cattle have arrived for slaughter, as well as about 60 tons of flour. The Germans have a water reservoir in the courtyard of the Museum in Caledonia Place as a precaution against fire.

After three years of Occupation the Island is in a state of destruction; railway tracks are running all over the country parishes and the harbours, while gun emplacements, etc., have sprung up in every conceivable spot. People are still being turned out of their homes and in certain open areas pylons have been erected to prevent planes landing. The roads are in a shocking state; huge tractors never intended for Jersey roads tear round the Island day after day. The troops seem very unhappy and almost without exception they declare the sooner the war is over the better, irrespective of who shall win; numbers of them anxiously await news of families in parts of Germany which are constantly bombed. The Gestapo is on the trail of persons suspected of having wireless sets, but they cannot find them all, and the news spreads as soon as it is broadcast; one thing we will never forgive the Germans for is taking away our wireless sets for they are still allowed to keep them in France. It is impossible to estimate the rise in the cost of living, but it must have risen by at least 300 per cent. An adult's rations at the moment are as follows (per week): Bread, 3 lb. 12 oz.; breakfast meal, 6 oz.; meat, 4 oz.; potatoes, 5 lb.; butter, 2 oz.; sugar, 3 oz.; salt, 3 oz.; milk, 3½ pints. Extra rations are drawn by persons holding doctor's certificates, such as invalids, expectant mothers, etc. As is inevitable, some people have made a pile of money out of the existing conditions, while others have had to spend all their savings. Many who formerly earned modest wages and have become black-marketeers have been able to purchase houses, farms, etc., but the authorities are known to be taking note of this with a view to appropriate taxation being imposed. In an article in the *E.P.* today a fairly accurate account of Island affairs after three years of German occupation was presented.

JULY 1943

July 1. The Germans celebrate three years of occupation by publishing a special four-page edition of their own newspaper; articles therein deal with local affairs, and one in particular

138

describes Jersey as an 'Outpost of the European Fortress'—it is conveniently forgotten that Jersey was once a stepping-stone to England! The fuel ration for this month and next is available only to persons who rely solely on special types of cooking apparatus, or invalids holding doctor's certificates.

July 2. Quantities of French material suitable for dresses, suits, etc., were released today and queues formed outside the textile shops; the prices were high but, even so, supply could not cope with the demand. The recently-escaped Russian worker has been captured.

July 3. The Germans celebrate by having a parade of troops through the town; this took about a quarter of an hour to pass a given spot, and some 2,000 took part, including artillery, cycle corps, etc. Warning is given to fishermen and others that a strip of coast from Grosnez to Plémont Point has been mined, this part of the coast now being closed from both the land side and the sea side. The Department of Labour announces that in order to help relatives of the local men now working in Alderney, arrangements have been made to forward collective parcels once weekly; these parcels are to be sent to the Labour Exchange, Conway Street by noon each Tuesday, postage to be paid by the Department.

July 4. Distant sounds of planes and bombing heard almost all day.

July 5. The Department of Labour appeals for whole- or part-time workers to help in picking the potato crop, labour to be paid at the rate of a shilling an hour. Rain is badly needed to swell the crop, and there is a considerable amount of blight. From today the retail price of potatoes is 1½d. per lb., but the ration has been dropped to 4½ lb. per head per week. Extras this week consist of a packet of 100 saccharin tablets and a bottle of red wine. Mackerel is being caught in fairly large quantities, but when it gets to the Fish Market the Germans have first pick. Messrs. Britton and Whinnerah present a comedy at the Opera House. Shows, concerts—good, bad or indifferent —are being staged in parish halls, church halls, etc., all over the Island, and it is amazing the amount of talent that has been discovered.

July 6. The Germans issue a warning to cyclists to have more regard to recently-published road regulations. According to this, riding two abreast is now permissible if it does not inconvenience traffic. Victoria College terminal service held at St. Helier's Parish Church.

July 7. A German notice says 'occasion has made it

necessary to order that charitable appeals and collections whether public or private, shall be subject to the approval of Field Command 515'—this does not apply to collections taken in churches and chapels during divine worship.

July 8. The Gestapo seizes a lot of black-market goods which were hidden on one of the incoming barges.

July 9. Jersey Girls' College hold terminal service at St. Helier's Parish Church—the first since the Occupation.

July 10. Farmer fined at the Royal Court for selling rhubarb at an excessive price. Welcome rain has arrived, though not in any quantity. Green vegetables are very scarce, but cucumbers and tomatoes have arrived from Guernsey, the whole of the latter being commandeered by the Germans.

July 11. A barrage balloon broke its moorings and floated over the Island; more and more ships are arriving with balloons attached. During the evening a convoy of 21 ships and barges left the harbour, many soldiers embarking; patrol vessels accompany these convoys and clear their guns as they leave harbour. Sunday Charity Concert No. 10 held at the Opera House.

July 12. A notice issued by the Medical Officer of Health announces that all forms of public entertainment have been prohibited by the Germans from the 14th inst. until August 10. This is to prevent the spread of disease, particularly diphtheria, and it is urged that all children under 14, and especially those in the group 1 to 6 years, be inoculated. The public is asked to register again for potatoes, a condition being that where in any household there is an amount exceeding 28 lb. per head, registration is not permitted. This week's extra rations are coffee substitute and macaroni (8 oz. of each).

July 13. A large number of cycles, mostly ladies, requisitioned by the Germans; owners of such are warned to take them to a specified place for inspection. Several residents who have been in jail for some time for offences in connection with the dissemination of news were removed to France today to be imprisoned; with them was Advocate Ogier, who returned to Jersey in May after the sentence of six months had been 'remitted'.

July 14. During the afternoon Allied planes were very high over the Island the Germans sounded the alarm in the Corbière area. An important official of the German medical service is here on a visit. It is understood that the Germans have taken over a large tract of land at Egypt (Trinity) for a training ground; three farms are involved and the dwellings are to be pulled down, the owners told to take away the woodwork. Lorries, cars under 12 h.p., and delivery vans are wanted by the Germans, as well as a number of saddle-horses from each parish.

July 15. Ammunition is being unloaded from a German 'hospital ship' which recently arrived here with a patrol-boat escort. There is a rush to buy tomatoes—both Jersey and Guernsey—and the Germans are commandeering large quantities. The recent Order regarding the closing of entertainments apparently does not apply to the German forces nor to the various cafés frequented by them; church services and auction sales are also excluded.

July 16. The Department of Agriculture notifies growers that it is now prepared to purchase green potatoes and chats.

July 17. The official prices are fixed for this year's cereal crops: wheat, 28s. per cwt.; oats, 22s. 6d.; barley, 32s. 6d.; rye, 39s. Some wheat sold recently on the black-market changed hands at over £20 a hundredweight. The compiler of this record saw a second-hand cycle-tyre purchased today for 35 marks (£3 14s. 9d.)! One of the cafés frequented by the Germans was raided at night and the females there had their identity cards taken from them; these were returned next morning at the Merton Hotel (military hospital), where the owners were medically examined.

July 18. Quantities of mackerel are being caught, German soldiers helping to catch some by throwing hand grenades into the water to blow the fish out, much to the delight of the children.

July 19. The Germans give notice that a farmer has been fined 200 marks (about £21) and sentenced to one week's imprisonment for selling potatoes to foreign workers. Attention is also drawn to an Order threatening heavy penalties for black-market activities. Sentences ranging from 21 months to two months were passed by German court martial on persons charged with being in possession of a wireless set or with spreading the news. This week's extra ration consist of jam for the A's and B's, red wine for those who want it, and 1 lb. of biscuits for everyone under 18 years of age—the gift of the French Secours Nationale. The M.O.H. again stresses the necessity of children being inoculated.

July 20. A German court martial has sentenced a resident to six months' imprisonment for advising a married woman whose husband is in the Army against going with soldiers. The female in question laid a complaint with the German authorities, and the man was subsequently sent to France. The Irishman who knocked down and killed a boy of 14 years in April last, has also been sentenced by the Germans to two years' imprisonment, although he tried to save himself by joining the Todts. Welcome rain has fallen today which was heavy enough to have a good effect upon the crops. The salt ration is now 4 oz. instead of 2 oz.

July 23. French woollen materials on sale in textile shops; this was of heavy quality and prices from £1 per yard. Many French cycles are now on the road, but the tyres are not of good quality.

July 24. Directions issued to farmers regarding the gathering of the cereal harvest, which should be good; a start has been made with the reaping of oats, and wheat is almost ready. The stacking of crops in such a way to minimise the danger from fire is also urged. A dairyman was fined £10 at the Royal Court today for milk adulteration.

July 26. Everyone highly delighted with the news from Italy of Mussolini's resignation. An Order has been issued to German soldiers permitting them to bathe only in groups and in the charge of N.C.O.s so that they may be found more easily when there is an alarm. This week's extras consist of macaroni (8 oz.) and margarine (4 oz.)

July 27. After a month, a batch of Red Cross letters arrive.

July 28. Early in the morning the German naval guns opened up in the west of the Island: it was reported a British convoy was in the area. A German notice gives further warning to owners of wireless sets and mentions sentences recently imposed, to be served in France. More severe penalties are threatened, and that even the death sentence may be imposed in certain cases. Attention is also drawn to punishments which can be imposed on employees who break the conditions contained in their signed contracts (with the Germans). St. Mary's Parish Assembly fixes the Rate for this year at 1s. 6d. per quarter.

July 29. British planes passed over the Island the Germans put up the heaviest and longest anti-aircraft barrage since the Occupation.

July 30. The Department of Essential Commodities warns the public to exercise the greatest care in the use of water; unless consumption is reduced the service will have to be restricted. The Children's Benefit Fund publicly acknowledged donations received from Channel Islands internees in Germany. St. Martin's Parish fixes the Rate at 2s. 6d. per quarter.

July 31. The Germans publish the following in today's *E.P.*:

142

NOTICE

Owing to the fact that provisions for the Channel Islands have not been disturbed by enemy action recently the rations from August 1 onwards will be restored to their former level.

Der Feldkommandant:
gez. KNACKFUSS, Oberst.

This means the bread ration will be restored to what it was previous to May 10, the full scale being as under:

General adult ration	4 lb. 8 oz.
Children (from 3 to 10)	3 lb. 0 oz.
Infants (from 1 to 3)	1 lb. 8 oz.
Male agricultural workers . . .	6 lb. 0 oz.
Female agricultural workers . . .	5 lb. 4 oz.
Reich-Germans	5 lb. 10 oz.
Adolescents general (10 to 18) . .	4 lb. 8 oz.
Adolescents male manual workers . .	6 lb. 0 oz.
Adolescent female workers . . .	5 lb. 4 oz.

Price of petrol increased to 5s. 4d. per gallon. There has been a number of cases of foreign workers escaping from camp and volunteering to work for farmers. Cereals are being gathered in some three weeks earlier than last year and threshing is about to commence; the wheat crop is very good in quality and quantity. The Germans are requisitioning more cars, etc.; these are taken to Springfield, and after the engines have been removed they are flattened (overrun by a tank) to make them less bulky for shipment. The railway from Gorey to Town is being extended along the top of the piers and to the Esplanade, where the narrow gauge track is being laid alongside the wide one. Several high German officials have gone on leave following the recent bombing of Hamburg, where their property has been destroyed.

AUGUST 1943

August 1. British planes in the vicinity of the Island; this is an everyday occurrence and the Germans now hoist a flag at the end of the Albert Pier to warn the workers to take cover.

August 2. August Bank Holiday. The weather was cloudy but

fine and warm. Cricket matches were played and everyone made the best of the day. Innumerable waggonettes, vans, etc., were to be seen on the road, carrying picnickers to and from various beaches. This week's extra rations are a piece of toilet soap per head and five boxes of matches per household.

August 3. Large quantities of locally-grown tobacco were taken to the local factories today for curing. The price is anywhere between three and five marks an ounce (6s. 4d. to 10s. 8d.).

August 4. Quantity of French melons on sale at 1s. 3d. per pound.

August 5. The German Feldkommandant (Colonel Knack-fuss) visits *The Evening Post*, where the German newspaper is printed for the Forces.

August 7. The Royal Court fines a farmer £80 for milk adulteration by 15 per cent. added water. More trousers for working men are made available by the Textile and Footwear Control.

August 9. This week's extras are ½ lb. of macaroni and a piece of household soap per head; soap has become a problem and the quality of the ration article makes it a little better than nothing.

August 10. Two parish assemblies fix the Rate for this year— St. Helier at 3s. 2d. per quarter and Grouville at 2s. 7d. Public entertainments commence again; the diphtheria epidemic is apparently abating. The Germans allow vraicking on Grève d'Azette beach for one day only. Several business-men have been interviewed by the Gestapo because a German soldier formerly stationed here has sent them letters complaining about everything in general and Hitler in particular; no further action was taken in the matter.

August 11. A German band gives an afternoon performance in the Royal Square.

August 12. British planes fly over the Island during the afternoon and are fired on. Young German sailor, aged 19, commits suicide at Havre-des-Pas Bathing Pool. Concert given at The Forum by members of the Todt Organisation, to which the local public are invited.

August 13. Persons sending parcels to deportees in Germany are warned not to include perishable greenstuffs or tomatoes.

August 15. The Germans held a sports meeting at the F.B. Fields, and at a concert in one of their soldiers' homes collections were taken for the bombed areas of Germany.

August 16. The Germans are taking numbers of wireless sets again and more cycles are to be requisitioned. This week's extra

144

rations consists of 100 saccharin tablets and a packet of washing powder; everyone under 18 years of age is to receive 4 oz. of cream chocolate, and red wine may be obtained without coupon. Mr. Jack Coombs presents a show at the Opera House.

August 17. Numbers of French colonial troops, mainly Sengalese, arrive to work on the quays, etc.; it is understood they are to replace the Spaniards who have been here for some time. These French prisoners are to be put in a camp alongside the District Office, Pier Road.

August 18. British planes over the Island practically all day.

August 19. More British planes in the vicinity of the Island, and terrific bombing is heard from the French coast.

August 20. A German Officer has committed suicide at College House (the Feldkommandantur); there have been many such cases of late, but detailed information is lacking, the Germans keeping things quiet. Numbers of Spanish workers leave the Island.

August 21. German Order registered 'restricting the sale of motor cars bearing a French registration number'. The Germans have issued instructions that all wheat which is in a fit condition is to be stacked. Fishing by boat has been cancelled and German leave has been stopped. The ban on children attending entertainments, etc., has been lifted for today to enable them to attend a matinée at the Opera House. On German instructions, the water supply is to be cut off from 9 p.m. until 6 a.m. German band plays in the Square.

August 23. News is received of the death of Advocate Ogier, in a German internment camp, to which he had been taken after having been discharged and allowed to return to Jersey following the case in which he and his son were taken to Paris for trial. This week's extras consist of macaroni ($\frac{1}{2}$ lb.) and coffee substitute ($\frac{1}{2}$ lb.).

August 24. Numbers of British planes in the vicinity of the Island during the afternoon, and bombing, gunfire, etc., heard from the French coast. Widespread robberies reported from St. Clement's Parish. Trinity fixes the Rate at 1s. 6d. per quarter and St. Lawrence at 1s. 3d. Sentences of twelve months and six months have been passed on local residents for Wireless Order infractions; a veterinary surgeon who used his car on a Sunday has had it confiscated and been fined 1,000 marks (over £100).

August 25. Special sitting of the States adopts an important measure relating to children's allowances. This was a modified version of the scheme which was presented to the States and lodged au Greffe on May 2, 1942. The German Field Commandant then refused to approve it. A measure which provided for the relaxation of some of the formalities connected with the making of Wills of real property was adopted in third reading. Also adopted in third reading was an amendment to the Law on Adulteration of Foodstuffs introducing penalties for a recidivist —a fine not exceeding £100 or three months' imprisonment. Three Jerseymen deported to Germany have been repatriated owing to ill-health and returned today, being accompanied by two Jersey 'orderlies' who must go back; friends of these men were pleased to have English cigarettes given them from parcels received in Germany through the Red Cross. St. Saviour's Parish fixes the Rate at 2s. per quarter.

August 26. Strong rumours are current in the Island that the mark is about to be depreciated.

August 27. The Department of Agriculture is advertising for a Vegetable Inspector, the man appointed to make a weekly report indicating the vegetable position. Among other advertisements is one of the Department of Education for persons teaching German and another for the Todt Organisation for interpreters, good wages and extra rations being offered. The price of paraffin, available to a few householders only, is to be 10d. per pint.

August 28. At the Royal Court a farmer was fined for selling potatoes without a licence, and a resident was fined £100 for making a false declaration regarding the amount of potatoes held by him; a farmer was also fined £5 for not declaring the birth of pigs. German band played in the Royal Square. No meat ration was issued this week.

August 29. In the early hours a barge going to Guernsey from France struck the rocks near Demi-des-Pas and foundered; later in the day all sorts of goods were washed up in St. Clement's Bay, and numbers of persons went home with onions, flour, cognac, butter, cheese, etc.

August 30. More salvaging going on today. German soldiers fired over the heads of some boys to frighten them, but at least one youngster had over twenty bottles of cognac. A notice is published by the Germans regarding the delivery of flotsam, jetsam and wrecks. Another notice warns people in the possession of firearms to give them up. A States notice published regarding procedure to be followed by parents who qualify for the children's allowances, recently approved. A memorial service is held at St. Mark's Church for Advocate Ogier, every section of the Island community being represented. This week's extras consists of ½ lb. of margarine and ½ lb. of bean flour; red wine is available on ration. The Island School of Dancing and Elocution presents a musical comedy at the Opera House.

August 31. The Germans have been making inquiries at some of the houses in the Samarès area regarding goods which have been picked up from the wreck. Human bones were found in the sand on Grouville Common, and, later on, more bones were found near La Folie Inn in sand that had been brought from Grouville Common; identity has not yet been established. One commodity badly needed is cycle tyres; hundreds of cycles have tyres extensively patched, while rubber garden hose meets the need in some cases. The majority of the Spanish workers have now left, their places being taken by the French colonial troops.

SEPTEMBER 1943

September 1. The water supply further curtailed, available only between 6 a.m. and 8 p.m. Fuel issue for this month only for invalids or persons with special cooking apparatus. The Germans issue a notice there is no truth in the rumour that the mark is to be reduced in value.

September 2. St. Peter's Parish Assembly fixes the Rate at 2s. 9d. per quarter; St. John's at 2s. per quarter.

September 3. The Royal Court imposes a fine of £100 with £20 costs on a dairyman for abstracting cream from milk.

September 4. A man sentenced by the Royal Court to six months' hard labour for selling furniture from an evacuated house in which he was tenant. A new call-up of males in the late 'teens and early twenties; they had to attend at College House for questioning in regard to their occupation, and some were told to have a bag packed and be ready to be sent to work for the Germans, presumably out of the Island.

September 6. Boat fishing is to be allowed again, and a German notice reminds boat fishermen that licences are to be renewed. The water supply continues to cause anxiety, and the pressure is to be reduced between 2 and 5.30 p.m. each day. Among reported robberies is one of two heifers from a field at St. Clement's; the hides and entrails were found on the beach. Extra ration for everyone under 18 of 4 oz. of sweets or two bars of nougat. German two-horse transport crashes into the hedge at St. Brelade's Hill and capsizes, one of the drivers being injured. Late in the evening Graf von Schmettow, the Island

Commandant, leaves for Guernsey to take over from General Mueller the duties of Commandant of the whole of the Channel Islands area; he was given a send-off by a guard of honour and a military band. A Colonel Heine is to take over the duties in Jersey.

September 7. A new vegetable prices list comes into operation; in spite of a glut of pears, the price is 10d. per lb., while apples and onions are to be 1s. and 6d. respectively.

September 8. Large number of Russian workers and Spaniards leave for France. The Forestry Section of the Department of Labour gives notice that farmers may again be granted permits to fell trees. St. Ouen's Parish Assembly fixes the Rate at 2s. per quarter. Today's big news was the B.B.C. announcement at 7 p.m. that Italy had surrendered unconditionally. It was astounding how quickly the news spread, and at Wests Cinema the audience knew by ten minutes past seven—this in spite of the penalties threatened for listening to the B.B.C.!

September 9. The Germans are looking glum today, and many state that everything is going very badly for them.

September 10. Department of Essential Commodities advertise for States representative at Granville; the German authorities have insisted on the dismissal of the present one. Thunderstorm and welcome rain, 1¼ inches falling in 24 hours.

September 11. A German-inspired article advises people who have cameras stored in places where they were told to take them some time ago, that, as there is danger of deterioration, it would be advisable to sell them to the Occupying Authority. German bands plays in the Royal Square.

September 12. More thunder, and a hailstorm causes some damage. Big German sports meeting at F.B. Fields.

September 13. Issue of piece of toilet soap per head and five boxes of matches per household. Old Victorians' Sports Club presents a scientific thriller at the Opera House. Large number of German troops leaves the Island.

September 15. Curfew hours altered—10 p.m. to 6 a.m., 9 p.m. to 6 a.m. in the Military Zone. Six horses belonging to the Department of Transport and Communications were sold in the Cattle Market today, one of them realising £350. British planes pass over the Island, the Germans putting up a very heavy barrage. St. Brelade's Parish fixes the Rate at 2s. 6d. per quarter.

September 18. Notice issued by the Superior Council regarding the conversion of motor vehicles to producer-gas, stating that it has become necessary to secure (a) lorries suitable for conversion to replace older vehicles now operating on essential civilian services; (b) farm tractors, and (c) parts of motor vehicles. More trousers for working men are being made available; among other goods from France is a large amount of handkerchiefs. The water supply is to be cut off from 7 p.m. to 7 a.m., with a reduction in pressure from 2 to 5.30 p.m.

September 19. Many harvest festivals held today (Sunday), the various churches being profusely decorated and the congregations very large.

September 20. Notice issued by the Department of Transport and Communications that arrangements have been made for the gathering of vraic during the season commencing October 1, and that a Vraic Controller has been appointed. This week's extras consist of ½ lb. macaroni and a packet of washing powder per head.

September 21. Large quantities of women's hosiery have arrived and distribution on ration is to commence with holders of ration books which still contain the March voucher. The Textile Department advises that many old boots, shoes or rubber wellingtons should be re-clogged. During the past two years no fewer than 10,000 pairs of footwear have been so treated. The Bailiff presents certificates for Chamber of Commerce examinations.

September 24. The body of an American airman has been found at Bonne Nuit Bay, but the Germans maintain strict secrecy. Long queues line up at shops for women's stockings.

September 25. In the small hours the Germans put up a heavy barrage when British planes pass over. An unusual case comes before the Royal Court when the Viscount is authorised to write to a woman threatening the discumberment of her property, it being stated that she cannot be placed in the debtors' prison owing to lack of accommodation.

September 27. The burial of the American airman takes place at Mont-à-l'Abbé Cemetery with the minimum of publicity. He is Sergt. A. E. Poitras and he did his training in Arizona; from the banknotes found in his possession it is presumed he had seen service in North Africa or Sicily. The grave had previously been dug and the undertaker was ordered to be at the cemetery at 4 a.m., at which hour the body was taken there. At 8 a.m. a German firing party arrived, and as the American was a Roman Catholic the burial service was read by Father Arscott; also present were the Bailiff of Jersey, the Attorney-General, the Constable of St. Helier and Doctor Shone. Wreaths were laid from the States, the Parish of St. Helier, the German Air Force, etc., but when the grave was uncovered for the lowering of the coffin it was found that a red, white and blue wreath was lying at the bottom, it having been placed there overnight! This week's extras consist of shaving soap for men, ½ lb. coffee substitute for everyone, and a jam ration commences alphabetically. The Green Room Club presents a farce at the Opera House. Farmers are notified by the Department of Transport and Communications that a few horses for ploughing, breezing, etc., are available at the rate of one horse and man for 30s. a day.

September 28. Many people visit the grave of the American airman at Mont-à-l'Abbé. The salt ration is again earthy stuff and has to be treated before being used.

September 29. A German soldier has been killed at Springfield by a land-mine and another seriously injured.

September 30. German courts-martial have been held today; a large number of Air Force personnel was involved in one case, and of the civilian cases sentences of nine, ten and twelve months respectively were passed on offenders against the Wireless Order. At a country sale a horse fetched £380. The month has ended with a considerable amount of whooping-cough among children. Large numbers of Todts are leaving almost every day, together with quantities of building material, concrete mixers, and even railway engines which have been in the Island only a matter of weeks. The line recently completed from Gorey to Town has hardly justified its existence, for on an average it is used about twice a week. Young local men are still being interviewed at College House and some have already been given jobs by the Germans; many of them have refused to work, but they cannot be put in jail as there is no room! There is more tobacco being smoked now than in former times. Among the goods recently received from France are thousands of wooden combs. Tea is the commodity fetching the highest price at present on the black market, £12 a lb. being an average figure; butter is 25s. per lb. (if it can be obtained), and pork 15s. per lb.

OCTOBER 1943

October 1. As the coal issued in the spring was for October, November and December, there will be no more issued this year. The average family receives one hundredweight of wood this month; owners of domestic appliances, such as hot-water boilers or slow-combustion stoves, may obtain a small quantity of anthracite dust, which they can mix with coal tar (obtainable at the Gas Works) in the proportion of two gallons of tar to one hundredweight of dust. Another notice is issued concerning electricity; four units per week are to be allowed per household instead of five as formerly; the additional rate granted to certain consumers remains unaltered, with the exception that the ration for electric cookers is reduced by 12½ per cent. and the use of electric refrigerators is prohibited until April 1, 1944. The Department of Transport and Communications is advertising for a few good lorries suitable for conversion to gasogene, for the maintenance of dairy and other essential services. Boat-owners are notified that all boats under 14 ft. in length, which are lying in the harbour of St. Helier, must be placed in rows on the quay, South Pier, or any other place allotted to them; boats of 14 ft. and over must be moored in rows in the French Harbour; all boats will then have a number painted on them.

October 2. Fines averaging about £20 each were inflicted at the Royal Court today on five farmers of St. Martin's for keeping unregistered pigs.

October 4. The Royal Court sentences a farmer to one month's imprisonment for milk adulteration (second offence), and another to a fine of £20; a fine of £5 is imposed in a case of illicit selling of saccharins. This week's extras consist of five bars of chocolate cream for adults and 4 oz. of sweets for children. Huge fire at St. Brelade's burns out a Todt shed over three hundred feet long containing stores, petrol and foodstuffs. The clocks go back one hour to Central European Time, we come into line with England.

October 5. Extensive robberies take place during the night: 25,000 cigarettes, tobacco, cigars and cigarillos, foodstuffs and clocks were among the things stolen. It is also learned a robbery has been effected at a German depôt; over 2½ tons of sugar were taken away in a motor lorry!

October 6. Alteration of the gas hours—7 a.m. to 1.30 p.m. and 5.30 p.m. to 10 p.m. Annual branchage visits are taking place.

October 7. Some of the stolen goods from recent robberies have been found in the Weighbridge Gardens, and some persons have been arrested in connection with the robbery of sugar from a German store.

October 8. Order published requiring every person having grown tobacco during 1943 to send in a return, Department of

Agriculture issues two notices—one asks for seed potatoes of the Royal variety for Sark, and the other indicates that, in future, the Department intends to tattoo cattle, pigs, horses and sheep.

October 9. Tragedy at St. Lawrence: 15-year-old boy dies on the way to hospital as the result of playing with an explosive he had found. The Royal Court fines two more farmers for keeping unregistered pigs and another for keeping an unregistered heifer.

October 11. Extras issued of 100 saccharins and 4 oz. of margarine for everybody and five boxes of matches per household. Messrs. Britton and Whinnerah present a thriller at the Opera House.

October 13. The public warned again about the water supply.

October 16. Another farmer was fined £20 at the Royal Court today for milk adulteration, while a shopkeeper was fined £10 for an infraction of the Rationing Order by selling sugar at 16s. 4d. per pound. Two boxes of matches issued with tobacco ration.

October 17. Some women who had let rooms to foreign workers were called to College House today and warned not to do so in future, under extreme penalties; these workers must live in the camps to which they are attached. Planes pass over the Island again during the evening and leaflets are dropped; these were in French and issued by the Americans.

October 18. The Royal Court fines a farmer £100 and £10 costs for neglecting to dig approximately three vergées of potatoes for delivery to the Department of Agriculture, a large quantity of the crop having been ploughed in; another was fined £10. Details issued of paraffin rationing. This week's extra is ½ lb. macaroni.

October 20. The Germans put up a very heavy barrage during the evening as Allied planes pass over.

October 22. Activity off the west coast by Allied planes, it being reported that a German ship was sunk during the early morning. The Department of Essential Services, by order of Field Command 515, publishes a questionnaire calling for details of 'wells in private houses, business premises, institutions and works, which could be used in the event of total destruction of the water mains by act of war'.

October 23. Number of Italian troops arrive, being played up the pier by their own band; they do not look very smart. Three farmers fined an average of £30 at the Royal Court for keeping unregistered pigs, a third being fined £30 with £10 costs for milk adulteration.

October 25. This week's only extra is a piece of toilet soap. Unique event in Jersey theatrical history takes place at the Opera House when the Green Room Club presents *The Paladins*, a light opera which is an entirely local production; the words by Horace Wyatt, music by Philip Larbalestier and production by Max Le Feuvre.

October 26. A robbery is reported from St. Clement's Parish Hall, where several wireless sets have been stolen; these sets were stored there after having been collected by German order in May of last year. The Italian troops who recently arrived are Badoglio troops and have been brought here to act as lackeys to the Germans.

October 27. More Italian troops arrive and a number of White Russians who are helping the Germans in what is termed 'an army of liberation'. German court martial passes sentence of five years' imprisonment on local woman and six months on her husband for alleged robberies from the German Post Office, of which they were caretakers. The Germans issue the usual notice that wreaths, etc., may be placed on soldiers' graves, etc., on All Saints' Day, All Souls' Day and Remembrance Day.

October 30. Royal Court fines a farmer £10 with £2 costs for neglecting to grow certain crops; a fine of £15 was imposed in another case concerning the non-declaration of pigs.

October 31. More Todts have left also large quantities of material; in some places loads of wood have been disposed of for 5s. and quantities of cement have also changed hands at very low figures—the Todts are making a little money before they leave! Wests Pictures have been ordered to hold an extra matinée each Tuesday, the profits to be paid to the German Propaganda Office. There has been a large number of Red Cross letters this month, and parcels of cigarettes from internees in Germany arrive occasionally for distribution among personal friends. Civil guards are in operation at present at Beauvoir, St. Saviour's and at St. Clement's Parish Hall. The month has been mild but damp, whooping cough is prevalent among the children.

NOVEMBER 1943

November 1. New textile ration books come into operation; large queues wait for permits for leather shoes which have arrived from France in considerable numbers. Fuel ration for

153

this month consists of wood only, and except in certain cases an average family receives two hundredweight.

November 3. Two important Orders issued by the Superior Council: One makes it an offence for any person, except those possessing a licence by the Department of Essential Commodities, to manufacture or sell tobacco or snuff. The other concerns sugar-beet syrup, which must contain 66 per cent. of soluble sugar-beet solids and labelled with the name of the retailer, etc.; the retail price is fixed at 5s. 6d. per lb.

November 4. Military funeral at St. Brelade's Cemetery of Oberleutnant Zepernick, a German officer had been here three years and was chief organiser of entertainment for the troops; he was fairly well known in the Island, his knowledge of English having brought him into contact with many local businessmen. He was killed when, near Vire, the R.A.F. attacked the train in which he was travelling home on leave.

November 5. Appeal issued for beech for clogging of shoes, which is required in quantities average 30 tons monthly; where trees have been taken others are planted in their place.

November 6. German Order registered by the Royal Court relating to the Manufacture of German Official Seals and Stamps. A fine of £35 with £5 costs was imposed concerning another Land Order infraction, and a fine of £15 with £5 costs for keeping pigs without the necessary licence. This week there have been long queues for permits for footwear, but some of the sizes have already run out. The boots and shoes are mostly of leather uppers with wooden soles, all-leather footwear being obtained on medical certificate only.

November 8. This week's extra is a piece of household soap. The Amateur Dramatic Club presents a comedy at the Opera House. The Germans have sentenced another local resident to six months for having a wireless set.

November 9. Six deportees have been sent back from Germany on the grounds of ill-health. The Germans demand another muster of locally-owned horses for inspection.

November 10. The Germans explode a British mine washed ashore at Fauvic; this resulted in many houses over a large area being seriously damaged—the damage being estimated at about £1,500.

November 11. Remembrance Day: Wreaths were placed on the Cenotaph, etc., and the Two Minutes' Silence was observed in the schools.

November 12. Information is published that some Jerseymen prisoners of war have been repatriated to England and that they passed through Sweden en route. Among the latest goods from France now on sale is a large number of suits for youths and thousands of neckties.

November 13. The Germans give notice that sharp-shooting in the direction of the coast will take place every Thursday from sunrise to sunset and every Friday from sunrise to 1 o'clock p.m. Facilities are being granted farmers for the gathering of vraic. No meat ration owing to non-arrival of supplies.

November 15. Extras issued of 3 oz. of cheese per head and ten boxes of matches per household.

November 16. Many bodies of British sailors or marines have and are being washed up around the coasts, these are men who lost their lives in a naval engagement in the Gulf of St. Malo, in which the cruiser *Charybdis* and a destroyer were sunk.

November 17. Impressive funeral service held at Mont-à-l'Abbé Cemetery at 9 a.m. as the last of the bodies of 29 British naval men were laid to rest in a common grave. The Dean conducted the service, and those present officially were the Bailiff, the Attorney-General, the Constable of St. Helier and representatives of the Red Cross and Order of St. John, the British Legion and the Navy League. The Germans had a firing party and a guard of honour from the Army and Navy drawn up at the side of the grave, and after the coffins, covered with the White Ensign, had been lowered into the grave, the Official wreaths were laid; these were from the States of Jersey, the British Red Cross and Order of St. John, the Parish of St. Helier, the British Legion, the Jersey Harbourmaster and Staff, the Navy League, the German Navy and the German Army. Later in the day a large number of wreaths sent by private citizens, firms and associations was deposited on the grave.

November 18. Many people visit the grave of the British sailors at Mont-à-l'Abbé and more wreaths are placed there.

November 19. The Jersey Green Room Club receives notification that it is dissolved and must cease to function; no reason is given.

November 20. A deputation of officials of the Green Room Club attend at College House and succeed in getting the original Order amended. The club is allowed to function for the specific purpose for which it was created—dramatic art, but it is permissible for the cast to hold a dance after each production. The Department of Essential Commodities makes directions under the Controlled Articles Order by virtue of which it is prohibited, after the 29th inst., to sell by auction carpets, linoleum, rugs and other floor coverings, whatever their value. Another pig case at the Royal Court, in which a woman is fined £20 with £2 costs. Two boxes of matches issued with the tobacco ration.

November 22. Half a pound of coffee substitute issued. German notice forbids horse-drawn vehicles being hired out to German units or for any other except agricultural purposes. The Germans advertise for a Miss Bercu, aged 24, of no nationality, who has been working for them and been missing since the 4th inst. Fifty-Fifty Club presents a comedy at the Opera House.

November 23. Early morning robberies reported; many farmhouses have been raided by a gang of foreign workers.

November 24. German court martial passes sentence on two local licensees; one is fined 5,000 reichsmarks (about £500) with six months' imprisonment in connection with the robbery of sugar in October, and the other is fined 200 reichsmarks (about £20) with two months' imprisonment for selling brandy alleged to be diluted at 3s. 2d. a tot.

November 26. Dedication of a plot of ground in the Howard Davis Park by the Dean of Jersey to be used as an Island of Jersey War Cemetery; in due course the bodies of those airmen and sailors already buried at Mont-à-l'Abbé will be re-interred there, also those of any others whom the misfortunes of war may bring to our shores. Many Island officials were present, headed by the Bailiff.

November 27. Meeting of the States to consider the Estimates. The total estimated expenditure of the financial year commencing February 1, 1944, is put at £757,936; revenue is estimated at £311,630, which, after adding £10,000 to the Statutory Reserve in accordance with Article 23 of the Finance Law (1924), will leave an estimated deficit of £456,306. The following recommendations were made: (1) That the rate of Income Tax be maintained at 4s. in the £; and (2) That a tax on local tobacco be imposed, to yield £7,000. Attention was drawn to the fact that no provision had been made for (a) payment made by the Pensions Department (all of which may be considered as recoverable), £90,000; (b) payments made to French nationals for military allowances and pensions, £5,000; and (c) contingent liabilities to the banks for amounts advanced against frozen assets. The surtax on salaries is to be dropped. In connection with the Tobacco Tax a 'projet' was lodged with a view to imposing a tax not exceeding 1s. per plant on all tobacco planted and for which a licence must be obtained. The latest Vegetable Prices Order raises the price of onions to 9d. per lb. and tomatoes to 1s.

November 29. First interment takes place in the Island War Cemetery, a British naval rating being buried there with full military honours; the German Navy furnished a firing party and guard of honour. The bodies of three more members of the crews of the cruiser *Charybdis* or of the unnamed destroyer sunk off the Islands were recovered today, and the re-interment of bodies buried in Mont-à-l'Abbé Cemetery has commenced. This week's extra is ½ lb. macaroni.

November 30. The matinée held at Wests each Tuesday is to cease, and instead of this the Germans announce that a limited number of seats is to be reserved for the local public for film performances at The Forum every day except Saturdays and Sundays. One humorous episode this month is that a guard of local residents, who had to spend the night at St. Clement's Parish Hall to watch over wireless sets, following a robbery, delivered some of them to friends in the small hours! Sugar-beet syrup is being made in large quantities, but not very much reaches the town-dweller. The Germans are fed-up with the war and every day evidence is forthcoming of their apathy; many of them due for leave have asked to be allowed to stay here, as their homes and towns exist no longer.

DECEMBER 1943

December 1. Fuel ration for this month consists of one hundredweight of coal and two hundredweight of wood for an average family. The tobacco ration for Christmas will be 50 cigarettes and 2 oz. of pipe tobacco; apart from this, the ration will remain as it has been for some time. Among latest robberies is one from a café of 7,360 reichsmarks (about £750) and eighty £1 Treasury notes.

December 2. Concert at the Opera House arranged by the Amateur Dramatic Club in aid of the Children's Benefit Fund raises nearly £120.

December 3. Royal Court inflicts £20 fine on a woman farmer for milk adulteration. The Germans are sending large quantities of toys to the bombed areas in Germany. They are also shipping ammunition, guns, etc.

December 4. Department of Agriculture fixes the price of home-grown straw at £10 per ton. Several cases occupy the Royal Court; fines of £40 and £20 were imposed on two farmers for milk adulteration; another was fined £75 with £10 costs for having three unregistered calves; two months' imprisonment was imposed on another for a fraudulent deal in pigs, and in another case a fine of £15 with £3 costs was imposed.

December 6. Issue of ½ lb. margarine and a piece of toilet soap per head. The salt ration is suspended. Green Room Club presents Shakespeare's *Merchant of Venice* at the Opera House. The actor who took the part of 'Shylock' was informed by the Germans that his interpretation of the part was not sufficiently repellent.

December 7. Early morning ceremony at the Island War Cemetery; burial of six more British naval ratings whose bodies have recently been washed ashore. The Dean and Father Arscott were the officiating clergy, and the Bailiff and other officials attended, the Germans supplying the usual guard of honour and a firing party. A total of 36 men of the Royal Navy, two of the Royal Air Force and one U.S.A. Air Force man has now been buried there, those originally interred at Mont-à-l'Abbé having now been transferred. Various schools take it in turn to keep the graves supplied with flowers.

December 8. The Constable of St. Helier acknowledges a donation of 224 reichsmarks (over £25) from Dutch seamen for the poor children of St. Helier. An inspector of the Jersey Motor Transport Company is undergoing sentence of two weeks imposed by the Germans for refusing to let three soldiers board an overloaded bus.

December 10. More robberies reported—pigs, a heifer and a goat—this time in the Mont-au-Prêtre and La Rocque districts. St. Clement's Parish fixes the Rate at 2s. per quarter.

December 11. Slight fall of snow. Two more pig cases before Court: one farmer fined £15 with £3 costs and another £20 with £3 costs. A farmer was also fined £5 with £1 costs for selling potatoes to the occupying forces without a licence after failure to send in his quota for the civil population; this case was brought before the civil court on the order of the Field Commandant. No meat this week.

December 12. Hundreds of leaflets found, mostly in the St. Saviour's area; these are in French and issued by the Americans. German soldiers are busy scouring the countryside to find them.

December 13. More robberies in the Mont-à-l'Abbé district, and thirteen cycles have been stolen in a week. Extra rations issued of 3 oz. of sweets for children and juveniles under 18 years of age; a packet of saccharins for everybody, and a red wine ration is available. Extra rations for Christmas may be obtained from now to the 25th; 4 oz. of sugar, 2 oz. of butter and double the potato ration (10 lb. instead of 5 lb.). All female adults are to receive a ration of 20 cigarettes.

December 14. Curfew hours for the holiday period have been posted in the parish boxes and are not to be published in the Press; these are midnight on December 24, 25, 26 and 27; 1 a.m. on December 31; and midnight on January 1.

December 15. Notice issued by the Department of Labour that it has been made responsible for placing tanks of salt water in certain parts of the town; this will be usable for cooking vegetables, etc., and available at the rate of 1d. per quart; it is advised the water be strained to remove particles of gravel or vraic. Salt is at a premium, and anything up to four marks (8s. 6d.) per pound is paid. A German notice states a local resident has been given six weeks' imprisonment for using for joy-rides a lorry which had not been licensed and which was not his own.

December 18. Meeting of the States: the proposed Tobacco Tax and Income Tax were the main items on the agenda. It was decided that the former should be imposed, the rate 5d. per plant. Other items included the grant of an honorarium of £350 to Mr. Jouault, who was a buyer in France in the early part of the Occupation. The Department of Agriculture advertises for an officer and assistant to carry out the tattooing of cattle, and the Department of Public Health appeals for mosquito netting, ballet dress fabrics or similar materials, which is urgently needed for surgical dressings. Notification of the extension of gas hours for the holiday period: December 24, 27 and 31, 7 a.m. to 1.30 p.m. and 5.30 p.m. to 1 o'clock the next morning; December 25, 26 and January 1, 7 a.m. until 1 o'clock next morning.

December 19. The usual Christmastide music is rendered in the churches; bands of carollers are also going about the town and country, having received permission from the Germans. A lot of soldiers are due to go on leave, but many sailings postponed at the last moment owing to bad transport conditions in France and R.A.F. activities over the sea.

December 20. A young lady, alleged to have thrown horse manure at a column of troops and sentenced recently to three months' imprisonment, appealed against the sentence at a court martial today, with the result that she had it doubled. The Spot Players present a thriller at the Opera House.

December 22. Notification that the water supply will not be curtailed during the holidays; electricity hours are extended until 1 a.m.

December 23. The Germans give a concert of Christmas music in Grove Place Chapel.

December 24. Christmas Eve: weather fine and mild. The town is crowded with people, but there is nothing to buy except second-hand goods and wooden toys, although the florists are doing good trade with chrysanthemums and seasonal plants. Times are especially hard for the small wage-earner who has a family to cope with, for children's toys are outrageously expensive; 1s. 6d. boxes of crackers have been selling at auction sales for two guineas!

December 25. Christmas Day: weather fine and mild. This has been the most difficult Christmas of the Occupation; foodstuffs have been very scarce and black-market prices so high that only those with large incomes could cope with them. Many rabbits have found their way to the festive board, for poultry is scarce and very dear—cockerels about £3; geese 10s. 8d. per lb. (five marks); turkeys £1 per lb. Pork is going at £1 1s. 4d. per lb. (10 marks) and beef at 15s. (6½ marks). A Christmas cake made with black-market ingredients is expensive, too, with butter at more than 25s. per lb., sugar about 16s. and eggs about 3s. 2d. (a mark and a half); supplies of the latter have been requisitioned for the Germans' hospitals. etc. The Germans have celebrated the festival much less ostentatiously than on former occasions, and have held church services at which Christmas trees took pride of place; some Russian workers also attended the morning service at St. John's Parish Church.

December 26. Boxing Day (Sunday): many carol services held in the churches. A Trinity farmer had a surprise in the early hours when British and French commando troops paid him a visit and stayed for about an hour; he could not ascertain from whence they came or how they got away, but there was a raid on France the same night. A German soldier has gassed himself at the house in Charing Cross where he was billeted.

December 27. Fire at Anne Port. The rear of a café occupied by German troops being burned out.

December 28. A farmer who refused to give up a heifer for slaughter was today fined £10 by the Royal Court, and the animal was ordered to be destroyed. The season's greetings were offered to the Bailiff and the Court by the Attorney-General, the hope being expressed that 1944 would be crowned with health, happiness and prosperity. The body of another British naval rating picked up at Bouley Bay. The Germans have a day of alarm, and at night manoeuvres are carried out; it was learned (through the Germans) that there had been a British

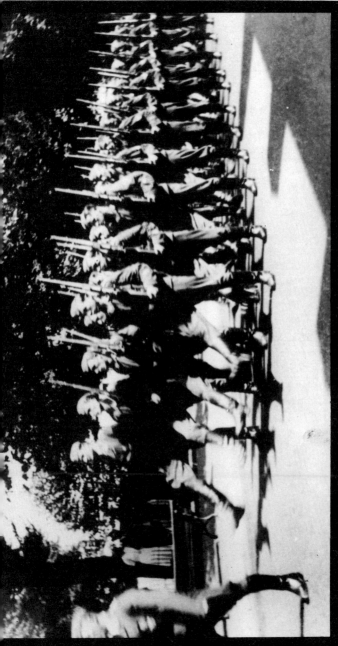

German troops marching into St. Helier

St. Helier Town Hall : Offices of Kommandantur

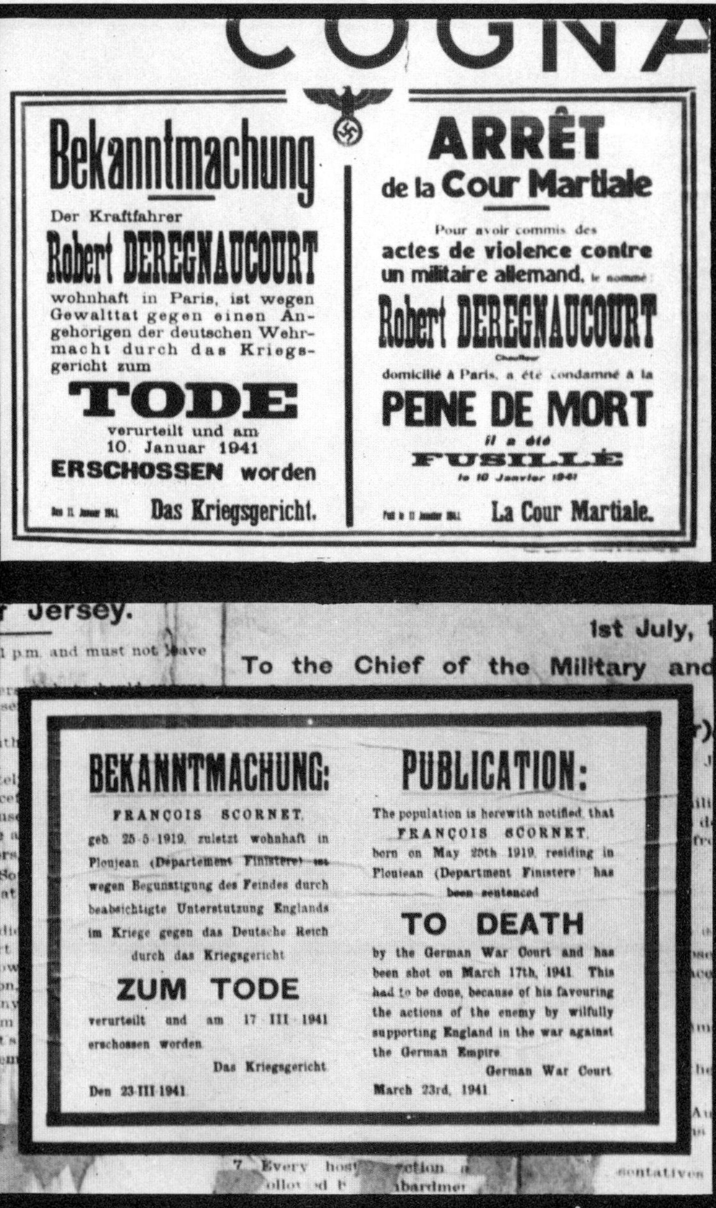

German posters declaring death sentences

German funeral of an Allied airman

Improvisation !

Above: A German relay race from West Park to F.B. Fields.
Below: The German Band playing in the Royal Parade, St. Helier.

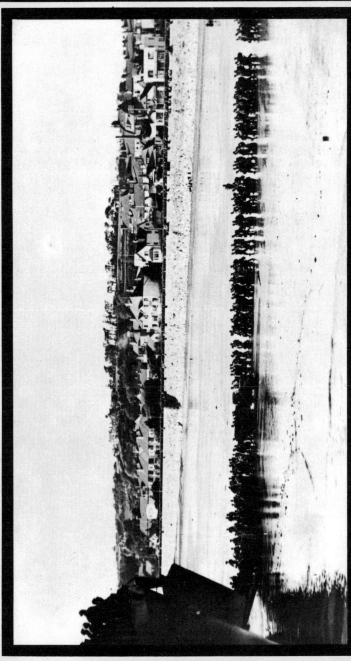

The long lines of German prisoners embarking ready to be shipped to England in 1945.

commando raid on Sark, the Germans claiming it had been a complete failure.

December 30. British planes pass over in the evening, and the Germans put up the heaviest barrage heard for some time; this was mainly in the north and east of the Island. Dramatic Section of the Jersey Green Room Club presents a pantomime at the Opera House.

December 31. At night many dances were held and everyone toasted the New Year in whatever could still be found in the cupboard. There has been a lot of brandy about lately, the doctors having been generous in prescribing it for their patients so as to prevent the Germans seizing any stocks they might suddenly take a fancy to. The rainfall for 1943 is seven inches down, which coupled with the wastage of water by the German contracting firms, has caused the water shortage. This year has seen the price of everything going up and up. The various charitable funds have been well supported and the institutions have also received their share of bounty. *The Evening Post* has admirably expressed our sentiments in its leading article: 'Standing today on the threshold of a new year, we gaze with brightened vision upon the days of 1944 which stretch out before us, and hope again springs up in our hearts as we long for the peace which will banish war and restore us to normal living conditions.'

JANUARY

January 1. New Year's Day: weather fine and mild, and everyone quite cheerful and optimistic. The fuel ration for an average family this month consists of two hundredweight of coal or coke and one hundredweight of wood, next month's coal ration being included in the issue.

January 2. The German police are searching the eastern parishes for a German soldier who shot an officer and then managed to escape; he went to an inn at La Rocque and asked for a suit of clothes, which was refused, and the Germans searching for him were angry with the licensee for not reporting the matter. The fugitive was subsequently found.

January 3. More cases of farmers keeping unregistered pigs occupied the attention of the Royal Court, heavier fines being imposed—in two cases the fine was £60 with £5 costs, in another £30 with £5 costs, and a third, which involved five pigs, a fine of £200 with £10 costs was imposed. A father and son were sentenced to three months respectively for robberies at St. John. This week's extra ration is ½ lb. of coffee substitute.

January 7. Quantities of black silk stockings are made available for the female population; coloured silk stockings are available for juveniles between the ages of 14 and 18. The Germans have been to some battery-charging firms and requisitioned two-volt batteries belonging to customers. They require about a hundred girl typists, and have visited some of the private schools to take names of former pupils who learned typing. The Germans have also published a warning that the observance of one-way traffic rules is to be more rigorously enforced.

January 8. The tobacco ration fixed at 12 cigarettes and 1 oz. of pipe tobacco for one week and 20 cigarettes for the next; the reason for the issue of 12 cigarettes instead of the former 10 is that packages of the required size are not available. The Royal Court sentences two young men to twelve and nine months' imprisonment respectively for extensive robberies. A German notice published warns the public that all main gas taps must be shut off in the event of air attacks or bombardment. A mine washed up at l'Etacq has been exploded, causing windows and window-frames to be blown out over a considerable area.

January 9. Another mine washed up at First Tower has had to be guarded by a policeman, as children were attempting to play with it; it was subsequently rendered harmless.

January 10. This week's extras consist of ½ lb. of macaroni and a jam ration (to commence alphabetically); shortage of jam pots is now a problem. Meetings of agriculturists are being held to discuss the sowing of crops for 1944; at one held at St. Saviour's today it was learned that there were 3,500 vergées (1,555 acres) less to cultivate, the land having been requisitioned by the Germans. The use of fertilisers and the question of labour was dealt with, and the observation was made that there are still too many lawns in private gardens.

January 11. Commencement of Rat Week; this pest is a scourge at the moment and an effort is being made to protect the food supply. It is also learned from a French source that two Frenchmen have invented a new insecticide—hexachloride of benzine—which is a most effective remedy for the Colorado beetle. Sentences ranging from five to twenty-one months have been passed on several people today by a German court martial for spreading B.B.C. news. The Guilds of St. Helier's and St. James's Church Players present a Nativity play at St. James's Church.

January 12. Two more mines washed up—one close to the slipway at La Mare and the other at Le Hocq; this makes five within a week.

January 14. At the request of the Department of Transport and Communications, the undertakers have agreed that the number of coaches for any one funeral shall be limited to three; this has become necessary owing to the present difficulty in obtaining sufficient fodder for the horses. British planes pass over the west of the Island in the evening and the Germans put up a barrage.

January 15. More cases before the Royal Court of farmers keeping unregistered pigs; in three instances fines of £40 with £5 costs were imposed. Quantity of saucepans from France on sale in the hardware shops, these being quickly sold out. After a long interval Camembert cheese is obtainable at some of the grocers' today.

January 16. The manager of Wests Cinema arrested by the Germans for being in possession of a wireless set; some of the recent sentences passed by court martial were on employees of Wests for the same offence. The Germans are also tightening up the curfew regulations and are stopping people in various parts of the Island and fining them—in many instances before cur-

163

few! About 10.30 p.m. one of the most disastrous fires for many years breaks out on the buildings of Messrs. A. de Gruchy and Co. Ltd., a large portion of the buildings being gutted. The town section of the Fire Brigade was augmented by the sub-sections from St. Aubin's and Gorey, and the German troops also lent a hand; it was half an hour, however, before water could be obtained, as the supply had been cut off at 5 p.m., as usual; water was obtained from the concrete tank recently constructed by the Germans in front of the Museum. The flames were seen almost all over the Island, and sections of the premises completely destroyed included the beautifully-appointed restaurant, the bakehouse, the library, the adjoining china shop and, across the arcade, the carpet shop. The restaurant was being used as the German quartermaster's stores.

January 17. Crowds of people visit the scene of last night's fire, and the Germans bar off part of New Street. Extra rations issued of 3½ oz. of cheese per head (which works out at about 4s. per lb.) and five boxes of matches per household. The Amateur Dramatic Club presents a comedy at the Opera House.

January 18. It is estimated that the damage caused by the fire at Messrs. A. de Gruchy and Co.'s premises will be in the neighbourhood of £100,000; among the losses was part of a number of etchings and paintings which had been on exhibition. The Germans are believed to have lost over two thousand uniforms.

January 19. Supplies of chalk and lime are being issued to growers making application for same as a dressing for the wheat crop, and there is another small issue of paraffin.

January 20. The Germans have taken over £80,000 in Treasury notes; these were from the various banks, and German officials collected the total from Barclay's Bank, in spite of vigorous protests.

January 21. Queues line up at the various footwear shops for men and women's shoes, issued without permit; these consist of leather uppers and wooden soles, at about 30s. per pair.

January 22. At the Royal Court a farmer is fined £3 with 10s. costs for refusing to hand over potatoes. First batch of Red Cross letters for this year arrives—15,000.

January 23. Today (Sunday) the Germans held a gun practice between Bel Royal and St. Aubin's, residents being warned to keep away from the sea side of the house. Terrific hailstorms today, with high winds.

January 24. This week's extras consist of a piece of toilet soap per head and 5 oz. of biscuits for all under the age of 18, the latter given free through the French Secours Nationale. A piece of pre-war soap will now fetch anything up to eight marks (17s.) for a 3d. tablet! Having had no salt for two months, a ration commences of 4 oz. for this week and thereafter 2 oz. per week; this commodity has been fetching enormous prices in the black market—up to four marks (8s. 6d.) per lb.!

January 25. The Germans again call attention to careless black-outs, especially in regard to cyclists, and declare there will be no more cautioning. A lot of French aluminium saucepans are on sale in the shops; these are of good quality, but, without lids, the prices are high, e.g., 15 marks (£1 12s. 0d.) for a four-pint container.

January 26. Many people going to work this morning picked up leaflets dropped by the R.A.F., especially in the Mont-à-l'Abbé and St. Saviour's districts. This leaflet was of quite recent issue, dated London, January 20, 1944; most of the items in it were already known to us, thanks to those who still risk listening-in with their forbidden wireless sets.

January 27. On the beach at West Park today some people have picked up tins of German-packed cocoa, presumably from a wreck.

January 31. Owing to another 25 per cent. cut in supplies of paper, the *E.P.* is now to be only a single sheet of two pages each day, except Thursdays, when there is no publication, and Satur-days, when four pages are allowed. The extra rations for this week consist of 4 oz. of margarine, 8 oz. of macaroni and 4 oz. of washing soda per head, and a packet of washing powder for everyone under 18 years of age. Première at the Opera House of a locally-written comedy by Mr. Winter Le Brocq entitled *Montparnasse*; it was presented by Messrs. E. Vivian Marett and Paul Williams. This month has been a very mild one, although rather damp. More charcoal-burning lorries, etc., are to be seen; the Germans are requisitioning a further 136 lorries, 87 cars and 19 motor cycles, some of these from the civil administration and the others from the civil reserve. Furniture in depositories can now be requisitioned by 'our friends' without a permit; a lot of furnishings are being sent away. There has been a search in St. Martin's Parish for a missing Russian boy, and some farmers have been to the Gestapo headquarters for questioning; they took pity on him when working in the district and he has lodged with different families at various times, but, they have denied having seen him. Some local residents who had to serve their time in France have been removed to Germany. The bakers have been notified that they must hold a supply of flour a week in advance. Wheat in the black market is about £15 per hundredweight. A small quantity of drugs has been received from the British Red Cross.

FEBRUARY 1944

February 1. The fuel ration for this month for an average family will be two hundredweight of coal (obtainable on the March and April coupons) and one hundredweight of wood. Reduction in the price of rationed tobacco, a blend of French tobacco and the locally-grown tobacco: cigarettes, 8d. for 12, 1s. 1d. for 20; pipe tobacco, 1s. 4½d. per oz. Black-market tobacco is now selling at 2½ marks an ounce (5s. 3½d.) and cigarette papers and flints are difficult to obtain. The Germans have arrested a member of the 'Jersey Democratic Movement' who had pamphlets on him outlining post-war policy.

February 2. The body of a British naval rating picked up in Rozel Bay, was buried in the new military cemetery at Howard Davis Park.

February 4. The gas hours, now from 7 to 8.30 a.m., 10.30 a.m. to 1.30 p.m. and 6 to 8 p.m.; this has upset almost everybody's domestic or business arrangements. The Germans declare that they do not expect to have a consignment of coal for February and that the supply for next month also is very doubtful. The Department of Transport and Communications advertises for old cork, which is urgently required for the re-packing of gasogene filters.

February 5. Another pig case at the Royal Court: farmer fined £90 with £5 costs. The Germans are to test the air-raid siren at the harbour every Saturday at noon.

February 7. This week's extra rations are a tin of French beans for everyone; ½ lb. of sweets for everyone under 18, and ¼ lb. of chocolate cream for adults.

February 8. Farmers from all over the Island had to take their motor lorries to Springfield today to be examined by the German Purchasing Commission; over a hundred were requisitioned. The fourth *E.P.* Occupation Almanac is published, and over 5,000 Red Cross letters have arrived. Owing to engine trouble, an American single-seater fighter makes a forced landing at Greenlands, St. Peter's, Joseph E. Krebs, of Milwaukee, Wisconsin, aged 23, was taken prisoner and the farmhouse near where he landed was searched; later he was removed to the Public Prison and then—he having slight injuries—to the German hospital at Merton Hotel, before being sent to a prisoner-of-war camp in France.

February 10. The Germans made a raid on a wood store kept by some Irishmen, following a big robbery of brandy from a German depôt; several arrests were made.

February 11. More hosiery is being made available to the female population, and quantities of French clothing for males are on sale;; the material is of inferior quality and very expensive.

February 12. Two men were fined £5 and £3 respectively, each with 10s. costs, at the Royal Court today for selling tobacco without a licence. A meeting of headmasters and teachers was held in the Old Committee Room of the States Buildings during the morning, when they were addressed by German officials on the need of furthering the teaching of German in the schools. Tube of flints for mechanical lighters issued on ration with the tobacco ration. Death of Mr. A. Harrison, co-proprietor and managing-editor of *The Evening Post*.

February 14. The Department of Transport and Communications advertises for lorries, motor cars (less than 14 h.p.), and motor cycles in good order, to replace those recently purchased by the German Buying Commission; today the Commission inspected more cars, etc., mostly those belonging to States officials, doctors, etc. Doctors are having a very busy time visiting patients, and if black-market petrol were not obtainable they would not to able to cover much ground. This week's rations are augmented by $\frac{1}{2}$ lb. of macaroni and $\frac{1}{2}$ lb. of coffee substitute for everybody and 100 saccharin tablets for adults. The Green Room Club presents a play at the Opera House.

February 15. Sounds of the heaviest bombing yet heard came from the direction of the French today; residents in the St. Martin's district report having seen hundreds of planes to the north-west in the early morning, and vibration was felt for some time all over the Island.

February 17. Owing to illness, the Ear, Nose and Throat Department of the General Hospital is closed until further notice.

February 18. The German Feldkommandant (Colonel Knackfuss) visits the communal kitchen and some of the restaurants in the town to see what sort of meals are being served; visits have also been paid to houses in the poorer districts.

February 19. Four men sentenced by the Royal Court for robbery of wheat; it is also learned that the Germans have sentenced a farmer to ten months' imprisonment for being in possession of German coal, and a well-known resident has been sentenced to three months' imprisonment for being in possession of German brandy—the sentence to be served when the Germans have won the war!

February 21. Three oz. of margarine issued per head, a wine ration for adults, and the jam ration re-commences (alphabetically). Robbery of a safe from the Transport Office containing papers, £440 in cash and cheques.

February 22. Fairly heavy fall of snow during the coldest day this winter.

February 23. The Bailiff issues an appeal for articles of clothing, blankets, etc., which can be utilised for the poor and needy. The Germans issue a notice forbidding sketching, drawing, painting, etc., of objects situated out of doors. The Germans start manoeuvres for a period of three days, and gunfire is continually heard all over the Island. Accident at La Mare, when a boy aged six years shoots his nine-year-old brother through the head with a German revolver he had found.

February 24. During firing practice a German shell fell short and caused a considerable amount of damage in Gorey Village.

February 25. In connection with the German manoeuvres, residents in a fairly large area at Les Platons had to be out of the district by 7 o'clock this morning and to remain so until noon.

February 26. Fines of £20 and £10 respectively imposed by the Royal Court on two farmers for keeping unregistered pigs; a fine of £10 was also imposed on a man accused of tapping an overhead electric cable and obtaining free supply. Quantity of sewing cotton, darning thread and hose being made available or ration, and the shops are displaying more and more French goods. The Germans have issued orders that all changes of ownership of horses which have taken place since the muster of horses held in November last, and all such changes in future must be reported immediately to Field Command 515. The manager of Wests has been sentenced to six months' imprisonment in connection with wireless sets found on the cinema premises; he was subsequently taken to Rouen.

February 27. British naval craft intercept a German convoy off Corbière and, firing on it, set on fire an armed trawler which blew up and sank, and damaged another; the Germans brought in a number of casualties.

February 28. Tin of green peas issued as an extra; the tinned

French beans which were recently on ration were not greatly in demand and may now be obtained at grocer's shops without coupons. The Fifty-Fifty Club presents a thriller at the Opera House.

February 29. The lack of warming foods is telling, and the health of the population leaves much to be desired; cases of scarlet fever are frequent, while almost everyone has suffered from colds, chilblains or 'flu, the doctors finding it difficult to keep pace with the demands made on their services. The number of families receiving the States child allowance is now 1,007, the number of children concerned being 2,290. The Children's Benefit Fund is doing excellent work in purchasing rations for people who cannot afford them. Where once little or none was ever seen, poverty and distress have taken a grip on a large section of the population; children with inadequate clothing and parents with pinched faces are to be met everywhere. A number of Red Cross parcels has been received during the months from friends in German internment camps who have found goods to spare, the recipients being highly delighted with tinned goods, etc., reminiscent of pre-Occupation days. The German Field Commandant and many of his staff are to leave the Island and make their headquarters at St. Lo; about five senior officers are to be left here under the command of K.V.R. von Aufsess, the Island thereby being administered from France. Many properties are being evacuated by the Germans, and large quantities of material continue to be shipped to France. A representative of the French Red Cross has been here in inquire into the welfare of French colonial troops. The jail is full with all sorts and conditions of men, charged with some infraction or other of a German Order, and there is a waiting-list of sentenced prisoners to be incarcerated in rotation as the cells are vacated. Owing to the absence of facilities for investment, the rate of interest paid by the Jersey Savings Bank and the Post Office Savings Bank is, from the end of this month to be reduced from 2½ per cent. to 1 per cent. on sums exceeding balances held by them on February 28, 1940.

MARCH 1944

March 1. The fuel ration for an average family this month consists of one hundredweight of wood. The Germans are after cycles again, owners receiving notice to take them to parish halls for inspection and valuation.

March 2. Five thousand Red Cross letters have arrived.

March 3. The Germans publish a long Currency Order; especial attention is drawn to the fact that the Channel Islands are to be regarded as a foreign country in so far as France is concerned; every import and export of currency without permission is liable to punishment.

March 4. The Bailiff's recent appeal for spare clothing and footwear has borne fruit. The civilian petrol supply must now be obtained at Barnes' Garage, Devonshire Place, and not from the Paragon Garage, David Place. The Saturday afternoon concerts by a German military band in the Royal Square have been resumed.

March 5. Morning and afternoon Allied planes over the Island at a great height; to see a German plane these days is an event!

March 6. This week's extras consist of ½ lb. of macaroni and 3 oz. of cheese per head. An extra pound of potatoes has been added free of charge to the ration to make up for bad ones. The Constables had to attend at College House to be informed the Germans would, in future, take a more serious view of farmers and other persons giving shelter to escaped Russian prisoners.

March 7. Paragraphs over the signature of the Field Commandant assert that there is still available in the Island approximately 750 lorries, 2,400 motor cars and 198 motor cycles; lists are to be prepared of serviceable and unserviceable vehicles, and an examination is to be made to find out which of these are to be designated as purely scrap; all such details to be available by March 25 at the latest.

March 11. Great scarcity of greenstuffs in the markets and shops today, swedes being the only available unrationed vegetable in any quantity. The Germans have a parade through the town in connection with Heroes' Day.

March 12. All day today (Sunday) the Germans have been holding 'memorial services' at The Forum in connection with Heroes' Day. Lord Justice du Parcq made an appeal for Channel Islands' refugees.

March 13. The General Hospital closed to visitors, there being cases of scarlet fever there. The Department of Health draws the attention of the public to the fact that requests for the services of doctors should be made before 9 a.m. if a visit is expected on the same day, and that no calls other than emergency calls to be made on Sundays. Arrival of about 350 tons of French wheat. This week's extra rations: five bars of chocolate cream for adults, 8 oz. of sweets for children and juveniles, and a piece of toilet soap for everybody. A 5d. bar of pre-war washing soap now fetches 18 marks (£1 18s. 6d.) in the black market!

March 15. Another series of robberies reported—a grain store broken into and meat stolen from butcher's shop; there having been attempts at entry into many other shops.

March 16. The Amateur Dramatic Club presents a drama at the Opera House; this was to have commenced on Monday, the 13th, but it had to be postponed as the Germans had requisitioned the Opera House for a visit by a German 'State' actress—Lil Dagover. This was a last minute arrangement, with no little inconvenience to the A.D.C., and it was unique by the fact that for the first time during the Occupation the Opera House was nicely heated—local companies performing there during the winters have had to shiver.

March 17. A few deportees to Germany returned today on account of ill-health, age, etc.; they were escorted by seven others, who were told they must work for the Germans, but it appears that this condition is not being too strictly enforced. They speak of the spirit of defeatism among the guards of the German camps, who supply the internees with wireless news every day. Most brought Red Cross parcels, and another batch of parcels has arrived for friends of internees at Laufen. One of the returning internees, who formerly lived in a bungalow at Corbière, found this had been demolished by the Germans. Today being St. Patrick's Day dances were held in the evening, mainly attended by the Irish residents, special curfew permits having been granted.

March 18. At the Royal Court a butcher was fined £500 and sentenced to one month's imprisonment for slaughtering a horse; the Attorney-General submitted that the horse had been traded in the black market and sold at an average price of five marks a pound (10s. 8d.)! The price of the tobacco ration increased to 1s. for 12 cigarettes and 1s. 9d. for an ounce of pipe tobacco, this alternating with twenty cigarettes at 1s. 8d.; two boxes of matches were issued with this week's ration. In connection with their 'Army Day' the Germans have been selling to soldiers little white labels to be attached to buttonholes, and have also hawked ice-creams for sale to civilians at a mark a time; trade was not very brisk!

March 20. The price of petrol increased to 5s. 6d. per gallon. The gas supply to be turned on at 6.30 a.m. instead of at 7 a.m. Half a pound of macaroni issued as an extra, also ten boxes of matches per household; the price of sugar fixed at 2½d. per ration of 3 oz.

March 21. Victoria College Terminal Service held at St. Helier's Parish Church. Main-crop potatoes are now being issued on ration. Black-market potatoes are fetching as much as £2 per cwt. Packets of dried carrots from France are on sale; there is a shortage of 'Bouillons', a highly-salted flavouring cube.

March 22. Notice issued by the Chief Registration Officer, on German instructions, that worn-out or defaced identity cards must be renewed; the fee for a duplicate card is 2s. 6d. and the Germans threaten to arrest any person whose card is considered not to be in good order.

March 23. Three Irishmen arrested for stealing a safe from an Italian café in Colomberie.

March 24. Arrival of a large number of replies to Red Cross letters. Local hairdresser arrested by the Germans on a charge of making 'miniature wireless sets'. Latest reported robbery is of about 200 lb. of meat.

March 25. Another pig case before the Royal Court, a farmer being fined £60 with £10 costs. A £10 fine was imposed on a young woman for ration frauds. The Textile and Footwear Control points out that second-hand or used clothing and footwear must not be sold direct to the retail trade, but must be sent to a special depôt, where it will be graded and distributed for sale through licensed retailers.

March 26. Mr. Churchill's review of the war situation was listened to by a quarter of the population, in spite of the wireless ban; many shorthand copies were made and these transcribed and distributed to friends next morning.

March 27. Another batch of Red Cross letters is being distributed—about 4,000. Island School of Dancing and Elocution presents a revue at the Opera House. Late at night the largest number of German planes heard for some time passed over the Island; the B.B.C. next morning announced that Bristol had been bombed.

March 28. This morning some of the streets of the town were littered with thousands of 12-page pamphlets printed in English and headed 'We Protest'; these contained pictures and cuttings from periodicals, mainly American, and extracts from speeches by politicians pointing out what a powerful enemy Germany is; some pamphlets were put in letter-boxes, but in view of the extremely obscene language printed in them the majority of people burned all they could get hold of. As a propaganda effort, this did the German cause more harm than good.

March 29. The Germans give notice that a purchasing commission in the Island is to examine all the remaining motor vehicles which are neither in circulation nor on the reserve; this means the requisitioning of every remaining motor vehicle, but it is known that hundreds are well hidden. Two German destroyers and a light cruiser are anchored in St. Aubin's Bay—the first seen for many months.

March 30. Death of the little boy named Wood who was shot by his brother with a German revolver last month; an inquest was held, the verdict being accidental death. Six German fighters swept over the Island today.

March 31. Charged with the illegal retention of wheat, a farmer was fined £150 with £10 costs at the Royal Court today; in addition, 1,033 lb. of wheat were confiscated and will be handed over to the Agricultural Department. Quantity of woollen material from France issued today on ration. Arrival of some French flour. Large numbers of people are obtaining brewers' yeast for use in various ways, and on some days hundreds of jam jars, etc., are filled at the two breweries, which have to make beer mainly for the Germans. The States Telephone Department has developed a much-appreciated system of relaying concerts, church services, etc., to the various institutions. Sovereigns are changing hands at £16 each. The local death-rate for March was 26.7 per 1,000.

APRIL 1944

April 1. No issue of fuel for this month except on medical grounds, etc.; the electricity ration is cut to 3½ units per household per week. In a pig case a breeder was fined £450 with £10 costs; a farmer was fined £50 with £5 costs for not giving notice of the death of a heifer, and another £35 with £5 costs for non-registration of a pig and heifer.

April 3. Clocks advanced one hour to conform with Central European Summer Time. This week's extras are chocolate cream for adults and juveniles, sweets for children, and a piece of household soap for everybody.

April 4. The combined Guilds of St. Helier's and St. James's Church Players present a Passion Play at St. James's Church.

April 5. Sale of horses in the Cattle Market; seven sold for £2,220, an average of £317.

April 6. The Germans have brought from France a large cargo of potatoes for their own consumption.

April 7. Good Friday: weather dull, turning to rain in the evening. The usual Passion music was performed in the churches, and a play written by a local author—*The House of Iscariot*—presented at the Opera House.

April 8. The town packed with people looking for something to buy for Easter, the only thing being large quantities of flowers. A pre-war two-shilling-size chocolate Easter egg, offered to the highest bidder in aid of the Children's Benefit Fund, fetched 100 marks (£10 13s. 8d.).

April 9. Easter Sunday: heavy rain in the early morning, but, from midday, glorious sunshine. The gas hours for today only: 6.30 a.m. to 1.30 p.m. and 6 to 8 p.m.

April 10. Easter Monday: fog in the morning, turning to glorious sunshine. The big attraction of the day was a football match at the F.B. Fields. Half a pound of macaroni and half a pound of coffee substitute issued as extras. The Green Room Club presents Grand Opera at the Opera House. Distribution of a large number of Red Cross letters—about 8,000.

April 11. Another cut in the gas hours, the supply being on only six and a half hours per day: 6.30 a.m. to 8 a.m.; 11 a.m. to 1 p.m.; 6.30 p.m. to 7.30 p.m. The Germans putting up large numbers of 'pylons'—lengths of railway line or girders—in fields where there is an area suitable for landing a plane; quite irrespective of whether crops are already planted, these pylons are buried to a depth of about five feet and some 100 feet apart. Royal Court fines two shopkeepers for selling goods without a licence. Many single Allied planes over the Island today. Daring robbery reported from St. Clement's, about £400 in British Treasury notes being stolen. Supplies of Vitamin D are being dispatched to the children of the Channel Islands through the Red Cross, enough to cover a six-month period.

April 12. The local hairdresser who was arrested for making miniature wireless sets—crystals—has been sentenced to six months' imprisonment.

April 15. Markets full of greenstuffs, for, in addition to the local produce thousands of cabbage and lettuce from Guernsey are on sale. Notices issued by the Department of Agriculture again call attention to transfers, etc., of livestock, disposal of produce, and the danger of warble-fly.

April 16. It is learned there has been a mutiny among German soldiers billeted at Portelet. Details were hard to obtain, but it was gathered a large number of men had been imprisoned at Fort Regent.

April 17. This week's extras: a piece of toilet soap for everybody and a ration of red wine for adults. A quantity of late-variety seed potatoes has arrived from France and these are obtainable at 21s. 4d. per cwt.

April 19. About 10 p.m. the Germans have a march through the town of about 40 troops carrying torches, and two military bands beat a tattoo (Grosse Zapfenstreich) in the Parade; the curfew was postponed until midnight so that the local population might witness this ceremony.

April 20. Allied planes have today celebrated Hitler's birthday, for there has been a continuous procession on their way to the French coast. St. Helier's Parish Assembly authorises the Constable to submit to the States a proposal to amend Article 1 of the 'Parish of St. Helier (General Purposes Loan) Law 1942' in such a manner that the amount of the loan which may be raised by the parish shall be increased from £45,000 to £150,000. German band plays in the Royal Square.

April 21. In various parts of the Island quantities of shredded silver paper foil were picked up, having been dropped by passing planes.*

April 22. The Full Court sentenced two Irishmen each to two years' hard labour in connection with the recent safe robbery. Single Allied planes over the Island today.

April 23. More Allied planes over again today. Many churches hold semi-patriotic services in commemoration of St. George's Day and with thoughts of the National Day of Prayer in England.

April 24. German planes pass over the Island at about 12.30 a.m., it being subsequently learned that Bristol had been attacked. Later in the day Allied planes were over. This week's extras: a packet of saccharin tablets for adults and ½ lb. of macaroni for everybody. German Order published forbidding interference with pylons erected in the fields. Messrs. Britton and Whinnerah present a farce at the Opera House.

April 25. The evening gas hour changed—6 to 7 instead of 6.30 to 7.30.

April 26. After midnight German planes were heard going to England. Allied planes were also heard in the early hours. During the morning leaflets printed in French were found. In the afternoon and evening more Allied planes were over, and were fired at by the German batteries as they flew low in the Grève d'Azette district. Curd is again available to the public, as well as skim milk.

---

* This foil—code name 'Window'—we were to learn later, was used by the R.A.F. to disturb the enemy's radio location.

April 27. German planes again pass over the Island. Later large numbers of Allied planes were in the vicinity and residents counted groups of over 100; quantities of silver paper strips were dropped by the planes and small parachutes with parcels of leaflets attached, these being quickly collected by the Germans. After twice attempting to leave the harbour all German shipping left again for France. The German soldier who shot an officer at La Rocque about three months ago faced a firing squad this morning and was later taken to the Strangers' Cemetery; the burial party got there before the hour appointed, smashed the gate-lock to force its way in, and then gave instructions for it to be repaired immediately.

April 28. It is learned that all German leave has been stopped.

April 29. Among the latest textile goods from France are cotton coats such as butchers wear, men's pyjamas and braces. New potatoes have made their appearance 'under the counter' at 1s. 6d. per pound. The price of paraffin for those who may purchase it is 1s. per pint. Meeting of the States: Jurat Dorey presented the Budget, which showed that receipts amounted to £235,444, and expenditure to £840,606, the deficiency having been met by bonds, issued under States guarantee, totalling £630,000. The sum of £798,130 had been borrowed during the year, bringing the total of the Islands debt to £3,645,690. Jurat Dorey pointed out that, although commercial transactions had sustained few losses, this might not continue, and that to meet this a reserve of £18,571 had been established. The flour subsidy had amounted to £90,398, loss on the 'soup kitchens' to £5,589, loss on the Textile Department to £2,177, and on the Milk Department the total loss over a period of two years amounted to £16,616. Owing to the change of currency in France, it was not now possible to send reichsmarks away to pay for purchases, so that there was an estimated accumulation in the Island of between £1,000,000 and £1,500,000 in reichsmarks. We must, said Jurat Dorey, visualise in the future an annual Budget of £1,000,000, instead of the old-time Budgets of £400,000-odd. Local tobacco was taxed at 5d. per plant; suggestions were made for the extension of sick-pay benefits, and the school-leaving age was fixed at 15 for another year. The Markets Inspector was given an increase in salary.

April 30. Many Allied planes over today. The Germans appear to be sending away large quantities of material, and some hangars have been pulled down and removed. On the landing field of the Airport itself felled trees have been rolled so as to obstruct any Allied planes that may attempt to land. Several owners of property occupied by the Germans have been notified there is likelihood of their property being de-requisitioned, and have been asked if they wish to have caretakers placed on the premises. Cars continued to be shipped and the doctors have had to give up two more.

MAY 1944

May 1. The Germans look on May Day as a general holiday; all the foreign workers are given the day off and publication of *The Evening Post* is forbidden. The curfew is from 11 p.m. to 5 a.m. There is no fuel ration this month except in special cases. This week's extra is a 5-oz. ration of cheese at 1s. 3d. A boy at St. Ouen's has had his hand badly injured as the result of playing with a detonator which exploded. The May Assizes opened today with a case concerning the theft of two cows at St. Brelades.

May 3. Case of rape reported from St. Mary's, a local married woman being half strangled by an Algerian; the man was subsequently arrested by the German police. Three of a family living at Five Oaks—father, son and daughter—have been arrested by the Germans for stealing large quantities of ammunition.

May 4. The Germans re-commence their 'sharpshooting' (gun practice) on a big scale, residents of certain districts being warned to leave their premises.

May 5. The Germans publish an Order making it a punishable offence for cyclists to ride two abreast. More pylons are being erected, the latest sites being some of the beaches, especially at Grouville. The Royal Jersey Golf Club has now had to cease functioning, as the whole of the course has been mined. The Department of Labour announces that nearly 80,000 trees have been planted to replace those cut down.

May 6. Local residents who have received letters from friends deported to Germany say these indicate there may be cases of repatriation to England. A pre-war 8-oz. jar of Marmite has changed hands for £8.

May 7. Single Allied aircraft over the Island today, and, for a change, a German plane flew over during the afternoon.

May 8. Extra rations this week of ½ lb. of macaroni per head and 4 oz. of sweets for children and juveniles. Mr. Jack Coombs presents a musical show at the Opera House. About 2 o'clock in the morning a terrific explosion was heard, and it was learned that an ammunition ship had been bombed between the Islands, there being only three survivors. Planes were over all day, with the accompanying sounds of bombing. The Germans apparently expect something to happen soon, for armed guards are to be kept at the telephone exchanges all night and soldiers have now to sleep in the trenches.

May 9. Warm weather has brought along spider crabs, and a supply to the Fish Market is commencing, the Germans having first pick.

May 10. Order issued by the Superior Council regarding the tobacco crop; by this the Department of Essential Commodities is empowered to purchase the whole of the 1944 crop, but every holder of a licence will be allowed to retain fifty plants for his own use; the Department will pay 10s. per lb. for good stuff, but less for tobacco of inferior quality. A German Red Cross ship is in the harbour today.

May 11. The Germans have another spasm of 'sharpshooting'; this always takes place on a Thursday, and people in defined areas are expected to evacuate their houses.

May 12. At 5 o'clock in the morning the Germans start a large-scale manoeuvre, waking everyone up with their firing; gardens and fields in some districts where there are growing crops were trampled over and damage done to fences, hedges, etc. Mines have been laid in fields at Archirondel, and persons are still being turned out of their homes for 'military reasons', as a rule without much warning. The Full Court sentenced a third Irishman to two years' hard labour for complicity in the robbery of a safe.

May 13. The retail price of new potatoes fixed at 7½d. per lb.; these may be obtained as half the ration if so desired.

May 14. Morning and evening Allied planes pass over.

May 15. The gas supply cut down to three hours a day: 6.45 to 7.30 a.m.; 11.30 a.m. to 1 p.m. and 6.15 to 7 p.m.; the early morning period is the most inconvenient, but this has to be to suit the Germans. Small quantities of coal arrive now and again. This week's extra ration consists solely of ½ lb. of washing soda per head. The Germans have placed sentries outside houses occupied by them in the country.

May 16. People who expected new potatoes as half of their ration this week will not get them, as the Germans have commandeered 50 per cent. of the greenhouse crop—some 50 tons. Gold, silver and securities in the local banks belonging to French and other foreign nationals are being packed ready to be transferred, on German orders, to Continental banks. The Germans are after lead, zinc and iron; with this object some master plumbers have been summoned to College House to be questioned regarding the sale of these commodities. Fourteen cannon have been taken from Elizabeth Castle.

May 17. Two of the family at Five Oaks recently arrested by the Germans for stealing quantities of ammunition have been released.* A hotel proprietor who was arrested recently is to answer charges relating to black-market activities and changing of Bank of England notes.

May 19. Full Court passes sentence of two years' hard labour on three men for pig-stealing. During the evening Allied planes pass over.

May 20. Apparently the Channel Islands have gone down in the German social scale, for from now on 'Feldkommandantur 515' is to be replaced by 'Platzkommandantur 1'. This is really only a transference of powers, for the high officials formerly here left the Island some time ago. Cases before courts martial are to be tried by the 'Festungskommandant' (Fortress Commandant), and the notice is signed by the Platzkommandant (Major Heider).

May 21. Two barges and an armed trawler (or patrol boat) were sunk off the south-west of the Island by Free French naval forces; over 100 casualties have been brought ashore; a few bodies are to be buried and the number of drowned is understood to be in the region of 25.

May 22. Half a pound of macaroni issued per head and 1½ oz. of French 'ginger' cake at 6d. per ration. The Amateur Dramatic Club presents a comedy at the Opera House. Arrival of about 3,000 Red Cross letters. The Germans have been moving foodstuffs, etc., from their usual stores and placing them in some of the tunnels which they have constructed, more especially in St. Peter's Valley and at Grands Vaux.†

---

* Jimmy Houiellebecq, the son, aged 17 years, was subsequently taken to a German concentration camp, where he died on January 20, 1945.

† Subsequently one of these tunnels—the largest in the Island—was found to be an underground hospital, constructed by Russian slave labour, the majority of whom had been marched across Europe. It took two and a half years to construct this hospital, which was hewn out of solid rock, many of the ill-treated labourers losing their lives by falling rock and being buried in the side walls. It was fully equipped and had its own air-conditioning, central heating and electric light plants. The other tunnels were for the storage of ammunition, one of them being the old railway tunnel at St. Aubin's.

179

May 23. British E-boats came close inshore in St. Aubin's Bay and dispersed a convoy of enemy shipping; there was a lot of gunfire, and one of the barges in the convoy ended up on the Dogs' Nest, but was brought into harbour later in the day. The harbour was filled with ships taking refuge, and when, in the evening, a large cargo boat left for France, she was escorted by seven armed vessels. The Germans are taking away numbers of the big gun turrets, using the Dutch 100-ton crane for loading. Plenty of Allied planes over today. German Order issued regarding the felling of trees, which is now strictly forbidden except on permit from the Platzkommandantur.

May 24. Many people wore roses today in honour of Empire Day. A man recently sentenced by the Germans to two months' imprisonment for alleged 'insults' to a German who was with a local woman, was given a further three months today as the result of an appeal. The Germans are placing in St. Aubin's Bay, near La Haule, poles on top of which are boxes containing explosive material which will be set off if touched by a boat or anything else. Six ounces of biscuits per head have been issued to schoolchildren—a gift from the French Secours Nationale.

May 27. Slight increase in the price of the tobacco ration: cigarettes, 1s. 1d. for 10, 1s. 9d. for 20; tobacco, 1s. 10d. per oz. Price of French gruel raised to 2s. per lb.; this commodity is obtainable only for infants. Royal Court deals with another case of an unregistered pig, a farmer being fined £20 with £5 costs.

May 28. Whit Sunday: weather very hot. A heavy explosion which was felt was learned to have been an ammunition dump near Rennes. Extra half hour of gas allowed on Sunday mornings until further notice.

May 29. Whit Monday: in the evening between four and five thousand people attended a football match at the F.B. Fields, the final of the Occupation Cup; the scenes were reminiscent of former Muratti days. This week's extras: half a pound of macaroni per head and five boxes of matches per household.

May 30. Many robberies have been reported over the weekend; among the objects stolen is hair cut from horses' tails by people who wanted to make brushes! The ration per person of new potatoes is half a pound, the other four and a half pounds being old ones, but extra potatoes may be obtained fairly easily at the controlled price (7½d.). The rainfall figure for the month is 0.34 of an inch, being the lowest for the month of May since 1927. The Germans are getting very strict on persons out after curfew and cyclists riding two abreast; for curfew infractions many fines have been imposed, and in several cases offenders have been kept in a German billet all night and next morning taken to College House to be fined. They are also checking on motor cars which may have escaped notice by the Purchasing Commission. A lady resident of St. Ouen's is in German hands for having given refuge to a young Russian for about two years; she fostered him like a son and he used to accompany her to town; the Germans did not find him, for he escaped, but to add to the lady's troubles they found a wireless set. A St. Martin's resident who also gave refuge to a Russian is undergoing sentence of five months' imprisonment. Black-market prices have increased; tea is going at £20 a pound, butter at 30s., bicarbonate of soda at 30s. and very inferior baking powder at 1s. a packet; meat is very scarce. Many sales of standing hay are taking place, at prices up to £70 per vergée. The new power station built by the Germans in St. Peter's Valley has been tried out during the month, and occasionally electricity generated there has been put on supply; but the plant is not yet satisfactory owing to the sabotage of French engineers who erected it.

JUNE 1944

June 1. This is the month when we expect things to happen! The Germans appear to think so, too, for they are continually having anti-invasion manoeuvres. Allied planes over today. There is no fuel ration for June, except by special permit, and the electricity ration has been further cut—the basic ration for lighting and domestic purposes is 2½ units per week, instead of 3½, with a sliding scale for cooking, e.g., a household with four in family is allowed 22 units per week. A German Order now in force prohibits the painting of woodwork of any building, except glasshouses and other buildings used for the growing of foodstuffs.

June 3. The Department of Agriculture issues a notice regarding conpulsory spraying of crops as a precaution against the Colorado beetle. Large quantities of crabs arrive in the Fish Market.

June 5. Everybody delighted to hear of the fall of Rome. The price of new potatoes fixed at 2d. per lb. This week's extras consist of ½ lb. of macaroni per head, a stick of shaving soap for male adults, and a jam ration re-commences (alphabetically). The Green Room Club presents a drama at the Opera House. Under a new German Order, the *E.P.* is to consist of two pages only per day, including Saturdays.

June 6. INVASION! From the early hours we guessed something unusual was happening, owing to the large number of planes passing over. The Germans put up a terrific anti-aircraft barrage, and one of their gun positions at St. John's was machine-gunned. The sound of planes and A.A. fire continued well into the morning, after which aircraft were heard almost all the time, but there was no more A.A. fire. The Germans have manned all their posts and parked waiting ambulances, lorries, etc., in various parts of the Island. Guards have been doubled outside their billets, Red Cross flags galore placed near hospitals, and one peculiar thing is the sight of soldiers wearing Red Cross armlets and equipped with steel helmets and rifles! The Germans immediately took over the telephone service, but in spite of this, news spread, smiling faces indicated that the day had arrived for which we had waited so long. The Todts working on the Victoria Statue railings have stopped work, and one of the first things the Germans did was to arrest some British ex-Army officers and hold them prisoner for a few hours. In today's paper the following was ordered to be printed:

PROCLAMATION
To the Population of the Island of Jersey

Germany's enemy is on the point of attacking French soil. I expect the population of Jersey to keep its head, to remain calm, and to refrain from any acts of sabotage and from hostile acts against the German Forces, even should the fighting spread to Jersey.

At the first signs of unrest or trouble I will close the streets to every traffic and will secure hostages.

Attacks against the German Forces will be punishable by death.

Der Kommandant der Festung Jersey.

Jersey, June 6, 1944.   (Signed) HEINE, Oberst.

All foreign workers have been taken off their jobs and workers on the quays sent home. The B.B.C. has announced that a wireless station in the Channel Islands has been destroyed, and this is taken to be the one at Fort George in Guernsey, which was bombed again yesterday. In some parts persons have been warned off the beach, and low-water fishing is suspended. No German places of entertainment, etc., are functioning. German secret police are now in uniform, and at the moment there are about 7,000 troops in the Island. Guards have been placed at the entrance to the gas works, electricity station, etc.

June 7. Rather a quiet night, although planes are now continually heard in the distance. The German officials at College House slept on the premises, and not in their billets. Civilian staffs of places where the Germans are billeted have been paid off. Over 100 Frenchmen who have worked here for some time were imprisoned in Fort Regent because they did not turn up for work yesterday; a few managed to escape, and those who were recaptured were manacled and taken back; they are guarded by members of the Todt Organisation. During the night the 8-inch guns at Les Landes fired out to sea, as warships were in the vicinity, off St. Ouen's Bay. About half a dozen small vessels arrived in the harbour and four of these left in the evening; German nurses and female canteen or office workers were embarked, and a few officers; some ammunition was also shipped, after being removed from Trinity Manor, where it had only recently been taken. German reports maintain there is fighting in the Channel Islands. There is hardly a soldier to be seen in the town, and those who are riding in lorries, etc., are fully armed. The majority of the troops have been spread around the coasts. A German Order closes down all theatres and cinemas 'in order to save electrical energy'; all dances and other public entertainments are cancelled, and curfew commences at 10 p.m. instead of 11 p.m. A new monthly publication makes its appearance, entitled *Jersey Theatre*. The public is once again warned about the water supply, which is still a serious problem; the rainfall for the last eight months was only 17 inches.

June 8. Planes have been passing over all night but were not fired at. The boats which left last evening returned this morning, accompanied by many others. By noon there were over 30 small ships, barges, etc., in the harbour. Later in the day most of the boats left and anchored in the bay. The Germans have cleared from many town billets, but on account of the number of new gun positions all over the country other billets have had to be found, and there are innumerable cases of people having soldiers foisted on them. Foreign workers are back at work today.

June 9. The Germans are taking away potatoes, and there is a considerable amount of shipping in the harbour. A Red Cross flag is flying outside the jail in Gloucester Street, a portion of which is to be used by the Germans for anticipated casualties. Trenches are being dug in all sorts of places, including the town parks, and more billeting is being arranged. A German notice published today declared that all beaches are out of bounds to the civil population until further notice. The Havre-des-Pas Bathing Pool, however, and the beach immediately behind are to remain open. More individual soldiers are again seen in town; they are fully armed, with rifles, steel helmets, and hand grenades slung around the neck. In consequence of the suspension of the telephone service, the Electricity Company publishes names of some of its employees who live out of town, to whom complaints may be made in an emergency.

June 10. The Germans apparently have decided not to fire on planes unless they are flying low. About 6.30 a.m. three patrol boats out of a group of six which were lying outside the harbour were attacked by Allied planes and one was damaged by machine-gun fire; the boats managed to get back into harbour. There is not much in the harbour today apart from these vessels and a few barges. The telephone service has been restored for the essential services, certain States officials and doctors. The Germans are still placing machine-gun posts all over the Island.

June 11. Many of the local churches are observing today (Sunday) as the Day of National Prayer. About 10.30 a.m. the naval guns at Noirmont fired out to sea; these are seldom used, and it seems certain Allied warships were close to the Island. The Germans have put up Red Cross flags at a large number of places, including soldiers' recreation homes, etc., which can hardly be described as hospitals. Underground hospitals are also fully equipped and ready for use. Many of the foreign workers are declaring they would welcome a British landing; nationals of occupied countries who are enrolled in the German Army are in agreement, and even some of the Germans have told residents they would give themselves up immediately. All day the Germans have been moving large stocks of flour and tinned goods from outlying depôts to stores in the town area near the harbours; they have also demanded information regarding stocks of flour and other essentials held by the civil authorities.

June 12. After a very quiet night Allied planes swooped down over the harbours at about 6.30 a.m. and bombs were dropped near patrol boats anchored off Elizabeth Castle; one bomb struck some earth against the castle walls, but the boats were not hit and they entered harbour later. A few barges came in during the day. Allied planes also machine-gunned gun emplacements at Mont-à-l'Abbé; a number of gasogene lorries have been commandeered today and there is to be a cut of 50 per cent. in the vehicles on the roads. Names of drivers of vans used for the delivery of essential commodities have to be submitted to the Germans, who also want returns of all livestock held in the Island. This week's extra rations consist of a packet of sweets for children and a piece of toilet soap for everybody. A large quantity of potatoes is to be sent to Germany. Although the beaches have been closed, a few places are accessible to farmers wishing to gather vraic. Fishing boats are allowed out at their own risk. Now that the invasion has been on for a week the atmosphere may be described as tense—we certainly are in the zone of operations now. Fully-armed soldiers are being continually rushed to new positions; even those who visit local barber shops keep their rifles between their knees while being shaved!

June 13. Plane activity heard but more distant than usual. The harbours are almost empty again today. Nearly every night the lighthouses at Mont Ubé and La Mare are in operation, and local cranemen have been warned they may be called at any time and must sleep near the harbours. The bus services are restricted to one bus in the morning and one in the evening; this means that only sixty persons can be carried on any route, so that priority permits are to be issued to genuine long-distance business people who are known to travel daily. Buses must be parked in town all night and not at country termini. All 'friendly aliens' have had to give up their wireless sets, and some belonging to Germans are also to be handed in. The local population is exceedingly cheerful and optimism is so great that certain shops are doing quite a trade in selling Union Jacks and emblems of a patriotic nature. The German Post Office is accepting no more letters for delivery to deportees, etc., in German internment camps. Black-market goods are very difficult to obtain, but among articles on sale from France is a large number of ladies' and gents' umbrellas. The first appreciable amount of rain for some time fell today: the wheat is looking very well, though unfortunately in many cases there is evidence of 'smut'.

June 14. Planes, planes, planes—from midnight onwards, but very little A.A. About 2.30 a.m. sounds of naval gunfire which shook the Island came from the direction of the Minquiers, and then from 4 o'clock onwards there was a lot of activity in the harbours. Three torpedo-boats or mine-sweepers were brought in during the morning and two were placed on the 'hard', both being torn open above the water-line. The third was so badly damaged that torpedoes had to be removed and put on shore. About 9 a.m. five escort vessels off Noirmont were attacked by Allied planes; one sank immediately and another a few minutes later. Still later in the morning planes bombed guns at St.

Ouen's and machine-gunned positions around the Airport. German A.A. opened up, and, unfortunately, one of the planes was hit and crashed into a house at Grantez, St. Ouen's; the house was burned out and the pilot (unidentified) burned to death. The Germans are calling in civilian curfew passes, the only exception being expectant mothers. Only German naval craft in the harbour.

June 15. Planes have passed over continually, and at about 9 a.m. a bomb was dropped on Elizabeth Castle; it is not known if any damage were done. Nowadays German anti-aircraft gunners are kept at their posts without respite. The Germans have mined several of their storehouses, etc., which could be destroyed in the case of an Allied attempt to capture the Island. Football matches which were to be played this week have been banned by the Germans.

June 16. Absence of aircraft until the afternoon, owing to bad weather. The body of the unidentified Allied airman who crashed at St. Ouen's two days ago was buried in the War Cemetery in Howard Davis Park this morning, the ceremony following the usual lines; the body had lain in St. Luke's Church overnight and the Germans sent a firing party. Only a few escort vessels are in harbour. A notice published today reduces the bread and meat rations from June 19. The bread ration is reduced to 4 lb. 4 oz. per week for all adults, whatever their occupation. Ordinary adolescents are to have 4 lb. 8 oz., while male and female adolescent manual workers will get 6 lb. and 5 lb. 4 oz. respectively; children and infants will continue to get 3 lb. and $1\frac{1}{2}$ lb. respectively. So that the meat supply may last as long as possible, there will be an issue every other week, but in the meatless weeks an extra 2 oz. of butter per head will be available. The salt ration is also cut to 1 oz. per week. At the moment the total rations for an adult are therefore as follows: $4\frac{1}{2}$ lb. bread, 5 lb. potatoes, 4 oz. of butter (in a meatless week), 3 oz. sugar, 7 oz. breakfast meal, 1 oz. salt—a total of 10 lb. 3 oz. The milk ration remains the same—half a pint per person per day, and one pint per day for juveniles.

June 17. Planes in the vicinity of the Island all day, with sounds of bombing from the adjacent coast. The Germans appear to be making preparations to defend the Island and mines are being placed everywhere. It is not known where the Germans are burying their casualties from the recent Allied air attacks, but no new graves have been dug in the German section of St. Brelade's Cemetery. Although the telephone service is only partly in operation, facilities are still available for church services to be relayed to various institutions. Children are buying marbles—on the black market—at twelve for half a mark (1s. 0½d.).

June 18. Sounds of gunfire closer as the Allies reach Barneville and Carteret, which are only about 15 miles away; many cyclists are visiting the north-eastern part of the Island in the hope of getting a glimpse of the battle. We were interested to learn that the correspondent of the National Broadcasting Company who, from Carteret, said that he could see Jersey, was named Larry Le Sueuer; also that troops captured by the Allies had recently come from the Channel Islands. Planes about all day and a lot of activity off the south coast. Some barges were attacked several times on the way from Granville and subsequently two came in, lashed together. A convoy was attacked by planes when off the Corbière, and out of eight ships at least three were damaged. During the morning several ambulances fetched casualties from boats in the harbour. Some French workers who had been imprisoned at Fort Regent by the Germans were observed today escaping down a wall bordering the 'Long Road'. It is also noted that Italian prisoners who have been allowed to roam the town at will, have now an armed escort for a very small group.

June 19. Several early-morning visits by planes. The German batteries opened up and two bombs were dropped at La Rocque, near a gun emplacement; widespread havoc was caused, a dozen houses being damaged; roofs were blown off and windows blown out of many others, and a crater was made near the roadway about ten feet deep and twenty feet across. Fortunately the casualties were slight. Residents of the damaged properties, helped by neighbours, commenced moving their furniture to other houses which were thought to be safer. Allied planes also did a considerable amount of machine-gunning in various parts of the Island. The Mont Ubé light remained lit all night. No extra rations issued this week, but the reduction in the bread ration has commenced. Reich-Germans are allowed 5 lb. of bread per head. Four years ago today the evacuation notice was published, and we are now in a similar state of tense excitement.

June 20. Rather reduced air activity today. The Germans are transferring large quantities of ammunition from Fort Regent to their tunnel in Grand Vaux, and they are also shifting cases of liquor from stores in town. There appears to be underground activity among the troops, and seditious propaganda has been widely circulated of late. The Germans published an article dealing with Allied air attacks on the Channel Islands, and

187

claim they recently shot down 12 machines, with six probables. The Department of Transport and Communications appeals for old cork, which is essential for maintenance of lorries converted to producer-gas. The harbour is full of all kinds of small craft, and late in the evening there arrived from the Cherbourg peninsula a large number of troops who are being evacuated to another part of France via Jersey.

June 21. Just after midnight German planes passed over; some of them were using the Airport. About 3.30 a.m. the German flak-ships off the harbour opened up and a low-flying German bomber was hit and set afire. Fortunately no one was injured among the civil population, but the whole crew of five perished—four on the spot and the fifth later in hospital. The wreckage was visited by scores of people, but they were chased off by sentries who fired warning shots. Shortly after the plane had crashed a large number of canisters was dropped by parachute in various parts of the Island; these canisters were four feet high, with a diameter of eighteen inches, and they contained ammunition, such as small-calibre shells; the only explanation was that they were dropped here in mistake for Cherbourg. In their descent a house at Samarès was badly damaged.

June 22. After a very quiet night, Allied planes re-commenced activity in the vicinity of the Island, the weather having improved. Before daylight German transport planes were using the Airport. The Island has been shaken all day by bombing and gunfire from the Cherbourg peninsula, and, probably, Alderney, which, we learned, had also been bombed. The Germans are loading barges with concrete blocks and preparing for demolition work. Seven small ships left for France, carrying a large number of Todts, foreign workers, etc.

June 23. German planes commenced arriving just after midnight and used the Airport. About 3 a.m. a terrific explosion was heard, and it was learned that there had been a naval brush off the south of the Island. A convoy from St. Malo was attacked by Allied planes, but managed to get away; when off Corbière, however, British E-boats closed in and a fight followed; the Germans lost two escort vessels, and a ship of about 60 tons carrying ammunition and petrol was torpedoed. It was learned the Germans had lost their mail, of which they have received none for the past three weeks. During the morning an American single-seater fighter came down at St. Ouen's owing to lack of petrol; the pilot was arrested and the plane put under guard.

June 24. Little air activity over the Island today, but sounds

188

of warfare from the adjacent coast are increasing. The Germans used the Airport in the early hours, transport planes arriving. There is a large number of naval craft in the harbour, the town being full of sailors. Crews of boats running from Jersey to France are not at all anxious to sail these days. The Germans have erected an anti-aircraft gun in a field alongside Overdale Isolation Hospital. A meeting of Constables was held today to discuss the measures to be undertaken if there is fighting in the Island. The Germans have passed sentence of two years' imprisonment on the lady from St. Ouen's—Mrs. Gould—who was recently arrested for giving refuge to a young Russian; lesser sentences were passed on three 'accomplices', but these are not to be served yet as the jail is full. A young man is undergoing a sentence of five months' imprisonment for having a wireless set, and another arrested some time ago for stealing ammunition has been sent to France. The Germans have given one of their officers—Sonderfuehrer Wolchen—the task of listening to telephone conversations (the part-service is still in operation). A limited quantity of kindling wood is to be made available to the public on ration—20 lb. for a mark (2s. 1½d.).

June 26. There was some shipping during the night, and the Mont Ubé beacon was lit; a boat which was loading cargo, including potatoes, has left, and the streets are clear of sailors. A list of first-aid posts is published today for people who may be injured through acts of war. Stallholders in the Old Market and part of the Fish Market have been warned they must vacate their stalls as this locale is to be prepared for communal feeding when the gas gives out. There has been very little air activity today—probably accounted for by the heaviest rainfall this year. The reduction in the bread ration now extends to people who formerly had special permits; ration is now the same as that for all other adults—4 lb. 4 oz.

June 27. Everybody is very pleased to hear of the fall of Cherbourg. The Constables of the Island, in collaboration with the Department of Public Health, are making provision for the lodging, etc., of persons whose homes may become uninhabitable by reason of war action; householders who can accommodate such distressed persons are asked to forward the necessary particulars; all food and clothing will be supplied by the authorities.

June 28. Allied planes passed over and the Germans fired from a few points. After this some German planes came in and landed at the Airport. In the early hours naval gunfire was heard from the south-west; a subsequent report announced that a British and a Canadian destroyer had engaged German heavily-armed trawlers off the Channel Islands, two being sunk and one probably sunk. Still later in the morning six fair-sized vessels, with an escort, arrived with 1,500 persons of all nationalities. It was learned they were foreign workers from Alderney, prisoners from a concentration camp in that Island, a few evacuees from Cherbourg and some foreign workers from Guernsey; military and naval personnel also arrived, as well as Jerseymen who had been working in Alderney. The prisoners were taken under armed escort to Fort Regent; some were in a pitiable state, and many were garbed in blue and white striped uniforms—Jews, Poles, Russians and even German political prisoners. The others, including many women, were lodged at some of the larger hotels, and quantities of mattresses and blankets were taken into West Park Pavilion.* A lot of German sailors were also about, and there were many cases of drunkenness.

June 29. There was no shipping during the night, but a large vessel arrived in the morning. Foreign workers swarmed the town again, and in the evening they were taken to the harbour. Indignation has been caused in the Island because about 20 local residents who had been sentenced by the Germans for various 'political' crimes were to be sent to France. It was learned at a later date that a German concentration camp was the destination of these poor unfortunates, some of whom were never to return.† About 11 p.m. everyone had embarked and 22 boats, barges and escort vessels left the harbour. During the evening all the boats sounded their sirens in honour of a German captain who had recently won the Iron Cross.

June 30. The boats which left for France last evening returned in the early hours and their passengers were taken back to their billets or to the Port Regent prison; it was learned that units of the British Navy had been sighted near St. Malo. A subsequent B.B.C. report announced that two heavily-armed German trawlers had been sunk. The workers were about town during

---

* The Pavilion was one of the first places the Germans occupied, using it as a transit camp for men travelling to and from France. Although a guard was on the door, the manager was allowed to go in and out and he saved the china and glass, the grand piano and the carpets.

† Among these people were Mrs. Gould, of St. Ouen's (see June 24), and her brother, Mr. Harold Le Druillenec. Mrs. Gould was taken to Ravensbrueck concentration camp (probably the most notorious in Germany), and no more was heard of that lady, while Mr. Le Druillenec was—as far as is known—the only Briton to come out of Belsen alive.

the day; a special performance was given for them at The Forum, and the Italian cafés were crowded, there being a rush on substitute coffee and synthetic lemonade. At night they embarked again, and this time the boats went by a different route. The local prisoners have also gone, fifteen in all; two of the original number have been allowed to remain here.

The end of the fourth year of Occupation finds us more optimistic than we have ever been. With the invasion now in full swing and the sounds of battle within hearing, we feel confident that our release will not be long delayed. The Germans appear to have relaxed a little; many are now to be seen in town without their equipment. There seems, too, to be a more restrained note in the news items which the *E.P.* is ordered to publish. During the past month planes in increasing numbers have been over the Island, and German convoys sailing to France have to dodge units of the British Navy. The recent rain has done good; the wheat crop ought to be the finest we have had and main-crop potatoes are going well.

JULY 1944

July 1. The Germans are searching for a young Irishman who was due for deportation and who escaped from the public prison. Several official notices published today: one warns the public that the gas supply will cease about the middle of August and that supplies of house coal will be very limited; provision is being made for communal cooking and/or communal feeding. There is to be a supplementary potato ration of two pounds for male manual and agricultural workers to compensate them for the reduction in their bread ration. Impôt officials are to inspect the tobacco crop, and penalties will be imposed for growing tobacco without a licence. A local tradesman has been fined £15 with £5 costs for attempting to sell a second-hand suit for £19, the clothing being sequestrated. The *E.P.* publishes a leading article referring to the four years of Occupation, which gives expression to what the majority of Jerseymen feel. It is indicative of the present mood of the Germans that it passed censorship without alteration: the regular censor, is away on manoeuvres at the moment. A fuel ration for July and August is available to persons holding special permits, but the quantity is halved.

July 2. Today the harbour is almost empty. Only one plane

was heard over the Island during the day; the weather is still very bad, with plenty of rain. The B.B.C. has announced that a German convoy off St. Malo was intercepted by British naval forces; two heavily-armed trawlers were sunk and some ships damaged. The body of a high German military officer was picked up by a local fisherman off Corbière today; it bore the Iron Cross and had not been in the water very long.

July 3. Two barges brought from Guernsey about 100 tons of tomatoes which flooded the local shops and found a ready sale at three pounds for a mark (8½d. per pound). The Germans now require seventeen head of local cattle per week to augment their meat supply. They have recently brought some from France, these are in fine condition and are being grazed at St. Peter's in the charge of a French cowman. Supplementary rations this week include 1 lb. 5 oz. of extra sugar for everyone for jam-making, half a pound of macaroni per head, and a packet of boiled sweets for children and juveniles. One boat left harbour late in the evening with the remainder of the foreign workers who arrived here from Alderney a week ago; the boat was escorted. Among those leaving was a young Jersey boy who mingled with the crowd so as to escape from the Island; he was on probation, as he took part in demonstrations when the deportees left in 1942, but expected to be called for again by the Gestapo. We learned that a few days after his arrival in France he managed to get out of the camp in which he had been placed and contacted the American forces at St. Lo, eventually arriving in England.

July 4. The only boat to enter the harbour was a hospital ship, formerly the *Bordeaux*, a German troop transport. Residents on the south coast saw flashes of naval gunfire, and a subsequent B.B.C. announcement declared that light naval forces had intercepted a German convoy off St. Helier and opened fire. For some days now single leaflets printed in England have been found in various parts of the Island warning the inhabitants to keep away from gun emplacements, etc., and to take cover in the event of any fighting; it is thought, these were intended for Alderney, and had got blown here. Some of the French workers have attempted to obtain work on farms; many of them are refugees from the Cherbourg area and are without homes; the Germans give warning that these people should not be helped as they are to be repatriated to their own country and that any assistance given them would aggravate the local food position. After an interval since the start of the invasion German police are again fining cyclists for riding abreast. Another requisition of cycles is being made. The weather continues to improve, and several times during the day Allied planes were over the Island.

July 5. Planes were over in great numbers during the night; there was no A.A. fire. Mails which are being delivered to the German troops probably arrived on the hospital ship yesterday; letters from Islanders deported to German camps—Biberach, Laufen and Wurzach, all in Southern Germany—have also been received. After a lull the Island is again being shaken by the effects of bombing or gunfire on the adjacent French coast; many fires may be seen at night by residents on the north and east coasts. One result of the invasion has been to send the black-market goods soaring to unprecedented levels, for it is realised the possibilities of getting goods from France are now very slender. The ban on entertainments remains, but the Germans have re-opened The Forum for the troops, a certain type of civilian grasping the opportunity to attend as well.

July 6. No boats went out during the night, but a couple of barges sneaked in, and are loading with potatoes, the bulk of which are for Guernsey. Planes were over in large numbers but they were not fired at. Very heavy bombing and gunfire were heard from France. Sleeping accommodation has been arranged at the Town Hall for policemen who may be away from home when a state of emergency is declared; the Bailiff and the Attorney-General have been informed that in the event of such an emergency they will have to stay in their homes until fetched by the Germans and then be accommodated in the States Building. All sorts of wild rumours are circulating in town and the bakers have been notified that they must bake an emergency supply of bread. A resident of St. Martin has been sentenced by the Germans to eleven months' imprisonment for having a wireless set, his wife to five months and his daughter to two months; his son was sentenced to three weeks' imprisonment for being in possession of a leaflet.

July 7. Planes were over in the early hours and at noon; more groups were about later in the day, and during the evening a single plane was overhead for a long time, presumably on reconnaissance. The two barges loading with potatoes have left. The following is an abbreviated summary of a notice published by the States under the heading 'Issue of Emergency Rations of Foodstuffs': The Occupying Authority has intimated that the military situation may at any time result in the declaration of a state of emergency within the Island. In the event of such a declaration two consequences will immediately follow—(1) the civil population will be required to remain indoors in their own homes, and (2) The distribution of foodstuffs will be entirely suspended. In these circumstances the Superior Council of the States has resolved, with the approval of the Occupying Authority, to issue forthwith to every member of the civil population a supply of foodstuffs to be kept as an emergency ration for use during any period when foodstuffs may not be normally obtainable. The foodstuffs, which are issued free, must not be consumed now, and anything perishable must be replaced from the normal ration; it is pointed out, too, that in the event of the possibility of the declaration of a state of emergency no longer existing, the emergency ration now issued will be taken into account in the issue of future normal rations. Each person is to receive 3 lb. of bread, 5 lb. of potatoes, 3 oz. of sugar, 2 oz. of butter, 8 oz. of macaroni, one tin of sardines, and for all children born on or after July 1, 1942, there will be 12 tins of condensed milk.

July 8. The large quantities of tomatoes from Guernsey and the local ones becoming more plentiful have caused a glut; greengrocers' shops are doing a roaring trade in tomatoes at 12 lb. for a mark (2s. 1½d.) and a motor lorry is making a tour of the town suburbs. The tobacco ration ceases today with an issue of 12 cigarettes; local tobacco is fetching two and three marks an ounce in the black market.

July 9. No shipping during the night, excepting the usual patrol boats. The weather is bad again. A large quantity of Guernsey tomatoes, loaded for France in ships which called here en route and then apparently could not get away, was brought into the town today and the shops were allowed to open to sell them, in spite of it being Sunday; over the week-end one store sold over 22 tons of tomatoes, 3½ tons of which were locally grown. It is believed that some 11,000 German soldiers, marines and Todt workers are now on the Island.

July 10. Following the B.B.C. instructions given yesterday, many people have commenced making crystal sets, but it is difficult to obtain the essential components. Stallholders in the Old Market, who were warned to leave as the market was to be converted into a communal dining hall when the gas supply runs out, have been notified these arrangements are cancelled for the time being. Three boxes of matches issued today as an extra, and the emergency rations are also being delivered. Many a cat is facing starvation for lack of the limpets with which it was formerly fed.

July 11. More planes than we have heard lately passed over in the the early hours; the weather continues to be very bad. Farmers with lorries are notified that petrol will be supplied only if not less than two tons of potatoes are carried. The Department of Public Health issues an augmented list of first-aid posts and points which will function after an alarm; at first-aid posts the services of a doctor will be available. The Germans announce a naval engagement in the Gulf of St. Malo, in which, as usual, they came off best; their patrol boats 'forced enemy destroyers to withdraw'. The Germans have been making inquiries about facilities for getting barges, etc., away from small harbours in the north and east of the Island, especially at St. Catherine's.

July 12. There has been a lot of plane activity. In some parts the Germans are cutting quantities of wheat and hay from places in which they are to dig trenches or make gun positions. All sorts of wild rumours are circulating in the town following reports that the Germans have cancelled some of their orders for supplies; the German bakery in Victoria Road has dispensed with the services of some of the girls who were employed there packing bread for export. We were interested that Mr. Eden has announced the repatriation of British civilians interned by the Germans in Germany or German-occupied territory, and wonder if this will include the local residents deported to Germany in 1942. There has been a large-scale round-up of persons accused by the Germans of having frequented a house in Queen's Road for the purpose of listening to the B.B.C. About 10 p.m. ships were seen approaching the Island from the southeast; the convoy entered harbour and was found to consist of a ship, which carried cargo, and seven escort vessels; a large quantity of flour, butter and eggs was unloaded.

July 13. Planes were over during the night, but the weather deteriorated again and there was no air activity all day. Two barges left for Guernsey with potatoes which had been loaded a few days ago; mail was also carried. From today the Germans have permitted Wests Cinema to re-open on Thursday and Sundays from 7 to 9 p.m.; civilians may also attend The Forum on Wednesdays and on Saturdays in the afternoon, to see the films now being shown to the troops. A few secret dances—rather thinly disguised as 'dancing classes'—are being held by local parties, and many sweepstakes are being run based on the day on which the Union Jack will be hoisted again. The Germans have re-commenced sports in a small way.

July 14. The Department of Transport of Communications announces the amount of petrol available for civil purposes is not sufficient to cover the transport of potatoes to St. Helier, and that no more will be issued after the 15th inst.; to meet farmers' requirements, a number of gasogene lorries has been made available, a charge of 9d. per barrel being made. A small amount of cotton material for women's summer frocks is on sale, and among black-market goods it is noted that nutmegs are selling at 2s. 1½d. each!

July 15. Planes were over during the night and one seemed to be circling for a long time. A group of German planes passed over from west to east—a large transport plane, escorted by seven fighters—and Allied machines were about all day, one group in the evening receiving a heavy A.A. barrage. The harbour is empty save for the usual half-dozen patrol boats and the hospital ship. Some leaflets in French have been picked up in various parts of the Island. A bad case of milk adulteration before the Royal Court resulted in a fine of £30 and costs being imposed. The public are notified they must register if they wish to avail themselves of the service arranged for cooking meals in bakers' ovens, when the fuel supply for domestic purposes comes to an end. One meal will be cooked per day per family.

July 17. There has been no movement of shipping, the harbour remaining almost empty. The Germans are still making arrests in connection with the Queen's Road wireless case. Appeals are being made for donations to the Children's Benefit Fund. The bakers are using a proportion of sea water for the making of bread. This week is quite a good one for extra rations, with ¼ lb. of coffee substitute and ½ lb. of macaroni for everybody, a packet of saccharin tablets for adults, and a jam ration commencing again alphabetically, the issue this time being described as 'jelly marmalade'.

July 18. Planes over all night and all day, the weather having improved considerably; there was only a little anti-aircraft fire. The Germans have been sharpshooting today from Elizabeth Castle* towards the beach. Large numbers of people are register-

---

* The fortifying of the Castle was carried out between 1942 and 1944, Russian and other forced labourers being employed on the works. The German garrison numbered about one hundred men. They were housed in the Officers' Quarters in the Lower Ward and the Governor's House in the Keep. Their kitchen was situated in the 1746 building at the southern end of the Lower Ward. Their batteries and shelters were fitted with every kind of scientific apparatus necessary to the comfort and protection of the occupants, and bottled Vichy water, stored in special compartments, formed their reserved supplies of drink!—*Elizabeth Castle*, by Major N. V. L. Rybot, D.S.O., F.S.A.

ing to have their food cooked in bakers' ovens when the gas supply finishes.

July 19. Planes at night and, after an early-morning fog had passed, large numbers over and around us all day; there was more A.A. fire than usual and some very heavy explosions were heard. A group of five escort vessels or E-boats came into harbour during the morning. The Opera House is to re-open on Tuesday and Saturday evenings for films and variety shows. The bakers are offering to make rusks out of the emergency bread ration, so that it will keep. The German naval guns at St. Martin's opened up today on Allied shipping off the French coast.

July 20. A convoy of eleven ships, including escort, arrived from Guernsey; a barge brought a large quantity of tomatoes and cucumbers, and a number of Todts have arrived on the way to France. Following the recent talk from the B.B.C. regarding the construction of crystal sets, it is estimated that there is more listening-in than at any time during the Occupation.

July 21. Sentences were passed by the Germans today in connection with infractions of the Wireless Order on several residents; they ranged from 18 months down to two months, and many are to be served at once. The Germans are making more 'look-outs'—fire-control points—in walls, etc., everywhere, for the purpose of sniping, the latest including some along the Esplanade and the Yacht Hotel basement.

July 22. The harbour was empty, save for a few escort vessels. It was heard with interest today that the B.B.C. had declared an area off the French coast, including the Channel Islands, is unsafe for fishermen, as in this area a free bombing policy was to come into force with immediate effect. The Germans are advertising for a young man who has been missing since the beginning of the month. The emergency ration of 12 tins of condensed milk is now extended to children born between July 1, 1941, and June 30, 1942. A ration of kindling wood is being made available to householders under the 'plan of emergency fuel allocations', and the public is advised to reserve this fuel. The Germans have warned farmers, etc., not to deal in unauthorised sales or exchanges of potatoes with members of the civil population, German units, or members of such units; they point out that potatoes are an essential item in the rationing scheme and that infractions of the Order will entail severe penalties. At the Royal Court today fines were imposed in two cases of keeping unregistered pigs—£20 in one and £30 in the other, both with costs. The Lending Department of the Public

Library sets up a new record with 775 issues in one day.

July 23. After a quiet night, planes were over several times during the day; the weather has improved somewhat and sounds of bombing or gunfire were heard from the French coast after a lull of a few days. Some medical supplies and footwear have arrived from France.

July 24. No extra rations issued this week. The Germans warn residents about hiding foreign workers and cite prosecutions which have recently come before the military courts. A further supply of ladies' stockings is to be made available; these have come from France, but, 'Summerland' is also turning out a fair quantity of silk stockings, and 200 pairs of sandals are now being manufactured there per week.

July 25. At about 11 a.m. we were treated to a glorious sight when we saw about 1,500 Allied planes passing to the south of the Island after an attack on the Cherbourg peninsula. A colony of Colorado beetles has been discovered in a patch of potatoes at Verclut, Grouville, under cultivation by the German army of Occupation, and precautions are being taken to confine the pest; unlike the farmers, the Germans have not bothered to spray, and even now will not burn the patch. Soldiers are searching the haulms to find the beetles. The Germans have opened up some of the beaches for bathing for the civil population between the hours of 9 a.m. and 6 p.m. In consequence of a new decree, the Germans are all giving the Nazi salute, instead of the military salute as formerly. The Department of Transport and Communications advertises for two lorry drivers to drive States vehicles in St. Malo. The Department of Agriculture publishes the prices to be paid for this year's cereal crop: Wheat, 28s.; oats, 22s. 6d.; barley, 32s. 6d.; rye, 39s. Victoria College Terminal Service held.

July 26. The Department of Public Health is making an appeal for bandages.

July 27. The Germans carried out their usual Thursday gun practice today. The B.B.C. has announced the renewal of the warning regarding fishing in the Channel Islands area.

July 28. Only one or two planes during the night and in the day. People in the eastern parishes could see explosions on the French coast as the Americans approached Coutances. St. Martin's Parish fixes the Rate at 2s. 6d. per quarter and St. Mary's at 1s. 6d.

July 29. With the occupation of Coutances, the Americans have now gone past this Island. A barge and a small vessel came in from Guernsey, bringing tomatoes, a small number of troops and Todt workers, and some French civilians. Wests and the Opera House are now allowed to be opened three times a week. In a notice regarding the new fuel ration books which are being issued, it is stated these now cover the whole of a household. At the Royal Court a man charged with growing tobacco without a licence was fined £25 with costs, and the crop is to be confiscated; a fine of £5 with costs was imposed on a grower for failing to deliver potatoes to the Potato Control.

July 30. A few aircraft over at night, but many during the day; one group flew very low over the west of the Island, and after the Germans had opened fire they machine-gunned gun positions. Some boats took away troops, workers and a young Englishman who was recently sentenced in connection with the Queen's Road wireless case. This week's extras: half a pound of macaroni. The two lorry drivers recently advertised for by the States to drive lorries in St. Malo have also left the Island; there was a large number of applicants. Many foreign workers are deserting and looking for jobs on farms, etc., requesting no pay but only their food, so anxious are they not to return to France.

July 31. During the morning thirteen boats, barges and escort vessels entered harbour, presumably from France; some coal and cattle arrived for the Germans, and among goods for the Department of Essential Commodities were much-needed salt and soap. The Island has got back more or less to conditions existing before the start of the invasion, especially now some places of entertainment have been re-opened. There appears to be no sign that the Germans are going to evacuate, though a few officers have been notified they must leave for France. Arrests are still being made of persons accused of listening to B.B.C. news bulletins. The Germans have also arrested two women and a man at St. Brelade's for spreading anti-Nazi propaganda. The women are French subjects and are alleged to have been responsible for pamphlets, etc., circulated among the troops; recently, packets of cigarette papers have been found bearing translated B.B.C. news. These women were eventually sentenced to death, but later reprieved, and they were liberated a quarter of an hour before Mr. Churchill's speech on VE-Day. The month has been a bad one for weather.

August 1. The harbour is full of shipping, and in the evening two boats of the minesweeper class went out. The telephone service is restored from 8 a.m. to 8 p.m. each day. St. Helier's Parish Assembly fixes the Rate at 3s. 2d. (no change). Details issued of arrangements made for communal cooking and catering which will come into effect when the gas supply finishes; at that time electric current for cooking purposes will also cease, as well as fuel for Aga cookers, etc. Oven space is being allocated at the various bakehouses, the charge for cooking to be 3d. per container; those who wish to avail themselves of communal restaurant facilities must give up part of their potato ration and the whole of their meat ration, which will be utilised in part provision of each meal.

August 2. Large numbers of planes were over all day, but, as usual, the Germans withheld their A.A. fire. The harbours are full of small naval craft, barges and cargo ships. A boat arrived from France today and some troops from Guernsey on their way to France. The Germans have commandeered the salt which arrived two days ago. St. Ouen's fixes the Rate at 2s. 3d.

August 3. Sounds of explosions on the French coast have continued into the early hours. A considerable amount of shipping has left for Guernsey, carrying cargo which included some cattle.

August 4. A quiet night and quiet day as regards planes. The B.B.C. announced today that St. Malo was cut off and that the position of the German garrison there and in the Channel Islands was very delicate; it was added there were signs that the Germans were trying to withdraw from the Channel Islands, but up to now there is no indication of it, as far as Jersey is concerned. A number of foreign workers, mostly Dutchmen, have apparently no chance of getting away, and the Germans are employing them on a road they are constructing in the Grands Vaux Valley.

August 5. A quiet night for planes, and not many in the day. In the morning eight ships entered harbour from France, these including three landing barges. Some troops arrived who had apparently been evacuated, and about twenty American prisoners were also brought; some of the latter were wounded and were taken to hospital, but the remainder were imprisoned. The B.B.C. announced there was no confirmation that troops were being withdrawn from the Channel Islands. St. Malo is now cut off and, as the Americans have reached Brest there is no chance of the Germans in these Islands getting away. Three barges left for Guernsey late in the evening. German Order registered by the Royal Court warning the public against making unauthorised use of the Red Cross or the Cross of Geneva, or using imitations calculated to deceive. They would do well to abide by this Order themselves! Several farmers fined for infractions of the Milk Control Order by not bringing in their milk at the appointed time. Fines of £25 and £5 were also imposed for tobacco-growing infractions. Among the latest wireless offenders is a policeman, and at St. Peter's there have been inquiries regarding people who have batteries charged regularly.

August 6. In the afternoon four large German torpedo-boats came into harbour at full speed, having managed to get away from France; the naval personnel were accommodated at one of the Weighbridge hotels and were soon about the streets of the town. In many churches today (Sunday) collections have been taken for the Children's Benefit Fund, which is still doing excellent work.

August 7. August Bank Holiday: glorious weather, but not much of the holiday spirit. A lot of bathing and there were many horse-drawn vehicles on the roads. The harbours are now full of all sorts of shipping—thirty-two ships of all kinds, exclusive of small naval craft. The hospital ship left for France in the late afternoon. The Germans look very gloomy, for they must know that they are virtual prisoners, but many declare they are glad that for them the war is over; the restrictions on them are relaxed somewhat, and many no longer carry equipment. German Military Police have made their re-appearance, looking for offenders against traffic regulations. This week's extras are sweets and toilet soap for juveniles.

August 8. Sounds of bombing, etc., continued throughout the night and day, with the drone of planes never absent; the warning sirens at German anti-aircraft posts were continually sounding and, as usual these days, some of the guns were never left unattended. The Germans are after foodstuffs for the troops, such as butter, and they are slaughtering a number of horses each week to be made into sausage meat. In the evening the hospital ship returned from St. Malo with wounded soldiers, and these were taken to the various German hospitals. Twenty American prisoners who were brought here and taken to the hospital a few days ago are still there, and wave to the passers-by from the windows.

August 9. At about 8 a.m. planes machine-gunned German gun positions at Elizabeth Castle; there were casualties. There has been some movement of shipping. In the early hours a convoy which left for Guernsey was attacked by American E-boats in the St. Helier roadstead. Casualties have been taken to hospital, and these together with the German wounded brought yesterday by the hospital ship (between two and three hundred) are giving the German doctors a busy time. The Opera House and Wests are now to open all the week, and this evening the Green Room Club presented a play at the Opera House. St. Brelade's fixes the Rate at 2s. 6d. By German Order, harvesting is to be carried on on Sundays, if necessary, so as to make the most of the fine weather. The Germans must also be given notice of changes of tenant of farms, and increases in rents are not allowed. The laundries give notice that they will have to remain closed each alternative week.

August 10. An Allied seaplane came down in St. Ouen's Bay to pick up survivors of yesterday's naval engagement, and the Germans fired on it as it took off with a heavy load. The harbours are crowded with all sorts of vessels; there are over fifty in all, and some have to be accommodated in the Old Harbour. Many of these have come from St. Malo and other ports on the French coast bringing large numbers of soldiers, sailors and Todt workers. Some have come from Guernsey and Alderney; there being a rumour that Alderney is being partly evacuated. Many hotels in the neighbourhood of the Weighbridge have filled up and the town is crowded with newcomers, sailors predominating. German sentries near the Weighbridge are not allowing anyone near the harbours. All day there has been a constant stream of traffic to the east of the Island, where 5.9 guns are being erected between La Coupe and Rozel.

August 11. Several planes over during the night, but some of these must have been German, as they were flying low and singly. The Germans are looking for billets in the Rozel districts for crews for the guns taken there yesterday. We have learned with interest that Channel Islands evacuees are getting ready to return home; this gives the impression that the Islands may soon be relieved. Some of the Americans recently brought here are convalescing and parcels are being sent to them in hospital or in prison; they have asked for a football, but the Germans are taking care they do not come into contact with local residents. The body of an American naval rating has been picked up at St. Ouen's. Petrol is not allowed to be consumed by lorries carrying potatoes or vegetables; horse-drawn vehicles or producer-gas lorries must be used.

August 12. The German medical staff is totally inadequate to deal with the large number of casualties recently brought in, which results in untold suffering for men who need urgent attention; help offered by local doctors has been refused. The body of an American airman has been picked up on the east coast. The Royal Court today with another tobacco-growing infraction, a fine of £8 being imposed. The Germans have published an Order forbidding the gleaning of corn while stooks are still standing and the field not raked. Portelet Bay is now open to bathers. This morning a rumour went round that some Americans were in a barber's shop near the Royal Square; in no time a crowd numbering several hundred gathered in the vicinity and resisted all efforts of the local police to move them along; German Military Police then took a hand and became very nasty when they found their efforts unavailing; as a final resource they took away the identity cards of about fifty people, who will have to fetch them from College House and, presumably, pay a fine. A young man has escaped from the German section of Gloucester Street Prison.

August 13. Not many planes during the night and only a few over in the day, but some terrific explosions took place in France today, the resultant vibrations being the strongest we have felt. No movement of shipping until the evening, when a convoy left for Guernsey. According to German sources Alderney has been almost completely evacuated. The Germans have placed a water tank on Grève d'Azette beach from which a pipe is run to their bakery in Victoria Road to supply sea water for use in the making of bread; this caused some amusement, for it was placed there at spring tide and had to be moved lower down the beach when the tide commenced to neap.

August 14. More signs of naval activity were seen to the south just after midnight; this is almost a nightly occurrence, with the guns at Noirmont joining in, and at times the whole of the south coast illuminated by searchlights. The extra rations for this week are $\frac{1}{2}$ lb. of macaroni and $\frac{1}{4}$ lb. of cheese per head; the cheese is to take the place of the extra butter recently issued in weeks when there is no meat. The Germans are to have an extra ton of butter per week, but they are making up for this by having skimmed milk, the cream from which goes to make the butter. From today the German bread ration is cut to half a pound per day. Those persons who had their identity cards taken away on Saturday fetched them from the College House today, where fines imposed varying according to the means of the offenders. Some of the American prisoners recently brought here are working at the Airport—weeding, etc.

August 15. It was announced today by the B.B.C. that Alderney was bombarded by H.M.S. *Rodney* on the 12th. Three American naval ratings were buried in the Island War Cemetery in Howard Davis Park this morning; their names were D. A. Bricker, R. E. Horsfield and R. W. Schaffroth. The Germans provided a naval firing party, but members of the public were excluded as the Germans thought there might be a demonstration. Grouville fixes the Rates at 2s. 7d. per quarter.

August 16. There has been no movement of shipping, and some of the smaller craft are to be taken to St. Aubin's Harbour. The Germans advertise for an Irishman and a Jerseyman who have been missing for some time, and give warnings of severe punishments for any persons sheltering them; they also admit that thirteen Russians are in hiding and warn farmers not to give them work or shelter. Some parcels of food have been smuggled in to the American prisoners who are feeling the change to German rations rather keenly; they are disgusted with these, especially the soup, which they call 'Nazi hog. swill', and they are all craving for 'candy'. The Germans want a large number of horses for eating purposes; to replace these they will 'lend' some of their lighter draught horses.

August 17. The Germans have issued an Order that all wheat is to be threshed first and oats, etc., afterwards; they want at the moment 10 tons of wheat, 600 tons of straw, and other goods. Some wheat is to be sent to Guernsey. The Germans have 600 horses in the Island, and it is estimated the number of soldiers, sailors, Todts, etc., is in the region of 14,000. Numbers of these fill the town every day and buy all the greenstuffs and fruit they can. The German sailors have been told they must undergo land training and will have to defend the Island to the very last man. The Germans must now obtain a permit to ride a cycle. The Parish of St. Peter fixes the Rate at 2s. 9d.

August 18. Five of the wounded Americans who were at the General Hospital have been removed to Merton Hotel, which is now the German main hospital. Kindling wood is selling at 10 marks a hundredweight (£1 1s. 4d.).

August 19. Two boats left harbour and have been moored at St. Aubin's. The Germans have placed four guns in the Parade and manholes continue to be dug in all sorts of places. At the Royal Court a grower was fined £10 for selling green peas above the fixed maximum price. The price of locally-grown tobacco is now controlled: leaf or unmanufactured, 16s. per lb.; manufactured (excluding cigars, cigarillos and cigarettes), 2s. 1½d. per oz.; cigarettes 2s. for 20. Many persons are being fined for bathing in prohibited areas; the usual procedure is adopted—identity cards taken away, to be fetched at College House, where the fines are collected. Conditions at the General Hospital remain appalling, but the Germans still refuse help from local doctors.

August 20. No air activity night or day. In the early hours some boats arrived from Alderney and Sark; all sorts of materials were landed, as well as horses, cattle, guns and ammunition. About 300 personnel also came, and all day there has been a stream of lorries taking guns, etc., to La Coupe, to swell the large number already in that district. There were 36 ships of all kinds in the harbours today, and it has been learned that the garrison at St. Malo was kept supplied with bread and water by a barge which left each night.

August 21. No air activity during the last 24 hours, and there was heavy rain all day. Dr. Shone, as representative of the Red Cross, is being allowed more freedom in visiting the American wounded or prisoners, and they are receiving parcels of foodstuffs, etc., quite regularly. The farmers are very annoyed over the Germans commandeering horses, for making into sausage meat; they want 350 in all, and will pay only up to 200 marks per animal (£21 17s. 4d.). As an alternative to payment they offer to loan one of their younger horses, the farmer being answerable to the Reich for 1,200 marks if anything happens to it while in his custody.

August 22. About 2 p.m. two planes from the direction of the French coast swooped down on gun emplacements at Sorel Point and machine-gunned the crews, there being a number of casualties. A German sailor who had deserted and had been living with a local woman in the Pier Road district was finally run to earth by the German Military Police. He managed to escape but later in the evening committed suicide. The Fifty-Fifty Club present a play at the Opera House.

August 23. There are over thirty ships of all kinds in the harbour, and the *Robert Mueller*, a 1,100-ton vessel, is being fed with oil from some of the other ships, while the *Bordeaux*, the 'Red Cross' boat, is to have some berths placed in her and the gun platform removed. Everyone overjoyed to learn of the liberation of Paris.

August 24. Although there were no planes during the day, there had been more than usual in the early hours, these being low-flying German machines coming from France. Later in the morning two small boats arrived and about twenty seriously wounded Germans were landed and taken to hospital many had beards of several days' growth and came from the Island of Cèzembre, off St. Malo, which is still holding out. It is understood that supplies are being sent at night to the garrison there. [St. Malo surrendered on the 16th.] Some of the minesweepers, etc., moored for some time in the harbours of St. Helier and St. Aubin, have had their depth charges and paravanes removed. Guns have also been removed, to be placed at strong-points all over the Island.

August 25. Heavy bombing heard as Brest is being severely attacked. Several prople in the Grève d'Azette district have been arrested by the Germans for wireless offences, one being a radio repairer. All day there have been propaganda meetings for German troops, sailors and marines at The Forum; they were told, inter alia, that they would soon be back in France—maybe this is quite correct! The Germans ordered the States today to provide the money necessary to pay their personnel, and arrangements for this purpose have been made with the various banks.

August 26. Few planes in the early hours, and none during the day. Late at night, the supply boat for Cézembre left harbour, only to return on account of Allied naval craft in the vicinity. The beach of St. Aubin's Bay, from the Grand Hotel to Bel Royal, has been opened for bathing from 9 a.m. to 6 p.m. At the Royal Court today fines were imposed in two cases for infraction of the Tobacco Law. The Colorado beetle has now been found at St. Brelade's and Longueville.

August 27. In the evening a brawl occurred among some sailors leaving a café in Colomberie, and ended by one of them being stabbed to death. There seems to be less discipline in the navy than in the army, and the sailors are not very pleased at having to be aboard ship at 10 p.m.

August 28. The sailor who was stabbed yesterday was buried this morning in the Strangers' Cemetery, without honours, as he was guilty of 'dishonouring the flag'. Forestry permits are being granted to farmers to enable them to fell trees for their personal use, in lieu of wood rations. The Germans give warning that no vegetables or fruit may be sold by farmers or growers directly to the forces or to individual members; this does not apply to greengrocers, etc., but the quantity to be sold by them is limited. This week there are extra rations per head of two bars of chocolate cream and 4 oz. of cheese.

August 29. Three boats left harbour today—for Gorey, where

they are to be laid up. The Germans offer a quantity of stable manure to farmers, preference being given to those who will be required to deliver straw to the German Forces. The Germans also invite applications from farmers who are willing to exchange old horses under the slaughter scheme, which, apparently, is being made voluntary instead of compulsory. A naval picket now patrols the town each evening.

August 30. St. Saviour's Parish Assembly fixes the Rate at 2s. per quarter.

August 31. Large-scale air activity has become a thing of the past. Apart from an occasional boat to or from Guernsey, shipping is static. Leaflets in German were dropped during the night by an Allied plane. Sailors were busy early picking them up, but not before many had been found by the troops and local residents, the latter keeping them for souvenirs. Trinity Parish fixes the Rate at 1s. 6d. per quarter. The Island being entirely cut off from supplies, conditions are gradually deteriorating, and not improved by the fact that the German Forces here number nearly sixteen thousand. Over six hundred of these are wounded, and the diminishing supply of medicaments is causing the German staff no little anxiety. Butter has gone right off the market, but some unscrupulous farmers are quite willing to sell it to the Germans at anything up to 25 marks (£2 13s. 5d.)! The Island is now in a state of siege, and on behalf of the Superior Council of the States the Bailiff has forwarded a Memorandum to the Occupying Authorities calling attention to the serious situation which will arise in the event of this being unduly prolonged. A report by the Medical Officer of Health (Dr. R. N. McKinstry) concluded as follows:

'It was recognised within a few hours of the invasion of Normandy by the Allied Forces that whatever might be the immediate or ultimate result of that military operation new factors faced those Island Authorities, civil and military, who were responsible for the lives of the civilian population. Constant consultations have taken place between the Insular Government and Occupying Authorities. Every phase of the, first slowly and then swiftly moving, course of the military operations in France has been carefully studied in relation to its bearing on the problem of the maintenance of life of the people of Jersey. It has, throughout these consultations, been apparent that the time would come, sooner or later, when the Occupying Authorities would desire to make the Insular Government aware of the date after which, in the opinion of the Occupying Authorities, the increasing state of siege could no longer be maintained with due regard to the maxims of International Law. The Insular Government has just heard with dismay that the Occupying Authorities are of opinion that the siege can be maintained until January 31, 1945. For the reasons stated in the foregoing Memorandum the Insular Government does not, and cannot, share that opinion, and declares in the most solemn manner possible that in the view of the Insular Government it is the bounden duty of the Occupying Authorities to re-examine the problem in its entirety and in the light of the observations contained in this Memorandum.

'Sooner or later the clash of arms will cease, and the Powers will meet not only to consider the means to an enduring peace, but also to pass judgment on the authorities, be they civil or military, upon whose conceptions of the principles of honour, justice and humanity, the fate of peoples and places, and not least of occupied peoples and places, has temporarily been determined. The Insular Government believes that, at that day, it or such of its members as survive will stand with a clear conscience born of the conviction that it has failed neither in its duty to the people of Jersey nor in its interpretation and observance of the rules of International Law.

'May the Insular Government be spared the duty of adding to the problems which will face the Powers an allegation that, by an unjustified prolongation of the siege of Jersey the military representatives of the German Government unnecessarily endangered the health, and indeed the lives, of the people of Jersey.'

SEPTEMBER 1944

September 1. Some leaflets, in German were dropped again during the night. About 1,500 German naval personnel attended a propaganda meeting at The Forum today; they marched there headed by a fife-and-drum band, and it is reported that, they were told that the naval personnel in Jersey would form the vanguard when the Germans re-took the Channel Ports! The German 'hospital ship' *Bordeaux* left harbour in the afternoon, and, later in the evening, a barge left for Gorey, but had to return on account of the stormy weather. The fuel ration for this month for an average family consists of half a hundredweight of anthracite dust (which may be mixed with tar, obtainable at the Gas Works), and a hundredweight of wood.

September 2. No planes and no shipping. The weather is very stormy and many people are gathering twigs in the country lanes to augment the meagre fuel ration. At the Royal Court today a farmer was fined £60, with costs for keeping pigs without a licence, and fines were imposed in three cases for growing tobacco plants in excess of those for which a licence had been obtained.

September 3. There is a report that the German hospital ship which left here two days ago has been intercepted, for she was due to return next day and has not yet done so. Today (Sunday) saw the commencement of harvest festival services.

September 4. The War news was overshadowed today by the fact that the gas supply terminated at 7.30 a.m. All sorts of arrangements for cooking have been adopted by householders and the communal feeding centres are catering for people who have forfeited their meat ration and a part of their potato ration, but some of the bakers' ovens do not function too well not having been used for a long time. Most people have taken a philosophical view of the situation, which is not without its humorous aspect, and some enterprising young men have opened up hot water supply depôts, this useful commodity being sold at 3d. per quart! There is enough gas to keep Mrs. Fraser's communal feeding centre going for some time, and the German newspaper is also to continue, which means that the special main put in for this purpose will enable the *E.P.* to be published also. The Jersey Gas Light Company has worked consistently to postpone the evil day when their supply to the public would cease, and, in common with the policy adopted by many local concerns, continually furnished the Germans with incorrect facts and figures when ordered to give account of the company's affairs.* For three nights from tonight the electricity

---

* This first started over three years ago when the Germans, in order to reduce consumption of coal gas for gas making to the total allocated by their headquarters in Paris, required the hours of gas supply to be restricted. As the Germans were under the (false) impression that the troops were using about half the gas manufactured, these coal allocations were 45 per cent. from German Army of Occupation in France supplies, and 55 per cent. from French civilian supplies. To avoid inconvenience to the civilian population of restricted hours of gas supply, the Gas Co. (under the authority of the Department of Essential Services) persuaded the Germans to allow them to 'ration' gas to the civilian population. This 'ration' of gas

supply is to be cut off from 11 o'clock until 7 a.m., as an experiment. The whole supply now comes from the coal-driven plant which was erected by the Germans in St. Peter's Valley, but which does not function too satisfactorily. This cutting off of electric power is a great inconvenience, particularly to nursing institutions and, perhaps most of all, to the Dispensary (Maternity Hospital), where they have to manage with a meagre supply of candles. The elementary schools resumed today after the summer holidays; the problem of clothing for children is very acute, and many are barefooted. Among today's advertisements is one for an experienced tanner.

September 5. Further restrictions are placed on the use of electricity—the use of permanent-waving apparatus is prohibited, and the following businesses and establishments may not use electricity on Mondays, Wednesdays and Thursdays (the days when most shops are shut): Auction rooms, bazaars, bookbinders, breweries, builders, carpenters, confectioners, cinemas, coachbuilders, dance halls, decorators, drapers, ironmongers, jewellers, marine store dealers, milliners, mineral water manufacturers, musical instrument dealers, opticians, painters, pawnbrokers, photographers, quarriers, second-hand dealers, stationers, tailors, tobacconists, theatres, woodworkers. St. Lawrence fixes the Rate at 1s. 3d. per quarter. Cyril Medland presents a musical revuette at the Opera House.

September 6. Several groups of planes were about during the day, and one machine is reported to have fired on a German gun position at Westmount. According to a German source, naval ships in harbour have been ordered not to fire on passing aircraft. A British destroyer was seen today off the West of the Island and the Germans fired at her. The bakers' ovens are now functioning very well and proving a great boon; many Gas Works employees are working in the bakehouses. The Germans are taking quantities of barbed wire from fields, etc., to place round their billets, and some has also been put round a door at their hospital at Merton Hotel. One German, when asked what the wire was needed for, said that it was to put round a con-

---

was worked out based on 55 per cent. of the coal used. Actually, throughout the Occupation, the civilian population consumed over 85 per cent. of the total gas made, so that 30 per cent. of the gas made was used by the civilian population unknown to the Germans. When in due course gas coal became more difficult to obtain, and following direct orders from Paris, restricted hours of gas supply had to be applied. It may be added that no gas consumer was ever prosecuted for exceeding his 'ration'.

centration camp for British, Canadian and American prisoners!

September 7. Gas lamps are now being cleaned, and an itinerant hot-water seller has made an appearance in the streets of the town. Ann Street Brewery is supplying hot water free of charge. Football started again today; the Germans also had a naval match on, this ending in a fight between two of the players. A week has now passed since the Germans received the States Memorandum; there has been no official reply, but it is believed it has been favourably received.

September 8. A few single planes about today. Another series of robberies has commenced, fowls and rabbits being among the goods stolen. Presentation made to Mr. C. J. d'Authreau, of the G.P.O., in recognition of his services in connection with the Bailiff's Enquiry and News Bureau; the presentation took the form of a picture by Edmund Blampied entitled: 'A Jersey Family Receiving a Red Cross Message'. Since the Bureau was opened in 1940 the number of original messages sent from Jersey was 92,041 and the replies received on the reverse of Jersey forms numbered 33,262; original messages received from England were 235,744 and the replies sent also totalled 235,744 —a very creditable achievement. A local resident who was recently arrested by the Germans for repairing wireless sets has been sentenced to two years' imprisonment. St. John's Parish fixes the Rate at 2s. 6d. per quarter.

September 9. By order of the Germans, the electricity supply is to be cut off at midnight until 6 a.m. Licences are revoked for a number of appliances, including refrigerators, but may be obtained for electric fires in cases of persons over 80 or under two years of age, as well as in serious medical cases. Two barges left for Guernsey laden with 900 tons of stores for the military, including flour, wheat, potatoes, hay and straw; eight escort vessels accompanied the barges, but five of them went only half-way and then returned, having been relieved by similar ships from Guernsey. The Germans have made several more arrests for wireless infractions, this time in the St. Brelade's area.

September 10. More leaflets have been dropped. From today the state of alarm which had existed since the invasion has ceased; German troops are no longer carrying arms and several restrictions placed on their movements are removed. A house-to-house search was made today in the neighbourhood of St. John's Church: as a result of this, the Germans re-captured three Russians who had been at large for some time.

September 11. What is now referred to as the 'mail plane' dropped its usual batch of leaflets during the night; this time they fell in the neighbourhood of Havre-des-Pas. An attempt to escape from the Island has had an unfortunate ending: three men tried to get to France from Icho Tower; they were using floats, and owing to difficulties which befell one of them they missed the tide that would have carried them to the French shore and drifted towards the Paternosters; they eventually landed at Grève-de-Lecq and were taken into custody by the Germans. The full telephone service has been restored. This week's 'extra' consists of 4 oz. of cheese, which is as usual, to replace the extra 2 oz. of butter issued during a meatless week.

September 12. Last night's leaflets fell mostly in the western parishes; the Germans have put a young lady in prison for two days for distributing leaflets to her friends. Sounds of distant bombing heard today—more than for some time. The Germans exploded a mine in the Beaumont district, one house suffering extensive damage to windows as the owner was out and therefore not warned. Some irresponsible person has sent anonymous letters to several local residents, accusing them of having collaborated with the Germans.

September 13. Leaflets in the Samarès district this time. The Germans have searched houses in New Street and Don Street; it is presumed that missing Russians were being looked for, as the search was not as thorough as it would have been for wireless sets. A small boat arrived from Guernsey with mail. Dancing is to be resumed again.

September 14. Although the 'mail plane' was heard, no leaflets have been found, and it is presumed they fell over the sea. During practice by light artillery on the beach near West Park some houses at First Tower were damaged by shellfire, one of them rather seriously. Four Allied bombers passed over during the afternoon. A meeting of medical practitioners has decided to appeal to the Germans to be allowed to send a ship to Cherbourg to get much-needed medical supplies, the shortage of which, especially anaesthetics, has become acute. The Germans today passed sentences of eight months and nine months respectively on two local residents for being in possession of wireless sets.

September 15. Several more robberies reported; pigs have been taken from many places in the country, and as shots have been heard in some cases there can be little doubt as to who the thieves are. German sailors in groups were in Valley-des-Vaux —picking blackberries! Arrangements are being made for infirm persons to have their meals taken to and from the bake-houses. The Department of Labour published a report of its various activities since its inception in 1940; it is a comprehensive document and discloses the many and serious problems which had to be faced at the commencement of the Occupation. In the words of the *E.P.* it 'should afford much food for thought to those who, at times, may have felt critical of the manner in which the Department undertook and dealt with a situation so completely without a precedent in the history of the Island'.

September 16. Two lots of leaflets found this morning—dated the 14th and 15th—most at Grouville and around Victoria College. The 'mail plane' was over again at about 10.15 p.m. with the next issue, these falling in the St. Brelade's district. A German ship in harbour is flying the quarantine flag. A young female resident and a Dutchman got away from the south coast after dark in a rubber boat. A letter was left behind stating they hoped eventually to reach England and they had taken information of conditions here.

September 17. The change in British Summer Time has inconvenienced owners of wireless sets, as it is now one hour behind Central European Time. Two barges arrived from Guernsey today with escort; they brought 330 ton of coal for the St. Peter's Power Station, and some munitions.

September 18. The newspaper plane was over at about 10 p.m.; leaflets were dropped at Grouville and Havre-des-Pas, but one container did not burst and the whole consignment fell in a field at Bagot; early next morning local residents got it away, before the Germans could find it, and in the evening an organised distribution was carried out in various places where troops are billeted. Residents in the west of the Island declare Allied warships are constantly off the coast. This week's extra rations consist of $\frac{1}{4}$ lb. of coffee substitute and $\frac{1}{2}$ lb. of macaroni per head, and another jam ration (orange and apple) commences alphabetically.

September 19. A correspondent complains about the high price of kindling wood; he alleges he has paid a mark (2s. 1½d.) for a hamper containing 3½ lb., which works out at about £70 per ton! Misfortune has befallen the couple who left the Island in a rubber boat on Saturday (the 16th), for, after being at sea since then and having spent about half that time on a rock, they landed at Corbière this evening under the impression that they were on the French coast. They were very surprised when a German guard asked them if they had come from Brest, and they were than taken into custody.

September 20. Residents of Le Hocq were awakened by cries for help coming from the sea before daylight; these gradually grew stronger and, as visibility became clearer, three figures were seen—two in the water and one marooned on a rock. The Germans at Rocque Berg could not provide much assistance, but focused searchlights as two local residents made attempts at rescue. A canoe was found to be useless, but a ship's raft was obtained and with this the person on the rock was rescued; the two others managed to get ashore by themselves, all being in an exhausted condition. They were found to be three youths out of a party of eight who had attempted to escape from the Island during the night in three canoes; one had become waterlogged and eventually sank, the three occupants attempting to regain the shore. The other five youths managed to get away. The three unsuccessful ones were immediately interrogated by the Germans and then taken to the German section of the German Hospital; later in the day they were subjected to a series of questionings. A young lady who, on seeing the youths in the ambulance, said to one of them 'Hard luck', was also detained by the Germans. An unfortunate circumstance, which may affect the position of these youths, is the fact that they were on two years' probation for having been involved in demonstrations when British subjects were deported two years ago. The Germans have published a notice warning that 'desertion to the enemies of the German Forces' is forbidden and will be severely punished as espionage. The Germans also give warning that it is forbidden to cross areas in which iron, concrete or wooden poles with connecting wires have been erected, with laden vans or similar vehicles, the height of which exceeds two metres, and that the tethering of cattle to these poles with connecting wires or pegging-out cattle in the immediate vicinity is dangerous. During the evening more German patrol boats then usual went out, but this did not prevent another party of four getting away, although details are lacking. The Amateur Dramatic Club is presenting a comedy at the Opera House, commencing on a Wednesday so as to comply with the recent orders regarding economy in electricity.

September 21. Those who were arrested yesterday for trying to escape from the Island are continually being taken for questioning from one German official to another, and as they go through the town under guard they give friends the 'thumbs-up' sign. Firing by German heavy guns has gone on all day, increasing towards the evening, when it is believed Allied naval craft were near. Three more got away tonight—the skipper of one of the barges, whose home is between Portbail and Carteret, a young Frenchman who had been working for the Germans, and the son of a St. John's farmer; they did everything quite

214

openly and used a boat from one of the German vessels which they had painted a different colour. They went from Fauvic, after having tested the motor of the boat in a farmer's yard, and the information they took with them included plans of fortifications and mining of the harbours. The Germans are trying out a new dodge in regard to cycles; they are stopping cyclists in various parts of the Island and after ascertaining the machine has good tyres, saddle, etc., take the number; the object of this appears to be that any cycles which may eventually be called in for requisitioning cannot be tampered with and parts changed. The news plane resumed its service tonight and leaflets were dropped in the outlying suburbs of the town, falling on many people who were hurrying home just before curfew.

September 22. The Germans have sentenced Detective-Constable Shenton to four months' imprisonment for being in possession of a wireless set, and to an extra week for having a camera. A young lady resident of St. Lawrence was sentenced to three months for distributing leaflets, and the present manager of Wests has to serve a sentence of two weeks for translating a leaflet. Spools of 500 metres of rayon sewing thread available on ration at 1s. 8d. each. More sounds of bombing were heard today than for some time.

September 23. The electricity supply is to be available again for the full 24 hours, but the public is reminded of the need for economy; this has been made possible through the arrival of coal from Guernsey last Sunday (the 17th). The public is again warned about the water supply. A party of five local men who went into Grouville Bay during curfew to get their nets ready for fishing was seen by a German guard after daybreak and held in custody for five hours before being transferred to town for questioning; the Germans thought it was an attempt at a getaway, but let them go after hearing their explanations. A relative of one of the party of five who escaped from Le Hocq on the 20th declares it has been announced over the Paris radio that they arrived safely in France, their names being mentioned. A barge laden with wheat left for Guernsey during the afternoon. The news plane was over about 9.30 p.m. and dropped its load in the Le Hocq district.

September 25. This week's extra rations consist of ½ lb. of macaroni and a ¼ lb. of cheese per head—the latter instead of the extra butter issued in a meatless week—and four boxes of matches per household. The retail price of sugar-beet syrup has been reduced from 5s. 6d. to 3s. 10d. per lb. During the evening the electricity supply failed in several districts. An explanation

215

published subsequently by the Electricity Company pointed out that the demand during the evening exceeded the capacity of the St. Peter's Power Station; in consequence it was necessary to reduce the supply and, in order to avoid undue inconvenience to the public, eight districts were cut off for ten minutes instead of one district for eighty minutes. This procedure is to continue whenever necessary, economy again being urged.

September 26. From a German source it was learned that a Canadian Major and member of the Canadian House of Parliament had recently arrived off Guernsey in a destroyer flying the white flag as a sign of truce. The story was that a pinnace took him into the harbour area, where he was met by a German boat; he asked to see the Commander in order to discuss the military situation, and, after some delay, received the reply that in the Commander's opinion there was no need for a discussion as he was fully aware of the military situation. The pinnace then returned and the destroyer steamed away. Souvenirs were said to have been exchanged between the crews of the pinnace and the German boat, and it was subsequently learned the Germans considered it was a breach of military etiquette to send a Major to interview a General! Following this information, the usual crop of rumours flooded the Island; one was to the effect that the Germans would capitulate within 48 hours, while another had it that the Bailiff had gone on a destroyer to interview the King behind Elizabeth Castle! Deputy Le Quesne, head of the Department of Labour, has been sentenced to seven months' imprisonment for being in possession of a wireless set, but he is to be allowed out one day per week to attend to business. An auction sale in aid of the Children's Benefit Fund has realised £153.

September 27. General von Schmettow, Military Commandant of the Channel Islands, who is stationed at Guernsey, arrived here today and is staying at Government House; he came from the sister Island on an 'artillery float' and landed at the Victoria Pier. The Germans advertise for women and girls to repair soldiers' clothing, for which they are offered good wages. The body of an American airman has been washed up at St. Ouen's.

September 28. General von Schmettow is holding conferences with German officials. In the late evening a party of five young men took a boat to Pontac with a view to escaping; they had stolen the necessary petrol from a German garage and the boat was transferred from town in a lorry. They were due to leave at about 9.30, but, owing to delay in getting the petrol, did not get away until 3 o'clock the next morning. Some time after they had arrived at Pontac, however, the Germans must have got to know that there was something going on, for searchlights and tracer-bullets lit up the area for a considerable time, the escapees sitting calmly under the sea-wall until the display was over.

September 29. General von Schmettow inspected sailors in training at Trinity during the morning. The Germans have arrested an Italian who has been their buyer of foodstuffs in the Island since the commencement of the Occupation; he was in possession of a wireless set, about two thousand British Treasury notes, and large quantities of German tobacco and cigarettes. Searches for wireless sets are continually going on. More and more crystal sets are being used, some being attached to telephones, and innumerable little gadgets have been made for connecting to radiogram amplifiers.

September 30. Major von Heldorff, adviser to the Military Commandant of the Channel Islands (General von Schmettow) interviewed the Bailiff at his Chambers this morning, von Heldorff was stationed in Jersey for some time, but transferred to Guernsey earlier in the year, and he has been in the Channel Islands long enough to know something of the conditions prevailing here. The body of the American airman found three days ago was buried in the War Cemetery at 9 a.m.; his name was William H. Parks. The usual service was held, the same officials being present, with the exception of Dr. Shone as representative of the Red Cross, who was replaced by Dr. Hanna. The Germans had deposed the former for having been found passing a note to American prisoners when he took them foodstuffs. The American Colonel who is a prisoner of war was allowed to be present at the ceremony, and, afterwards, to talk with the Bailiff and other officials. At their request for exercise, the Americans were taken to the grounds of Victoria College today, but the Germans locked the gates at each end so that they would not come into contact with local residents. The month of September finds the Islanders rather depressed and inclined to take a gloomy view of the approaching winter. Fuel is one of the problems affecting most people, though it must be admitted the bakers' ovens are a great boon; apart from a few isolated instances, they are doing wonderfully well. The problem of footwear is also acute, all available leather now having been used up, while clothing devoid of patches or darns is thought the hallmark of distinction. Apparently the news plane has now ceased its visits, no leaflets having been dropped for a week. There are about two dozen ships in the harbour, in addition to small craft, but there is little or no activity; numbers of sailors are now billeted at Fort Regent. Sentences are still being passed on local residents for all sorts of petty offences, such as wearing a red-white-and-blue favour in the button-hole, but in most cases wireless infractions are more severely dealt with, though many sentences are remitted after part has been served. Whether this is due to a general relaxation on the part of the Germans or to the fact that the jails are overcrowded, one is not certain, but it is considered an honour to belong to the ever-growing body of those who are now facetiously termed 'Old Glostonians'!* At the moment there is an abundance of apples, but pears are very scarce. Groups of Germans are always out blackberrying and raiding orchards or pear trees; they also buy large quantities of sugar-beet with which to make syrup for mixing with the fruit, as they are badly off for sugar. The following list of prices generally prevailing for black-market foodstuffs and other essential commodities makes interesting reading after 4½ years of occupation: Butter, £4 5s. 6d. per lb.; sugar, £1 1s. 4d. per lb.; flour, 4s. 3d. per lb.; salt, 10s. 8d. per lb.; beef, 17s. 1d. per lb.; pork, £1 1s. 4d. per lb.; tea, £20 per lb.; eggs, 2s. 1½d. to 3s. 2d. each; bread, 6s. 4½d. per 2-lb loaf; saccharins (packet of 200), £1 1s. 4d. per packet; potatoes, £1 10s. 0d. per cwt.; wheat, £8 per cwt.; potato flour, 6s. 4½d. per lb.; firewood, 7s. 6d. per barrel of 20 lb.; matches, 1s. 0½d. per box; candles, 2s. 1½d. each; soap—toilet, £1 per tablet, washing, £3 per bar; cigarettes, 12s. 9½d. for 20; tobacco, 6s. 4½d. per oz.; whisky, £10 per bottle; hot water, 3d. per quart.

OCTOBER 1944

October 1. The fuel ration for this month consists of one hundredweight of wood blocks for an average family, with a small quantity of coal in special cases on medical recommendation. A single plane was over the Island during the afternoon and a British or Allied cruiser was sighted off St. Brelade's. The Department of Public Health is making an appeal for clinical thermometers.

October 2. The clocks have gone back today with the end of Central European Summer Time and we are now in line with

---

* The local prison is situated in Gloucester Street.

British Summer Time. From midnight the electricity supply was cut off until 6 a.m.; it was cut off again from 1 to 6 p.m., and again at 11 p.m. until 5 a.m. tomorrow. Great inconvenience was caused to many businesses through the afternoon cut, for there was no warning. The Germans have been placing anti-tank defences around the harbour area and in many places are strengthening their barbed-wire barricades. They want twenty head of cattle from each parish per month, and contemplate sending a German official round with the milk testers. Many bakers have run out of yeast and are now using sour dough as an alternative. The only extra ration for this week is a piece of toilet soap for the children and juveniles; adults have not had a toilet soap ration for three months.

October 3. Owing to boiler trouble at St. Peter's Power Station, until further notice the electricity supply will be cut off during the following hours: 1 p.m. to 6 p.m., 11 p.m. to 7 a.m. It has been learned that the five young men who escaped from the Island on September 28th have arrived safely, a code message having been received through the Paris radio. Today's *E.P.* contained one of the best bits of information we have read since the start of the Occupation, the following having been handed to the editor for publication:

re SUPPLIES FOR THE
CHANNEL ISLANDERS

In order to keep the population informed about the question of supplies, and to stop injurious rumours, the Commander of the Channel Islands has authorised this paper to publish the following information:

The Channel Isles had virtually been cut off from all supplies already a month before the invasion. From that moment the population lived on the produce of the Island, and from stocks which had been formed according to instructions from the Occupying Power. In view of the possibility of a state of siege, agriculture and industry had been adapted as far as feasible to make the fortresses self-supporting.

As the population, however, cannot be supplied indefinitely from the stocks of the fortresses, or from the produce harvested or manufactured within them, the Commander of the Channel Isles some time ago took the precaution of getting into touch with superior authorities, and has informed the German Government of the situation.

This action was appreciably facilitated by reports about the most essential commodities, supplies of which were running out in the near future, submitted by the Bailiff in the interest of the population of Jersey.

The German Government has intimated its intention of taking the necessary steps in this matter with the Protecting Power. For this purpose the Commander of the Channel Isles has submitted a report about the Island's monthly requirements of essential commodities.

Any action the Protecting Power may decide to take on this information is now, of course, beyond the control of the Occupying Authorities.

October 4. Although many people are sceptical regarding yesterday's information concerning the possibility of getting supplies to the Channel Islands, the majority are greatly relieved that something is being done to ease the situation. Another change has been made in the hours of electricity supply, which will remain on all the time until the end of the week; many districts now have their supply cut off, however, when the load becomes too great. This is usually in the evenings, and the period of cut-off varies from ten minutes to half an hour, the sudden plunging of everything into darkness causing no little inconvenience. This evening the Green Room Club commenced a four-day run of a comedy at the Opera House; the lights were cut off for half an hour during the performance, but this had been anticipated and an emergency system was used consisting of three motor-car headlamps in the orchestra well and lights from car batteries in the wings. A small quantity of poultry food, consisting of winnowings, offals, etc., is to be made available from time to time for small poultry-keepers who do not grow cereal crops; this is conditional on the surrender of three eggs for 28 lb. and six eggs for 56 lb., the eggs to go to the various institutions; the number of poultry kept must be stated. For some time the Germans have been requisitioning 50 eggs from each parish once every twelve weeks, paying 6d. for each egg, but this has now been increased to 100. The water situation has become acute and the Fire Brigade has had to pump water from Le Mourier Valley into the Handois Reservoir as this had got very low; the consumption of water by the Germans without any regard to economy and their interference with several streams when making fortifications have combined with the lack of rain in the last twelve months to create a problem which gives cause for great anxiety. It was announced through the B.B.C.

that a question regarding the Channel Islands in the House of Commons received the following answer: 'The Germans in the Channel Islands have been given the chance to surrender, but have refused; there is nothing to show that they are not treating civilians properly.'

October 6. Several official notices issued. Maximum prices for kindling wood fixed at 2s. 1½d. of rough, uncut kindling wood, and 3s. 2d. for 20 lb. of kindling wood cut up and ready for use. Infants' wear permits are to be called in for examination in order to facilitate the manufacture of essential baby clothing from available stocks of material. A ration of flints for mechanical lighters is to be issued, which works out at the rate of one for each holder of a tobacco ration card. The supply of French 'biscottes'—pieces of toasted bread issued to invalids in lieu of part of their bread ration—has now ceased. A German Red Cross plane arrived at the Airport during the morning and left later in the day; the Bailiff's Enquiry and News Office was informed and a small parcel of priority Red Cross messages was collected for dispatch. An advertisement in today's paper offers £5 6s. 10d. for a cycle tyre. The Germans today imposed a levy on the State of a further 1¼ million marks; this makes a total to date of 6 million marks, which is over £600,000.

October 7. The Royal Court today imposed a fine of £20 with £5 costs for a Tobacco Tax infraction; £30 with £5 costs for keeping a pig without a licence and fines of £1 and £10 respectively in two cases of ration book frauds. Further cuts are to be made in the public water supply, which is to be turned on for five hours only per day—7 to 8.30 a.m., 11.30 to 1.30 p.m., 5 to 6.30 p.m., with a variation of times for certain districts. The Germans have commenced stopping cyclists in the outlying districts and examining their baskets for black-market goods; if anything is found and no satisfactory answer is forthcoming, the goods are confiscated and the cyclist's identity card is taken away, to be fetched from College House.

October 8. From today until further notice, the electricity supply will be cut off from 1 p.m. to 7 p.m. in order to conserve the Island's fuel stocks; it is pointed out that when the demand exceeds the capacity of the St. Peter's Power Station each district will be cut off for a short period, as in the past, and stringent economy is again urged. The crews of the German naval craft in the harbour held a miniature regatta in the harbour at high water. At night a young man and a young lady made their escape from the Island, leaving St. Martin's in a boat at about 10.30.

October 9. In one of the first B.B.C. news bulletins today it was stated that plans were being put into operation for the commencement of the Channel Islands air service after the Islands 'had been liberated'. More explosions were heard from the French coast during the day, and the theory was propounded that mines were being exploded in that area. The rations for this week are augmented by $\frac{1}{2}$ lb. of macaroni and $\frac{1}{4}$ lb. of cheese per head, the latter in lieu of the extra butter previously issued in a meatless week. General von Schmettow, Military Commandant of the Channel Islands, who has been on a visit here for some days, returned to Guernsey this morning on the 'artillery float'; since his arrival there has been a tightening-up of discipline, particularly in regard to naval personnel. Deputy Edward Le Quesne, head of the Department of Labour, went to jail today to commence his sentence of seven months, but it is understood if he behaves himself he will do only two weeks and the remainder after the war! Three lots of young men left the Island in the evening from points along the east coast; one of the boats was taken to the starting point in broad daylight! Many letters have been taken by those escaping to relatives of local residents.

October 10. The engineer and manager of the Jersey Electricity Co. gives a detailed reply to an observation that warning should be given of the cutting off the supply each evening. He states that permission has been obtained from the Germans to cut off each district at the same time every night for a week, due notice being given; in conclusion, consumers are warned that they must be prepared for shut-downs at any time, without notice. Now that kindling wood prices are controlled, none can be purchased, it having disappeared 'under the counter' to be sold at higher prices. Wood merchants, however, declare that the controlled price is insufficient, as enormous sums have to be paid at sales of wood, thus greatly affecting the retail selling price. The German shop which has for a long time been open for members of the Forces on Burton's premises has run out of supplies, and today workmen were cleaning German lettering off the windows. Orders have been given by the Germans that a pilot boat is to be got ready to meet the Red Cross ships when they arrive! The Germans have extra patrols around coastal districts in the evening, but in spite of this a party of four young men got away from a point in Grouville Bay. Sentences have been passed of six and twelve months respectively on the young girl and a Dutchman who made an unsuccessful escape from the Island on September 16. A sentence of 15 months had previously been imposed on another would-be 'escapee' who got into difficulty off the Paternosters on September 11.

October 11. The party of four who tried to escape last evening have met with disaster. It appears that the boat became swamped and that they had to put into Anne Port. When they had got ashore they brought up the motor of the boat and other equipment, but the Germans, hearing movements, sent up Verey lights and challenged the figures they saw on the beach; there was no reply and shots were fired, one of the party, Douglas Le Marchand, aged 19 years, being killed. The remainder were arrested, and with the boat taken to town, then put into prison. A German plane was over the Island in the early hours and Allied planes were in the neighbourhood of the south coast at odd times during the afternoon. There is a theory that these planes may be searching for the companions of some who have managed to get to the French coast. An appeal is made today for old motor tyres, 'owing to the lack of leather for repairing footwear and the urgent need for a substitute'. The German Censor has been tightening up lately on advertisements which contain a hidden meaning or are offensive to the Occupying Authorities; several of these have slipped through from time to time, but today the whole of the *E.P.* edition had to be reprinted because an advertisement inserted by the Jersey Gas Company did not meet with the Censor's approval.

October 12. The Germans have ordered that no cereals are to be sown for harvesting in 1945, all ground lying fallow to be planted in vegetables only; this will mean that about 600 ton of wheat kept for seed will be available to them for 'other purposes'. The weather continues stormy, but a small boat arrived from Guernsey with mail for the German troops, which had been flown to Guernsey a couple of days ago; she also brought grapes for the troops. A bag containing letters addressed to relatives of local residents has been picked up on the east coast. These are some which were to have been taken away by 'escapees' and apparently dropped on the beach, for they were quite dry when found. It is learned that young Douglas Le Marchand was shot through the head, but the Germans are guarding all particulars of the affair with great secrecy.

October 13. The Germans publish a notice stating that they have fined a local resident 200 marks (£21 17s. 4d.) for buying butter on the black-market. Re-registration with retailers for potatoes is ordered, application being conditional on not more than 28 lb. being held by each member of a household. St. Mark's Church celebrates its centenary.

October 14. The Germans this morning made a large-scale raid on persons coming into town from the country, to ascertain if they were carrying black-market goods. The Feldgendarmerie were established at approaches to town, particularly West Park and Georgetown; vans and baskets were searched and large quantities of goods taken away. At West Park the haul was particularly heavy, the shelter being used for the temporary storage of the various articles found; these included all classes of rationed goods, such as butter, milk, etc., and also some unrationed goods, such as eggs and apples. There were protests and a lot of uncomplimentary remarks; identity cards were taken from persons who were cheeky, and in cases where the quantity of goods was considered excessive. The cards must be fetched from College House, where explanations as to the possession of the goods involved are to be offered. German soldiers were also searched, for they have lately been buying heavily on the black-market with the extra money they receive as 'siege pay'. The news spread quickly and various ruses were adopted to pass the barriers with goods intact, alternative routes to town being used. The Attorney-General went to College House to protest, and was assured it was a mistake and would cease immediately; it was admitted there had been many robberies by the troops, and as the Feldgendarmerie had received a rap on the knuckles for not being more vigilant, the consequence was they had become over-zealous. Cycles were also taken from cyclists riding two abreast today, the Germans handing over 50 marks for each machine. Four more escapees got away during the night in a 12 ft. boat from Grouville Bay; they were a local youth, a French skipper and two French engineers; eight others got away at about the same time from Le Hocq beach. Residents on the north-east coast declare that the Carteret lighthouse is now lit every night.

October 15. From today the electricity supply is to be cut off from 1 p.m. to 6 p.m., with the exception of Sundays, when it will be on all day so that the Germans may enjoy wireless entertainments in their billets and concerts at The Forum. The time of cut-off in each district changes every week, due notice being given in the Press. Many people went to College today to fetch their identity cards; in some cases fines were imposed, and in others some of the goods, such as flour obtained from gleanings, were returned. From a German source it is learned that during the morning four men arrived on the beach at Gorey; they fixed sails on a boat and in broad daylight went off under the nose of the German guards. At 8.30 p.m. there was a

224

general alert which lasted for a few hours; the Germans manned all their posts. It was subsequently learned that Allied warships were in the vicinity of the Island, and the Germans feared a landing.

October 16. The lad Douglas Le Marchand was buried this morning. The funeral service was held at St. Thomas's Church at 8 o'clock, but the public had been kept in ignorance of the hour of the service as the Germans feared a demonstration. There was a large number of wreaths. In today's paper the Germans issued the following warning:

'Between 5 and 6 o'clock in the morning of October 11, the commander of a patrol in the eastern part of the Island noticed a dark, moving object on the beach about 250 yards from the coast. In the flare of a Verey light which was sent up it was possible to make out four or five people who were busy with a boat and who took cover from the flare of the light. As no answer was given to a challenge and the persons tried to escape, they were fired at. A civilian was killed and the other three were captured and arrested. They proved to be local young men who were trying to escape from the Island.

'Attention is again drawn to the notice by the Fortress Commandant of September 20th, 1944, giving warning against leaving the Island. Anyone aiding an escape, such as supplying a boat to be taken by lack of precaution, is also liable to punishment. Anyone going on the beaches round the coast during the darkness of night is playing with his life. He risks being fired upon without warning.'

The local resident who sold the boat in this case has been arrested and placed in jail. Half a pound of coffee substitute issued this week.

October 17. The Germans withdraw permission for the civilian population to bathe from the beaches of Grouville Bay, St. Clement's Bay, St. Aubin's Bay, Portelet Bay and the Bathing Pool, with immediate effect. Bathing at other points around the Island is forbidden, as before, and the civilian population is forbidden to go on to the beaches anywhere. Commanders of strongpoints are empowered to grant permission to limpet-gatherers who are known to them to go on the beaches in day-time; gathering vraic is allowed as before. A man who was moving a boat in a lorry has been arrested by the Germans, as have five youths who were to have used the boat. Mr. Cyril Medland presents a musical show at the Opera

House, but this is affected somewhat by the cutting of the electricity supply.

October 18. The Germans published the following in today's paper under the heading 'What Constitutes the Black Market?':

'The Platzkommandantur makes the following statement:

'Rationed goods must not be freely dealt in, either by sale, barter or gift. All foodstuffs fall under the heading of rationed goods except poultry, eggs, vegetables and fruit.

'The sale of vegetables and fruit to the troops can only be made by dealers in the town and country. Producers (farmers and gardeners), on the other hand, are forbidden to sell vegetables and fruit to members of the Forces. Dealers are only allowed to sell to a member of the Forces sufficient fruit for the man's own use, i.e., one kilo per head (2¼ lb.). Wholesale purchase for units is forbidden. These measures are taken in the interests of the civilian population and to guarantee sufficient vegetables for them.

'For this reason, the sale by farmers of sugar-beet and apples to the troops is particularly forbidden. The only exceptions are in the event of the purchaser producing and giving up a permit stamped by the Platzkommandantur I.

'As every kind of cereal is on the list of rationed goods, the giving up of cereals by the producer, be it by sale, barter or gift, is forbidden. Farmers are only entitled to retain for their own use what is left over in the threshing. The retaining of large quantities is not allowed. The milling of the grain by the mills is limited to 28 lb.

'Every attempt to retain larger supplies of rationed or unrationed foodstuffs for sale or purchase at a higher price is an offence against the community, and will be dealt with by stern measures.'

The meaning of this notice is not quite clear, but it seems to be an attempt to explain away last Saturday's hold-up of persons going into town.

October 19. The Germans are watching cyclists again to see that their lamps are properly blacked-out, a reminder having been issued that the slit through which light is emitted must remain as before—4 centimetres by 1 centimetre. The German notice of yesterday dealing with the non-supply of goods to the troops by shopkeepers amounts to nothing, for soldiers are now furnished with permits in virtue of which they demand all sorts of vegetables, apples, etc., in large quantities.

October 20. The Germans have placed their own inspectors on the threshing machines to see that no 'hanky-panky' goes on; these are soldiers who were formerly farmers, and, apparently, with the exception of one, they can be easily handled, some even helping with the work. They openly declare they are not interested in what happens to the wheat and that as long as they are well looked after will not see anything!

October 21. An attempt has been made to get away from the Island by a party of youths who some time ago stole the boat from the Waterworks Company's reservoir at St. Lawrence. They were to have put off from the little Bay of Bel Val, near St. Catherine's, but apparently the attempt did not go according to plan, for the Germans found the boat abandoned and confiscated it. A ration of 10 lb. of kindling wood is to be issued for one week; this is priced at 1s. 0½d., and consists mostly of chopped-up green logs. At the Royal Court today a fine was imposed of £30 with £5 costs for keeping an unregistered pig. These cases have been less frequent of late. The Germans have authorised the Bailiff to make the usual announcement regarding the placing of wreaths on cenotaphs and soldiers' graves on All Saints' Day, All Souls' Day and Remembrance Day.

October 22. The Germans visited a house today in the course of their investigations regarding some people whom they believed to be preparing to leave the Island. A search revealed a wireless set and the family was arrested and placed in jail; later, however, two were released. At the moment the jail has 105 occupants, and many have had pieces of furniture sent in so as to be more comfortable! In the afternoon an 'artillery float' left for Guernsey with some high German officials, and at night another four people escaped from the north-east coast; these were a local man and a girl and two Dutchmen.

October 23. A barge arrived from Guernsey during the night; the cargo included 200 tons of coal (Guernsey, by the way, still has gas), 600 cases of grapes for the Germans, a small quantity of wool and some ammunition. Some mail also arrived, mostly for the Germans; they get very little home news these days, but publish in their newspaper a list of members of the Forces to whom greetings from home have been sent. Half a pound of macaroni per head is being issued this week as an extra, and there is also to be a meat ration. [For some time there has been meat every other week only, and in the meatless weeks we had 2 oz. of butter and then 4 oz. of cheese, but cheese stocks are exhausted.] The *E.P.* warns the public against an individual who is selling packets of washing powder as baking powder, with the result that food has been rendered uneatable. The black-market price of baking powder or bi-carbonate of soda is about 20 marks a pound (£2 2s. 8d.). This month has been very wet up to now, and in the past eleven days the rainfall has measured 2.69 inches. A special meeting of the Superior Council today discussed demands by the Germans for 20 ton of butter and 30 ton of coal and coke. Protests by the Bailiff resulted in the quantity of coal and coke being cut down by four ton, and a threat that, if the protest against the requisitioning of butter were persisted in, the Germans might find it necessary to requisition supplies of whole milk, instead of skim as at present.

October 24. By directions of the Platzkommandant, a new Order is issued entitled Control of Mills (Jersey) Order, 1944; this prohibits the carrying on of the business of miller except under licence, and licence-holders may not accept from any one person more than 28 lb. of cereals for milling, unless a permit from the Department of Agriculture is forthcoming. The wholesale price of eggs is fixed at 7½d. each and the retail price at 8d.; this seems a ridiculous order when the average price of an egg is a mark and a half (3s. 2d.)! During the afternoon a German Red Cross plane arrived at the Airport, this giving rise to all sorts of rumours. At night a party left the Island from Grève d'Azette; they took a large number of letters.

October 25. A local resident who was serving a sentence of 15 months for attempting to escape from the Island made a daring escape today. A German who was interested in some fishing tackle he had for sale took him from the jail to his residence to fetch a net; when they got there the prisoner managed to lock a door with the German on the other side of it, and made good his escape. There were strong German patrols in some of the coastal districts during the evening, it probably being thought a second attempt to get away would be made, and though this resulted in one party being prevented from escaping, other attempts were successful. One party left from St. Aubin's Bay and two from the Le Hocq district. A party of three who left from Fauvic, however, were fired at by the Germans and had to come ashore at Gorey, where they abandoned their boat and made good their escape.

October 26. There have been several cases reported of late of houses of persons suspected of collaboration with the Germans having been daubed with tar and windows broken; a climax was reached during the night, for several places both in the town and the country received attention. One shop was badly damaged and the proprietor of another was covered with a tarry substance when he looked out of an upstairs window; some private houses also had swastikas painted on them, and many windows were broken. Sentences were passed today on would-be escapees; the members of a party which came to grief at Le Hocq last month were each sentenced to 12 months, and one, the owner of the boat, was, in addition, fined 10,000 marks (£1,000). The three whose companion was shot when they tried to escape at the beginning of this month were sentenced to ten months, and the man who sold them the boat to five months. During the day a single plane was over the Island at various times.

October 27. The Germans give notice that all boats, no matter of what type (even collapsible boats and floats), and all outboard motors, must be reported to them by the end of the month; exact details must be given as to the whereabouts of boats and motors, and previous failure to report boats or changes of ownership will not be punished. A single plane was over the Island during the afternoon and evening. The electricity supply was not cut off in the evening as the Germans had night manoeuvres and they also had to listen to a speech by Goebbels.

October 28. More houses have been daubed with tar and the Germans have published the following notice:

'During the recent nights the repeated daubing of houses has occurred, carried out by young men under cover of darkness. In spite of the state of siege, the curfew hours have been generously maintained at the same hours as during the summer time. In the event of a continuation of these activities by irresponsible elements, an extension of the hours of curfew will have to be considered. The population, which will have to suffer an extension of the curfew hours, will have to thank for these measures the activities of these young men.'

The Germans today used the windows of a shop in King Street to display a large quantity of goods found in one of the houses they have been searching, together with notices deploring black-market activities and stating that these goods would be sent to the 'soup kitchen'. There is no doubt the display was a wonderful one after four years of occupation, but it must be admitted that a large portion could well have been obtained by legitimate means. Much indignation is being expressed at the conduct of some local people who attended a birthday dinner given by a German; they are being ostracised and the houses of some of them have already been daubed with tar.

October 29. In spite of the German warning, tar-daubing goes on, some houses having swastikas 'painted' on them.

October 30. The Germans have published an article dealing with food hoarding and black-marketing, with particular reference to the display of goods on Saturday (the 28th); this article was written by an individual who has been supplying the Germans for some time with material for a weekly jibe against the local authorities under the heading of 'The Man in the Street', and who, it is hoped, will be brought to book in due course. Following the recent requisitioning of paraffin by the Germans, persons holding paraffin ration cards (i.e., persons without gas or electricity) are notified that the cards are available, for only half a pint per month instead of a pint. The sugar ration is also cut all round by one ounce, the scale now being: Adults, 2 oz. per week; juveniles and children, 5 oz.; invalids (supplementary), 6 oz. The only extra issued this week is a stick of shaving soap for male adults, the first since June 4. A special meeting of the Superior Council was held to discuss the situation as there had been no reply to the Memorandum and nothing had been heard from the Protecting Power; the draft of a further communication to the Protecting Power was approved. Another matter discussed was the need for more police at night in view of the wholesale robberies which are now taking place. At about 8 p.m. there was witnessed the first air activity for some time. A large plane flew over the Island with all its navigation lights on; it circled twice and it appeared as if the pilot were looking for a place to land. Everyone thought it was a German mail plane, but after it had been overhead for some time the Germans opened up and fired; the plane was hit and came down into the sea off the north coast.

October 31. The plane which was shot down last night is now learned to have been an American one, and it is presumed the pilot mistook his bearings; it crashed into the sea off Bouley Bay Harbour, and the captain alone was saved. Five bodies were washed up at Bouley Bay today and have been taken to the General Hospital mortuary to await burial. A protest has been made to the Germans regarding the goods taken from a local resident and displayed on the 28th, but none have been handed back. At the annual general meeting of Brig-y-Don Children's Convalescent and Holiday Home today, Dr. Mac-Kinstry, the M.O.H. gave some thought-provoking figures in relation to child welfare under existing conditions. Up to the age of six the food rations proved not unsatisfactory, and heights and weights were normal, but from six to ten years the rations were inadequate and badly balanced, so that on reaching school-leaving age boys were about half an inch shorter in height and seven pounds lighter in weight than normally, girls being similarly affected, though not quite to the same extent. In addition, tuberculosis had become rife, particularly bone-tuberculosis, which as a rule is rare in Jersey. The results of all this would not terminate with the Occupation, but would remain for many years to come. The Germans issue a notice warning the public that it is forbidden to remove sign-posts or notice-boards of any kind. They have lately lost a number of these boards, which make excellent firewood. Robberies of wood are frequent, and gates are rapidly disappearing. Numbers of trees are also being felled to keep the meagre ration going, and soles for footwear are being manufactured from beech. Among these are some from the magnificent avenue of beeches leading to Beau Desert, opposite St. Saviour's Schools. Furniture is commanding high prices at sales, and much is being purchased for firewood. Many poster hoardings have been taken down and sold. The Germans themselves are also in a bad way for fuel supplies and groups of soldiers are to be seen all over the Island digging or blasting roots of trees which had previously been felled. Fortunately, the Gas Works has not been able to ship tar since the Occupation, and householders are buying large quantities to mix with coal dust, ashes, etc. Many of the prison sentences now being served have been remitted or reduced; it is not known whether this is a sign of leniency or of inadequacy of accommodation in the prison! A joke is going the rounds. The war is over and everything is set for the great victory parade. Suddenly General Eisenhower gallops to the head of the procession and cries, 'Stop! We have forgotten to relieve the Channel Islands!' Yes, that's how we feel at the moment.

NOVEMBER 1944

November 1. The fuel ration for an average family consists of 1½ cwt. of wood. The Germans issue two notices; one deals with the reporting of motor-boat engines, and the other with food hoarding. The latter, under the heading of 'What Stocks are Permissible', reads as follows:

'It is well known to the German authorities that the

civilian population before the war and before the Occupation laid in stocks in order to be prepared to face bad times. Naturally, these stocks will not be touched. There is no objection to other small supplies which do not exceed what a careful and considerate housewife can collect for her family.

'It is, however, objectionable if huge stores are hoarded simply out of selfishness and by making use of one's wealth, profession or business in order to live a gluttonous existence in the midst of want. In cases of huge black-market transactions no consideration will be taken of pre-war stores in the hoard. It will be assumed that these stores have been amassed or recently obtained out of greed or for bartering in the black-market.

'It would be an unjust and incomplete punishment if, in cases of immense enrichment with rationed goods, the selfish motive were not judged as a whole and punished by confiscation of all the hoard.

'In Germany, which has once experienced a hunger blockade during the World War of 1914–1918, public opinion demands verdicts of imprisonment with hard labour or even the death sentence against hoarders who have acted contrary to the interests of the community.'

A notice issued by the Department of Agriculture demands notification within 24 hours of the theft or disappearance of any bull, cow, heifer, calf, horse, pig or sheep, and the Textile and Footwear Control publishes a list of articles, accessories and footwear which may be obtained during the new rationing period commencing today. Mr. 'Scottie' Gosling is presenting a musical show at the Opera House. A local policeman has been sentenced by the Germans to four months' imprisonment for arguing with a pro-German, an additional complaint being that he had refused to salute German officers! Four men were released from jail today before they had completed their sentences. The elementary schools resumed today after the mid-term holidays, their hours now being 10 to 12.15 and 1.45 to 3.30. An inquiry has been opened and adjourned in connection with a shocking tragedy at Longueville in which a woman was found to have been strangled by her husband, who then hanged himself; it was revealed the woman had for some time been consorting with German soldiers, and the verdict subsequently was one of 'murder and felo de se'. Two barges left for Guernsey today, laden with wheat, potatoes, etc., of which 150 tons of wheat and 10 tons of potatoes were for the civilian population; a small

232

quantity of oats was also taken.

November 2. Following complaints by crews of German boats which are laid up that they have inadequate heating, small quantities of coal and wood were delivered to the vessels today. The electric light was cut off from 4 a.m. today to 7 a.m. and again at 10.15 p.m. to enable St. Peter's plant to be repaired.

November 3. Another body—the sixth—from the plane which crashed into the sea off Bouley Bay Harbour on October 30, has been washed up. The States barge, equipped with diving apparatus and having a French diver on board, has been taken to Bouley Bay by the Germans in an attempt to ascertain if the plane was carrying important documents. A notice issued by the Department of Essential Services gives warning that if the St. Peter's Power Station breaks down and the Queen's Road plant must be used, the stocks of diesel oil will permit of a supply of electricity only from 9 a.m. to noon and from 7 p.m. to 10.15 p.m. The Germans have given permission for members of the public to have access to the beaches for the purpose of fetching salt water, the permission to be granted by the officer in charge of the nearest military post. A tobacco ration is being issued for one week; this is 1 oz., at 1s. 6½d., and is from confiscated stocks and other tobacco purchased by the Department of Essential Commodities. The Germans are advertising for women and girls for knitting, working at home for good wages. Nine more prisoners released today; they were serving sentences for wireless infractions and will have to complete them 'after the war'! A party of youths was imprisoned today for being in possession of firearms and a quantity of explosives stolen from the Germans.

November 4. At the Royal Court today sentence of six months' imprisonment was passed on a cycle thief; it was emphasised that this is a very serious offence—eleven cycles have been stolen during the past week in St. Helier alone. The Court also imposed fines on two farmers for keeping unregistered pigs—£200 and £30 respectively—and a man charged with an infraction of the Tobacco Tax Law was fined £500. It was reported today that at a farm sale a horse has fetched the sum of £500!

November 6. The burial took place this morning of the six Americans whose bodies had been washed up following the recent plane crash at Bouley Bay; they were 2nd-Lieut. E. G. J. Pallantine, E. J. Pycz, T. J. Manning, W. M. Kearns, J. J. Stout and W. W. Anderson. The Dean and Father Arscott officiated, two of the victims being Roman Catholics. The usual officials were present and wreaths laid. Among those at the ceremony were the captain of the aircraft—Lieut. Blacker—and the senior officer of the American prisoners in the Island—Colonel Reybold. This week's extra is 1 lb. of macaroni per head and there is a meat ration, although this week is supposed to be a meatless one. The Germans publish a notice requiring that one-half of the 'privileged ration' of oats for 12 months retained by horse owners shall be surrendered and used for the manufacture of breakfast food for the civilian population. Horse-owners had been allowed to retain, during the 1944 harvest, oats on the basis of 13 cwt. per horse. The experiment has recently been made of using oats in bread-making, but this has not proved successful. Owing to technical difficulties, millers are no longer able to produce white flour, and their customers have to be content with wholemeal.

November 7. Tar-daubing still goes on and wood robberies continue, the latest development being the stripping of untenanted houses. The Department of Transport and Communications draws the notice of the public to the following extracts from an Order received from the Platzkommandantur, dated November 1, 1944:

' (a) Use of Cars and Motor Cycles. (1) Cars and motor cycles may only be used on journeys of absolute necessity. (2) A taxi may only be used as an auxiliary ambulance for the transport to and from the Hospital (or nursing homes) of persons unable to walk. (3) Doctors may only use their cars when called to persons confined to bed who are unable to come to their surgeries.
' (b) Use of Lorries. A lorry is to be employed only when work cannot be carried out by a horse-drawn vehicle. Horse-drawn vehicles may no longer be used for outings. All pleasure drives are to be discontinued. Farmers may bring their agricultural produce into town by their horse-drawn vehicles. It is suggested that a collective transport service be formed in districts so that in the event of one farmer not being in a position to bring his produce to market he can be assisted by a neighbour. It is not permissible for potatoes, tomatoes or other vegetables to be transported by petrol-driven lorries.
' (c) The sale and purchase of motor vehicles of all kinds between civilians is forbidden until after the end of the war.'

November 8. Graf von Schmettow, Military Commander of

the Channel Islands, arrived in the Island from Guernsey on an artillery float, which took six hours to make the crossing, owing to the very bad weather. Two barges also arrived with over 500 tons of coal between them. The Germans have taken another 100 tons of potatoes. Today is the anniversary of the formation of the Nazi Party and propaganda meetings were held at The Forum. The Germans have questioned some lads who are suspected of having been involved in tar-daubing activities.

November 9. Graf von Schmettow is meeting other German officials; two big parades of sailors have been addressed on the Albert Pier. A few aircraft were over the Island during the day, and at about midnight a plane passed over the town at almost roof-top height; the Germans have declared this was a mail-carrier.

November 10. von Schmettow had a conference during the evening which lasted several hours. A party of five got away from Fauvic at night in spite of increased German patrols. Fauvic has become a favourite starting-point for escapees; many willing helpers are always ready to give assistance, and tales of the 'Fauvic Embarkation Port' and the brave men who never counted the risk will surely be told in happier times.'*

November 11. Today—Remembrance Day—several official wreaths were laid on the Cenotaph and graves in the Island War Cemetery in Howard Davis Park. The Department of Agriculture, following directions of the Platzkommandant, gives notices to all persons who have grown potatoes in 1944 and who have any seed potatoes in their possession that they must furnish a return of the number of boxes of such potatoes held by them at midnight on November 18. The Germans forbid the boarding-up of windows, and are advertising for women who have sewing-machines and are able to sew. Two boats left from Fauvic during the evening with six young men; there were about thirty people on the beach to see them off and help lift one of the boats over the sea-wall. This party took with them valuable information regarding conditions in the Island, as well as letters of introduction to influential Jerseymen residing in England, and the whole expedition was carefully planned. A pre-arranged signal from Portbail Lighthouse has been observed

---

* When freedom of speech was restored, many high tributes were paid to residents in the district who had helped escapees, and one of them—Deputy W. J. Bertram (nicknamed 'The Harbourmaster')—was awarded the B.E.M. by the British Government, and the American Medal of Freedom for assisting the escape of two American officers.

by friends of recent escapees, this denoting their safe arrival.

November 12. The Bailiff and the Attorney-General had an interview again today with high German officials and were assured that a message from the Bailiff would be sent to the Protecting Power; the Germans are understood to be at a loss to account for the fact that no notice has been taken of a former communication. At night a party of four got away from St. Martin's, but the weather was not propitious.

November 13. About 8 a.m. a German convoy of five armed trawlers left for Guernsey; a number of sailors was on board, having been transferred to Guernsey on account of signs of unrest among them. von Schmettow was expected to return, but has delayed his departure. No extra rations this week, no issue of the meagre salt ration, and the last sugar ration for adults and invalids. More sea-water depôts have been opened. Two Victoria College prefects who went to Gorey to look at a boat in which they were contemplating leaving the Island have been arrested by the Germans; their homes were searched, wireless sets and ammunition being found; the father of one boy and the father and sister of the other have also been imprisoned.

November 14. It is learned that a message from the Bailiff was transmitted last night from Guernsey; it was sent in German and not in code. The electricity supply is now liable to be cut off for half-hour periods. A local café frequented by Germans has had stones thrown through the windows, and tarring continues. A paragraph published today over the Bailiff's signature states that arrangements have been made for a weekly dispatch of Red Cross messages. Under the heading 'Four men drowned in attempting to leave the Island' the Germans publish the following:

'In spite of strict prohibition, four Islanders again tried to leave the Island yesterday in order to avoid the common fate of the inhabitants. Their boat was driven ashore and dashed to pieces against the cliffs of the north coast. They themselves were drowned. The population will only have to put to the credit of such irresponsible persons if the occupying authorities are now forced to take stricter measures for the enforcement of their orders.'

There is no doubt the party left from Rozel two nights ago—three men and a woman—and local eye-witnesses declare the boat was seen dashing against the rocks off Saline Bay, but no help could be given on account of mines. A single plane was over the east of the Island during the morning and was fired on from Gorey; friends of some of the recent escapees declare that this was a pre-arranged flight to notify them of their safe arrival. The Amateur Dramatic Club is presenting a comedy at the Opera House.

November 15. First meeting of the States since April. The Estimates were tabled for discussion at a future date; the House approved the creation of an auxiliary police force of 40 men in an attempt to check the rapid increase of robberies; the salary of the Special Administrator was discussed and a measure was adopted providing for an increase in the Parish of St. Helier's General Purposes Loan from £45,000 to £150,000. The Deputies' term of office was extended for another year. The Dispensary reveals that 1,092 babies have been born there. Two bodies have been washed up on the north coast. The Germans have been searching a number of farms, and they have confiscated a fair amount of food. They sent a form to the *E.P.* to-day to be printed for circulation among the farming community; strict instructions were given that no word of this was to leak out; but the necessary information was broadcast in record time!

November 16. The Germans have taken back the form which they handed to the *E.P.* yesterday; maybe they guessed the information would leak out and realised they had made a faux pas! Farmers everywhere today have been hiding their stocks of those commodities which it is anticipated the Germans will rob, and wholesale removals are being carried out. The body of another American airman has been washed up at Bouley Bay—the seventh from the plane shot down. The Germans gave a recital of music at Aquila Road Methodist Chapel, civilians being invited.

November 17. An inquest was held today on the bodies of two young men named Gorvel and Bisson, washed up two days ago; the verdict was 'that they were accidentally drowned while attempting to leave the Island, contrary to the orders of the Occupying Authorities, when the boat which they had taken, in defiance of orders, from Gorey Harbour capsized and was dashed on to the rocks at La Saline Bay, St. John'. There were four in the boat altogether, including Bisson's wife; the Germans handed the bodies over to the civil authorities for the inquest, but have issued instructions that the funerals are to be kept secret so that there may be no demonstrations. It was stated in evidence that the boat was watched drifting for two hours until it dashed against a rock, but the Germans made no attempt to rescue the occupants. The Germans have also published a notice to the effect they have imposed sentences of from five to fifteen months' imprisonment in four cases of attempted escape from the Island.

November 18. The seventh American was buried this morning in the Island War Cemetery, the usual procedure being followed. The body was that of Radio Operator Joseph E. Fisset; the pilot of the machine—the only one saved out of twelve—attended, and civilians were allowed in the cemetery after the burial. A busy morning at the Royal Court; fines were imposed as follows: for the illicit felling of trees, £20 and £5 costs; for milk adulteration, £40 plus the Analyst's fees; for keeping unregistered pigs, £90 and £10 costs; for the illicit sale of wheat, £5 and £1 costs; for the illicit sale of potatoes, £10 and £1 costs. By German order, private milling is being stopped for the time being, and there were queues of people waiting to get their 'gleanings' ground at the various millers. The Germans now want from eight to ten tons of meat per week; this means that out of one hundred animals that must be slaughtered to fulfil the needs of the whole Island they will take about seventy.

November 19. From today (Sunday) the electricity supply is to be cut off for a further half-hour period in the evenings if the load is too heavy; this should increase the price of candles, which are already changing hands at 30s.! Some more appropriate titles for sermons were announced for one of the churches today: 11 a.m., 'Lighted Dwellings'; 4 p.m., 'Wits' End Corner'; the anthem was to be 'Had we but hearkened'!

November 20. The Germans commenced to search farms. Persons suspected of black-market dealings, received more attention. The farmer was given a form to sign and the quantities of such commodities entered on the form must not be touched. It was fortunate that the farmers had warning of this latest move, and they have been busy during the last few days hiding stocks of potatoes and cereals. Apparently the Germans had themselves printed the forms by means of duplicators. The body of young Gorvel was buried today at St. Martin's; the Germans allowed attendance at the church, where there were members of the Municipality, but gave strict orders that no procession was to follow the hearse. The Germans give notice of further sentences—ranging from ten to twelve months—imposed for attempts to leave the Island. Two persons accused of rendering assistance received sentence of five and six months' respectively, and for failure to report boats two others were sentenced to imprisonment and a third fined 500 marks (£53). The laundries have now closed, owing to lack of fuel; one is to be kept open, for nursing institutions, and another for German

238

work. This week's extra is ½ lb. of coffee substitute, but the sugar ration for children and juveniles is further reduced to 4 oz.; there is, however, a supplementary ration of 7 oz. for bottle-fed infants.

November 21. The funeral of young Bisson, another victim of the recent attempt to leave the Island, was held this morning; the service was at St. Thomas's Church and the interment at St. Saviour's; one of the Gestapo agents and some of the Feld-gendarmerie were present, and no one, apart from the mourners, was allowed in the cemetery.

November 22. The Germans publish the following in the *E.P.*: 'As a result of negotiations instituted by the Occupying Authorities re supplies for the civilian population, a delivery of medical supplies, soap and food parcels has been promised as a first measure.' The *E.P.* reminds its readers that two months ago it was announced the German authorities had taken up the question of supplies for the Channel Islands, and that, helped by a report from the Bailiff, the German Government had intimated its intention of bringing the matter to the notice of the Protecting Power; '... no word was heard until on November 13 last we were officially informed that the German authorities had made arrangements for the transmission to the Protecting Power of a direct appeal or message from the Bailiff. In this message, which was broadcast a week ago, details were given as to the present position of supplies.' All sorts of wild rumours followed as the result of today's statement. Among today's advertisements is one inserted by the Department of Labour asking for open-topped galvanised cisterns for supplying salt water for the use of the population. A resident of St. Mary is advertising, at 2s. 1½d. per pint, liquid yeast, which is guaranteed to take the place of baking powder. Fantastic prices are being offered for bicarbonate of soda, among the latest being 30 marks (£3 4s. 1d.), plus half a pound of tobacco, for a pound of bicarb.

November 23. The searching of farms goes on. The Germans had their usual gun practice today on a scale larger than for some time. Mothers with babies have been getting an extra pint of milk per day for the first six months; they have now been notified that, on a German Order, this is to cease, except in the case of a mother nursing the baby herself.

November 24. The rainfall in the past eight days is over three inches. Various States offices are to close earlier because of no lighting. A special ration of 3 lb. of invalid bread is to be made available to invalids instead of their ordinary ration; this means that an invalid will receive 1¼ lb. less in weight.

November 25. The Department of Agriculture has published the following notice, based on an order from the Germans: 'Preservation of the Oat Fields. I request that the farmers be ordered to preserve all crops arising from oats strewn wild where these are in good condition and where, in the meantime, grass seed has not been sown. Further, I request that you will order that the turnip leaves are not to be ploughed in, as is often done, but that before harvesting the turnips for feeding the cattle, the leaves be gathered, washed and used as additional cattle food.' The Department of Transport and Communications issues a notice stating it has been informed by the Germans that a taxi used for the conveyance of sick persons to and from hospitals, etc., must be withdrawn from service and the ambulance used instead. The Department of Education, in view of the bad weather and defective clothing and footwear informs parents that no proceedings will be taken against them if their children are kept at home in bad weather. The *E.P.* pays tribute to the men who, in atrocious weather, have carried on with their task of making the new North Road from Saline Bay to Rozel.* The Royal Court today fined a shopkeeper £200 for selling a suit of clothes at £32 and offering for sale an overcoat at £64! A meeting of the joint Council of the R.J.A. & H.S. and the Farmers' Union was held today, when the latest German demands were discussed. Out of only twelve tons of butter still in store, the Germans want eight; production, at the moment, is only 25 cwt. per week, and the 2 oz. ration absorbs about 48 cwt. It was suggested that farmers should give up their butter ration, as they are getting extra milk. The recent demand for more meat does not help as it means that a number of milch cows must be slaughtered; the Germans are willing, however, to count offal in the weight, and will also take old horses. The number of cows in milk in 1939 was 4,853 and in 1944 6,441; young stock in 1939 totalled 4,448 and in 1944 2,801, a deficiency of 1,647. The farmers will be permitted to sow 100 tons of wheat (about 1,000 vergèes), but this must come from civilian stocks, which would mean the bread ration being reduced almost immediately to 3 lb. 2 oz. Foodstuffs in store for the use of the civilian population after January 31, 1945, have been blocked by the Germans and must not be touched.

November 26. A German plane landed at the Airport. Later

* It was revealed by British officials after the Liberation that this road showed clearly on photographs taken by reconnaissance planes, and was a source of great perplexity, for it was naturally thought that the Germans were responsible for its construction.

in the day some mail for the troops and civilians was brought by speed-boat from Guernsey, and an artillery float left for that Island during the afternoon. From today the electricity supply will be cut off each Sunday afternoon, except in the district where The Forum is situated when soldiers' concerts, etc., are being held.

November 27. The Germans have lifted their ban on the milling of gleanings belonging to private people; only 14 lb. is allowed at a time and the miller must keep a register of names, which will be open to inspection. An oil barge has arrived from Guernsey to take some oil off another barge lying in the harbour, and medical supplies for civilian use have been received from Guernsey. A ration of 100 saccharin tablets issued to adults. Among today's advertisements is one asking if anyone has facilities for pressing sunflower seeds.

November 28. A verdict of accidental drowning returned at the inquest concerning a young man named Luciennes, one of the party of four who recently attempted to leave the Island; a body is still to be recovered—that of Bisson's wife. The Germans give notice that at 1 p.m. today a Russian got away while at work, and the population is warned not to lodge, feed or in any way help the escaped prisoner. The Fifty-Fifty Club presents a comedy at the Opera House.

November 29. Two more have been drowned while attempting to escape. A German notice states that during the night November 27–28 three young men tried to get to France in a boat they had obtained by false pretences; it drifted and was thrown against the cliffs; two were drowned and the third now awaits punishment. The Estimates for the financial year commencing February 1, 1945, were presented to the States today and made interesting reading. The figures were given as in the table on page 242.

The cost of the Army of Occupation amounted to £93,660, and Jurat Dorey, President of the Department of Finance and Economics, pointed out that besides that sum the German Authorities are periodically making levies in reichsmarks to meet the proportionate costs of occupation; up to the present these levies had amounted to eleven million reichsmarks, or something like one and a half million pounds. He also referred to the difficulties in connection with our purchases in France in consequence of the prohibition on the export of reichsmarks; it had become necessary to borrow money from the Office des Changes in Paris to the extent of £433,412 to pay for the purchases. Revenue was slightly down as compared with last year;

	£	s.	d.
Total estimated expenditure . .	801,037	4	0
Total estimated revenue . .	283,335	3	2
	£517,702	0	10
Add: Statutory reserves, in accordance with Article 23 of the Finance Law, 1924 . .	10,000	0	0
Estimated deficit	£527,702	0	10

In these Estimates no provision has been made for:

(a) Payments made by Pensions Department (all of which may be considerd as recoverable): £90,000.

(b) Payments made to French nationals for military payments and allowances: £5,000.

(c) Contingent liabilities to the banks for amounts advanced against frozen assets.

the Tobacco Tax had yielded £7,000. Expenditure had slightly increased, this in the main being due to poor relief showing a rise from £30,000 to £40,000. Income Tax was recommended to remain at 4s. in the £. A proposition was adopted to establish a Remand Home for a certain type of delinquent; Mr. Oscar Le Q. Mourant was appointed new Principal Agent of the Impôt in place of Mr. J. C. Filleul, who has died in England, and a proposition was approved for the acquisition of land required for the construction of the North Marine Drive.

November 30. The funeral of young Luciennes took place this morning, the service at St. Thomas's Church and the burial at St. Martin's. A boat arrived in St. Helier's Harbour today—from St. Aubin's!—and discharged a single-seater American plane which came down some months ago and was to have been shipped to France. The Germans had anti-aircraft practice today, the target being a balloon; this is the first time for several weeks. Trees are being felled all over the Island—both officially and unofficially—and it is not safe to leave anything lying about that will burn. Some of the wooded slopes of the Island at times looks like fair-grounds when indiscriminate felling is going on, but, knowing the real need of the people, the authorities often turn a blind eye. Thinking the plant in St. Peter's Valley was solely for the use of the Germans, the French engineers certainly 'made a good job of it'! The Germans declare they are hungry, and there is little doubt they are responsible for many of the robberies now going on everywhere; their rations have been further cut and pay has been halved so as to stop black-market activities. Parties of Germans rake over the fields with trenching tools to search for any potatoes that may have been overlooked. They have also been buying old furniture to strip coverings for the making of shirts, etc. During the month a large number of sailors has been changed over with soldiers from Guernsey. Tarring still goes on, many innocent people have been victims of spite and some had had 'Iron Crosses' sent to them. The Germans are making a kind of whisky from rotten potatoes, Calvados from cider, and a light lager beer; a tot of black-market brandy in a public house now costs 2½ marks (5s. 4d.). The Germans have declared Villa Millbrook is to be put in order to house a commission. Candles are known to have been sold for 30s. each, tobacco is going for 12s. 6d. an ounce, and a 2½d. tin of Brasso was sold at an auction sale for 20 marks (£2 2s. 9d.). It is estimated that so far between 150 and 200 people have managed to escape from the Island. Local dance bands are playing the latest hits!

DECEMBER 1944

December 1. The fuel ration for this month has not yet been decided; some people have not yet received last month's ration; in addition, the needs of institutions and bakehouses must be met first: the General Hospital alone wants 200 tons a month and the bakehouses burn 10,000 bundles of faggots and 270 tons of wood in five weeks. The electricity hours have changed once more; the current will be on only from 7.30 a.m. to 12.30 p.m. and 6 to 11 p.m., with five periods during which it may be cut off. Nursing mothers and persons over 70 are being allowed half a pint of paraffin for a month's ration. Another American from the shot-down plane—William E. Westemeier, whose body was washed up at Samarès—was buried this morning with the usual ceremony; no one was allowed in the vicinity of the Island War Cemetery. [This was the last American to be buried there.] Some of the Honorary Police have had their curfew passes restored.

December 2. The Germans, having given permission for 100 tons of wheat to be sown from civilian stocks, any farmer who wishes to do so is requested to inform the Department of Agriculture. The Germans have commenced taking foodstuffs from the farms, and a notice published by them reads as follows:

Among the stores which were registered, the following are blocked:

1. Potatoes, including pig potatoes.
2. Seed potatoes.
3. Wheat and oats, as well as mixed corn.
4. Sugarbeet.

Farmers may dispose of all other quantities and produce.

The soldiers are ordered to take away at the same time the horse ration of 6 cwt. of oats, which is to be delivered to the States.

Farmers will receive payment for the produce given up against the receipts given at the time of delivery.

Payment will be made by the Platzkommandantur, Room 13, parish by parish. The parishes will be informed.

Der Kommandant der Festung Jersey.

Jersey, den 1.12.44.   gez. HEINE, Oberst.

A further notice forbids producers and greengrocers to sell or give any produce (vegetables, beet, etc.) and fruit either to units or to individual members of the Forces; exceptions only by permit from the Platzkommandantur. At the Royal Court today fines were imposed of £30 and £5 costs for keeping unregistered pigs, and £20 with the costs of the analysis for milk adulteration. A ration of 15 cigarettes was issued today.

December 4. Juveniles and children receive their last sugar ration; bottle-fed babies are to continue their 11-oz. ration until further notice. The American prisoners were exercised in Howard Davis Park during the afternoon; the gates were shut, but many people caught sight of them and exchanged a friendly word. About 6 p.m. a plane which was showing its navigation lights shot over the Island at a low level and the Germans put up a very heavy barrage; some people were injured by falling shrapnel. A notice issued by the Foresty Section of the Department of Labour warns the public of action if anyone is found wilfully mutilating the young trees which have been planted.

December 5. An inquest was held on the body of Mrs. Bisson, the fourth member of the party which tried to escape from the Island on November 12th; it was found on the beach near the Braye Slip, St. Brelade's, and the same verdict was returned—accidental drowning. A part of Castle Irwell Hotel, Millbrook, has been requisitioned by the Germans for the accommodation of 'officials'. In addition to requisitioning stock which they had blocked, the Germans now expect farmers to use vans, etc., for delivery; in many cases the farmer is using a horse 'loaned' by

244

the Germans in exchange for an old one which has been made into sausage meat, and it is difficult to wriggle out of the situation. Some barges are loading with wheat and potatoes for Guernsey. Among ridiculous prices at auction sales, £4 15s. was paid today for 12 new coloured crayons and a case of about three pencils!

December 6. An artillery float arrived during the night from Guernsey, and among those now in the Island are Admiral von Hueffmeier and Col. von Heldorff, Chief of Staff and Military Adviser respectively to Graf von Schmettow, Military Commander of the Channel Islands, who is stationed in Guernsey. The Admiral is staying at the British Hotel, outside which an armed guard has been mounted. The Germans have notified the civil authorities that a Red Cross ship is due to leave Lisbon on the 7th for the Channel Islands. Several large stores have been listed as receiving depôts. The bread ration for all adolescents, including adolescent manual workers, has been reduced to the level of everyone else (4 lb. 4 oz.), and the butter ration has been stopped for 'persons who have cattle in their custody, members of their households, and others who draw the special higher milk ration . . .' The public is also notified that, owing to further alterations in the hours of electricity, the processing of milk has become practically impossible and deliveries delayed; retailers cannot be held responsible for sour milk or for the late deliveries. Parish of St. Clement fixes the Rate at 2s.

December 7. The funeral of Mrs. Bisson took place this morning; the service was at St. Thomas's Church and the interment at St. Saviour's Cemetery, the Germans taking the usual precautions to prevent a crowd gathering. Some more mail has arrived for the Germans. The Constable of St. Helier notifies the inhabitants of the parish that 'by reason of a curtailment of the number of horses at our disposal, and being very limited with mechanical transport, I regret it will be impossible to maintain even the inadequate amount of dust collection of the past weeks'. The Germans have stopped their newspaper one day a week (Thursdays) in order to help in fuel economy. The air-raid shelters in the Parade have suffered owing to the wet weather and have been rendered almost useless; parish workmen are now on the job of filling them in.

December 8. Under the headline. 'Red Cross Supplies on the Way' the Bailiff has issued the following statement:

I am officially informed by the German Military Authorities that a Red Cross ship was, weather permitting, due to

245

leave Lisbon on Thursday, December 7th for the Channel Islands. The ship will call at Guernsey first en route for Jersey.

The Germans also give notice that Red Cross letters for the Channel Islands civilian internees in Germany will be taken by the 'Red Cross ships which are expected to arrive within the next few days'; four pages may be written and the letters posted at the Head Office, Broad Street, by 6 p.m. on the 11th inst.; the usual 25-word Red Cross message may be handed in at the Bailiff's Enquiry and News Office, for transportation by air through Germany to the addressees. The Department of Agriculture gives notice that, following instructions from the German Platzkommandantur, the milk ration of all adults will not be supplied on one day in seven; the rations for children, juveniles and persons entitled to special rations on medical permit remain unchanged. The 'milkless day' will vary according to the dairy making delivery. The Germans are advertising for large quantities of fir and pine trees for use as Christmas trees.

December 9. During the night there has been a lot of tar-daubing in all parts of the town. Planes were over several times during the day and the Germans opened up on two occasions. The Bailiff has made another appeal for used clothing. At the Royal Court more fines were imposed in two cases of keeping unregistered pigs; £40 and £30 respectively. The Saturday Football League has decided that, 'until living conditions improve', all matches under its aegis will be restricted to 1 hour 20 minutes, i.e. 35 minutes each half. The American prisoners of war in the Island have collected a sum of over £50, to be divided among local charities as a mark of their appreciation of a Thanksgiving Day dinner sent to them by some local ladies; the charities concerned are *The Evening Post* Christmas Fund, the Children's Benefit Fund and the Winter Relief Fund. The curfew hours for the holiday period have been published as follows: December 24, 25, 26 and January 1, midnight; on December 31 the curfew hour will be 1 o'clock next morning. High German officials who have been here for some days returned to Guernsey on an artillery float; they were accompanied by some of the local German administration, who are said to have gone to meet the Red Cross ship expected any day. More householders are keeping their Christmas dinner in back yards, gardens, etc., following rumours that the Germans are going to take poultry from the farms, and today the latter have published an official notice stating that the solders who are engaged in registering and carting away blocked farm produce have been ordered to count poultry on farms; the notice continues: 'This census is simply meant to find out the number of poultry in the Island. Notice is hereby given that the rumour that poultry would be confiscated except from two to six per head is quite without foundation. Useless and senseless slaughter of poultry must therefore be discontinued immediately.'

December 10. The usual quiet Sunday. The weather continues to be atrocious, with rain, hail, thunder and lightning.

December 11. The Department of Transport and Communications invites farmers to send in their names if they are willing to supply horses, vans and drivers, for a short period to help as additional transport when the Red Cross ship arrives. The electricity supply is extended in the mornings until 12.45 to enable the Germans to hear their news bulletin at 12.30. Today sees the last issue of supplementary rations for the majority of heavy workers; the supplementary rations of butter and meat will in future be issued only to: Firemen of shovel-loading boilers, welders and acetylene cutters working under difficult circumstances, trimmers, workers on generators, boiler fitters, sewer-men. In the evening the Germans held their postponed Soldiers' Radio Revue at The Forum. Parties of carollers have appeared in country districts and town suburbs.

December 12. B.B.C. news bulletins today have given the information that supplies are to be sent to the Channel Islands; everyone is overjoyed. Victoria College Terminal Service held at St. Mark's Church instead of St. Helier's as owing to the electricity being cut off in the afternoon the Town Church organ cannot be used. The Germans are advertising for paraffin lamps and two-volt batteries. The Green Room Club presents a comedy at the Opera House.

December 13. The electricity supply has been on all night in some districts as there was some movement of shipping; about 7.30 a.m. two barges with wheat and potatoes for German troops in Guernsey left in company with two artillery floats; 40 tons of sugar-beet was also taken. The Germans have made an alteration in their Order of December 1, 1944, whereby it is now stated members of the Forces are permitted, as previously, to purchase fruit in the market and from greengrocers' shops at the rate of 1 kilo. The fuel ration for December is 1 cwt. of wood for an average family. Medical permits are valid for a wood ration instead of the usual coal; all registered wood merchants must give priority to those and to householders in town and suburban areas. Good news today, is the following notice:

The Befehlshaber has informed me that the Home Secretary has made the following statement in the House of Commons:

Supplies of food, medicines and soap are to be shipped to the Channel Islands. The German Government had approached the British Government with a view to sending supplies to the Channel Islands. In view of reports received, the British Government had decided that it was right to send additional supplies of medicines, soaps and food parcels. The food parcels would take the shape of those sent to prisoners of war. Final arrangements had not been completed, but it was believed the ship would be ready to sail next week. She was a Swedish vessel sailing from Lisbon. It was hoped a representative of the International Red Cross would be able to sail and carry out further investigations into the actual situation of the population of the Islands and arrange for further supplies.

13/12/1944.   A. M. COUTANCHE, Bailiff.

December 14. Open verdict returned at an inquiry concerning a decomposed male body found washed up at Portelet. It is learned a German soldier has committed suicide. The Germans had their usual gun practice today, and other explosions heard were caused by soldiers blasting tree roots.

December 15. An artillery float has arrived from Guernsey, bringing a small quantity of medical supplies and mail. Following the recent Order allowing the troops to purchase fruit again, a shop in Conway Street was besieged by Germans clamouring for apples. List of names published of the new auxiliary policemen, and the Germans have issued telephone numbers of Feldgendarmerie stations which have been set up 'in order to prevent further thefts in the country'. Owing to breakdown, the electricity supply did not commence until 6.50 p.m. due to cut-offs, some districts get only 3½ hours' light.

December 16. In spite of their notice published a week ago ridiculing a rumour that they were to confiscate poultry, the Germans have now demanded 2,000 head of poultry to be collected for them and delivered alive by Friday, December 22; the collection must be made by parish officials, each parish having its quota. The Germans also want one-fifth of the seed potatoes held by farmers. St. Clement's Parish gives notice that, owing to the impossibility of obtaining horse transport, the collection of house refuse is to be discontinued until further notice, and the Parish of St. Helier issues a warning against children using catapults, of which there has been much use lately. In the list of donations to the *E.P.* Christmas Fund appears the sum of £29 7s. 7d. from 'the Dutch seamen'. At the Royal Court today another case of keeping unregistered pigs was presented, the fines imposed amounting to £65 with £5 costs.

December 17. Following yesterday's Order regarding poultry, there has been much 'shuffling'; town-dwellers are visiting country friends to fetch their Christmas dinners. There has been a considerable amount of 'twigging' following a very high wind which blew all night. German soldiers gave a choral concert at The Forum.

December 18. A tin of tunny fish issued to everybody on ration, and an extra flour ration. Double meat and flour (break-fast meal) rations may be drawn this week, but persons doing so will have none next week! The Germans are after cattle for meat for the troops. The new auxiliary police were addressed by the Bailiff this morning and have commenced their duties.

December 18. As it is possible that the production of the top outer cover of the 1944 food ration book may be used in con-nection with the distribution of Red Cross parcels, the public is advised to have them ready for immediate production if neces-sary. The following notice was handed to the *E.P.* by the Food Control for publication, but the German Censor would not allow it to appear:

RED CROSS PARCELS: UNLIKELY TO ARRIVE FOR CHRISTMAS

The ship carrying Red Cross parcels for the Channel Islands has not yet arrived at Guernsey; it is consequently feared that the distribution of these parcels is not likely to be possible before Christmas. This will cause a good deal of dis-appointment to the population, who were hoping to have their Christmas made brighter by the extra food, etc. especi-ally in view of the fact that no supplementary rations other than those advertised have been sanctioned. The sanction of the Occupying Authorities has to be obtained for every ounce of supplementary rations which may be issued to the public. The Medical Board is also limited in the quantity of food, etc., which may be allocated each month to the sick and in-valid.

December 20. The Germans have informed the local authorities that the Red Cross ship bringing supplies to the Channel Islands is due to leave Lisbon today. They also publish a notice informing fishermen with or without boats or equipment that they have the opportunity of carrying out their profession under favourable conditions; personal or written application must be made to College House. Apparently they are trying to encourage fishermen for of late all fishing has ceased. The Council of the J.F.A. has prohibited all junior football, and the Department of Transport and Communications is advertising for 6- 12-volt batteries to maintain the milk supply.

December 21. The B.B.C. has announced that the Red Cross ship has left Lisbon. The Germans have again searched many farms and taken whatever they wanted.

December 22. The two thousand head of poultry were taken to the parish today to be collected by the Germans; everyone called on to supply these birds has picked out the most scraggy. The B.B.C. announced more details today about the Red Cross parcels; they are Canadian-packed, and a resident of Portugal has given a large quantity of salt. Six Germans have been picked up in a boat off the Ecrehos, having escaped from an American prison at St. Malo. Schools broke up today for the Christmas holidays and will not resume until January 25, as they have no means of heating. Electricity hours for the holiday period: On Christmas Day the supply will be on from 7.30 a.m. to midnight; December 24 and 26 the evening period will be extended until midnight; December 31 until 1 o'clock next morning; the usual cut-off periods will operate, with additional ones if necessary. The Germans issue an Order to the effect that no private plants for the generating of electricity for water pumps, glasshouses, swamping, lighting, etc., may be sold or bought from this date; this Order refers to all generating plants worked with petrol or with Diesel oil; accessories of such plants, e.g. batteries (including the acid contained therein) and switchboards, are included in the Order. This means the Germans will requisition these plants; they have already set up windmills to drive small dynamos when the electricity supply ceases, and they have a big supply of Diesel oil from ships which are laid up.

December 23. Last 'shopping' day before Christmas. There was little to buy, the only things not second-hand being highly-prices wooden toys, flowers, home-made Christmas cards and calendars; black-market meat is at a price beyond all reason; pork goes for nearly £2 a lb. There is great comfort, to know that Red Cross parcels are on the way, and we are pleased Guernsey will get theirs first, for they are in much greater need.

The Germans have requisitioned all they could to make their celebrations a success, and on the pretext of looking for a boat searched several houses in the Samarès district today from top to bottom and took foodstuffs they fancied from people's cupboards. Some were unlucky to be caught with a wireless set, and have been sent to jail, swelling the large number already there. Foreign workers brought here by the Germans are having a very lean time, and offer almost anything to obtain something to eat; a Dutch skipper off one of the barges is known to have paid ten marks each for two female cats for his Christmas dinner! Fines were imposed at the Royal Court on two persons charged with infractions of the Livestock Order. The Amateur Dramatic Club has been rehearsing a concert for the American prisoners, for which the Germans had given permission, but then withdrew at the last moment. One of the Americans—Lieut. Hass—has tried to escape and he has been placed in solitary confinement. The electricity supply was on until midnight.

December 24. Christmas Eve, being Sunday, Christmas music has been rendered in a number of churches; some programmes were relayed to the institutions. The German Harbour Police are still searching in the Samarès district, and several persons had to attend at the Harbour Office at La Folie for questioning. A previous German Order allowed civilians to have 28 lb. of wheat milled for their own use, but the Harbour Police declare the local population should not have extra foodstuff in their houses while the Germans have to live on carrots and potatoes. Curfew did not commence until midnight, with the electricity supply also on until then.

December 25. Christmas Day: weather beautiful—cold and frosty, but bright sunshine. Planes were over in the early hours. Everyone made the most of this, we hope, last Christmas under such conditions. The bakehouses had a bumper day and carried out their task to everyone's satisfaction, the display of dishes being remarkable and a credit to people's ingenuity after four and a half years of occupation. Not all the Germans fared too well, and a local resident was stopped by a sailor in town and asked if he had any tobacco. 'Yes,' was the reply, 'but none for you.' 'None for us,' said the sailor, 'that's all we hear. We have a fowl between seven of us, a handful of potatoes, no tobacco, and Calvados mixed with cognac. The officers have a fowl between two of them and all the champagne and cognac they want. Wait until we get back to Germany!' To which the local resident replied, 'Why wait?' The electricity supply was on all day until midnight, the public having been asked not to use current except for light. Curfew did not commence until midnight, and there was a brilliant moon.

December 26. Boxing Day: weather remains the same. A large crowd attended a football match in the afternoon, and in the evening many private dances were held; there has been a number of these during the Christmas period. In the evening the Green Room Club presented the pantomime *Aladdin* at the Opera House; this is to run until January 6. Curfew began again at midnight, with light until that time also, but there were cut-offs again. A Miss Waddell has been admitted to hospital suffering from loss of blood through a wound in the thigh, she having been shot by someone when she went on to the verandah of her house at Portelet to investigate noises made by intruders.

December 27. The *E.P.* could not be published today as a breakdown at the St. Peter's Power Station prevented an extension of the electricity supply. Various clubs, etc., have given concerts to the inmates of the various institutions, and a number of these has been relayed through the States Telephone Service, which is doing excellent work. Several robberies have been reported; these include a number of pigs. The *E.P.* Christmas Fund has passed its previous record; many persons in receipt of the money vouchers were also given potatoes and fuel, the gift of generous donors, and one resident gave a thousand boxes of matches. Department of Labour employees have now commenced to fell the Royal Crescent trees and those in other crescents and terraces of the town; some trees in Green Street Cemetery are also being removed, and the Foresty Section of the Department of Labour gives notice that it has requisitioned all branchless standing trees. The problem of fuel remains acute, and many people are spending £2 a week on kindling wood alone! A German patrol boat came into harbour during the morning with mail; it returned later with the Bailiff, who went to Guernsey to attend a conference between civil officials of the Channel Islands and a Red Cross Commission, it being learned with thankfulness that the Red Cross ship *Vega* had arrived there earlier in the day; the Bailiff was accompanied by Baron von Aufsess, a member of the German Administration Staff at College House.

December 28. The Bailiff has telephoned from Guernsey to the Attorney-General stating he will return from there on Saturday with the Red Cross ship. Miss Waddell, who was shot at Portelet by a German on Christmas night and admitted to hospital next morning suffering from loss of blood from a thigh wound, has died. The Germans have 'loaned' a quantity of coal to the General Hospital to keep the electricity supply plant going; for some time wood soaked in tar has had to be used and this has involved a considerable amount of extra labour and inconvenience; conditions at the Hospital have become appalling, due to the lack of sufficient electric power.

December 29. Statement issued dealing with the expected arrival of the Red Cross ship and the return of the Bailiff, who has conferred in Guernsey with representatives of the International Red Cross. An inquiry was held today concerning the finding near St. Catherine's of the body of John Francis Larbalestier, who was drowned on November 28 while attempting to leave the Island in company with his brother Bernard (also believed drowned) and a friend, Peter Noel, who was saved; the jury returned an open verdict. Peter Noel is still in prison, where he was placed by the Germans. The Germans have issued a notice calling for the surrender of all private stocks of lubricating oil; car owners may keep three gallons for each car that has been licensed for the road; with immediate effect, lubricating oil is to be regarded as a rationed commodity, and any black marketing is prohibited, punishments being threatened. The Germans also advertise for shoemakers' sewing machines. Next week's rations may be obtained in advance so as to help transport facilities.

December 30. The funeral service for John Francis Larbalestier was held this morning at St. Simon's Church, the Germans taking the usual precautions. Summerland gives notice that owing to the scarcity of suitable wood and the amount of clogging repairs already in hand no further clogging can be accepted. Up to December 1 the number of articles manufactured by Summerland this year amounted to 136,042, an increase on last year of 8,971. The omnibus service ceased completely today owing to the exhaustion of anthracite and charcoal stocks. Among latest reported robberies is one of 95 pounds of butter from Messrs. Orviss's Beresford Street Branch. After weeks of anxious waiting, the International Red Cross ship *Vega* entered St. Helier's Harbour and took up her berth at the end of the Albert Pier; she was flying the flag of the International Red Cross at her foremast, her house flag at the main and the Swedish flag astern, while on her superstructure were two illuminated red crosses. On board were two members of the International Red Cross Commission—Colonel Iselin, of the Swiss Army, Chief Representative of the Red Cross at Lisbon, and M. Callias, Delegate of the International Red Cross; during the vessel's stay here they will be accommodated on board. Just previous to the *Vega*'s arrival the Bailiff of Jersey had returned to the Island in the captain's cabin of a German E-boat which had been placed at his disposal by the German authorities, and was on the quay to welcome the ship. Not a great crowd saw her enter harbour, but there would have been many more if the time of arrival had been known, for, unfortunately, rumour changed this hourly. A description of the arrival was relayed from the tower of St. Helier's Parish Church, being greatly appreciated by inmates in the institutions. In a leading article wishing its readers a Happy New Year, the *E.P.* wrote that '. . . only those who have knowledge of how so many of the poorer inhabitants have lived during the past months can imagine what this will mean. Medical supplies, foodstuffs, soap, all urgently needed, are being provided, and a commission will decide what other supplies are required. So the year ends a brighter note, and we enter the New Year with the knowledge that, though hard and difficult times still have to be faced, our position is less serious than it might have been.'

December 31. The discharge of the *Vega*—which, by the way, was a frequent visitor before the war with hay and straw—commenced at 8.30 this morning, and by the end of the day 250 tons had been unshipped. German sailors and marines worked on the unloading, and members of St. John Ambulance Brigade were on the quay to render assistance and accompany the trolleys laden with parcels to Martland's store on the Esplanade, where they were checked and stored before being eventually passed to the grocers for distribution. A German soldier was on the lorry and the route to the store was patrolled by German troops, the civil police and members of St. John Ambulance Brigade. The transport was undertaken by volunteer farmers, who harnessed their horses to merchants' trolley. There was a limited number of special diet or invalid parcels, the gift of the British Red Cross, a quantity of salt, soap and medical stores, the gift of a small quantity of tobacco and cigarettes from the New Zealand Red Cross, and a number of layettes, the gift of 'The Lady Campbell Fund', created by the wife of the British Ambassador at Lisbon. The contents of a sample parcel was given as follows: 6 oz. chocolate, 20 biscuits, 4 oz. tea, 20 oz. butter, 6 oz. sugar, 2 oz. of milk powder, 16-oz. tin marmalade, 14-oz. tin of corned beef, 13-oz. tin of ham or pork, 10-oz. tin of salmon, 5-oz. tin of sardines, 8-oz. tin of raisins, 6-oz. tin of prunes, 4-oz. tin of cheese, 3-oz. tablet of soap, 1 oz. pepper and salt. Crowds of people visited the neighbourhood of the harbour to see the ship being unloaded and to watch the trolleys with their crates of parcels. This morning there was an official reception of the Commissioners by Colonel Heine, Commander-in-Charge of the garrison at Jersey; the Bailiff and the Attorney-General were also present. At 4 o'clock this afternoon a conference of a similar nature to that held in Guernsey took place at Fort d'Auvergne Hotel, the whole of the members of the Superior Council being present, together with Drs. R. N. McKinstry (M.O.H.), H. J. Shone, J. R. Hanna and E. A. C. Drécourt, the latter representing the French Red Cross. All that transpired in Guernsey was passed under review from Jersey's point of view and unanimous agreement was reached on all questions affecting the interests of the two Islands. The following facts emerged from the conferences and were subsequently published by the *E.P.*:

1. It is hoped to maintain the *Vega* on the Lisbon–C.I. service and it is estimated that the round trip, including the loading at Lisbon and the discharge in the Islands, will take about one month. In these circumstances the conference in Jersey—in consultation with the Commissioners—has been considering what is the ideal cargo, and representations accordingly have been made to the Powers concerned. The ideal monthly cargo has been decided upon as:

> 500 tons of flour,
> 1 Red Cross parcel for every person once a month,
> Medical supplies.

A priority issue of footwear and clothing for manual workers has also been asked for, as have an allocation of candles, matches, flints for lighters and yeast. Seeds, leather and boot-repairing equipment are also being requested.

2. The conference recognised that the fuel problem was one of equal gravity with that of foodstuffs, and our Island authorities were glad to learn that negotiations in this respect are taking place with the belligerent Powers through the Protecting Power. The conference considered that gas coal would best meet our needs as supplying not only gas for cooking but also coke for fuel.

3. The question of the maintenance of a supply of electricity was discussed, but this presents serious problems.

4. An important point dealt with was the voluntary evacuation of persons requiring special medical treatment. This was agreed to both by the German authorities and the Commissioners; arrangements are being made and a notice will

shortly appear in the Press informing relatives how such evacuation may be brought about.

5. The present Commissioners have no authority for dealing with prisoners of war in the Channel Islands, but intend opening up negotiations in order that future cargoes may include parcels for the American and French colonial troops in the Island.

6. Negotiations are to be opened for the carrying of Red Cross mail from England via Lisbon, short messages, similar to Field Service postcards. Mail from internees and prisoners of war have arrived on the *Vega*.

To help the work of unloading the *Vega*, the electricity supply was left on all day and until 1 o'clock next morning, as it was New Year's Eve, curfew being delayed until that hour as well. Some very cold weather this month, with temperatures at times several degrees below freezing point; the fuel problem has been most acute, and some folk have had to cut up blankets with which to make underclothing. Farmers have been notified that they may plant 4,000 tons of seed potatoes, but are reluctant to do so as it is probable they will be taken out of the ground, which has often occurred. Some Germans have offered 300 marks (over £30) for a Red Cross parcel, and they are shooting seagulls for food. Searches of farms have resulted in all sorts of ruses being adopted, in one case a farmer's wife pretending to be ill in bed and having a newly-slaughtered pig alongside her wrapped in a sheet! The Germans continue to set up windmills for driving dynamos. Some telephone exchanges have not been working all the month, as the electric supply has been insufficient for battery charging, which takes much longer. More cyclists are overcoming tyre difficulties by having outer covers fitted made from motor-car inner tubes. 'Jersey' boots are now being worn by many children; although crude in appearance, they keep out the wet quite effectively. Apart from an occasional patrol boat which carries mail between the Islands, shipping is at a standstill. Various charities have been well supported, the *E.P.* Christmas Fund making a new record with a sum of over £600. The trials of the Occupation are telling on everyone, and many quite young men have been affected through overstrain caused by the perpetual heavy work which must be undertaken in order to live, mostly the carting and sawing of wood. The jail continues to receive new inhabitants; arrests for Wireless Order infractions predominate, but it is learned that at least one prisoner has installed a crystal set in his cell!

January 1. The year starts on an optimistic note. Unloading of the *Vega* did not take place today, but there were conferences with the Red Cross Commissioners. The weather was cold but sunny; a football match in the afternoon and a visit to the harbours to see the Red Cross ship were the only attractions. Curfew did not commence until midnight. During the evening there were drunken soldiers and sailors about the town, and a couple of ugly scenes developed. The B.B.C. mentioned the Channel Islands today in a New Year broadcast. Extra rations for invalids have been stopped with the exception of milk, and for everyone this week there will be no meat ration.

January 2. Discharge of the *Vega*'s cargo commenced at 8.30 this morning and finished at 3 p.m. Those who helped to unload received soup, sausage and biscuits from the crew, the Germans eating as though it were the first food they had ever seen. German secret police have been searching parcels, the only things they were seen to remove being English newspapers used as wrapping round the layettes sent by Lady Campbell. The *E.P.* has published an interview with the Bailiff concerning conferences held with the Red Cross Commissioners, the heads of the Islands, and German representatives. A leading article under the heading 'The Island is Grateful' gave good advice to recipients of the parcels to avoid recklessness in their use. Expressions of appreciation for what the Red Cross has already done and what is hoped will be done in the future can be shown through a Red Cross Fund which is to be opened. During the day the Red Cross Commission visited various places, including the communal kitchens. Mrs. Fraser's kitchen, which has been maintained by gas since the general cut-off at the beginning of September last, has now gone over to steam cooking. The Germans have given permission, an inquest was held today on the body of Miss Waddell.

January 3. A message from the Bailiff to the people of Jersey was published today. This gave further details regarding the Red Cross supplies and advice as to their use. The Bailiff states that 'valuable as the food parcels are, we require many other additional commodities if a reasonable standard of life is to be maintained, especially now that stocks of food, including flour and potatoes, under the control of the Insular Government, are nearly exhausted'. Every member of the community is urged to treat his or her parcel as an iron ration, and to make it last as long as possible. Another distribution is to be made as soon as it is prudent to do so. Plans are to be made for the distribution of the soap, salt, tobacco and layettes, and in conclusion the warning is given that persons making dishonourable use of their Red Cross gift would be debarred from receiving any share in the future. Details regarding the first distribution of parcels have also been published. It is to be spread over four days and receipt for the parcels will be the cover of the 1944 ration book. The invalid's parcel will be available to children under two years of age, persons of 90 years of age and over, gastric ulcer patients, and, if supplies permit, other special cases recommended by a medical practitioner and approved by the Medical Board. The parcels were taken to the shops today, members of the St. John Ambulance Brigade and volunteers being on the trolleys. Within twenty-four hours of its opening the *E.P.* list of the Red Cross Fund acknowledged the receipt of over £1,000! Further conferences with the Red Cross Commissioners were held today.

January 4. The distribution of Red Cross parcels to the public commenced this morning, and is being speedily carried out. Parcels vary slightly in contents and at least half contain no soap, but there is to be a ration from the supply brought in bulk. All sorts of conveyances are being used to fetch them from the shops—boxcarts, perambulators, cycle trailers, etc., and farmers' vans are collectings numbers for distribution to friends. The special invalids' parcels are issued at Boots the Chemists, these containing comforts such as Ovaltine, Horlicks and Rowntree's cocoa. The *Vega* left on the return journey to Lisbon about noon, the Commission going with her. A report of conditions in the Channel Islands is to be presented to the British Government. The Germans have been present at every conference, but this has not prevented some very straight talking. There is a possibility that the *Vega* may have to lay up for a short spell, as she sustained damage to her keel in Guernsey Harbour as the result of being placed in an unsuitable berth. A newly-born child has been named after the ship. Money is pouring in for the Red Cross Fund and the parishes are organising house-to-house collections.

January 5. The Department of Public Health publishes a notice on the possible evacuation of certain classes of invalids who would benefit by treatment not available in Jersey; the patient must travel alone, not necessarily to England; a hospital ship will probably be used, the earliest possible date being two to three months hence, and Jersey's quota will be 60. The Germans are after cycles again, individual owners being warned to take them to College House for inspection. They are also commandeering paper from stationers and printers. The troops now have organised 'limpet parties'; about twenty were seen today on the rocks behind Havre-des-Pas Pool—billycans were first filled and then emptied into a large bucket, after which the squad lined up and marched up Roseville Street with their 'catch'! The Germans have lost a quantity of meat and have been searching butcher shops, with the result that one butcher was arrested.

January 6. In the first five days the *E.P.* Red Cross Fund list has acknowledged over a thousand pounds a day. The parcels are nearly all distributed, and the housewives are happy to be able to vary the menu. In consequence of these supplies, black-market goods have almost disappeared, especially tea and butter, the former commodity being one of the most appreciated after four years of substitutes. The plywood containers in which the parcels were packed in sixteens are to be distributed to the poor for wood. The Germans have fined a farmer for not growing enough potatoes; a resident was sentenced to two months for refusing to disclose where he had obtained oats, and another for 'inciting the Germans to revolt', and the usual number of convictions for infractions of the wireless order. They have also given notice that army horses may be used for field cultivation, farmers to make application to their Constables. A fine of £30 and £5 costs was imposed at the Royal Court today in another case of keeping an unregistered pig.

January 7. In several churches Sunday thanksgiving services were held for the Red Cross supplies. In many churches the electrically-blown organs could not be used and it was difficult to see, for new electricity supply hours came into operation today; these are from 6.15 p.m. to 10.30 p.m. only, and no current may be used for any power purposes except for the operation of sewage and water-pumps. Notice has been given to residents in districts supplied through booster stations of the hours during which pumped supplies are available, and owing to these further electricity restrictions the telephone service is to be cut to an essential minimum; this affects sub-exchanges mostly, and the Central Exchange is to function as usual. During the afternoon an American fighter plane was shot down at St. Brelade's; it crashed in a minefield; the pilot baled out and came down over the sea; his plight was witnessed by a young Jerseyman named De La Haye, who went to his rescue on a float. The float began to break up as they neared the shore and

De La Haye placed the American on a rock and then swam ashore for help; a German who had also attempted rescue got on to the rock as well, and a boat eventually took them off and brought them ashore.*

January 8. The new electricity time-table has been suspended for two days. All sorts of gadgets are being used for creating light; the Germans have erected windmills to drive dynamos, and installed several small oil-driven plants. Steamrollers have been brought into service to drive various plants; two are at flour mills and another is being used to charge batteries for the Telephone Exchange, while Summerland is using a steam engine which formerly drove a thresher. The Hospital, which still runs its own plant, is supplying current to some other buildings, and laundry for other institutions is also being done there; the private laundry doing this has had to close down. The Germans have issued a notice declaring that two American prisoners of war escaped this morning—Captain Clark and Lieut. Haas; warning is given to anyone who may offer them help that this will be punished by the death penalty. A full description of the Americans was published in the Press, and during the day German patrols searched many houses in the Havre-des-Pas district; people have been stopped and asked for their identity cards, these including occupants of a mourning coach following a hearse. Lieut. Haas has attempted to escape once before. The Germans have released a quantity of potatoes for civilian consumption. There is a meat ration this week. Residents in certain areas of Grouville and St. Saviour's were warned to leave their houses this morning on account of gun practice, but this did not take place. The weather has again turned cold and sleet is falling.

January 9. For some time it has been known that a few German officials at College House have deplored the behaviour of units who have searched private houses and taken stocks of foodstuffs; as a result, a notice has been published stipulating what households may possess—each member of a household may have not more than ten tins or jars of tinned or potted meat, fowl, fish or fat, and not more than twenty tins or jars of fruit or vegetables; any excess must be distributed to civilians in less fortunate circumstances or offered to the soup kitchens. Tins from Red Cross parcels, as well as any home-made fruit or vegetable preserves, are excluded; invalids requiring special diet

---

* John De La Haye received a letter in appreciation of his gallantry from the Bailiff of Jersey, and was presented with the Bronze Medal of the Jersey Humane Society; on Liberation Day, 1946, he was awarded the American Medal of Freedom.

may retain stores in excess of the above figures and may, through their doctor, obtain permission to do so from College House. Similarly, not more than 14 lb. of flour and 4 lb. of sugar may be retained for every member of a household; any excess to be distributed as above. This means that a considerable quantity of goods may be held without fear of it being confiscated. The Germans are still searching for the Americans, houses in the Red Bouillon district receiving attention today; posters have been circulated with a description of the wanted men, and unfortunate results of these house-to-house searches is that some residents were caught with wireless sets. The fuel ration for January is a hundredweight of wood for holders of a medical permit.

January 10. German order issued stating that 'the food position in the besieged fortress makes necessary a reduction in the number of dogs'; only one dog over three months old may be kept on each farm or private household; all dogs exceeding this number must be killed by the 20th inst. Certified kennels breeding dogs are exempted by this order, and persons desiring to keep a second pedigree dog must apply for the necessary licence to the Constable of their parish. Owing to the change in the electricity hours, the *E.P.* has to be printed in the evening previous to the day of publication.

January 11. The Germans imposed a number of sentences today for alleged offences—these included persons whose houses had recently been searched and who would not divulge where they had obtained flour or wheat; others for being possessors of crystal sets, and some who had written letters to England which had been lost by would-be escapees and found by the Germans. There is a waiting list for the jail.

January 12. Two more German notices: one calls on owners of installations for generating electric current to furnish particulars of these; the other requires registration of all new or almost new tyres for motor cycles, motor cars and lorries which are not in use. These tyres now appear on the list of rationed goods and black marketing in them in punishable. The Germans have stopped taking cycles for the time being. They have also dug around tree-roots in the Royal Crescent preparatory to removal; two trees have been left standing by their orders 'so as to preserve the beauty of the crescent'. Details were published today of the Red Cross supplies brought by the *Vega*—the Canadian Red Cross sent 77,384 parcels; the British Red Cross sent 2,700 'diet' parcels, about 7,060 lb. of salt and about 27,000 tablets of soap, also 52 cases of medical supplies; the New Zealand Red Cross sent 15 cases of tobacco (88 lb. in 2-oz. packets) and cigarettes (32,244 packets of 10 each); Lady Campbell's fund sent four cases of layettes.

January 13. More German notices: these state that part of the stores of potatoes held by farmers has been de-blocked in favour of the Department of Agriculture, which body will issue instructions as to how these will be dealt with; farmers are also made responsible for the safety of their stores, in particular seed potatoes, which must be placed in rooms which can be locked and which are situated in the immediate vicinity of their dwelling houses; barns and outbuildings at a considerable distance from the farm are to be emptied. The Platzkommandantur has ordered the ration of electric current for the civilian population to be reduced, with immediate effect, from $2\frac{1}{2}$ to 1 kw. (unit) per week per family. The Germans are to grant facilities for letters to be sent to prisoners of war—one per month. From today the majority of telephone subscribers connected to the Central Exchange have been cut off, only essential services being permitted.

January 14. St. John Ambulance Brigade held a Red Cross thanksgiving service at St. Helier's Parish Church today; this body, which is allowed to function and wear uniform, has done excellent work during the Occupation. The epidemic of indiscriminate tree-felling reached its climax today when numbers of people armed with saws and axes attacked the trees along St. Aubin's Road which border the Lower Park, almost every one of the trees being hewn down. The Germans were very annoyed about it, and although it was a Sunday afternoon insisted on the Bailiff and Attorney-General visiting the scene. The Germans took away many identity cards, which will have to be fetched at College House. Dry wood is being ripped from untenanted houses, sleepers along the German track from Don Bridge to Corbière disappear overnight; and among the 'acquisitions' must be included the wooden gates of St. Luke's Church! With the evenings lengthening, the electric supply is to commence later—6.30 instead of 6.15.

January 15. Three orders concerning rations today, all by order of the Platzkommandant. 1. No butter is to be issued as from today; this applies to all butter rations—the normal, the invalid's, heavy worker's and Reichs-German's supplementary. 2. There is to be a meat ration every alternate week. 3. The milk ration is to be issued to the adult population only on four days out of seven. This means the milk ration for children, juveniles and persons entitled to special rations on medical permit remain unchanged, but that adults will get only two pints per week.

Persons whose identity cards were taken yesterday for illicit wood-cutting had them returned today but the wood was confiscated. Another German notice states that the Commandant of the Fortress has prohibited the use of electric power for water-pumps in private houses; water-pumps on farms and on commercial premises, etc., must be converted to hand-pumps by the 25th inst. Two barges are being loaded with potatoes and wheat for the German troops in Guernsey; the Superior Council has agreed to loan fifty tons of flour for the civil population of that Island. The Department of Agriculture has notified growers that they may obtain a small quantity of fertiliser for glasshouse potatoes. To enable the cranes to be used, the district which includes the harbours must be supplied with electric power with the result that residents in that area take full advantage. The *E.P.* list of the Red Cross Fund has now reached over £10,000.

January 16. The layettes given to the Island by Lady Campbell's Fund are being distributed to new and expectant mothers. Among the *Vega*'s cargo was a small number of parcels from New Zealand, but these have not yet been distributed. A variety entertainment was presented at the Opera House this evening by Doug. Power; the Opera House and Wests are still carrying on, and many entertainments are being held in aid of the Red Cross Fund.

January 17. A German court martial today acquitted some local residents who had appealed against sentences for refusal to reveal where they had obtained flour or wheat found in recent searches of their houses; and they were told their goods would be restored. Sentences ranging from weeks to months were passed in other cases, which included Wireless Order infractions. Some numbers on the Central Exchange have been restored, these in addition to essentials. The following notice re the cutting of wood is published over the signature of the Commandant of the Fortress of Jersey:

Unauthorised tree-cutting in the Island has recently increased to such an extent that it has led to spoliation of the Island and unequal distribution of the wood, so that the whole wood question has been taken over as from now by the Occupying Authorities. It is therefore ordered as follows:

(1) With immediate effect all illicit cutting and gathering of wood is forbidden for all, whether owner or occupier of the land on which it stands, also in private grounds and farms, public parks and roads.

(2) Anyone found cutting or gathering wood with saw or

axe without permission will be punished. The tools and all the wood will be confiscated.

(3) The cutting down of trees and transport will only be permitted to the authorised wood cutters and transport workers of the States with a new permit from the Platzkommandantur I, St. Helier, and only when they are cutting the wood or carting it away from the recognised localities during working hours.

(4) The troops are authorised to take wood and tools from any despoilers of trees. Further orders for the protection of the troops and the population will follow.

Anyone infringing the above Order will be punished according to Par. 22 of the Order for the Protection of the Occupying Forces of December 12, 1942.

January 18. A verdict of death from cardiac failure supervening on pulmonary congestion, accelerated by malnutrition, was returned at an inquest on the body of a woman of 70 who was recently found dead; doctors' evidence showed she weighed only three stone.

January 19. The American prisoners who escaped on the 8th inst. got away from the Island during the night. The Germans give notice that a court martial has sentenced a farmer to three months because he declared that fowls which were registered had been stolen, his story being discredited. Local officials are convinced he was telling the truth. The re-opening of all colleges and schools under the control of the Department of Education has been postponed until February 8 owing to the continued cold weather and lack of fuel; many private schools are due to commence, pupils supplying fuel for the fires. Red Cross soap issued to the public and greatly appreciated; two tablets are allotted each household.

January 20. Ten cigarettes for all adults were issued today from Red Cross supplies; these were de Rezke, manufactured in New Zealand. The Germans give notice that a resident has been fined 250 marks (about £25) for using his lorry for a 'pleasure trip'—transporting a football team; another resident has been fined 360 marks (about £30) for using electric current during the evening, contrary to prohibition. At the Royal Court today a youth was ordered to have eighteen strokes of the birch for stealing a Red Cross parcel. Due to the fuel shortage, country smiths can no longer get supplies, and the Germans have offered space in their forges to smiths who wish to shoe customers' shoes or repair agricultural implements. A westerly gale which has been raging for some time was today accompanied by sleet squalls.

January 22. By order of the Germans, the Parish of St. Helier advertises for 30 cross-cut saws, 50 axes and 50 iron wedges for use in supplying the civilian population of St. Helier with wood. At the Police Court today three persons were charged with stripping the wood from an untenanted house for use as firewood. Large quantities of boxwood and potato barrels are also being bought for the purpose. Several residents received varying sentences today for infractions of the Wireless Order. Some skim milk may now be obtained on milkless days. The Red Cross supply of salt issued—2 oz. per head. The barges laden with wheat, flour and potatoes for Guernsey have left.

January 23. Notice is given by the Department of Essential Services that, owing to the coal stock for the St. Peter's Power Station being practically exhausted, the supply of electric current is expected to cease on Thursday night, January 25th, at 10.30. The next monthly ration of half a pint of paraffin for invalids and nursing mothers will be the last. The Germans have stopped food, fuel and other necessities being sent to political prisoners; this had been allowed for some time.

January 24. There has been much activity today in connection with the electricity situation; the Germans have intimated they would be willing to provide oil to keep part of Queen's Road Power Station running, but about 80 per cent. of the supply would be required for military purposes. The Electricity Company has refused participation in any scheme unless the supply is shared equally by the civilian population and the military. Further developments are awaited. The Germans have also issued their first order re the felling of trees; this states that trees marked by them for the civilian population can only be felled under the control of the Department of Labour, which must issue special permits bearing the Platzkommandantur stamp. The *E.P.'s* fifth Occupation Almanac was issued today. The public must register through their grocers for further supplies of Red Cross parcels. A group of five planes passed over the south of the Island this afternoon the Germans firing at them. The Department of Agriculture has made directions prohibiting the planting of potatoes in the open ground; this does not affect planting of potatoes under glass.

January 25. More meetings between the Electricity Company officials and the Germans took place today; the latter have declared they will run one of the generators at the Queen's road Power Station for their own use and they have placed engineers in charge; the Electricity Company has left two of its staff at the works to watch the company's interests. The Germans have stated they will run some essential civilian services and their linesmen have commenced fixing overhead cables. Among the places affected by the cessation of the electricity supply are the Opera House and Wests, which will close down after tonight; dances have also been stopped. The Germans are requisitioning private power plants and are searching for stolen Diesel oil, especially around Gorey. The electricity supply terminated at 10.30 p.m.

January 26. On this first evening without electricity, many people have started going to bed early; we never studied sunrise and sunset so much. Crystal sets have come into their own now that mains sets cannot be used, and are fetching high prices. The Germans have made inquiries as to when the *Vega* is due to leave Lisbon, and the arrangement is that the next Red Cross parcels will not be issued until it is known she has left again for the Island.

January 27. The Electricity Company thanks its customers for past support and gives advice about storage of electrical equipment. The *E.P.* gives notice that it may have to suspend publication. The Constable of St. Helier warns householders to take precautions against would-be thieves at night, and they are advised, as there is no telephone service of any account, to make the noisiest alarm if intruders are heard. At the Police Court today a woman was sentenced to a month's imprisonment for stealing from a Red Cross parcel. After being stopped for a time, Summerland announces that clogging of boots and shoes of certain sizes can be resumed.

January 29. German electricians, assisted by foreign workers, are installing cables to keep some essential services going. The Germans are again commandeering bicycles; many people have failed to renew their bicycle licences in the hope that their machines will not be traced through the parish books. Extra rations issued this week of $\frac{1}{2}$ lb. of rice for all children and juveniles, and $\frac{1}{4}$ lb. of bean flour for everybody. There was no publication of the *E.P.* today.

January 30. Planes were over in the early hours. The Germans had a meeting at The Forum this morning to celebrate the twelfth anniversary of Hitler's coming to power. There has also been a meeting of German doctors, they are greatly concerned with the health of the troops and lack of medical supplies; many soldiers are looking extremely ill, and some have collapsed in the street; they now have reveille an hour later and must rest in the afternoon, while all sport is stopped. Another notice published today gives the names of civil forestry officers from whom information may be obtained regarding the felling of trees. The *E.P.* published three times a week—Tuesdays, Thursdays and Saturdays.

January 31. The total to date of the Island Red Cross Fund is over £25,000. The police have raided premises in Wesley Street and found illicit stills used for the manufacture of Calvados* or some similar spirit. January has been a long, dreary month, with low temperatures and falls of sleet and snow. People with supplies of paraffin or candles are lucky, for the majority of the population goes to bed early, to stay there until daylight. Some professions such as dentists and photographers, cannot undertake work unless customers provide paraffin. The Germans have connected the Telephone Exchange with the electricity supply from the generator they are running at Queen's Road Power station, and the supply is from 2 to 10 p.m. each day. After a lapse, night patrols are out again to catch people after curfew. The jail is still full, but food may be smuggled in once again. Two boys have been beaten up by the Harbour Police (or water rats, as they are called) for alleged tar-daubing. Robberies continue on a large scale; bakehouses are the latest attraction, and it is beyond doubt this is the work of Germans. Dogs and cats are being missed daily, these forming part of many a German menu, while some soldiers are so hungry that they eat raw swedes; at a baker's shop one offered five marks (10s. 8d.) for a piece of bread, and from the farmers they are continually begging for food. The health of the population as a whole is very poor; minor ailments, such as poisoned fingers, broken chilblains, or worms, are very prevalent, while nursing homes have seldom a vacant bed. The death rate for January was 35.6 per 1,000. Soup has been doled out daily to schoolchildren, and young children may obtain a small quantity of honey, sugar-beet syrup or dripping, on medical certificate. The Germans appear to be making ready four torpedo-boat destroyers; masts and other gear have been removed and coaling has commenced, the suggestion being they will try to get away at night. Hatches, etc., off many of the French barges are being used for fuel. The Germans have dug man-holes all over the place; these are meant to give cover to soldiers if the Island is attacked, but residents of parishes having no dust collection find them very handy!

---

* This 'calvados' was made from distilled cider by both Germans and the civilian population, especially in the country; a fair amount was manufactured and some of it was extremely potent.

February 1. No fuel ration issued this month, but it is understood the Germans are to grant permits to people wishing to buy a tree to fell. There is a shortage of wood even for the bakehouses; some of the crates containing Red Cross parcels have had to be used. The Department of Agriculture gives notice that the recent prohibition of potato planting in the open ground does not apply to private gardens. The Germans issue a notice to the effect that farmers unable to find seed for all their fields must let a small portion of the same to units of the Occupying Forces wishing to rent them; the rent is fixed at 30 reichsmarks (£3 4s. 1d.) per vergée and a short written agreement has to be entered into with the unit concerned. Warning is also given to employers that they are not permitted to employ foreign labour not domiciled in the Island without permission from the Platzkommandantur. The Germans have demanded a large quantity of swedes and turnips, each parish having to contribute a substantial quota. The Gas Works is still experiencing a rush on tar and the maximum amount obtainable per person has had to be fixed at two gallons.

February 2. Planes were over in the early hours and there was some activity at the Airport. The Bailiff was informed by the Germans today that there was no likelihood of flour supplies being sent by the Red Cross; there is only enough flour for another week, and the men at the mills have been given notice. In the afternoon the *E.P.* was handed for publication a notice from the Superior Council which stated that, in compliance with an order of the Military Commander of the Channel Islands, bread rations would, with effect from Monday next (February 5, 1945), be reduced to the following amounts: 1 lb. per week for infants (up to 3 years); 1½ lb. for children (3 to 10 years) and invalids (special white bread); 2 lb. for all other categories. The public is informed that the supplies of flour under the control of the States would have been sufficient to maintain the bread ration on the old scale only up to February 10; the reduction now ordered will make possible the issue of a ration (on the reduced scale) up to February 17, 1945.

February 3. More air activity in the early hours. Deep depression has settled on the population in view of the imminent halving of the bread ration. In many undertakings workmen have signified their intention of working shorter hours, while some are threatening to strike. The Germans have a ration of 4 lb. of bread per week and are presumed still to hold a large proportion of the two thousand tons of wheat which they recently 'blocked'. It is thought they should have enough flour to keep themselves and the civilian population for six months on a 4-lb. ration. This afternoon a bill was posted in the *E.P.* window to the effect that it had been officially learned that the *Vega* on her next voyage would bring parcels for prisoners of war in the Islands, and it was learned through the Germans that she had left Lisbon. Two small boats arrived from Guernsey today; they brought mail and about 20 troops. Five cigarettes were issued today to male adults; they were manufactured from plants confiscated by the Royal Court and tobacco purchased by the States. A farmer was fined £20 at the Royal Court today for keeping an unregistered pig; these cases are not so numerous as they were.

February 5. Red Cross parcels are being taken to the shops for the second issue, these having been brought by the *Vega* on her first visit; the same arrangements regarding distribution were made. The reduced bread ration came into operation today; parents with children are especially hit, not knowing how to satisfy their families.

February 6. A message from the Bailiff was published by the *E.P.* today, the full text being as under:

> The Council has asked me, by means of this message, to make known to the public that, in accordance with an order received from the German Military Authorities, the civil bread ration must be reduced by half.
>
> The public is aware that when, after long and difficult negotiations, the representatives of the International Red Cross came here shortly after Christmas, they were accurately informed of the position of stocks in the Island and were urgently asked to arrange for the sending to the Island of the flour necessary to maintain the civil bread ration.
>
> Day by day we have anxiously awaited news.
>
> Unfortunately, as I write, the position is that there is no official news whatever that ships are on their way to us with flour, food parcels, or the many other stocks for which we asked.
>
> The stocks of flour and of grain under our own control would not maintain the civil bread ration on the existing scale beyond the 10th of February.
>
> The proposed cut should make possible a continuation of the bread ration for a week after February 10.

If help does not reach us by then, either by the actual arrival of flour of by promise of future supplies, the bread ration must cease entirely.

I have been given facilities for making an urgent appeal to the International Red Cross, and we shall continue to do everything in our power to bring relief to the public.

It is under these circumstances that the second distribution of food parcels, already announced in the Press, will be carried out.

We know how difficult it is to refrain from immediate enjoyment of the contents of the parcels, but we would be lacking in our duty if we failed to make the public aware of the gravity of the position.

With the present issue of parcels, our store is exhausted except for a few hundred parcels, some deficient, which remain over.

It is impossible to say when a further issue will be possible.

The public is reminded that facilities for the distribution of soap have long been in existence. Every effort is being made to increase the supplies available.

2/2/45.   A. M. COUTANCHE.

The publication of the above message has been unavoidably delayed. I am informed by the German Military Authorities that news has been received that on her next visit to the Channel Islands the *Vega* will bring food parcels for prisoners of war, but will NOT bring flour.

A. M. COUTANCHE, Bailiff.

It was learned during the morning that the *Vega* has arrived at Guernsey. Due to the latest cut, postmen are to make only three deliveries per week; other workers' hours are also reduced. The Germans have given notice that the forces require a large number of axes to carry out wood cutting; householders with more than one axe in their possession must deliver them to the forces against payment, these to be taken to parish halls; offenders against the order will be punished. An American speedboat, used by Germans who escaped from Granville recently, is missing from the harbour. It has been rumoured that some sailors were to make a getaway; if this were the case, their plans were upset by Allied planes which were off the Island during the night.

February 7. Three local youths have escaped from Gloucester Street Prison, where they were serving sentence for trying to escape from the Island. The local prison governor and the German jailers have been interrogated several times by College House officials. German police, in searching the youths' homes, found the brother of one in possession of a crystal set. The second distribution of Red Cross parcels is taking place. These are extended to foreign workers, who show their gratitude by contributing to the Red Cross Fund. A nine-year-old boy has been killed in one of the Parade air-raid shelters; these were being filled in some time ago, but the Germans stopped the work. The little chap had gone there for kindling wood and through knocking away a wooden upright the roof fell in.

February 8. From today (Thursday) all football matches have been cancelled; with the meagre bread ration the playing of football would impose too severe a strain on the health of the players. Among recently reported robberies is one involving the altar candles from St. Andrew's Church. The President of the Department of Agriculture is to attend meetings of farmers in the parish halls to ascertain what stocks of potatoes they can deliver for the civilian population and to examine documents in their possession covering deliveries of potatoes to the German Forces. The German soldiers have been warned about using sea water for cooking vegetables, it being suspected this has caused boils. Schools under the control of the States have re-opened; until the end of the month the hours will be from 10 a.m. to 12.30 p.m. Soup and milk are being distributed to the school-children. The teaching of German, which was always spasmodic, has now been discontinued for as long as the schools have only one session per day.*

---

* It may be of interest here to quote from a pamphlet entitled 'The Channel Islands Schools During the German Occupation:

'Early in 1942, a volunteer class for German was held after school hours in some schools. It was the considered opinion of the teachers that it was preferable to have our own teachers giving instruction in the language rather than that our schools should be contaminated by some pompous propagandist of the German Forces.

'So feeble was the response to learn German voluntarily that the Education Department had at last to inform head teachers that, ordered by the Field Commandant, the compulsory teaching of German in the schools would commence on the 15th February, 1943. The German Education Officer, one Bleul, had been a master in some college in the Argentine, and had let the Education Secretary know that he was accustomed to be on friendly terms with English masters at the college. He found no teacher friends in Jersey though—he was shunned severely—and

271

February 9. The Weighbridge today presented a scene reminiscent of former potato seasons, farmers' vans going 'over the bridge' with loads of swedes and turnips recently requisitioned. The Germans are now paying for poultry commandeered at Christmas—6s. 6d. per head. At the last of a series of concerts held at St. Ouen's in aid of the Red Cross Fund an auction sale was held this evening; astounding prices were paid—£1 18s. 5½d. for an egg, and £9 8s. 0d. for a quarter of a pound of tobacco!

February 10. The last Saturday buses ran today. A notice by the Department of Agriculture calls on growers to give a statement of what seed potatoes they possess and the area of land required for planting same. A further notice by the Department calls for more precautions by cattle-owners to ensure cleanliness of milk and the need for keeping milk cool, as quantities are received in town in a condition unfit for distribution. Milk roundsmen, etc., are being allowed 1½ pints of milk per day and an extra ½ lb. of flour per week. Accommodation will be available on the *Vega* for mail for civilian internees in Germany; instructions are given concerning special forms obtainable at the Bailiff's Enquiry and News Office.

February 11. Despite bad weather, many people went near the harbours today to see the *Vega*, but she did not arrive. Two more youths have escaped from prison; a third was shot in the leg by a German guard and re-captured.

February 12. The Germans have run an electric cable to one of the dairies to provide power for milk pasteurisation. Numbers of young people are being arrested for possessing crystal sets or a one-valve set run off an accumulator, and the Germans have arrested some youths on suspicion of having stolen explosives and firearms. The electricity supply was switched on for about half a minute at 9.45 this evening.

February 13. The Red Cross ship *Vega* arrived on her second visit at 10.45 this morning. Her berth was at the Albert Pier and arrangements for transporting the cargo were the same. This time she was unloaded by French colonial troops who are prisoners of war. There was trouble between the German authorities and the cranemen; the latter were willing to unload the *Vega*, but not to load a barge taking foodstuffs to the Guernsey garrison, and they were dismissed. Electric power generated with Diesel

when he ordered heads to report on the teaching of German he had many rude shocks. He just could not make out how we could have the nerve after years of German arrogance to tell him what we thought of his "bright idea". '

oil brought by the *Vega* was used for the cranes. Mons. Callias, International Red Cross delegate, came with the *Vega*, and meetings will be held with the German and civil authorities. Colonel von Heldorff has also arrived from Guernsey to take part in these meetings. Among the *Vega*'s cargo—mainly food parcels packed in Canada and New Zealand—are American-packed parcels for American and French prisoners of war; clothing has also arrived for the latter. Reports of a small boat being on the rocks off the east coast and closing of part of the coast road while bodies said to have been washed up at La Rocque were being transferred to hospital.

February 14. The discharge of the *Vega* goes on, and a message from the Bailiff has been handed to the *E.P.* for publication, as follows:

The latest news with regard to flour comes to the Island in a letter written to me by Colonel Iselin, Lisbon, delegate of the International Red Cross, from Lisbon on February 1, 1945.

Monsieur Callias, who has again come to the Channel Islands with the *Vega*, has no later news.

After referring to the delay caused by the need of repairing the *Vega* and to his regret at being unable to send any soap, Colonel Iselin adds:

'Furthermore—and this is worse—*Vega* will not bring you any flour, although there is flour available in Lisbon, I wish to add that I have continually stressed the point how important it was that flour should reach you now, but the British Red Cross Society in London—for reasons unknown to me—have decided that the flour shall be loaded on the third voyage only. Instead you will receive a proportionally higher number of standard parcels. It must be hoped that the consequences this change may have will not be too serious.'

The bill of lading shows *Vega* as carrying 85,344 food parcels for Jersey, in addition to diet parcels, and small quantities of tobacco, cigarettes, medicaments, salt and leather for boot-repairing.

It is hoped to make the next distribution of food parcels on February 20, and a notice will appear in the Press on Saturday.

February 14, 1945.   A. M. COUTANCHE,
                                                Bailiff.

February 15. There is a meat ration this week—really a

273

meatless one—for the local authorities have done some wangling. Due to lack of refrigeration because of no electricity supply, distribution of meat will in future be divided; shops in the market will supply customers in the middle of the week and outside shops at the end, this alternating. The Germans now have dogs and cats killed and dressed at the Slaughter House, and many residents have lost their pets. Planes were over during the day; there have been continual sounds of heavy gunfire or explosions coming from the French coast. Grocers' shops are to remain closed on Thursdays; apart from the Red Cross parcels, the only article handled in these establishments is breakfast meal. A film to be shown to civilians at The Forum this evening was not screened owing to a breakdown of the electricity supply (The Forum is fed by a line from the Power Station); the film was advertised as *This is to Certify*, the Germans have mistaken the Board of Censors' certificate for the title.

February 16. The *Vega* returned to Lisbon today, and we all hope she will soon come back with flour. Some bakers have supplied extra bread to customers from surplus flour; this has not met with official approval and has been stopped, it being hoped a small general ration may be issued. Since the ration has been 2 lb. per week, workmen in several undertakings have had their hours reduced to a minimum. Black-market prices for wheat and potatoes have soared; wheat has changed hands at £30 per hundredweight and potatoes at over £4 per bag. The Red Cross delegate was delighted with Jersey's contribution to the Red Cross Fund, which exceeds £30,000. A committee of responsible persons has been formed to deal with the contents of broken parcels, etc., and extras will be distributed to the needy.

February 17. The Germans have issued a notice that stocks exceeding five litres of spirits and ten litres of wine, including champagne, per household, as well as supplies of soap exceeding two tablets per head, will be confiscated in favour of hospitals and institutions. A notice from the Department of Essential Commodities removes the prohibition on sales by auction of linoleum, rugs and other floor coverings. Locally grown grapefruit is on sale in a King Street shop in aid of the Red Cross Fund. The barge which was loading with foodstuffs for the Guernsey garrison left the harbour today, and a number of sailors who came here recently for manoeuvres also returned. At the Royal Court today fines were imposed in two cases of tree-felling without a permit; sentences of six and nine months' imprisonment were imposed on two cycle thieves.

February 18. Some fishermen who risked putting down a net

on the east coast had a good haul of 800 lb. of fish; most of this was bartered, what was over being sold for three marks a pound (6s. 4½d.) Along St. Ouen's Bay recently hundreds of dead squid have been washed up, believed due to last month's very cold weather. The Germans have been busy carting them away for food.

February 19. One pound of bread is being issued to everyone from surplus flour, the last until supplies arrive from Lisbon; the whole is being made at one bakehouse in order to save fuel. The bread situation is eased somewhat, this by a double potato ration (10 lb.), issued 'on the quiet'; unfortunately a large proportion has to be thrown away as potatoes are bad. Tar is no longer available to the public.

February 20. The third issue of Red Cross parcels made today; those distributed in town were Canadian, while those issued in the country were mainly New Zealand, many of the latter being affected by damp. Children under two years of age, who may have an invalid's parcel instead, receiving a tablet of soap. About 2,000 Red Cross messages are being delivered; these are from England and were brought by the *Vega*, in addition to messages from internees and prisoners of war in Germany. An allocation of a hundredweight of wood is being made to holders of a medical permit; to be countersigned by a German 'tree inspector'.

February 21. A plane was over in the early hours. Some mail has arrived from Guernsey, and the Germans are taking butter away on a patrol boat; a number of officers have recently left the Island, proceeding to Guernsey by sea and then being transferred to Lorient or St. Nazaire by plane. The Airport here is little used.

February 22. During the night hundreds of houses in town and country have had swastikas 'painted' on them with tar; this was the work of German marines, who did a systematic job. Many householders tried to remove these swastikas or paint them over, and some turned them into Union Jacks. At a country sale today £32 was paid for 100 bundles of wood faggots. On Thursdays St. Helier is a town of the dead with nearly every shop closed.

February 23. The German military authorities are annoyed about the swastika-painting by the marines; the latter are stated to be getting undisciplined. The Germans are advertising for farmers willing to grow tobacco for the Forces; they are also prepared to receive orders from farmers requiring horses for ploughing, etc. A party of five escaped from La Rocque during the evening; they had taken their boat there previously and had made careful preparations.

February 24. The Germans renew their warning to farmers about employing foreign workers, and remind householders they must not let rooms to them. Mail may be sent to civilian internees in Germany, this to be taken by the *Vega* on her next journey. The Department of Agriculture is unable to accept delivery of potatoes until further notice, because of German instructions. The latter have only enough potatoes to last until the end of May; in consequence, civilian supplies must be curtailed. The local authorities hope to keep the ration going until next season; many farmers are not planting seed potatoes, for as soon as they are in the ground the Germans come at night and dig them out. Cart axles are wanted by the Department of Labour for making wedges essential for fuel production. Hours of water supply in the town are now: 7 to 9, 11.30 to 12.30 and 5 to 7.

February 25. Single planes during the day—a quiet one apart from this; Sundays have become monotonously depressing. Members of the St. John Ambulance Brigade are examining and re-packing some New Zealand parcels to be issued next week, as a large number of these are damaged.

February 26. Six ounces of salt for everyone this week from Red Cross supplies; 3 oz. of macaroni issued per head, and another meat ration in a 'meatless' week, it being hoped to continue this. The Germans have lifted their control of goods still held by the civilian authorities. No bread issued this week, but the double potato ration was repeated. Men working for the Todt Organisation have been put on removing swastikas from houses; in many cases the 'removal aggravates the defacement, and some are being chipped off with chisels.

February 27. Session of the States: Main business was the granting of £20,000 for subsidising tradesmen to enable them to keep their staffs, on the basis of £1 1s. 4d. for each male adult employee, 15s. for each female, and 10s. 8d. for each juvenile. The Bailiff was requested to transmit a resolution to the Red Cross Authorities expressing the States gratitude. Trades not affected by the subsidy are bakery, greengrocery, milk distribution and second-hand shops. Other business before the House concerned the establishment of a Remand Home for young men under 20 who are awaiting trial or requiring to be dealt with otherwise than by imprisonment. A report of the Social Assurance Committee on a scheme to extend benefits to cover sickness was lodged au Greffe, and the session concluded with the adoption of a resolution of thanks to the Red Cross for sending much-needed supplies to the Channel Islands. Two notices were published by the Department of Public Health today: the first concerned the evacuation of invalids from the Island to England, negotiations being in progress between Great Britain and the German Government; those eligible will be persons of unsound mind, persons suffering from tuberculosis and persons requiring investigation or treatment not available on the Island. The second notice gives details of Red Cross medical supplies and the method of distribution—proprietaries, patent medicines and surgical sundries are to be distributed by the Chemists' Association at full prices, all moneys received to be paid to the Red Cross Fund; baby foods, vitamin preparations and aspirins are to be issued on medical certificate only, approved by the Medical Board; other drugs which have been received are such as will only be used on prescription in cases of real medical need; small quantities of toilet or household soap which have arrived will be allotted as follows: every child that is born will be presented with a tablet of soap; every doctor, nurse, or other person certified to be in actual attendance on the sick will receive one tablet; and some will be put aside for use in the operating theatres of the Island; the household soap will be distributed to sick-institutions and to district nurses for distribution to the sick poor in their care. Other items, which include shaving soap and toothpaste, are being kept in store until other supplies arrive. It is understood the whole of these supplies were intended to restock Boots' shops in the Channel Islands and were awaiting shipment at Southampton after the liberation of the Islands; when the Red Cross sent an S.O.S. for medical supplies these were sent immediately to Lisbon. The Germans have issued a long statement regarding tree-felling; they declare the Island has been divided into ten zones for the purpose; each zone under the control of a German expert, who decides what trees may or may not be cut down. Some German naval officers and ratings had to attend a court martial today; there have been cases of insubordination of late. At night two German soldiers escaped from Gloucester Street Prison.

February 28. Graf von Schmettow, Military Commander of the Channel Islands, stationed at Guernsey, has been replaced by Admiral Hueffmeier; Col. von Heldorff goes with von Schmettow, and the Platzkommandant for Jersey (Major Heider) has been replaced by the Harbour Commandant here (Korvetten Kapitän von Kleve). The reason given by the Germans for this change is that all ports still held by them must be under naval command, local opinion views the changes with mixed feelings, for Admiral Hueffmeier is known to be a rabid Nazi. There has been a fracas in the College grounds between soldiers and sailors, knives being used. Two naval officers have been arrested for their part in painting swastikas. German patrols have been out today searching for an escaped Russian. There is an underground movement at work, and today numbers of typewritten pamphlets were found about the town; these were in German and made a scathing attack on the Nazis, Hitler in particular, pointing out the futility of continuing the struggle, especially in Jersey. Officers were stated to be ready to lead an insurrection when the time is ripe, and warning was given to do nothing until further orders. Copies of these leaflets were soon translated and large numbers circulated among the civilian population. We have come to the end of a very mild month, with a great deal of fog. The Germans are searching for persons who augmented their fuel supplies with sleepers from the Todt railways. Empty houses continue to be stripped of woodwork. Some farmers have sown wheat, but the majority have not yet received permission to plant potatoes. The Germans have also proper squads of limpet-pickers, their 'catch' helping—with sugar-beet!—to flavour 'soup'! Several essential services have been connected with the electricity supply; we are getting used to doing without light or going to bed early. One type of 'lighting' has been made with boxes of bluestone, these giving a phosphorescent glow. Black-market Diesel oil is selling at 50 marks a gallon (£5 6s. 10d.)! The whole Island is grateful for Red Cross supplies, without which we would be faring badly.

March 1945

March 1. The first of the month brings the news, through the B.B.C. that the Red Cross ship *Vega* has again left for the Channel Islands; this is welcome, for she is bringing flour.

March 2. 'Summer Time' is to come into force from midnight tonight, but as the *E.P.* giving the information will not be published until tomorrow (Saturday) the majority of the population will not know about the change, which is a month ahead of last year, and only for the Channel Islands. The local authorities had an interview with the new Platzkommandant today. A single plane was over during the afternoon.

March 3. As anticipated, the sudden change to 'Summer Time' has upset a lot of people who knew nothing about it, and the losing of an hour's daylight in the morning is especially deplored by farmers. During the night, Union Jacks, French Tricolours and V-signs have been painted in red, white and blue in many parts of the town; some of these were works of art and must have taken a long time to do. Fifty cigarettes or 2 oz. of tobacco issued from Red Cross supplies to everyone over 18, a gift from New Zealand; most people had cigarettes, as there was only a small amount of tobacco. Attempted robberies of these supplies have been frustrated. The following Order to the German Forces was published today:

At noon, on 28th February, 1945, I have taken over the command of the Channel Islands and of the Fortress of Guernsey from General Graf von Schmettow, who has been called home for reasons of health. I have only one aim: to hold out until final victory. I believe in the mission of our Fuehrer and of our people. I shall serve them with immutable loyalty. Hail our beloved Fuehrer.

HUFFMEIER,
Vice-Admiral and Commander of the Channel Islands.

March 4. Numbers of planes were off the Island at various times during the day. The Germans are attempting to catch fish with tennis court netting suspended on poles.

March 5. Fourth distribution of Red Cross parcels; this time they were all New Zealand, and the usual arrangements were carried out. No bread again this week, but the potato ration remains doubled; there is also meat and a ration of cooking oil—half a pint for adults and a quarter of a pint for everyone under 18.

March 6. The *Vega* has arrived at Guernsey with flour. No more applications for trees or for forestry permits can be accepted until the 20th inst., and would-be growers of tobacco are reminded it is necessary to obtain a licence.

March 7. A fire broke out at the Palace Hotel this morning; when this spread to an ammunition dump there was a violent explosion which shook the town and did widespread damage. In the immediate vicinity many houses suffered damage to windows, doors, ceilings, etc., and flying débris was found in neighbouring fields. In addition, fifteen gas meters exploded, and ammunition was heard going off until late in the evening, the Fire Brigade having an unenviable task. The main part of the building was gutted. The Germans have been at the Palace since the start of the Occupation. At night a shed at the Todt depôt at Georgetown caught fire and was burnt out. The Germans suspect sabotage.

March 8. The Home Secretary in the House of Commons today gave details regarding Red Cross supplies for the Channel Islands. Planes were over in numbers today, especially in the north-west. Aircraft is in the vicinity of the Island almost every day, but the Germans do not fire unless they are flying low.

March 9. The Germans made a commando raid on Granville during the night and claim to have done all sorts of wonderful things; some of those who went on the expedition have been decorated with the Iron Cross. The B.B.C. has admitted the raid and said there were casualties on both sides. The Germans brought back a ship with them—the *Eskwood*, a coal boat of 800 tons which traded here before the war; she had discharged her cargo at Granville and was in ballast. About 30 prisoners were captured, the majority being American, and the Germans 'released' 55 of their own men, bringing them here to limpet soup and boiled swedes! The Germans lost two small boats and 16 men, but they claim to have sunk nearly 5,000 tons of shipping, destroyed the locks, and set the town and docks on fire. The Red Cross ship *Vega* arrived in harbour on her third visit at 4.30 p.m. bringing flour as her main cargo—5,029 sacks.

March 10. The *Vega* commenced discharging this morning, being unloaded again by French colonial troops, St. John Ambulance Brigade personnel supervising. The flour was taken to the Red Cross store (Martlands) and after checking, was immediately taken to the bakers. Additional cargo consisted of 43,278 food parcels, 1,068 diet parcels, 126 cases of soap, 94 sacks of salt, yeast, medical supplies and sundries. She also brought Diesel oil to work the cranes and petrol for the ambulances. Proprietary goods which had been brought among the medical supplies on the last visit were on sale to the public at chemist shops today; there were the usual queues and very soon most articles were sold out. Shoe repairs with Red Cross leather may now be obtained on medical permit. The Red Cross delegate who arrived with the *Vega*—a new man—has not been allowed to land, as his papers are stated to be not in order. A local resident who escaped from the Germans on October 25 and has been in hiding since then got away from Fauvic tonight.

March 11. The *Vega* finished discharging today. Some bread has already been delivered and gratefully received; the loaves are such as we have not seen for four years and are a joy to behold, being double the size of those we have been getting. Sour dough was used instead of yeast for this issue as supplies of this are still on the ship. Coke was used for the baking, the Gas Works having kept a supply hidden from the Germans. At some churches a loaf was exhibited and there were special prayers of thankfulness. Appropriately enough, today was 'Refreshment Sunday', and the Gospel of the Day was the Feeding of the multitude. In the evening great interest was taken in a service held by Channel Islands refugees in Westminster Hall, the reception—mostly on crystal sets—being very good.

March 12. The baker shops looked well today with bread displayed on the shelves, and the Germans gazed on this in wonder. The ration is to be 4 lb. for adults, 3 lb. for everyone under 10, with the exception of babies under two years, who get 1½ lb.; a shilling is to be charged for a 4-lb. loaf, as this flour is to be purchased from the British Government. With the advent of bread after being without for three weeks the potato ration goes back to 5 lb., and this week there is to be no meat. An extra ration of 4 oz. of split peas is being made. Postal deliveries are again six times a week instead of three. The *E.P.* has now to be set by hand, a long and tedious job.

March 13. Red Cross messages brought by the *Vega* are being delivered; the majority are several months old. The Germans invite farmers and growers in need of vegetable seeds to apply at the Platzkommandantur, taking paper bags with them. Several farmers whose produce has been requisitioned by the Germans have received permits to purchase a pair of house shoes and a box of matches at the Quartermaster's store on the Esplanade!

March 14. More changes made in the German Command: the Fortress Commandant—Major Heine—is to go to Guernsey, his place to be taken by General Wolff. The recent appointment of Admiral Hueffmeier as Commander-in-Chief of the Channel Islands has made this necessary, as Graf von Schmettow, whose place he took, was a military man. General Wolff, who is to reside at Government House, has come to the Channel Islands from Berlin. The delegate of the International Red Cross— Mons. Marietta—was allowed off the *Vega* today and had conversations with local and German officials; he did not land at Guernsey; this was unfortunate, for the plight of that Island is extremely bad and he could not learn of its needs.

March 15. The *Vega* left this morning on her return to Lisbon. Facilities are now in being for her to take a small amount of Red Cross messages each time. The recommendation that Dr. J. R. Hanna be appointed representative in Jersey of the British Red Cross and the Order of St. John has been approved by London, and the Bailiff has received a message to this effect. An inquest was held today concerning a woman burned to death following an attempt to light a lamp containing Diesel oil and petrol.

March 16. The Germans have made a demand for 200 tons of potatoes and 100 head of cattle 'for Guernsey'; following representations made by the Bailiff and the Attorney-General, they agreed to accept 100 tons (of which 20 tons could be swedes) and the cattle requisition was shelved, an assurance being given that this would be the last requisition from 1944 crops. More leaflets aimed at spreading disaffection among the troops were found today; these were in stronger terms than others, and particularly threatened Nazi officers. The Germans have imposed sentences ranging from two weeks to several months on a number of people, chiefly for wireless offences, and one young lady 'suspected of helping American prisoners to escape' was sentenced to four months.

March 17. For the first time for many months, a German Air Force Band played in the Royal Square during the afternoon; the performance was attended by the new Commandant of the troops—General Wolff. The Germans have temporarily vacated the Ritz Hotel, which they have used since they arrived here. Farmers have been warned about a recurrence of the warble fly.

March 18. Planes were over at all hours of the day. In the evening a fire destroyed a German-occupied garage in St. John's Road; two lorries and a motor cycle were burnt out, and explosions caused by the ignition of small arms ammunition. The tide over the week-end has been favourable for ormering, and some fair catches have been made. It is impossible to purchase these, the majority being used for barter—in some cases an ormer for an egg.

March 19. Planes were over in the early hours. Schools under States control have commenced an afternoon session—2 to 3.30—in addition to the morning one. From Red Cross supplies, 6 oz. of salt issued to everyone, and a piece of household soap (Sunlight or Puritan) to all women and to children and juveniles up to 18; 2½d. per ration was charged both for the salt and the soap, this money to be refunded eventually to the British Government, as only the parcels are gifts. A distribution of the outer wooden cases of the parcels was made, these making excellent firewood. From civilian stocks still held everyone can have a ration of tinned peas. A display of goods from Red Cross parcels in a King Street shop has been stopped, as it is considered an ill-timed gesture while the local authorities are fighting further requisitioning. The German military police are searching for armed Russians who have escaped.

March 20. The Germans have demanded more cattle; these are to be supplied by the Parishes, for shipment to Guernsey. Local representatives had to attend College House today to receive various recommendations following the visit of a German 'dairy expert'. The following figures will be of interest:

> Minimum German requirements for their troops—Skim milk, 1,500 to 1,750 pots per day; full milk, 100 pots per day; butter, 20 cwt. per day (29 tons per month); curd 30 cwt. per day.
>
> Requirements for the civil population—Full milk, 2,500 to 2,750 pots per day for the sick, nursing mothers, children and institutions; butter 6½ cwt. per day (9 tons per month).

This would mean there will be no full milk for adults but a 2-oz. butter ration instead, and it may be possible to obtain a small quantity of skim milk. The issue of permits for tree-felling was resumed today; after about a thousand had been granted there was another suspension until further notice.

March 21. The local authorities have been informed by the Germans that a British collier named the *Susan* is due to arrive from England any day with coal and coke. A meeting of the Council of the Jersey Football Association decided that all competitive football be abandoned for this season.

March 22. Barges are loading potatoes for Guernsey and 186 head of cattle for meat for German troops there; the full number of cattle demanded has not been obtained as some parishes defaulted. Soldiers are also leaving by these barges; it is believed another commando raid is being planned, this time on Cherbourg, with Alderney as the base. Many squads of soldiers were gathering nettles today, they having done this for some time on a smaller scale; the weed is for medicines, etc. A man was sentenced to a month's imprisonment for stealing a loaf. A statement from the Bailiff published today gives the reason why some Red Cross supplies are to be paid for—there is a distinction between goods sent by the International Red Cross and those supplied by the British Government.

March 23. Following the recent recommendations regarding the milk supply, the staffs of Don Street Dairy and of other dairies have threatened to strike if they are put into effect, but the matter appears to have been shelved for the time being. German military police had a shock early this morning when they saw two Union Jacks suspended between the towers of Victoria College! They removed them immediately and subsequently interrogated the Acting Head (Mr. P. A. Tatam). Large numbers of planes were around today, and the Germans sounded their sirens several times. For many days there have been sounds of heavy bombing from the French coast.

March 24. Further inquiries into yesterday's Union Jack affair at Victoria College; we learned subsequently that they had been hoisted by two O.V.s. Many planes about again.

March 25. The Germans had a good catch of snipe at St. Brelade's Bay in improvised nets; to make these they have visited many tennis courts and poultry runs.

March 26. Many people had a pleasant surprise today when told they could buy almost unlimited quantities of milk; this was on instructions from the chief dairy—Don Street—as the Germans had not sent their weekly ration of coal for use in separating. The coal was sent later, and the official who gave the order for the public to have the milk before it went bad had to attend at College House for questioning, the outcome being that a German official was reprimanded. From civilian stocks everyone can have a $\frac{1}{4}$ lb. of dried haricots.

March 27. The Germans had a big meeting at The Forum this morning, when they were addressed by Vice-Admiral Hueffmeier, the Commander-in-Chief of the Channel Islands. He told them they were to hold the Islands until they had orders to give them up, that rations would be further reduced, and, in order to conserve fuel for next winter, they would have to do without fires! Older residents witnessing German arrivals for the meeting were reminded of Grand Review days of fifty years ago, when box-carts, etc., were used, for there were only two motor cars among the whole gathering. As the assembly was going on, farmers' horses were taking trolley loads of Red Cross parcels to grocer shops for the fifth distribution—this issue was entirely Canadian, excepting invalid diet parcels for children under two and people over ninety, which are gifts of the British Red Cross.

March 28. The German communiqué is no longer published in their newspaper, the reason they give is that it can be heard on the radio and space is required for articles of greater interest!

March 29. Everyone was interested this morning in a programme broadcast for the Channel Islands; this was a review of Channel Islanders in Britain and words of encouragement for those at home.

March 30. Good Friday: brilliant sunshine but the wind keen at times. The usual sacred music was rendered in churches, but this year there was no outstanding programme. In the afternoon a large crowd attended a football match at the F.B. Fields between the St. John Ambulance Brigade and the Fire Brigade.

March 31. Good trade was done today in Easter flowers, and large queues formed at greengrocers for lettuce, cauliflowers and young cabbage, there being a scarcity of fresh vegetables. The banks were busy with people paying in marks, following a rumour that they may slump—1,000 to the £ sterling. The Bailiff and Attorney-General attended a meeting at College House today in connection with the recent milk recommendations the German dairy expert was in truculent mood, but so were the local representatives, and the meeting was postponed with no decision having been arrived at. The Germans also held a meeting of all fishermen, who were invited to fish on the basis of 30 per cent. for themselves and 70 per cent. for the Germans, retail prices being paid; those who refused had their boats and gear confiscated. Ten Red Cross cigarettes issued to all male adults. Following further reductions in the petrol allowance for civilian use, the *E.P.* delivery vans went out for the last time today; in future, deliveries will be made to agents by the dairy lorries. A German band played in the Royal Square this afternoon. The weather has been exceptionally fine for March, with no rain worth mentioning, and growers have everything well in advance. A few new potatoes are 'under the counter'—at 2s. 1½d. per lb.! The Germans are planting seeds and vegetables in the ground they have acquired; some of this in the town area includes the Royal Crescent and other such places, where cabbages have been planted. The new Military Commander—General Wolff—has instituted further restrictions for the troops; officers are mostly affected—they are to give up their cars, and there has been a change in messing, officers and men being together. Altogether, the German soldier is not having a happy time, with scanty news from home, very little food, and a tightening of discipline. Civilians continue to be sentenced, though some sentences are curtailed to allow more to go to jail. The good news of these days has prompted a rush for flagstaffs, red-white-and-blue ribbon, etc.; many schoolboys are wearing rosettes under their coats. The Red Cross Fund has now reached £45,000; concerts, etc., are continually held in its aid—one series at St. Peter's brought in over £500—and there are also numerous raffles and lotteries. Children, who always seek something novel, have replaced the collections of cigarette

285

cards with labels from Red Cross parcels. For black-market tobacco the Germans will pay 20 marks an ounce—over £34 a pound ! ! ! There is no limit to the number of plants which may be grown this year. *Battle Dress*, by Gun Buster, is an English book going the rounds, it having by some means come from the SS *Eskwood*, which the Germans captured at Granville during their commando raid at the beginning of the month.

APRIL 1945

April 1. Easter Sunday: weather dull and showery, but bright intervals. There were good church attendances. Curfew commenced at midnight.

April 2. Easter Monday: disappointing day, with rain most of the time. A netball game and a football match were the only functions to attend during the day, and a few private dances in the evening, the curfew again commencing at midnight. An extra ration of tinned sardines is available this week from stocks still held. There have been several week-end robberies, which included a large quantity of tobacco. Double British Summer Time has come into operation today, this being of great interest to wireless fans.

April 3. A further 'milk meeting' was held today between local officials and the Germans, the outcome being that the position would remain as it is for a fortnight, but the farmers were to be urged to increase supplies to such an extent that there would be no need for a change in the civilian rations.

April 4. Heavy explosions heard as the Germans demolish walls of the Palace Hotel considered dangerous following the recent fire.

April 5. The Germans commenced payment to farmers for potatoes, swedes and straw which has had to be supplied to the Forces. A German Order forbids the cutting of all pasture 'in order to ensure an increased hay crop, which will be retained by farmers as calf fodder'. Two interesting small advertisements appeared in the *E.P.* today: one for a Union Jack and the other for an American flag. Four Dutchmen who had been working for the Germans escaped from the Island today.

April 6. Following a recent visit to the prison by General Wolff, the local authorities have had to acquire another building—the Chelsea Hotel, Gloucester Street—for the accommodation of people who have been sentenced by the Germans but have not yet been incarcerated owing to the jail being full; the threatened alternative to this was to send them to a concentration camp in Alderney.

April 7. Another German Order: guards and patrols, in order more effectively to prevent thefts from fields or glasshouses, will arrest thieves during the day and will make use of their firearms if they should try to escape; and during the night on no account to challenge but to shoot straight at any person 'committing larceny (i.e. stooping and taking vegetables or potatoes or breaking into a glasshouse)'. A German band played in the Royal Square this afternoon; some children who stood to listen were wearing red-white-and-blue rosettes! In the evening a German orchestra gave a concert at the Opera House.

April 8. The Red Cross ship *Vega* arrived at about 5 p.m. on her fourth visit; the usual Swiss representatives did not come this time, but two Swiss doctors—M.M. J. P. Cuenod and E. Wyss Dunant; in addition to medical supplies a varied cargo consisted of 28,904 Canadian food parcels, 6,300 invalid diet parcels, 352,543 kilos of flour, yeast, sugar, soap, candles, matches, flints, seeds, salt, kerosene, clothing, footwear, leather, rubber and nails. The Germans today shot an N.C.O. for 'desertion'. Planes were over the Island several times.

April 9. The *Vega* commenced discharging this morning, arrangements as last time. German soldiers who, with a St. John Ambulance man, accompanied each trolley to the Red Cross depôt were equipped with spoons to scoop up flour and put it in their billycans. Supplementary rations from stock still held were issued today; 4 oz. of split peas for everybody, 100 saccharin tablets for adults, and two boxes of matches per household. Boxes of matches have recently changed hands at 5s. each! The Germans have taken possession of Don Street Dairy, the products of which are now almost wholly for their own consumption; the Milk Control staff has moved to other premises, but the dairy staff will carry on until such time as the threatened cut in rations come into effect and the dairy no longer deals with civilian supplies.

April 10. During the early hours of this morning German soldiers stole two sacks of flour from a bakehouse at First Tower, holding up at the point of the bayonet two auxiliary police who were on guard. A similar attempt was made at the Red Cross parcel depôt. We have certainly seen the decline of the German Army—the swag bag has been substituted for swagger, and they have even descended to picking up cigarette-ends! The German A.A. opened up on some planes which flew low over the harbour area about 8 a.m., and more planes were over at night. The *Vega* has finished unloading. Victoria College Terminal Service was held at St. Mark's Church, this afternoon, a collection for the Red Cross exceeding £100.

April 11. The Germans are searching for a Russian who has escaped; there has been some trouble among Russians incorporated in the German Army, and camps to accommodate these are in course of preparation at the north of the Island and at Grouville. The Germans have commenced requisitioning a large number of houses for billeting troops in various parts; this seems to be part of a new plan to get concentrations of troops at focal points. The new German staff considers invasion a possibility, and there has been a strengthening of defences. A German has been identified as having been implicated in the theft of flour at First Tower yesterday. Planes were over the Island in the late evening.

April 12. The medical delegates of the International Red Cross who arrived on the *Vega* have given details concerning the arrangements for the evacuation of invalids. The evacuation will be voluntary, Jersey's quota being 600; males between 15 and 60 will be examined by German doctors, a neutral medical commission refereeing in case of dispute; the hospital ship will arrive in six to eight weeks' time, the cost of transport being borne by the British Government; only those who are themselves eligible on medical grounds can accompany patients, and the evacuation is for British residents only. The German authorities pointed out that conditions on the Islands may get worse and it may be impossible to maintain medical extras at the present level, also many medicaments may be unobtainable; they feel that they are not responsible for the well-being of those sick who do not avail themselves of this opportunity. The Forestry Section of the Department of Labour is unable to allocate any further trees or issue permits for private felling. This is to safeguard fuel supplies for bakehouses.

April 13. Everyone regrets the news of Mr. Roosevelt's death. Heavy explosions heard from the French coast; it is presumed mines are being cleared. Large numbers of planes have been around the Island continually.

April 14. Meeting of the States for the presentation of the Budget for the financial year commencing February, 1945, together with results of trading transactions to December 31, 1944. The financial situation was reviewed by Jurat Dorey, who pointed out that the Public Debt, including cost of the Occupation was now over five million pounds. The total expenditure was fixed at £801,037, and the effect of maintaining Income Tax at 4s. in the £ and imposing a tax on locally-grown tobacco (5d. per plant) would make the estimated revenue amount to £283,335 and the presumed deficit £517,702, to which must be added the sum of £10,000 for statutory reserve. Jurat Dorey said it was feared that shortage of fuel and other supplies would compel the communal kitchens and restaurants to close down soon. An Income Tax amendment was carried by 32 votes to 7 to prevent the evasion of taxation, particularly by persons who had made excessive profits during the Occupation. Other business included the adoption of the Social Assurance report, the scheme now being extended to cover sick benefit; the report of the M.O.H. was tabled; postponement of States Scholarships for the year 1945 was decided upon, and several lesser items received attention. At the Royal Court fines of £40 with £5 costs were imposed in two cases of keeping unregistered pigs. A German band played in the Royal Square during the afternoon, and Allied planes were over again.

April 15. The *Vega* left on the morning tide. The two Swiss doctors returned; they have examined patients at some of the institutions.

April 16. Three ounces of macaroni issued this week as an extra, this from stock. The body of an infant child has been found at St. Martin's; the jury at a subsequent inquiry brought in an open verdict, the body having probably been there for many years. We are experiencing exceptional weather for this time of the year; shade temperature today was 78 degrees.

April 17. Sixth issue of Red Cross parcels; on her last visit the *Vega* did not bring sufficient and the number had to be made up from those in stock. With the invalid's special diet parcel, children under two years had a piece of Red Cross toilet soap.

April 18. Baron von Aufsess, who has been on the German administrative staff here for a long time and proved to be one of the more 'reasonable' officials the local authorities have had to deal with, has been recalled, and left the Island today. Some more cattle was shipped to Guernsey. About 10.45 p.m. an Allied plane passed over and dropped flares.

April 19. The German Commander of the Channel Islands—Admiral Hueffmeier—who is in Guernsey, has sent a message to the effect that the proposed increase in supplies for the German Forces to 10 pots of milk per week must be forthcoming by the 25th inst.; responsibility for non-compliance with this Order will be punished, the threat of imprisonment in Alderney being

289

issued. Local officials met the Germans, and a series of meetings commenced between these officials and representative farmers; the latter were urged to cut out private supplies so that the adult population as a whole would not suffer, for they would lose their milk ration entirely if the Germans' demand could not be met by any other means. Today's German communiqué stated that in the last few days heavy naval coast batteries on Alderney have had under fire tank and petrol dumps in the north-west part of the Cotentin peninsula, discovered by a German commando troop in a night operation. The Germans have further restricted water consumption; special permits must be obtained for the use of water for gardens or greenhouses. Among today's advertisements is the offer of £50 for a lady's semi-sports cycle. The Germans held a tattoo on the Royal Parade late in the evening in honour of Hitler's birthday, the curfew not commencing until 11 o'clock. An Allied plane was taking photographs over the west of the Island tonight.*

April 20. It is learned through the B.B.C. that Channel Islanders were at the Buchenwald concentration camp. The Germans celebrated Hitler's birthday by hoisting the Nazi flag at Fort Regent and with a band and choir concert in the Royal Square. Planes over continually.

April 21. The milk meetings have continued, and today a warning was issued to milk roundsmen to curtail extra supplies to friends, etc., the threat of punishment by being sent to Alderney being made. The use of drinking water is prohibited for washing cars, etc., building purposes and watering of glass-houses, this being supplementary to the notice of two days ago; the hours of the water supply are now 7.30 to 9 a.m., 11.30 a.m. to 1 p.m., 5 to 6.30 p.m. There has been a marked increase in air activity during the past week. The Germans today sentenced to death a young Guernsey girl, who is resident here, for sheltering a German deserter; her brother was sentenced to three years' imprisonment.

April 22. To meet the German demands for increased milk supplies, another milkless day for adults was imposed today (Sunday), this without warning, and making four per week. A concert was given to the American prisoners in the South Hill Gymnasium; this was part of an effort by some local residents to entertain prisoners of war, including Algerians. The Germans are getting plenty of entertainment in the form of lectures; one delivered at St. Martin's today informed the troops that the

* Some of these photographs may now be seen at the Museum of the Société Jersiaise.

Russians would never take Berlin, and that their duty was to defend the Island until the very last. German police have resumed activities in fining cyclists not observing road regulations. Planes were over at various times.

April 23. St. George's Day: many people wore a red rose. The last potato ration was issued today—1½ lb. per head—but the bread ration was increased by 1 lb. to 5 lb.; persons so desiring may obtain a limited quantity of flour in lieu of bread at the rate of 1½ lb. in the place of a 2-lb. loaf. A ration of canned milk was issued to adults, and from Red Cross supplies the following very welcome commodities were issued: 6 oz. salt for everyone (1½d. per ration); a box of matches for everyone (1d.); a candle for adults and juveniles (1d.); a half-tablet of soap for adults and juveniles (6d.). The paraffin brought by the *Vega* is being issued to nursing mothers, invalids, persons over 70 years of age, etc. Eleven bakehouses were closed today; communal kitchens and the registered restaurants have closed down, but the former will continue to serve soup daily. The Germans today commenced lifting potatoes from greenhouses.

April 24. Another leaflet is being circulated among the Germans. A youth was, en Police Correctionnelle today, fined £25 for being an intermediary in the sale of black-market butter to the Germans at 35 marks (£3 15s.) per lb. Meetings in connection with the milk crisis continue and the 'Fortress Commandant' published the following notice:

(1). With immediate effect, it is hereby ordered that all farmers and cow-keepers must deliver, without reserve, the whole of the milk produced by their cows, with the exception of the milk which they are lawfully entitled to retain. Deliveries will be controlled by inspectors of the Forces and of the States.

(2). Farmers and cow-keepers who commit an infraction of this Order will have their cows and grassland confiscated without compensation. Moreover, infractions may be punished according to Para. 22 of the Order for the Protection of the Occupying Authority, by imprisonment or fine.

At a meeting of the Principals and Officers of the Parish of St. Helier the accounts for the St. Helier Poor Law Commission were adopted; the estimated requirements for the current year were shown as £48,400, the increase over last year being accounted for by the fact that £3,000 more was spent on emergency relief than was expected.

April 25. New restrictions in the milk supply came into force today: Juveniles from 15 upwards, instead of 18, now have the same rations as adults—half a pint on four days of the week (they formerly got a pint every day); no more extra milk is to be issued to schoolchildren, and invalids over 65 are not to receive any extra either, but there may be applications in special cases. Producers of milk, members of their households and others who retain or draw the special higher milk ration ('free supplies') may no longer draw their meat ration. Planes have droned overhead at various times.

April 26. The Germans are now getting a very poor news service for their paper, most being received from a station broadcasting news at dictation speed in the early hours. Planes were over again today.

April 27. The Germans have reduced their demands for 10,000 pots of milk per week to 9,000. Six farmers have had their herds confiscated for not supplying all the milk they should. The Germans today shot a German deserter; the girl who sheltered him, accompanied by her mother, was allowed at the funeral service; her sentence of death has been commuted to ten years' imprisonment following representations by the Bailiff.

April 28. Details issued regarding the seeds brought by the *Vega*; these are to be obtainable (on coupon) for use in private gardens only and not for raising vegetables for sale; a quantity of mangold and cattle swede seeds is to be obtained by persons having cattle in their custody. A German notice states that the retail sale of foodstuffs, with the exception of potatoes, meat, charcuterie, milk and milk products, is permitted to members of the Forces during the afternoon only; 'the purchase of foodstuffs of any kind from the producer (farmer, market-gardener, etc.) is forbidden as before. It is likewise forbidden to enter farms, etc., for the purchase of foodstuffs of any kind'. Another German notice reminds civilians that the sale and purchase of motor vehicles of all kinds is forbidden until the end of the war. Today was the closing day for applications from invalids wishing to be evacuated; persons who have applied at the banks for letters of credit have been refused. Interesting session of the Royal Court: Two Frenchmen each sentenced to 12 months' imprisonment with hard labour for stealing 110 lb. of tobacco; a farmer was fined £20 with £5 costs for refusing to give up a heifer calf; a farmer's wife was fined £100 for selling butter in contravention of the Rationing Order, it being proved that this butter was eventually purchased by 'strangers' (Germans) at 40 marks (£4 5s.) a pound; three auxiliary policemen pleaded guilty to charges of robbery, sentence being deferred as a fourth pleaded not guilty, and all will be tried 'en Police Correctionelle'; and the Full Court gave judgment in a case of selling a second-hand suit at £21 7s. 4d., in contravention of the textile rationing orders: a fine of £50 with £10 costs was imposed, the shopkeeper being fined £10 with £2 costs. A unique event occurred at the *E.P.* today when papers in three languages were published—the *E.P.* in English; *Les Chroniques* in French and the Germans had their own for the troops. A German band played in the Royal Square in the afternoon.

April 29. Great excitement today following the news that there had been offers of unconditional surrender to Britain and America.

April 30. Four ounces of dried beans were available for everybody, ½ lb. of sugar from Red Cross supplies (6d.). There was an argument on the Weighbridge this morning between some German naval ratings and officers; this developed into a shouting competition, and one of the sailors was taken into the J.M.T. garage, put up against the wall and shot, part of the vicinity being barred to traffic for some time afterwards. The temperature this morning was around 40 degrees, and sleet, hail and snow have fallen at various times of the day, in contrast to the middle of the month, when the temperature reached 78 in the shade. There has been a re-shuffle of troops with Guernsey, and more have come to this Island; numbers of houses have been requisitioned during the month in all parts of the Island. Hunger is written on the Germans' faces, and there are reports of many soldiers absolutely starving, while begging from door to door is by no means infrequent. Claims are being dealt with of persons who have had trees on their properties felled by the Germans. The soldiers smoke mostly coltsfoot, and they will pay anything for tobacco, as much as 40 marks (£42 14s. 8d.)! per lb. Wireless sets no longer being used by the Forces have been collected and stored in the Masonic Temple. There has been increased air activity during April. Some excellent efforts have been made to swell the Red Cross Fund: the *E.P.* list now exceeds £20,000, with the Island list over £64,000; a '*Vega* draw' has brought in about £5,000. One series of concerts, which was followed by auction sales, raised over £2,000. The local authorities have prohibited the sale of foodstuffs at these auction sales.

MAY 1945

May 1. The temperature this morning was just above freezing point and there had been a fall of snow during the night. The Germans did not celebrate May Day in their usual fashion, but there was a concert at The Forum in the afternoon, and the town was packed with troops who were buying all they could. Some shops were openly selling Union Jacks and other patriotic emblems, and people were carrying these through the streets with the Germans looking on. A local resident has been arrested for the alleged spreading of anti-Nazi propaganda. A portrait of Mr. Churchill, the work of a Russian, has been sold at a Red Cross auction for 400 marks (about £53). Late at night came the news of Hitler's death.

May 2. The Germans looked exceedingly glum today; flags were at half-mast and a memorial service was held at The Forum, lasting only twenty minutes. The Forum is to remain closed for a week as an act of mourning for Hitler, and at various points a proclamation by Admiral Doenitz was read to German units. A single Allied plane passed over in the morning. According to the Germans, a searchlight near Cap La Hague sent a message in Morse to the garrison on Alderney early this morning inviting them to discuss conditions of surrender, but this was refused. It is learned from German official sources in this Island, that the possibility of the Germans holding out for a prolonged period is becoming less likely.

May 3. As 'an urgent increase in prison staff is contemplated', the Prison Board has invited applications for the post of warders. Details were published today regarding the distribution of clothing or footwear supplies sent by the Red Cross: persons in need of this (some new and some second-hand) have to apply in writing for any of the garments enumerated and only if they have not already had similar garments on their current textile ration books; working men's boots or repairs (soles and heels) may be obtained without permit, no one being allowed to have both boots and repairs, but the quantity of shoes (for all ages) being small necessitates the issue of these on permit, application to be made at the States Dépôt; coupons and vouchers must be surrendered for these goods, which are to be paid for. A young German shot himself at the General Hospital early this morning and died. At a concert given in the evening to American prisoners of war, the senior officer (a colonel) thanked the artistes and presented bouquets to the ladies of the party; he said he hoped the time would soon arrive when he could meet his Jersey friends without his 'chaperone'. The Bailiff has asked the Germans for various concessions, but it is understood these have been refused.

May 4. The town was full of all sorts of rumours today about the Germans being on the point of surrender, most of these stories being traced to the Germans themselves. Some go to great lengths to impress us that they are Poles, Czechs, Austrians, etc.—anything but German, and certainly not Nazis. During the afternoon the town was packed with troops; some were trying to buy vegetables, but the remainder had nothing to do, nowhere to go and were depressed by the scarcity of news reaching them. They are having difficulty in filling their newspaper, for their news service taken from wireless broadcasts is almost nil. There was another bakehouse robbery during the night, a large number of loaves being stolen. In the late evening came the news of the wholesale surrender of the German forces in north-west Germany; this caused great excitement.

May 5. Another day of rumours, with the town packed with people; there were long queues for the footwear brought by the *Vega*, this being on sale from today, and large crowds gathered in the Royal Square in anticipation of the Bailiff having something to say; it was learned that he wished to address the crowd, but the German authorities would not permit this. Other crowds gathered outside the *E.P.* in expectation of a special edition, while shops selling flags, etc., were besieged with purchasers; this assumed great proportions, and so many people were carrying flags and wearing emblems that an order from College House prohibited the sale. Rumours were so strong in places that the war was over that flags were actually hoisted. The banks were busy—as they have been for some time—with people paying in marks to get rid of them. It was learned that the Germans had cleared the Airport. The Department of Transport and Communications has issued instructions to various personnel to be in readiness for essential work at any time. The German Commander of the Channel Islands— Admiral Hueffmeier—arrived by boat during the afternoon, and there were meetings with German and local officials. An order to the Germans not to fire on any planes came into effect at 5 p.m. At the Royal Court a person who sold two eggs for 12s. 9d. was fined £10 with £2 costs, and two persons were sentenced to two months and three months respectively for thefts from Red Cross supplies. The States met in the afternoon to consider various items recently lodged au Greffe and other matters of urgent importance.

May 6. Planes over during the day gave rise to a fresh crop of rumours. The Bailiff and the Attorney-General met the Admiral during the morning and he left for Guernsey again in the afternoon. Some of the Gestapo have gone into uniform and have now mingled with the troops. An elderly woman was taken to hospital today after having been assaulted in her home by a German soldier in search of food.

May 7. From about 6 a.m. there were large queues outside the shops selling boots brought by the *Vega*. A German official called at the office of the Department of Agriculture this morning to inform the authorities that the Germans were not at all satisfied with the milk situation; their requests for increased milk supplies had not been met, and threats were made if these were not forthcoming. Many arrangements have now been made by public and private enterprises in anticipation of the end of the Occupation, and everyone has been waiting anxiously for some official statement; the only one forthcoming, was a message from the Bailiff, who was continually in touch with the Occupying Authorities, urging the population to keep calm and dignified and refrain from any sort of demonstration. There was a meeting of the Superior Council during the morning, when many important matters were dealt with; as the Bailiff was going to meet the German Commander later in the day, concessions to be asked for were settled in principle, among these being the release of political prisoners. This request was granted and at 6 p.m. thirty were released. Gas Works employees who have been working at the various bakehouses had to return today as the retorts were to be fired with some fuel which had been kept aside for the purpose. Four ounces of dried peas were issued to everyone today and the bread ration has been increased to 6 lb. per head, except for infants, this helping greatly now that there is no potato ration. In town and country finishing touches were being put to flagstaffs, and everyone got busy after the announcement that Victory-in-Europe Day would be tomorrow, but the position here is not clear as the Germans are still in occupation; there has been no slackening in warlike preparations on their part, for today new gun emplacements were being made in various parts of the Island, and at night defence posts and guns were manned and searchlights swept the seas.

May 8. It appeared early this morning that nothing was going to happen, and there was keen disappointment; our spirits rose, when it was learned the schoolchildren had been sent home and that loud-speakers were being erected in various parts of the town. Then the *E.P.* came out with the following message from the Bailiff:

I appeal to you to maintain your calm and dignity in the hours which lie ahead and to refrain from all forms of demonstrations.

It is my earnest wish that all services should be held in all places of worship in the same manner as services are being held in the United Kingdom and in other parts of the Empire.

I feel that the conclusion of the Prime Minister's speech this afternoon will be the appropriate moment for the hoisting of flags, and I make the strongest appeal to you, in the interests of public orders, not to fly flags before that time.

I was present last evening at the release from custody of the majority of the political prisoners, and I am doing all in my power to obtain the immediate release of the remainder of them.

I shall make known to you immediately any further developments.

A. M. COUTANCHE,

May 8, 1945. Bailiff.

From that moment we never looked back; everyone was excited and busy getting their bunting ready for the afternoon, and by 3 o'clock thousands had gathered in the Royal Square. As the Town Church clock struck three a cheer went up at the announcement that Mr. Churchill was to speak; his statement was punctuated by cheers, especially when he referred to 'our dear Channel Islands', and when, at the conclusion, the Bailiff hoisted the Union Jack and Jersey flag over the Courthouse, enthusiasm knew no bounds, and many wept unashamedly. The Bailiff then told the assembly how the end of hostilities would affect the Island; he first asked them 'to join him in offering thanks to Almighty God for the deliverance of this dear Island of ours'. He then made announcements about various services to be held, reminded them that the King was to speak at 9 p.m., and that there would be no further restriction on the use of wireless in their homes! The Bailiff said that some political prisoners had been released; that American and British prisoners of war were to be set free, and that he was going to visit the French colonial prisoners in their camp. He then said that the German authorities had told him that a British Commission was on the way, but the greatest cheer was raised when it was learned that units of the British Navy were approaching the Channel Islands. After appealing for good behaviour and to remain calm and dignified, the Bailiff led the singing of the National Anthem, but emotion stifled many a voice. The Bailiff had a great reception when he went off in his car, on his way to visit the French camp. By then flags had been unfurled all over the Island and church bells were ringing out for joy. The whole atmosphere had changed—wireless sets had appeared from nowhere, their owners putting them in front windows to entertain passers-by; cameras were clicking all over the place, and one was soon dodging motor cars or motor cycles which had for five years been hidden away from the Germans. The Electricity Company turned up trumps* and the light was on until very late, this being appreciated by owners of wireless sets and those who held parties or impromptu dances. It was funny to see young men coming out of jail carrying their beds, to hear people openly discussing the news, to let off fireworks (yes, there were some!), to ignore the curfew, and forget the black-out, but on everyone's lips were the words 'Is it true?' The discipline of the Germans was excellent; they had had their last newspaper, had been carrying out demolitions of a minor nature, and throughout the afternoon and evening released stores of foodstuffs for their immediate consumption. At some of the Todt depôts large numbers of people were carting off furniture for firewood; wooden buildings were pulled down and those who had been left in charge were giving things away. In the midst of all this the *Vega* entered harbour to be unloaded by members of the School of Physical Culture. A notice published by the Depart-

---

* It may be of interest here to state that when the Germans first came to the Island they brought with them a cut and dried electricity rationing scheme, in which each household was allowed three lights only and one electric fire. The Department of Essential Services and the company fought this, and finally got the Germans to allow consumers two-thirds of their 1939 consumption. This remained in force until March, 1943, when, to avoid having to prosecute consumers who had exceeded their ration, the company succeeded in getting the original rationing scheme cancelled, and a new one instituted on a per capita basis. The company continued to maintain the public supply until the coal stocks were exhausted in January, 1945. After this the Germans wanted to use the last 60 tons of fuel oil for generating electricity for their own use, but because they would not allow 50 per cent. of this to go to the civil population, the company refused to run the power station, and three engines were subsequently requisitioned and operated by the Germans.

ment of Finance and Economics, on German instructions, invites owners of wooden or corrugated iron bungalows or sheds which have been 'physically removed' by the Germans to send in their claims.

May 9. Another great day. H.M.S. *Beagle* rounded Noirmont at 10 a.m., and some time after this the Bailiff received a message to go to College House to talk over the phone with Colonel Power, O.B.E., Chief Civil Affairs Officer on the Staff of Brigadier-General A. E. Snow, Officer Commanding Armed Forces of the Channel Islands, Colonel Power being in Guernsey. Later a message from the *Beagle* was received stating that the presence of the General Commanding the German Forces in Jersey was required on board, and the Bailiff was to accompany him. They left harbour in a German naval pinnace, the Attorney-General and the Solicitor-General being with the Bailiff; the German Commander (General Wolff) had members of his staff with him. On reaching the *Beagle* the Bailiff and Crown Officers met Brigadier Snow, Rear-Admiral Stuart and officers of the ship, while the German officers met British military representatives to discuss the arrangements for the formal surrender of the Island. From the *Beagle* the Bailiff sent two messages; the first to His Majesty the King as follows:

'With my humble duty, I send to Your Majesty this assurance of the devotion of the States and People of Jersey to Your Majesty's throne and person.

'We have kept ourselves informed of the Armed Forces of Your Majesty and of Your Majesty's Allies, and of the ceaseless efforts of the workers behind them, and on this day of our liberation we rejoice that we can once more take our place and play our part within Your Majesty's Empire';

and the second to the Prime Minister (Mr. Churchill):

'The people of Jersey assembled yesterday, Tuesday, 8th May, in the Royal Square to listen to your broadcast will ever remember your affectionate reference to "Our dear Channel Islands", and on this day of liberation I address to you, in the name of the States and People of Jersey, our undying gratitude for your inspired leadership of the British Commonwealth of Nations, which led to the victory of the Allied cause in Europe and to the liberation of the Channel Islands.'

A terrific cheer went up from the crowd which had assembled

around the harbours when a British naval pinnace came through the pierheads and later two naval officers who landed, Lieut. R. Milne and Surgeon-Lieut. Macdonald, entered a car; when they got to the barrier at the landward end of the Albert Pier the police could not prevent them being mobbed. On arrival at the Harbour Office our first 'liberators' went upstairs and hung a Union Jack out of one of the windows; there was deafening cheers, the National Anthem was sung, and the toughest witness could not restrain his emotion. In the early afternoon formations of the R.A.F. came over the Island and some time afterwards the first troops landed as the advance party; elements of many regiments continued to arrive, and these received a wonderful welcome. The officer in charge was Colonel W. V. A. Robinson, M.C., who was to be Officer Commanding the Forces in Jersey; he made straight for the Pomme d'Or as his headquarters where the German naval personnel had held sway for five years, and addressed the crowd from the balcony, after which the Union Jack was hoisted by Capt. H. G. Richmond, Harbourmaster of Jersey. Many Jersey boys were among those who arrived, and each and every one received a great reception. The first Jersey officer to land was Captain Hugh Le Brocq, who left the Island with the Militia in 1940, and to him fell the happy task of hoisting the Union Jack on Fort Regent. Colonel Robinson told the *E.P.* in a subsequent interview that the German General who had made the surrender to General Snow had been ordered to meet the colonel at the Pomme d'Or at 4.30; the orders were given that the Germans had to be cleared from the quays and Fort Regent by 6 p.m., and that the town, except for the Hospital and certain dumps, was to be clear by nightfall, arms and ammunition to be left in places specially indicated. The German Commander was allowed two per cent. of small arms to be used by guards at the dumps. The Tommies who have arrived all wear a special shoulder flash consisting of a shield with the three leopards. The life of Jersey has already undergone a radical change; a milk ration every day is being restored, the electric light is now on all the time, and buses have made their appearance, while to discuss the news freely is a luxury we have not enjoyed for five years. A further distribution was made today of the outer wooden cases of the Red Cross parcels for firewood. One distribution which received condemnation, was made early this morning, when some irresponsible people broke into the Masonic Temple and gave away large numbers of the wireless sets which had been taken there by the Germans for storage.

Now that all the prisoners of war have been released they are being warmly welcomed by everyone, and several, including Russians, who have been in hiding for a considerable time, have come into the open again. The *E.P.* went back to a four-page paper today, the leading article under the heading 'Thank God!' having 'Gratitude' as its theme.

May 10. The ceremony of hoisting the flag took place in the Royal Square this morning before an enthusiastic crowd which was addressed by Colonel Robinson and the Bailiff. A Royal Artillery guard of honour was drawn up facing the Royal Courthouse, and the States officials were there, headed by the Royal Mace, the Island's most cherished possession, the gift of King Charles II. When the flag fluttered out the guard of honour presented arms, the band of St. James's Boys' Brigade struck up the National Anthem, and the crowd sang with deep feeling. The Bailiff then said that 'the moment we have waited for has come' and read a message—the first received in the Island for five years—from the Commander-in-Chief, Plymouth; great cheers greeted the information that in the name of the Islanders the Bailiff had sent messages to His Majesty the King and to Mr. Churchill. Colonel Robinson, then addressed the crowd and said that the days when they were told 'I am the Military Commander and I order you' have gone; he praised the Islanders for their fortitude and appealed to them to allow his troops more elbow room to bring food, clothing, vitamins and the like which are so badly needed. At the conclusion of the ceremony the guard of honour marched around the town headed by the St. James's band, being greeted everywhere with enthusiasm. Cinemas have re-opened with 'scratch' programmes, and a concert was given at the Opera House this evening for released prisoners of war; the Americans are due to embark for Granville, on the way home, and they expressed their appreciation of the hospitality received at the hands of the Islanders. In the afternoon the captain and crew of the *Vega* were presented with solid silver replicas of Jersey milk cans, the presentation being made by the Bailiff on behalf of St. Ouen's Football Club. In the afternoon the first Allied planes landed at the Airport. Since the hour of liberation there have been incidents involving females who had consorted with the German Forces and who had earned the name of 'Jerry-bag'; collaborators and black-marketeers have also received rough treatment, but regrettable scenes took place this evening when one or two of these women were severely handled, and possibly but for the intervention of the troops would have been murdered. One woman whose association with the Germans was known has applied to the Prison Authorities to be taken into protective custody.

May 11. Today's *E.P.* carried a number of items consequent upon the change-over to British control. Inhabitants were warned about demolitions and requested to leave the roadways clear for the movement of transport; they were also warned not to pillage or loot any property formerly in the possession of the German Forces. The Bailiff, together with the Officer Commanding, appealed to the public to maintain order. The replies to the Bailiff's messages to His Majesty the King and Mr. Churchill were published, and also a statement that it was desired by the Officer Commanding and the Bailiff that Saturday, May 12, 1945 (tomorrow) be observed as an unofficial public holiday. Numbers of Germans were made to clean up their former billets or offices, etc., and the officers were not spared; doctors and medical staffs wore Red Cross armlets. The seventh issue of Red Cross parcels commenced today. The Full Court met in the morning to register two Orders-in-Council, British military and naval personnel being on the Bench; four auxiliary policemen were sentenced each to 12 months for burglary. The Gestapo were rounded up this afternoon, the name of the chief being Wolff.

May 12. Crowds watched the arrival of sailors and soldiers from assault-boats or 'Ducks', these coming from part of a convoy of over fifty ships which had been sent to the Channel Islands; on board this convoy were ten Channel Islands pilots, and part of the headquarters staff travelled in the Great Western Railway cross-channel steamer *St. Helier*. Tank-landing craft came up right under the sea-wall of St. Aubin's Bay, and these discharged all sorts of vehicles. Among the first ashore was Commander T. Le B. Pirouet, R.N.R., who was in charge of the landing operation. More and more men arrived all day, and these received a great welcome—everyone cheered, children clamoured for autographs, and the soldiers and sailors were very generous in showering chocolate, sweets and cigarettes on newmade friends. Many Jerseymen were in the parties, and these received a special welcome, news of relatives on the mainland being sought by all. Numbers of British and American correspondents were soon ferreting for stories to send to their papers, and they found many ready talkers. An historic ceremony took place in the Royal Square at 6 p.m.: the States Banner headed a procession of the Assembly to a position near the statue, where a special dais had been erected from which Brigadier A. E. Snow,

O.B.E., Military Commander of the Channel Islands, read the following proclamation:

People of the Channel Islands: It having pleased His Majesty by Order in Council to vest in the officer commanding the armed forces in the Channel Islands all powers necessary for the success of our operation, the safety of our forces, and the safety and well-being of his subjects in the Islands, I, Alfred Earnest Snow, as the officer commanding the forces, give you greeting on your liberation from the enemy.

I rely upon you all to work cheerfully and loyally to restore the normal life in your Islands. Your ready compliance with such regulations and orders as may from time to time be issued by me or on my behalf will be in the best interests of the Islands. It will be my firm purpose so to exercise my authority that your own Government may rapidly be restored to your Islands and that you may enjoy in peace and prosperity your customary rights, laws and institutions.

A. E. SNOW, Brigadier,

Officer Commanding the Armed Forces,

Channel Islands.

GOD SAVE THE KING.

This was followed by a message of Greeting from His Majesty the King:

Buckingham Palace.

To my most loyal people in the Channel Islands, I send my heartfelt greetings.

Ever since my armed forces had to be withdrawn you have, I know, looked forward with the same confidence as I have to the time of deliverance. We have never been divided in spirit. Our hopes and fears, anxieties and determination, have been the same, and we have been bound together by an unshakable conviction that the day would come when the Islands, the oldest possession of the Crown, would be liberated from enemy occupation. That day has now come, and, with all my Peoples, I cordially welcome you on your restoration to freedom and to your rightful place with the free nations of the world.

Channel Islanders in their thousands are fighting in my service for the cause of civilisation with their traditional loyalty, courage and devotion. Their task is not yet ended; but for you a new task begins at once—to rebuild the fortunes of your beautiful Islands in anticipation of reunion with relatives, friends and neighbours who have been parted from you by the circumstances of war. In this task you can count on the fullest support of my Government.

It is my desire that your ancient privileges and institutions should be maintained, and that you would resume as soon as possible your accustomed system of government. Meantime, the immediate situation requires that responsibility for the safety of the Islands and the well-being of the inhabitants should rest upon the Commander of the Armed Forces stationed in the Islands. I feel confident that the Civil Authorities, who have carried so heavy a burden during the past years, will gladly co-operate with him in maintaining good government and securing the distribution of the supplies which he is bringing with him.

It is my earnest hope that the Islands, reinstated in their ancestral relationship to the Crown, will soon regain their former happiness and prosperity.

(Signed) GEORGE R.I.

Brigadier Snow concluded by expressing thanks for the way in which the Forces had been received. Among those at the ceremony was Colonel H. R. Power, Chief Civil Affairs Officer for the Channel Islands, Rear-Admiral Stuart and a Russian officer. The band of the Duke of Cornwall's Light Infantry was present, and a guard of honour of Royal Marines and men of the Hampshire Regiment. In the evening the Weighbridge resembled a fairground with hundreds of people 'seeing the sights' and many being taken to the ships in the roads. From their boats in the harbour German sailors looked on this scene with sad expressions. Various officials have been interviewing bank managers, and others, with a view to getting the Island's affairs started again. Bus services have re-commenced and the telephone service almost fully restored.

May 13. The billeting of troops has gone on apace, and it is pleasing to see them occupying billets used by the Germans up to a week ago. German prisoners have tasks which include helping to unload supply ships bringing 2,000 tons of goods to the Islands. The first batch of German prisoners was taken away in the evening, these leaving in 'Ducks' for the ships in the roads. It is learned that the German garrison in the Channel Islands numbered between 27,000 and 30,000, the Islands being—for their size, the most strongly-fortified places in the world. All over the Island today thanksgiving services were held; the

Bailiff, Crown Officers, and the new military and civil heads attending St. Helier's Parish Church. Numbers of English newspapers have been distributed and it is anticipated there will soon be a regular service. The work of rounding up stray Germans goes on.

May 14. From midnight the rule of the road has reverted to 'Keep Left', and the one-way traffic system in parts of the town has ceased. Two warnings have been issued today—one against looting and the other that mines are being exploded; German military defence works are also put out of bounds owing to the danger of booby traps. A message to the Channel Islands has been received from the City of London, and free postcards are available for Islanders to communicate with the mainland. The most cheering news is that gas may be available in four weeks' time. Large quantities of food, coal and other supplies are being unloaded and taken to the various depôts. The States met today to adopt an Address in reply to His Majesty's Message, and the Royal Court sat to register four Defence (Channel Islands) Regulations. The price of petrol ex-States pumps is reduced to 3s. per gallon, and 3s. 8d. per gallon in two-gallon cans at dealers. Five Orders by the Military Authorities were published today—Control of Explosives Order, Control of Communications, Embarkation, Disembarkation and Firearms. The Military Authorities are taking precautions to avoid an outbreak of typhus among the visiting forces in these Islands, they being more like to contract the scourge than the inhabitants. There has been a 'spot of bother' with a nest of Germans armed with a machine-gun at La Preference, St. Martin's, but it did not take long to clean this up. A 'Victory Revue' is being presented at The Forum by Mr. Donald Journeaux, the rehearsals having been held up during the Occupation. A tin of tunny fish per head issued from stocks held by the States.

May 15. Visit to the Island by Mr. H. S. Morrison, the British Home Secretary, who was accompanied by Lord Munster, Parliamentary Under-Secretary. Mr. Morrison addressed the States Assembly and, afterwards, a huge crowd in the Royal Square. He paid tributes to the Bailiff and the States for the work they had done during the Occupation, and praised the courage and fortitude of the Islanders. Mr. Morrison gave the assurance that the British Government would do all it could to restore the Islands to their former position. Two Orders are published for the restoration of sterling in the Island; reichsmarks will be exchanged into sterling, at the rate of 9.36 to the £; during the next three days all reichsmarks should be deposited at the five banks; after the 18th they will no longer be legal tender; until the free circulation of sterling returns, cash drawings will be limited to £5 per person per week, except in the case of employers of labour, who can draw normal amounts to pay wages; persons who have deposited reichsmarks and are not normally bank customers may draw cash up to £5 a week until their balances are exhausted or until the whole amount can be redeemed when sufficient sterling is available, whichever is the earlier date. Petrol lorries may now be hired for essential work through the Transport Office, at 6s. 3d. per hour. The *E.P.* published an eight-page paper today.

May 16. The shop windows are a delight to behold, for they contain displays of the goods which will be released to the public in the next few days. Another warning about looting is published, and the Honorary Police have to do duty at some former German ammunition dumps. Messages of greeting continued to be received, among the latest being from the Archbishop of York (Dr. Garbett, the former Bishop of Winchester), Lord Justice du Parcq and C. T. Le Quesne, K.C. A Defence Regulation was published today concerning wireless telegraphy. Loudspeakers have been placed in various places as part of a public address system by which orders, news bulletins, music, etc., can be broadcast. The Liberating Forces have established a transmitter station at Bagot, and the Signal Corps is to move into College House. Applications can be made for wireless sets, electric fires and cameras surrendered to the Germans; it is pointed out, that many of these may be out of the Island. The German hospitals have been cleared and disinfected; houses in which Germans were billeted were found to be in a very bad condition. There were large queues at the banks today to change reichsmarks for sterling; to handle British currency again is quite a thrill. The Dutch seamen in the Island have been advised to find work of some sort until arrangements can be made to get them away. The first of a series of recorded messages from Channel Islanders was broadcast tonight by the States Telephone Department.

May 17. The mail service has been restored; from this afternoon telegrams are to be received at the G.P.O. Several Jersey officers are here on leave, and two French prisoners of war returned to the Island today in a fishing-boat from St. Malo. The first woman to arrive in the Island after the Occupation is Second Officer Diana Evans of the W.R.N.S. Large queues again waited outside the banks to exchange reichsmarks, the time limit having to be extended until May 23rd. Custodians of herds are asked to inform their retailers of their requirements of skim and butter milk—at reduced prices! Today's *E.P.* pays tribute to the housewives of Jersey, who carried on so nobly during difficult days.

May 18. The distribution commenced today of free gifts from the British Government; these were 30 cigarettes and a box of matches for all adults; 4 oz. tea for adults and juveniles; 3 oz. chocolate for children and juveniles, and 8 oz. household soap for adults. All aliens who have come to the Island since May 10, 1940, must report at Fort Regent; the notice states that arrangements will be made for their accommodation and feeding. The Electricity Company, after consulting the Military Authorities, gives notices that domestic appliances may be unsealed, but urges rigid economy. The Military Authorities have also pointed out that permits for travel to the United Kingdom and Guernsey can only be granted in exceptional cases. The Red Cross Fund has reached £85,000. It has been stated that the value of the *Vega*'s cargoes to the Channel Islands exceeds £500,000. Owners or occupiers of property requisitioned by the enemy may now substantiate their claims of ownership and obtain the keys (if any).

May 19. Cameras which were surrendered to the Germans were handed back to their owners today. During the day some Jersey airmen in the R.A.F. came over the Island and dropped parcels for relatives. In the evening there was a special ceremony to mark the first showing of English films; during the next fortnight admission to see various documentary films at the three cinemas will be free. Owners of motor vehicles or cycles purchased and paid for by the German authorities are to be given the option of re-purchasing same if such are still in the Island; owners of vehicles requisitioned and not paid for will be advised individually how to obtain their property. Persons who have removed furniture, etc., from property recently occupied by the enemy must return same, including that given away by the Germans. Numbers of American sailors were about the town today. Most of the Germans have been taken away, there are about a thousand left to clear up mines, clean buildings, etc., and it is learned that several Germans are missing and these are being rounded up. Drastic cuts have been made in the price of vegetables. There was a meeting of the States today. The Aliens Officer was appointed to deal with the applications of persons who desire to leave the Island. Following a request by Brigadier Snow, a body of members was appointed as the Competent Military Authority to deal with certain matters that might be delegated to them; during the discussion that ensued it was suggested that there had been too much haste in dispensing with the Superior Council. The Department of Finance and Economics recommended the disposal of stocks, and its Act of April 14, 1945, was repealed. A request for survey of extensions to the Airport was submitted and agreed to. A proposal that the States approach the Military Authorities with a view to giving effect to the Law on National Service was carried, the Bailiff saying that over 500 young men had called on him at his Chambers with a view to joining His Majesty's Forces. Deputy Bertram was thanked by the House for the part he played in helping the escape from the Island of American prisoners of war. Jurat Brée thanked the farmers for what they had done during the Occupation, and gave some interesting figures: 40,000 inhabitants and 15,000 Germans were kept going with potatoes, cereals, vegetables and milk, in spite of difficulties, but the speaker admitted there was a small percentage of farmers who had not done all they could. The productive acreage of arable land had been reduced by between 3,000 and 4,000 vergées, and the 15,000 'locusts' consumed more than the 40,000 inhabitants.

May 20. Whit Sunday: weather disappointing, with heavy showers and bright intervals. This morning the French prisoners of war who were in captivity here placed wreaths on the Cenotaph and at the Island War Cemetery at Howard Davis Park.* During the past week there have been heavy mails, and today the first parcels from the mainland were handled. Ships were still being discharged, and clothing and coal are among the latest cargoes; some coal was delivered to merchants for issue to bakehouses and persons holding special permits. Two German soldiers were killed when removing mines.

May 21. Whit Monday: the weather improved somewhat. In the afternoon there was a football match in which a Forces XI was beaten by an Island team; in the evening the cinemas were well attended and there were several dances at which the Forces were guests. During the day the town was very busy with grocers' and butchers' shops open to deal with the new general weekly rations which commenced today; housewives were delighted at being able to purchase goods they had not seen for

---

* Subsequently each grave in this cemetery was surmounted with an oak cross, the material and labour having been given by local residents. The bodies of the U.S. servicemen were handed over to the American authorities in June, 1946, and were taken home for re-interment.

years, and the people who were to have sausages for dinner was legion. The full list of rations now available is: 2 oz. of tea for adults and juveniles, 3 oz. of chocolate for children and juveniles, 3 oz. of lard and 3 oz. margarine for everyone, 1 lb. of biscuits for everyone, 4 oz. of cereals for everyone, 20 oz. of canned meat for everyone (there will be fresh meat on occasions), two 5-oz. packets of dried egg for children only, 2 oz. of salt for everyone, and a packet of soap powder for everyone, this alternating weekly with varieties of soap. The bread ration for infants is increased from 1½ lb. to 2 lb. A ration of one hundred-weight of wood is also available on certain coupons, this being from German stocks which are now the property of the British Government.

May 22. There were large queues this morning for clothing and footwear (a lot of which comes as a gift from America), the textile shops having a busy time; in future, these shops are to open every day except Thursday. The public is informed how to obtain permission to travel on compassionate grounds, etc., and a warning is given regarding interference with ammunition left by the Germans. Government experts have arrived: Sir Daniel Cabot (Chief Veterinary Officer), Dr. W. F. Bewlay, O.B.E. (Department of Agriculture), Dr. Banks (Department of Health), and Dr. McGee (Nutrition). The columns of the *E.P.* are particularly interesting, with news of relatives and friends from all over the world; equal interest can be taken in the advertisement, which show how business undertakings are making great efforts to restore the trade of the Island. Greetings on the Island's liberation have been received from all over the world, and great satisfaction is felt at the news of the large number of Jerseymen who have distinguished themselves. Many residents had their electric fires returned to them this evening, but the return of wireless sets has had to be deferred as there is a lot of sorting out to be done.

May 23. From today German currency ceased to be legal tender. Persons in receipt of British Imperial, Dominions or Colonial pensions and allowances, etc., are at present requested to attend regularly at Post Offices for payment. All persons or firms wishing to make application for permits for import goods to the Island may now do so. Among today's advertisements is one for a lighthouse keeper for Corbière. New potatoes are on sale (unrationed) at 7½d. per lb. The first party of local residents to travel to the mainland on compassionate grounds left the Island today by air. Our 'liberators' have been ordered to carry

309

arms, owing to signs of trouble among some of the Germans left here.

May 24. Empire Day. In the afternoon there was a parade of the liberating forces, who marched through part of the town headed by the band of the Duke of Cornwall's Light Infantry; all sorts of Army vehicles followed the infantry, and cheering crowds greeted the parade all along the route. A States delegation has returned from a one-day visit to Guernsey to confer with Guernsey authorities and the Civil Affairs Commission in that Island regarding the re-opening of trade between the Channel Islands and the United Kingdom.

May 25. Some of the bakers are making rolls, and white flour is being sold over the counter at 4d. per lb. Although the official date is Monday next (28), bread may be purchased in any quantity. The laundries announce that they will re-open on June 4. Grocers are re-commencing deliveries. The Germans left have now been grouped in one camp at St. Peter's.

May 26. A Jersey Airways plane arrived at the Airport today, bringing officials on a brief survey visit. A warning has been issued to persons possessing firearms or ammunition. Owners of agricultural land requisitioned by the Germans are required to send in a return of such land. A minor sensation was caused by the display in a King Street jeweller's shop of a dish of old gold bought during the Occupation and hidden from the Germans; it will now be sent to England. In the Royal Square this afternoon there was a performance by—no! not a German band this time!—the Duke of Cornwall's Light Infantry, one of a series of concerts being given in various parts of the Island. We were all thrilled to hear that the King and Queen are to visit the Channel Islands on June 6.

May 27. A large crowd attended a drumhead service on the Weighbridge this morning, the band of the D.C.L.I. accompanying the hymns. In the evening the band gave a concert at The Forum.

May 28. Changes made in the rationing: The ration of 4 oz. of various cereals per week is cancelled 8 oz. of oatmeal will be issued. This week there is to be a supplementary ration of 4 oz. of fresh meat, and every week until further notice a supplementary butter ration of 2 oz. Commencing today, 100 cigarettes or 4 oz. of tobacco were available as a fortnightly ration (cigarettes 8d. and 9d. for 10 and tobacco varying from 1s. 2d. to 1s. 6d. per oz.); in addition, there were two boxes of matches per head. The Union Jack was hoisted on the Minquiers this morning by Brigadier Snow. The Senior Civil Affairs Officer has given information of clothing to be available shortly and the methods for obtaining same; there will be quantities representing a year's supply on the United Kingdom basis, and persons having sufficient funds may draw from their bank account or beyond the limits imposed on sterling withdrawals from their credits for reichsmarks recently deposited; those who have no such funds at their disposal may make application to the Constable of their parish. In the evening 'Stars of the Army' presented a programme at Wests.

May 29. Visit by Admiral Sir Ralph Leatham, K.C.B., Commander-in-Chief, Plymouth; he was greeted by Admiral C. Stuart, Naval Officer in Charge, Channel Islands, Brigadier Snow and Captain S. Fremantle, Resident Naval Officer, Jersey. There were long queues in town today for the Red Cross clothing now being sold, and in the evening large crowds continued to besiege the cinemas.

May 30. Department of Public Health advises inoculation against diphtheria, especially in the case of children. The work of removing mines goes on; it is estimated there were 50,000. Also receiving attention are the huge underground tunnels which the Germans made; some of these are of enormous size, and will be 'show places' for a long time to come (see footnote on page 179).

May 31. Oranges were on sale in the shops today on ration of 1½ lb. per head, a consignment of 2,000 cases having arrived from Britain; sweets, 3,000 boxes of apples and 600 boxes of onions are also due. German nickel coins—nick-named 'washers' —are still acceptable up to the value of 1s. until arrangements have been made for a supply of copper coins. Another Currency Order was published today, also warnings against possessions of dangerous drugs from former German medical supplies and the finding of or tampering with military equipment. Persons desiring surgical appliances are asked to state the nature of their requirements. The troops are again going about unarmed. It is learned that 1,822 Britons from the Channel Islands who were deported in 1942 have arrived in England from Biberach. The first mail to arrive by air was received today. The Island Red Cross Fund stands at over £94,000.

JUNE 1945

June 1. The Department of Labour gives notice that the Military Authorities are anxious to give priority of return to those evacuees who are key men and women in the various businesses and professions.

June 2. Notice published dealing with the issue of priority permits for the importation of essential goods. Ministry of Information sound film programmes are being shown in the various parish halls. Reports by British experts declare that the Channel Islands' crops are almost free from pests. An evening taxi service is advertised at 2s. per mile. At the Royal Court today a severe warning was given against the retention of firearms, two persons found in possession of revolvers being fined £25 each. The States sat specially this afternoon to consider several matters of urgency: Their Majesties' reply to the loyal address was received and the day of the Royal Visit— June 6—declared a Bank Holiday. Several taxation measures were dealt with in regard to tobacco, beer, spirits and wines, these to come into effect immediately. A grant of £2 is to be made to each child already in receipt of an allowance, for the purpose of purchasing clothing. A food subsidy was suggested owing to the increased cost of living, and other items included the granting of sums of money to meet the requirements of a purchasing commission and for the Hospital medical services; the return of evacuees; a monetary gift from Tanganyika, and consideration of a suggestion from the Chamber of Commerce that Liberation Day—May 9th—be made an annual holiday.

June 3. The Roman Catholics held their Corpus Christi procession through the streets this afternoon. Rehearsals were carried out today for the forthcoming Royal Visit. Cargoes of house and gas coal are being discharged; it is understood that the public gas supply will be restored on June 12th.

June 4. New clothing ration books issued; these are the same as British ones, but we are being allowed 60 points instead of the 24 available on the mainland. This is to help us get ahead with essential clothing. Huge queues were outside textile shops all day, especially where stockings were being sold. The banking hours extended—10 a.m. to 3 p.m. A commodity which has been in great demand, but very scarce for a long time, was issued on ration—3 oz. of baking powder per head.

June 5. An 'In Memoriam' Mass was celebrated at St. Mary and St. Peter's Church this morning for Mr. C. C. Painter and his son Peter, who died in German prison camps. Subsequently news was received of other Jersey residents who were 'removed' to German camps and died there. An air mail service is now in regular operation, and delivery is being awaited of a huge batch of parcels which is held up at Guernsey on the way here. Four Germans in hiding were rounded up today. There is to be a supplementary ration of 1 lb. of marmalade and ½ lb. of dried fruit. A cargo of Red Cross food parcels was brought later in the month by the SS. *Marianne*; three other ships—the *Glen*, the *Zuidland* and the *Dorothy Weber*—brought tobacco and cigarettes as part cargo.

The following is the full list of supplies received here through the Red Cross:

Canadian food parcels	234,888
New Zealand food parcels	53,024
British and Scottish food parcels	125,394
Invalid (or diet) parcels	12,726
	426,032
*British Red Cross food parcels for British prisoners of war	192
American Red Cross food parcels for American and French prisoners of war	3,868
Medical supplies (packages)	357
Soap (tablets)	229,183
Salt (lb.)	88,745
Sugar (lb.)	100,222
Flour (tons)	1,388
Yeast (lb.)	6,900
Honey for children (from Her Royal Highness Princess Elizabeth) (lb.)	876
Biscuits (lb.)	71,400
Diesel oil (barrels)	43
Petrol (barrels)	4
Kerosene (gallons)	4,363
Candles	38,883
Matches (boxes)	39,168
Flints	39,000
Seeds (various) (bags)	77
Cigarettes	13,901,480
Tobacco (lb.)	3,515
Tobacco for British prisoners of war (case)	1

* The number of British prisoners of war here was very small, these dating only from the German commando raid on Granville three months ago.

CLOTHING

Men's garments	42,315
Women's garments	45,659
Boys' garments	16,000
Girls' garments	20,573
Children's garments	13,709
Layettes	528
From America for the French prisoners of war (cases)	12

FOOTWEAR, Etc.

Boots (pairs)	9,941
Shoes (pairs)	11,818
Leather (bends)	150
Cut soles (pairs)	684
Heels (pairs)	584
Rubber sheets (for soles)	537
Nails (for boot and shoe repairs) (lb.)	2,925

A case containing clothing, footwear, etc., was received from the Women's War Relief Work Organisation, Lisbon, and sundries included a small quantity of haberdashery and toilet requisites.

June 6. The Royal Visit postponed for twenty-four hours owing to unfavourable weather conditions on the mainland. There has had to be a revision of the arrangements as Their Majesties are to travel by sea instead of by air as was originally intended. A meeting of the States fixed June 7 as a Bank Holiday, the milk and baking trades being especially affected by the change. Coal or coke in varying quantities may be obtained by persons holding special fuel ration coupons; coal is £4 ton and coke £3 15s. 0d. Alteration made in the procedure of application for priority permits for the return of evacuees; this is now to be made on the mainland. After the *E.P.* has been set almost entirely by hand for nearly three months, the linotype machines were used again today. The general gas supply will be restored on the 10th inst.

June 7. THE ROYAL VISIT—grand and fitting climax to a month of rejoicing. Their Majesties King George VI and Queen Elizabeth visited Jersey today and were given an enthusiastic welcome. They came ashore at 11.15 a.m. in a launch from H.M.S. *Jamaica* and were met at the Albert Pier by Island and military officials. Then they drove to Trinity Church and from there returned to town via the eastern parishes. His Majesty replied to a Loyal Address in the States, and afterwards, on the way to Government House, the King and Queen stopped in St. Saviour's Road to talk with ex-Service men, next-of-kin of those who had lost their lives in the war, and other representative groups. After lunch they drove to the Airport, and left by air for Guernsey at 3 o'clock. It was a beautiful day, and the route of the Royal Progress was such that everyone could get a good view.

WEEKLY FOOD RATIONS TO THE POPULATION FROM JULY 1, 1940

(DATE OF OCCUPATION)

Re-printed from *The Evening Post* of July 4, 1946

Period	Butter or Margarine oz.	Cooking Fats oz.	Flour oz.	Sugar (Adults) oz.	Sugar (Children and Juveniles) oz.	Salt oz.	Tea (Adults and Juveniles only) oz.	Meat (Adults and Juveniles) oz.	Meat (Children) oz.
8 July 1940	4	4		4	4			12	6
22 July 1940	4	4		4	4		4	12	6
28 Oct. 1940	4	4		4	4		2	12	6
11 Nov. 1940	4	4	8	4	8	2	2	12	6
25 Nov. 1940	4	Nil	8	4	8	2	2	12	6
1 Feb. 1941	2	Nil	8	4	8	2	2	12	6
7 Apr. 1941	2	Nil	8	3	6	2	1	12	2
12 July 1941	4	Nil	6	3	6	3	1	4	2
30 Aug. 1941	2	Nil	6	3	6	3	1	4	4
13 Dec. 1941	4	Nil	6	3	6	4	Nil	8	2
21 Feb. 1942	4	Nil	6	3	6	4	Nil	4	4
7 Mar. 1942	2	Nil	7	3	6	4	Nil	4	2
18 July 1942	2	Nil	7	3	6	2	Nil	6	3
31 Oct. 1942	2	Nil	7	3	6	4	Nil	6	3
30 Jan. 1943	2	Nil	7	3	6	4	Nil	4	2
11 Dec. 1943	2	Nil	7	3	6	Nil	Nil	4	2

Period	Flour oz.	Butter oz.	Sugar (Adults) oz.	Sugar (Children and Juveniles) oz.	Salt oz.	Meat (Adults and Juveniles) oz.	Meat (Children) oz.	Controlled Articles
5 Feb. 1944–22 June 1944	7	2	3	6	2	4	2	As from April 14, 1941, one or two of the undermentioned commodities were issued each week: Macaroni, Cheese, Coffee substitute, Split Peas, Haricots, Canned Vegetables, Sardines, Tunny fish. As from June 16, 1941, until October 14, 1944, 1 lb. Jam per head approximately every eight weeks.
24 June 1944–19 Oct. 1944	7	2	3	6	1	2	1	
21 Oct. 1944–2 Nov. 1944	7	2	3	6	1	4	2	
4 Nov. 1944–23 Nov. 1944	7	2	2	5	1	4	2	
25 Nov. 1944–14 Dec. 1944	7	2	Nil	4	Nil	4	2	
16 Dec. 1944–18 Jan. 1945	7	2	Nil	Nil	Nil	4	2	
20 Jan. 1945–8 Feb. 1945	7	Nil	Nil	Nil	Nil	2	1	
10 Feb. 1945–15 Mar. 1945	7	Nil	Nil	Nil	Nil	4	2	
17 Mar. 1945–19 May 1945	7	Nil	Nil	Nil	Nil	2	1	

As from November 26, 1941, and to such time as Butter or fresh Meat was available, prior to the Liberation of the Channel Islands, Male Heavy Workers were entitled to a supplementary ration of 3½ oz. Meat and 2½ oz. Butter weekly. As from June 9, 1941, and until the present time, children under 3 years of age have been receiving French Gruel as follows: Infants from birth to 12 weeks, 8 oz. every 2 weeks; from 12 weeks to 27 weeks, 1 lb. every 3 weeks; from 27 weeks to 3 years, 8 oz. weekly. As from March/April, 1941, bottle-fed babies under the age of 12 months received a supplementary 6 oz. of Sugar per week, and from December 16, 1944, a total weekly allowance of 11 oz.

Period	Male Manual Worker		Female Manual Worker		General		Juveniles 3–10 yrs.		Children Birth–3 yrs.		Male Heavy Workers under 21 yrs.		Female Heavy Workers under 21 yrs.	
	lb.	oz.	lb.	oz.	lb.	oz.	lb.	oz.	lb.	oz.	lb.	oz.	lb.	oz.
4 Aug. 1941	6	0	5	4	4	8	3	0	1	8				
24 May 1943	4	12	4	4	3	12	3	0	1	8				
2 Aug. 1943	6	0	5	4	4	8	3	0	1	8	6	0	5	4
19 June 1944	4	4	4	4	4	4	3	0	1	8	6	0	5	4
					(under 21 years) 4 8 / 4 4									
11 Dec. 1944	4	4	4	4	4	4	3	0	1	8	4	4	4	4

19–24 Feb. 1945: One pound only to all categories.
26 Feb.–10 Mar. 1945: No bread ration was available.

On March 12, 1945, the Red Cross ship *Vega*, having brought flour, the bread ration was restored to 4 lb. for adults, 3 lb. for everyone under 10, with the exception of babies, who got 1½ lb.

A SELECTION OF FINE READING AVAILABLE IN CORGI BOOKS

Novels

☐ 552 07981 2 THE GAMES — *Hugh Atkinson* 7/6
☐ 552 07763 1 ANOTHER COUNTRY — *James Baldwin* 5/-
☐ 552 07885 9 CONFESSIONS OF A SPENT YOUTH — *Vance Bourjaily* 7/6
☐ 552 07938 3 THE NAKED LUNCH — *William Burroughs* 7/6
☐ 552 07317 6 THE CHINESE ROOM — *Vivian Connell* 5/-
☐ 552 08056 X KATIE MULHOLLAND — *Catherine Cookson* 7/6
☐ 552 07777 1 THE WAR BABIES — *Gwen Davis* 5/-
☐ 552 01278 5 THE GINGER MAN — *J. P. Donleavy* 5/-
☐ 552 07488 8 BOYS AND GIRLS TOGETHER — *William Goldman* 7/6
☐ 552 07958 5 THE WELL OF LONELINESS — *Radclyffe Hall* 7/6
☐ 552 01500 8 CATCH 22 — *Joseph Heller* 5/-
☐ 552 07904 9 THE CONSULTANT — *Alec Hilton* 5/-
☐ 552 08054 3 PINKTOES — *Chester Himes* 5/-
☐ 552 07913 5 MOTHERS AND DAUGHTERS — *Evan Hunter* 7/6
☐ 552 08074 8 THE ROAD TO REVELATION — *Norah Lofts* 5/-
☐ 552 08002 0 MY SISTER, MY BRIDE — *Edwina Mark* 5/-
☐ 552 08015 2 FLESH AND BLOOD — *Nan Maynard* 4/-
☐ 552 08092 6 THINKING GIRL — *Norma Meacock* 5/-
☐ 552 07594 9 HAWAII (colour illustrations) — *James A. Michener* 10/6
☐ 552 07500 0 THE SOURCE — *James A. Michener* 12/6
☐ 552 07766 6 APPOINTMENT IN SAMARRA — *John O'Hara* 5/-
☐ 552 07954 5 RUN FOR THE TREES — *James Rand* 7/6
☐ 552 08075 6 THE WHITE COLT — *David Rook* 4/-
☐ 552 01162 2 A STONE FOR DANNY FISHER — *Harold Robbins* 5/-
☐ 552 07655 4 THE HONEY BADGER — *Robert Ruark* 7/6
☐ 552 08022 5 THE DEVIL'S SUMMER — *Edmund Schiddel* 7/6
☐ 552 07807 7 VALLEY OF THE DOLLS — *Jacqueline Susann* 7/6
☐ 552 07883 2 THE CARETAKERS — *Dariel Telfer* 5/-
☐ 552 07921 9 THE BASTARD Vol. I — *Brigitte von Tessin* 7/6
☐ 552 07922 7 THE BASTARD Vol. II — *Brigitte von Tessin* 7/6
☐ 552 07937 5 THE DETECTIVE — *Roderick Thorp* 7/6
☐ 552 07352 0 EXODUS — *Leon Uris* 7/6
☐ 552 08091 8 TOPAZ — *Leon Uris* 7/6
☐ 552 08073 X THE PRACTICE — *Stanley Winchester* 7/6
☐ 552 07116 1 FOREVER AMBER Vol. I — *Kathleen Winsor* 5/-
☐ 552 07117 X FOREVER AMBER Vol. II — *Kathleen Winsor* 5/-
☐ 552 07790 9 THE BEFORE MIDNIGHT SCHOLAR — *Li Yu* 7/6

War

☐ 552 07936 7 THE DEVIL'S BRIGADE *George Walton and Robert Adleman* 5/-
☐ 552 08061 6 TOJO: THE LAST BANZAI (illus.) — *Courtney Browne* 5/-
☐ 552 08097 7 JAPAN'S LONGEST DAY *Compiled by the Pacific War Research Society* 7/6
☐ 552 08045 4 NOTHING IMPORTANT EVER DIES — *Romain Gary* 3/6
☐ 552 07871 9 COMRADES OF WAR — *Sven Hassel* 5/-
☐ 552 07959 6 THREE CAME HOME — *Agnes Keith* 5/-
☐ 552 07986 3 HIROSHIMA REEF — *Eric Lambert* 5/-
☐ 552 07726 7 THE DIRTY DOZEN — *E. M. Nathanson* 7/6
☐ 552 07476 4 THE SCOURGE OF THE SWASTIKA (illustrated) *Lord Russell of Liverpool* 5/-
☐ 552 08096 9 NIGHTMARE OF THE DARK — *Edwin Silberstang* 5/-
☐ 552 08078 0 TREBLINKA (illustrated) — *Jean Francois Steiner* 7/6

Romance

☐ 552 08050 0 THE DOCTORS OF DOWNLANDS — *Sheila Brandon* 3/6
☐ 552 08103 5 DR. ROSS OF HARTON — *Alice Dwyer-Joyce* 3/6
☐ 552 08067 5 A SIMPLE DUTY — *Hilary Neal* 3/6
☐ 552 08084 5 WHAT WE'RE HERE FOR — *Bess Norton* 3/6
☐ 552 08051 9 JUNGLE NURSE — *Irene Roberts* 3/6

Science Fiction

- ☐ 552 08037 3   NEW WRITINGS IN S.F.13   *John Carnell* 3/6
- ☐ 552 08085 3   THE AUTUMN ACCELERATOR (The Invaders) *Peter Leslie* 4/–
- ☐ 552 08068 3   TIME FOR A CHANGE   *J. T. McIntosh* 4/–
- ☐ 552 07682 1   THE SHAPE OF THINGS TO COME   *H. G. Wells* 7/6

General

- ☐ 552 07704 6   THE VIRILITY DIET   *Dr. George Belham* 5/–
- ☐ 552 07566 3   SEXUAL LIFE IN ENGLAND   *Dr. Ivan Bloch* 9/6
- ☐ 552 08086 1   ENQUIRE WITHIN   *Reference* 7/6
- ☐ 552 07593 0   UNMARRIED LOVE   *Dr. Eustace Chesser* 5/–
- ☐ 552 07949 9   GROW UP—AND LIVE   *Dr. Eustace Chesser* 3/6
- ☐ 552 07996 0   THE ISLAND RACE (illus. in colour) *Winston S. Churchill* 30/–
- ☐ 552 06000 3   BARBARELLA (illustrated)   *Jean Claude Forest* 30/–
- ☐ 552 07804 2   THE BIRTH CONTROLLERS   *Peter Fryer* 7/6
- ☐ 552 08087 X   THE COMPLETE ILLUSTRATED BOOK OF THE
  PSYCHIC SCIENCES *Walter B. Gibson & Litzka R. Gibson* 7/6
- ☐ 552 07400 4   MY LIFE AND LOVES   *Frank Harris* 12/6
- ☐ 552 07745 3   COWBOY KATE (illustrated)   *Sam Haskins* 21/–
- ☐ 552 01541 5   MAN AND SEX   *Kaufman and Borgeson* 5/–
- ☐ 552 07916 2   SEXUAL RESPONSE IN WOMEN *Drs. E. and P. Kronhausen* 9/6
- ☐ 552 07820 4   THE CATHOLIC MARRIAGE   *William A. Lynch* 5/–
- ☐ 552 08069 1   THE OTHER VICTORIANS   *Stephen Marcus* 10/–
- ☐ 552 07965 0   SOHO NIGHT AND DAY (illus.)   *Norman and Bernard* 7/6
- ☐ 552 07145 5   THE THIRD EYE   *T. Lobsang Rampa* 5/–
- ☐ 552 08105 1   BEYOND THE TENTH   *T. Lobsang Rampa* 5/–
- ☐ 552 08089 6   MOVIES ON T.V.   *Steve Scheur* 7/6
- ☐ 552 08038 1   EROS DENIED (illustrated)   *Wayland Young* 7/6
- ☐ 552 07918 9   BRUCE TEGNER'S COMPLETE BOOK OF KARATE   6/–

Westerns

- ☐ 552 08049 7   SINGING GUNS   *Max Brand* 3/6
- ☐ 552 08082 9   SUDDEN—APACHE FIGHTER *Frederick H. Christian* 4/–
- ☐ 552 08101 9   COLD DECK, HOT LEAD   *J. T. Edson* 3/6
- ☐ 552 08102 7   THE FLOATING OUTFIT   *J. T. Edson* 3/6
- ☐ 552 08133 7   WAGONS TO BACKSIGHT   *J. T. Edson* 3/6
- ☐ 552 08134 5   THE HALF BREED   *J. T. Edson* 3/6
- ☐ 552 08066 7   MACKENNA'S GOLD   *Will Henry* 3/6
- ☐ 552 08083 7   THE SHACKLED GUN   *L. P. Holmes* 3/6
- ☐ 552 07934 0   SHALAKO   *Louis L'Amour* 3/6
- ☐ 552 08007 1   CHANCY   *Louis L'Amour* 3/6

Crime

- ☐ 552 07872 7   THE KREMLIN LETTER   *Noel Behn* 5/–
- ☐ 552 08032 2   DOOMSDAY ENGLAND   *Michael Cooney* 5/–
- ☐ 552 08099 3   A CLUTCH OF COPPERS   *John Creasey* 3/6
- ☐ 552 08047 0   THE BARON AGAIN   *John Creasey* 3/6
- ☐ 552 08004 7   MADRIGAL   *John Gardner* 5/–
- ☐ 552 07905 7   HIDEAWAY   *John Gardner* 3/6
- ☐ 552 08030 6   MR. SCIPIO   *Tudor Gates* 5/–
- ☐ 552 08062 4   THE MONEY THAT MONEY CAN'T BUY *James Munro* 5/–
- ☐ 552 07973 1   THE BODY LOVERS   *Mickey Spillane* 5/–
- ☐ 552 07831 X   THE BY-PASS CONTROL   *Mickey Spillane* 3/6
- ☐ 552 08079 9   THE KILLING OF FRANCIE LAKE   *Julian Symons* 4/–
- ☐ 552 08080 2   BLAND BEGINNING   *Julian Symons* 4/–
- ☐ 552 08081 0   THE COLOUR OF MURDER   *Julian Symons* 4/–

All these books are available at your bookshop or newsagent: or can be ordered direct from the publisher. Just tick the titles you want and fill in the form below.

CORGI BOOKS, Cash Sales Department, J. Barnicoat (Falmouth) Ltd., P.O. Box 11, Falmouth, Cornwall.

Please send cheque or postal order. No currency, and allow 6d. per book to cover the cost of postage and packing in U.K., 9d. per copy overseas.

NAME ....

ADDRESS ....

(MAR. 69) ....